Reconfiguring Myth and Narrative in Contemporary Opera

MUSICAL MEANING AND INTERPRETATION
Robert S. Hatten, editor

YAYOI UNO EVERETT

Reconfiguring Myth and Narrative in Contemporary Opera

Osvaldo Golijov, Kaija Saariaho,
John Adams, and Tan Dun

INDIANA UNIVERSITY PRESS

Bloomington & Indianapolis

This book is a publication of

Indiana University Press
Office of Scholarly Publishing
Herman B Wells Library 350
1320 East 10th Street
Bloomington, Indiana 47405 USA

iupress.indiana.edu

Manufactured in the United States of America

Library of Congress Cataloging-in-Publication Data

Everett, Yayoi Uno, author.
    Reconfiguring myth and narrative in contemporary
opera : Osvaldo Golijov, Kaija Saariaho, John
Adams, and Tan Dun / Yayoi Uno Everett.
    pages cm — (Musical meaning and interpretation)
    Includes bibliographical references and index.
    ISBN 978-0-253-01799-4 (cloth : alkaline paper) —
ISBN 978-0-253-01805-2 (ebook) 1. Operas—21st century—
Analysis, appreciation. 2. Golijov, Osvaldo, 1960– Ainadamar.
3. Saariaho, Kaija. Adriana Mater. 4. Adams, John, 1947–
Doctor Atomic. 5. Tan, Dun, 1957– First emperor. I. Title.
II. Series: Musical meaning and interpretation.
    MT95.E84 2016
    782.109'05—dc23

                                    2015019678

1 2 3 4 5   20 19 18 17 16 15

To Hideo and Shoko Uno

La barbarie, ce n'est pas "l'Autre"; elle est en nous, en chacun de nous, tapie comme un fauve, prête à bondir, et c'est à nous de la débusquer et de la dompter. Il me semble que la musique, la littérature, et l'art en général, ont un rôle essentiel à jouer dans ce combat qui ne s'arrêtera jamais.

Barbarism is not the Other; it resides in us, in each of us, lurking like a wild beast ready to jump, and it's up to us to uncover and tame it. It seems to me that music, literature, and the arts in general have a vital role to play in this never-ending battle.

Amin Maalouf, Adriana Mater

Contents

Preface

The inspiration for writing this book came from lively debates I have had with friends and colleagues following performances of new operas at various venues over the course of ten years. Often, the underlying questions centered on whether the opera was successful in its treatment of music, portrayal of characters, narrative proportion, and staging. Back in 2003, I recall debating the profound stasis and circularity in Kaija Saariaho's *L'Amour de loin* at its premiere in Amsterdam's IJstheater; while my Dutch colleague dismissed the opera on the basis that "the music goes nowhere," I defended the absence of teleology as an essential feature of the musical drama. At the Lincoln Center's 2005 premiere of Brian Ferneyhough's *Shadowtime*, my friends and I similarly debated whether this concert-opera, chronicling Walter Benjamin's war trauma in a fragmented sequence of dialogues, monologues, and instrumental pieces, constituted a legitimate opera; the booing and hissing from the audience at the end of the performance indicated that an opera awash in angular, atonal language without flowing lines, and lacking narrative continuity could not be called an opera. Following the Lyrical Opera of Chicago's 2007 premiere of John Adams's *Doctor Atomic* in Chicago, a composer colleague and I disagreed on the theatrical excesses and the lengthy proportion of the second act in Peter Sellars's mise-en-scène. "Why does it have to go on for so long?" she asked, to which I replied that it had to do with creating a portal into the mythic experience of an operatic apocalypse.

These diverging responses to live performances attest to the fact that opera involves a complex negotiation with the libretto, music, action, lighting, and other aspects of the production. Considering these issues, this book addresses new developments in operatic production that have become commonplace since the 1980s; while music and libretto constitute the initial source material, they operate in counterpoint with variable production components of the director's mise-en-scène, including choreography, lighting, props, and filmic projections. The signifying capacity of music and text may be greatly altered by the performative components of an opera's mise-en-scène. But why have these new operas stirred up hours of heated debate? What lies at the root of our disagreements in our interpretive experience of opera?

In the last two decades, scholarship on opera has expanded its range of critical discourse by taking into account gender, cultural, literary, psychoanalytic, and media theories. In *Unsung Voices* (1991), Carolyn Abbate examines the performative dimensions of opera by exploring what she calls the "narrating voice." In *Feminine Endings* (1991), Susan McClary offers a gender-based discourse centered on desire, pleasure, and the body in her analysis of the "feminine" in works ranging from Monteverdi's *Orfeo* to Madonna's music videos. Slavoj Žižek and Mladen Dolar's *Opera's Second Death* (2002) explores operatic representations of death and its mythical framework through the psychoanalytical lens of Freud and Lacan. Similarly, Lawrence Kramer examines operatic moments in which "the sensory richness of music" assumes the function of the Lacanian Real – the unsymbolizable kernel of forbidden/ecstatic pleasure (2006: 270). Combining media and semiotic perspectives, Marcia Citron analyzes filmic operas (Ponnelle's *Madame Butterfly*) and operatic films (the *Godfather* trilogy and *Moonstruck*) in *When Opera Meets Film* (2010); she adopts Wolf Werner's concept of *intermediality* to explore the relationship between film and opera as well as hybrid systems of signification that arise from the interplay of media.

Prompted by such studies, this book contributes to current discourse on opera as media by examining mythic narratives of operas composed and produced in the first decade of the twenty-first century. Although the historical contexts and compositional approaches vary, the four operas selected for close reading share a common theme by foregrounding human conflicts that arise from war. In Golijov's *Ainadamar* (2003), actress Margarita Xirgu wrestles with the ill-fated execution of García Lorca during the Spanish Civil War (chapter 2). In Kaija Saariaho's *Adriana Mater* (2006), Adriana raises a child born of rape during a nameless war, and the opera makes an oblique reference to the Serbo-Croatian War (chapter 3). John Adams's *Doctor Atomic* (2006) explores scientist Robert Oppenheimer's moral struggle in bringing about the nuclear age (chapter 4). Finally, in Tan Dun's *The First Emperor* (2006–07), Qin Shi Huang faces a moral dilemma of choosing between duty and love after unifying China as its first Emperor (chapter 5). These operas draw on collective memories of war as a means for reflection and dialogue. Within the imagined plots and fictionalized settings, they transform historical figures into contemporary subjects, inviting the audience to identify with their aspirations and struggles from a transhistorical perspective by moving outside the frame of reference of a particular social or historical context. In these narratives, the main character often stands as a symbol of a more archetypal figure; for example, García Lorca and Xirgu are both represented as Christ-like figures, Adriana as Mater Dolorosa, Oppenheimer as Faust, and Qin Shi Huang as Mao Zedong. Furthermore, by presenting historical subjects in quasi-mythological settings, these opera invite audiences to contemplate the moral and ethical questions raised by war and human conflict.

In qualifying these works as *contemporary* opera, there are fundamental questions that need to be addressed with respect to how postwar operas have transformed narrative conventions from the past. First, postwar aesthetic trends have brought a fundamental shift in the narrative conventions of opera. As visual media gained in popularity and technical perfection during the twentieth century, the older live performance media modernized by "abandoning realism, returning to prototypical myths and moralities, favoring inner expression over clear narrative, experimenting with nonlinearity, and using stage action as a metaphor rather than as a simulation of reality" (Salzman and Desi 2008: 63).

Earlier twentieth-century operas, such as Prokofiev's *Love for Three Oranges* (1919), Puccini's *Turandot* (1925), and Carlisle Floyd's *Susanna* (1955), are based on a conventional narrative formula in which tension generated from conflict and expectations of resolution builds and sustains dramatic continuity. In comparison, diverse postwar operas have adopted non-linear or refractory forms of narrative, reconfiguring historical figures and myths into postmodern subjects through the deployment of filmic and electronic devices, *tableaux vivants,* fragmentation, collage, parody, and minimalist musical idioms. In the genre of "anti-operas" composed by Maxwell Davies, Harrison Birtwistle, György Ligeti and others in the late 1960s, operatic conventions are dismantled through parody, distortion, satire, and irony (Everett 2004). With *Einstein on the Beach* (1976), Philip Glass and Robert Wilson ushered in a new operatic form, allowing libretto, music, and stage settings to function independently within the total work of art through Jungian associations and other symbols. Birtwistle's *Mask of Orpheus* (1975–86) presents a postmodern fusion of music, drama, myth, mime, and electronics within a cyclical narrative form (Cross 2009). In the comic vein, John Corigliano's *Ghosts of Versailles* (1986) offers a nostalgic, conciliatory strain of postmodernism, in which the playwright Beaumarchais courts the ghost of Marie Antoinette; here, the contrasting elements – the eclectic borrowing of musical styles and merging of narratives – comment on each other "in making the whole much more than a sum of its parts" (Clendinning 2002: 133). In such contexts, multiple narratives and intertextual references are brought together to create an ironic collision of aesthetic styles and musical idioms.

Second, new forms of media and technology have transformed the spatiotemporal experience of attending to opera. Stage directors have transformed the settings of classical and grand operas by generating postmodern collisions of time and place, as witnessed by Peter Sellars's setting of Mozart's *Marriage of Figaro* in New York City's Trump Tower, Michael Mayer's setting of Verdi's *Rigoletto* in 1960's Las Vegas, and so forth. The Long Beach Opera's 2012 production of Osvaldo Golijov's *Ainadamar* reenacts Federico García Lorca's 1936 execution by projecting film footage of the Falangist Ruiz Alonso, accompanied by sounds of gunshots, flamenco music, and a radio broadcast of the Falangist's fascistic speech. Filmic projection, in fact, has become a standard part of the operatic mise-en-scène, as exemplified by Dominick Argento's *The Dream of Valentino* (1994), in which a surrealistically distorted image of Valentino's face is projected onto multiple screens. In Louis Andriessen's *Writing to Vermeer* (1999), Peter Greenaway uses gushing water on stage, filmic projection, and electronic distortion of Lully's *Le Bourgeois Gentilhomme* to portray the French invasion of Delft in the seventeenth century (Everett 2006). Character representation based on *doubling* is another strategy used frequently in postmodern productions, as witnessed by Sven-Eric Bechtolf's staging of *Pelléas et Mélisande* for the Zurich Opera (2006) where each character is accompanied by its mannequin double. Such adaptations shed new light on the production and consumption of opera as a popular genre, one that is continually shaped and transformed by new media and aesthetic trends (Sutcliffe 2005).

Third, the diversification in the modes of dissemination has transformed the ways in which we consume opera as media. In my own lifetime, my experience of opera has witnessed a dramatic shift, from listening to recordings with score in hand to viewing high-definition (HD) broadcasts of operas in a movie theater or on a television screen. The HD broadcast of live opera, with variable camera angles, shots, and edited sequence, forces us to engage with operatic narrative in a totally different manner from earlier experiences of imagining the story through sound alone. Another form of technical mediation can be found in the popularization of film opera, in which the singing takes place in a naturalistic setting away from the operatic stage. Such strategies have been used in Joseph Losey's directing of Mozart's *Don Giovanni* (1979), Francesco Rosi's *Carmen* (1984), Miklós Szinetár's *Bluebeard's Castle* (1981), Frédéric Mitterand's *Madame Butterfly* (1995), Penny Woolcock's *The Death of Klinghoffer* (2003), and so forth. In this genre, the visual dimension of the film dominates over the aural experience of opera. The *remediation* of art forms, as Jay Bolter and Richard Grusin refer to the representation of one form of media in another, has significant impact on how we examine narrative structure and meaning (2001).

Central to my investigation is determining how contemporary opera reconfigures familiar myths and narratives in its mediated form. Twenty-first-century operas so far have tended to strike a middle ground between radical postmodernism and traditional narrative conventions, while aiming to create a multivalent narrative through innovative use of media and unconventional plot formation. For example, the libretto of Adams's *Doctor Atomic* draws from books and documents that were found in Robert Oppenheimer's library, ranging from unclassified government documents on the atomic bomb to poems by Charles Baudelaire and the Bhagavad Gita. In *Ainadamar*, Lorca's life leading up to his execution during the Spanish Civil War is reenacted as a narrative embedded within Xirgu's remembrance prior to her death in Uruguay. In Saariaho's *Adriana Mater*, the rich soundscape created by the wordless choir represents the voices of the "haunted soldiers" in dream sequences that blur the boundary between dream and reality. Electronic effects are used strategically to signal the fall of the atomic bomb in *Doctor Atomic* and assassination of Lorca in Golijov's *Ainadamar*. Tan and Golijov incorporate improvisatory practices based on oral traditions (Beijing opera, flamenco music), while moving beyond the paradigms of exotic opera from the past.

This book provides a case study for multimodal analysis of contemporary operas from the perspectives of semiotic theory, literary criticism, psychoanalytic studies, and multimedia theories. For the semiotic analysis of music, I engage in a dialogue with other books from the series *Musical Meaning and Interpretation*. In particular, my theoretical framework adopts and builds on concepts developed by Andrew Davis's *Il Trittico, Turandot, and Puccini's Late Style* (2010), Byron Almén's *A Theory of Musical Narrative* (2008), Michael Klein's *Intertextuality in Western Art Music* (2005), Michael Klein and Nicholas Reyland's *Music and Narrative Since 1900* (2012), Raymond Monelle's *The Musical Topic* (2006), and Robert Hatten's *Interpreting Musical Gestures, Topics, and Tropes* (2004) and

Musical Meaning in Beethoven (1994). Chapter 1 provides a theoretical exposition of multimodal discourse on opera by examining structuralist and semiotic approaches to the study of myth and narrative, psychoanalytic approaches to understanding the role of the unconscious in myth, and multimodal approaches toward analyzing operatic narrative. In this context, I discuss the specific strategies used by composers and librettists to transform operatic subjects into archetypal, mythic figures and examine how the director's mise-en-scène adds new elements that render the narrative multivalent. Chapter 2 focuses on the mythical treatment of Lorca in Golijov's *Ainadamar,* with attention to the spatialization of sound effects (acoustic vs. electronic) in the depiction of a lost time and place in history. It examines four distinct productions of *Ainadamar* to illustrate how widely the narrative trajectory changes when the opera is adapted, for example, into an oratorio or into a meta-theater with dance. Chapter 3 draws largely on semiotic and psychoanalytical theories and explores issues of trauma and ambivalence in Saariaho's *Adriana Mater;* it focuses on the acousmatic function of Saariaho's music and the non-linear structure of narrative to convey the effects of trauma. Chapter 4 examines how Adams's post-minimalist music, in conjunction with Sellars's libretto and staging, recreates a Faustian parable in Adams's *Doctor Atomic.* Lastly, chapter 5 examines the archetypal representation of Qin Shi Huang (the Qin dynasty Emperor) as an antihero in Tan's *The First Emperor* and the controversial reception of this opera in light of discourses on exoticism and transcultural music. Wherever relevant and available, I incorporate aesthetic or ideological positions advanced by composers, librettists, and music directors in the production of these operas, as well as those by critics and scholars in their reception.

Acknowledgments

First and foremost, I convey my deepest gratitude to Robert Hatten for his support and enthusiasm during the entire process of writing this book on contemporary operas. His encouraging words and openness to new ways of thinking about opera kept me going during challenging times. I also thank Kaija Saariaho for her generosity in providing me with sketches, interviews, and an archival video for *Adriana Mater* during my visits to Paris between 2009 and 2013. Additionally, I am grateful to Ha Jin for interviews on writing the libretto to *The First Emperor,* Carmen-Helena Telléz for inviting me to Indiana University to discuss her production of *Ainadamar,* and John Adams for providing me access to scores and supporting materials for *Doctor Atomic.* My research would not have been complete without Cindy Layman at the Santa Fe Opera and Silke Meyer and Barbar Aumüller at the Staatstheater Darmstadt, for making archival videos and photos of the exemplary productions of *Ainadamar* available.

Next, the project would have not come to fruition without the yearlong Fellowship from The Fox Center for the Humanities at Emory University during 2010–11. I thank Martina Brownley (director) and Keith Anthony (associate director) as well as the following colleagues for the stimulating exchange of ideas on opera and narrative theories during my residency: Judith Miller (history), Dalia Judovitz (French and Italian studies), Sandra Blakely (classics), Davis Hankins (religion), Walter Melion (art history), and Robert Spano (conductor of Atlanta Symphony Orchestra and Professor in Residence at Emory). I also thank Emily Kader for her editorial assistance, Catherine Marin for her assistance in translating French texts, Claire Wu for the translation of Chinese texts, and Caleb Lewis for the translation of Spanish texts.

Within the music discipline, I thank the Society for Music Theory for the subvention grant to pay for expenses related to securing copyright permissions of scores and photos. I also thank Marianne Kielian-Gilbert (Indiana University) for her feedback on Saariaho's opera at the 2009 Society for Semiotics in America, and Susan McClary (Case Western University) for her comments on my presentation at the Feminist Music and Theory conference in 2011, followed by her incisive comments and suggestions for revision. I am also indebted to Michael Klein (Temple University), Philip Rupprecht (Duke University), Nancy Rao (Rutgers University), and Amy Bauer (University of California at Irvine) for sharing their thoughts on critical issues that pertain to the reception of postwar music and opera during the past five years.

I also thank my husband, Steve Everett, and my parents, Hideo and Shoko Uno, for their support and encouragement along the way.

Lastly, I thank the following publishers for their kind permission to reprint musical examples from the following operas:

· *Ainadamar* by Osvaldo Golijov
  © 2008 by Imagern CV, administered by Hendon Music, Inc., a Boosey & Hawkes company. Reprinted by permission of Boosey & Hawkes, Inc., an Imagern company.

· *Doctor Atomic* by John Adams
  © 2005 by Hendon Music, Inc., a Boosey & Hawkes company. Reprinted by permission of Boosey & Hawkes, Inc., an Imagern company.

· *Adriana Mater* by Kaija Saariaho
  © 2006 Chester Music Limited.
  All rights reserved. International copyright secured.
  Reprinted by permission.

· *The First Emperor* by Tan Dun and Ha Jin
  © 2006 G. Schirmer, Inc. (ASCAP)
  All rights reserved. International copyright secured.
  Reprinted by permission.

Abbreviations

Instruments

al.fl	alto flute
bcl	bass clarinet
bdrum	bass drum
bsn	bassoon
cb	contrabass
cbsn	contrabassoon
cel	celesta
cemb	cembalo
chim	chime
chor	chorus
cl	clarinet
clv	clavescrot, crotales
EH	English horn
fem chor	female chorus
fl	flute
glsp	glockenspiel
gtr	guitar
hrn	horn
hrp	harp
kb	keyboard
ob	oboe
picc	piccolo
pno	piano
scymb	suspended cymbal
sdrum	snare drum
str	strings
tam	tam tam
tba	tuba
tbls	tubular bells
timp	timpani
trb	trombone
tri	triangle
trp	trumpet
vla	viola
vlc	cello

vln   violin
xyl   xylophone

Registral designation of pitch is based on the system established by the Acoustical Society of America, e.g., C1 = lowest C on the piano, C4 = middle C, etc.

    0:0'00″ = timing (hour/minute/second) for DVDs. In a multiple DVD set, #1 re-
fers to DVD 1, #2 to DVD 2, and so forth.

Reconfiguring Myth and Narrative in Contemporary Opera

1 Toward a Multimodal Discourse on Opera

"We see shredded strips of blood-red ribbon hanging on his face. Groping, with a blank stare, [Oedipus] stumbles under the scaffolding and ramps that compose the somber stage set, until he is walking knee-deep in a pool of dark water, surrounded by ghostly figures. The chanting of the chorus has come to an end. We watch the water dripping from above, then hear the sound of cleansing pouring rain. The king's almost primitive self-sacrifice has made him human; Thebes's plague is brought to an end" (Rothstein 1993). Edward Rothstein's review of Julie Taymor's filmic production of Stravinsky's *Oedipus Rex* (1993) vividly describes the theatrical excesses of the concluding scene. This narrative production is a retelling of a myth twice removed; without distorting the essence of Sophocles' tragedy, Taymor expands the mythical stature of Oedipus by adding new layers to the Ciceronian Latin of Jean Cocteau's libretto and the neo-classical formality of Stravinsky's score. Taymor's mise-en-scène infuses the opera-oratorio with extraordinary power through her deployment of masks and puppets, Oedipus's dancing double, and extraneous narration in the style of Japanese classical drama. The life-size puppet uncannily mirrors Oedipus's every gesture, dramatizing the tragic fate of the Theban king.

Taymor's production of *Oedipus Rex* is multilayered in the sense that her concept of staging builds additional interpretive layers onto Cocteau's libretto and Stravinsky's music from different cultural perspectives. Rothstein argues that the additional cultural layers (e.g., the Butoh dancer, puppets, and clay-covered chorus) transform the mythic elements of the tale by reconfiguring the "primitive energy" of Parisian avant-garde aesthetics into a globalized myth remade for a twenty-first-century audience. I would go further, as does Taymor by claiming that the Japanese narrator's framing of the opera transforms the oratorio into a hybrid cultural production. Her staging successfully defamiliarizes Cocteau's avant-garde aesthetics and infuses the ancient myth with rituals taken from Noh drama, Butoh dance, and Indonesian *wayang kulit* (puppet theater).[1] The retelling of the myth in this production is provocative precisely because the cultural references interact without one overpowering the others.

The multiplicity of cultural meanings generated from Taymor's production of *Oedipus Rex* has fast become the norm for operatic production rather than the exception. Productions of operas, both old and new, are continually shaped and transformed by new media and aesthetic trends; this view accords with David

Levin's claim that opera has emerged as "an unsettled site of signification," requiring the audience to attend to a surfeit of competing systems (2007: 3). Each operatic production is unique in the sense that the multimedial elements – music, libretto, film, objects, lighting, mime, and/or dance – operate as interdependent structural and semantic components that shape the narrative production of the whole. Taymor's *Oedipus Rex* also calls into question how the production components actively *reconfigure* the narrative of the initial source material – the libretto and music. So how do we begin to theorize the narrative strategies we bring as viewers and analysts to our holistic engagement with opera? How does our engagement with the production figure into the operatic discourse?

Geoffrey Leech and Michael Short define *discourse* as "linguistic communication seen as a transaction between speaker and hearer, as an interpersonal activity whose form is determined by its social purpose. Text is linguistic communication seen simply as a message coded in its auditory or visual medium" (Mills 1997: 4). Their definition emphasizes the dialogical aspect of the communication involved; if we assume that both parties share a common knowledge base and interpretive framework (the *code,* in semiotic terms) for carrying on a dialogue about a particular subject, then *discourse* is a transaction between the sender and the receiver defined by a particular form (Eco 1976: 49). Operatic discourse is further complicated by multiple and variable factors that shape the communication process between production and reception. Production, in itself, can be divided into pre-production (librettist and composer), production (director, set and lighting designer, and/or choreographer), and post-production (editorial work for filmic version, if relevant). Under reception, we can include the audience's embodied experience of the performance as well as reviews and scholastic literature that shape our critical response to the work.[2] As a music theorist, my investigation typically begins with a close study of the score, libretto, critical commentary, and previews, followed by attending a live production (theatrical or high-definition broadcast) to study the director's interpretive aims as communicated through the work's production modes (staging, singing, acting, costumes, props, lighting, etc.). This may be further enriched by interview(s) with the composer, librettist, director, and/or dramaturge. More often than not, the process involves reconciling colliding perspectives; the postmodern staging of a particular work may add new cultural and ideological layers to those of the libretto and music, as exemplified by Taymor's staging of Stravinsky and Cocteau's *Oedipus Rex.*

Taking these variable factors into account, we can construct a dynamic model of musical discourse for the analysis of contemporary operas, as illustrated in figure 1.1. Music and libretto constitute the initial source material at the pre-production stage. With newly commissioned operas, the source material often undergoes change once it enters into the production stage – a portion of the libretto may be omitted or modified and the music may be substantially revised. Under production, mise-en-scène literally means to "put in the scene"; Patrice Pavis defines it as the "concretization of the dramatic text, using actors and the stage space, into a duration that is experienced by the spectators" (1998: 364). In

(Pre)   **Production**   *(Post)*   **Reception**

Libretto	*Mise-en-scène*		Embodied experience
Music ◄--►	Staging ◄--► Film		
	Previews	◄────►	
	Program		Critical reviews;
	notes		scholarly literature

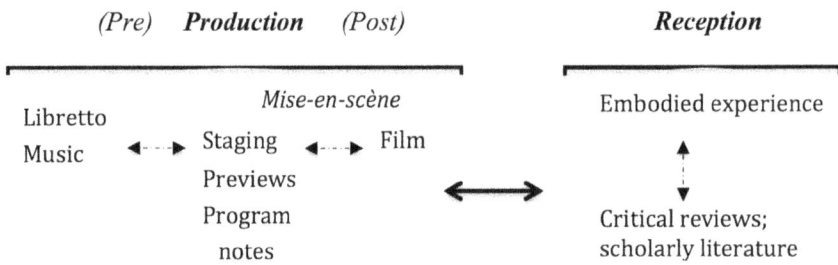

Figure 1.1. A Model for Operatic Discourse

theater, it includes props, scenery, acting, lighting, costumes, and/or music – as shaped by the stage direction. Previews and program notes also fall under production in that their primary function is to communicate the collaborators' aesthetic intentions to the audience. When a particular production is made available in high-definition broadcast, then released into a film, it belongs to the post-production stage. Mise-en-scène, in this context, includes everything that defines the composition of the shot – rhythm, framing, movement of the camera, lighting, sound, and set design. In lieu of the holistic visual perspective that theater affords the viewer, film shapes the content and form of storytelling through a prescribed sequence of shots and camera angles.

As is frequently the case with new operas, the reception of their premiere informs future production in a circular fashion, as indicated by the bi-directional arrows. In the case of Golijov's *Ainadamar*, its 2003 premiere at Tanglewood prompted an extensive revision by Peter Sellars for the Santa Fe production in 2005; its immense popularity led to new productions of the opera by various directors and opera companies between 2007 and 2012. In the case of Tan Dun's *The First Emperor*, the critical reception of its Metropolitan Opera premiere in 2006 led to an extensively revised version a year later. Its reception was also marked by a collision of ideologies surrounding the perception of Qin Shi Huang, as will be discussed.

Building onto this audience/analyst-centered model of discourse, I argue that *multimodality* presents an important basis from which to examine operatic production in its totality. As a starting point, Gunther Kress and Theo van Leeuwen distinguish multimodality from multimedia in the following terms: Multimedia refers to how different physical media (e.g., print, airwaves, radio) are brought together to convey information; multimodality has to do with how we utilize different sensory modes – indexing verbal, visual, and aural resources that are evoked by the media – and the system of choices we use to construct meaning (2001: 67). For my purposes, multimediality will refer to the encoding of media elements from the perspective of production, while multimodality will refer to decoding these elements from an interpreter's standpoint. Ruth Page, in relating multimodality to the viewer's construction of narrative, categorizes the multimodal dimensions schematically into textual resources (words, images, sound, movement), platform of delivery (digital screen, printed page, cinema, face-to-face), physical environment (private, public, inside/outside, light/dark), and sensory modalities (sight, hearing, touch, smell, taste) (2010: 7). She claims that narratives delivered in different physical environments generate different meanings and bring to light the comprehensive way in which narratives need to be examined in relationship to different modal contexts.

In fact, current research in neuroscience demonstrates that sensory modalities are *not* processed separately, but in an interactive and integrated manner.[3] Alison Gibbons, in her study of the multimodal reading of graphic novels, contends that even if verbal and pictorial recognition occurs in different regions of the brain or neocortex, we construct textual meaning through the co-occurrence of modalities (2010: 100–101). She then explains how the reading of a graphic novel is in itself an embodied activity that relies on a plurality of semiotic modes. For example, she provides a graphic text accompanied by a visual frame from the beginning of Steve Tomasula's graphic novel *VAS: An Opera in Flatland*. It contains a boxed and italicized text that reads "first pain," accompanied by a large starburst shape underneath. Gibbons argues that the reader's embodied experience is significantly enhanced through the physical sensation of pain evoked by the starburst shape; even in the absence of an agent at the onset of reading, "the visual immediacy of the representation of the paper cut thus induces the reader to envisage the event in relation to the self" (104).

Film composers generate soundtracks to evoke embodied response in viewers through the coordination of sound and moving image. Exaggerated sound effects often accompany action sequences and affect the viewer's response through a co-occurrence of visual and aural modalities. Think of filmic shots that depict physical violence, where non-diegetic or amplified diegetic sounds are designed to elicit an embodied experience of fright or suspense more vividly in the viewer than if it were evoked by the visual dimension alone.[4] Interestingly enough, turning off the soundtrack significantly diminishes the impact. Later in this chapter, I will bring up the concept of *intermediality* as a framework for illustrating how different media elements depend on and refer to each other in co-articulating the structure of narrative.

In viewing opera, our multimodal experience is further complicated by the multiplicity of elements that shape our embodied experience: text, music, filmic images, choreography, action, lighting, and other production components. As a way to map these elements onto specific categories, I invoke Lars Elleström's four modalities: 1) *material* refers to the corporeal interface of the medium (e.g., human bodies, digital screen); 2) *sensorial* to the physical and mental acts of perceiving the interface through sensory faculties (seeing, hearing, feeling, tasting, smelling); 3) *spatiotemporal* to the structuring of the sensorial perception of the interface with respect to space and time, and 4) *semiotic* to the creation of meaning in the medium by way of sign interpretation (2010: 35–36). Building on Elleström, I refer to the viewer's perceptual grouping of media elements according to one or more of the four modal categories as a *semiotic field:* as an area of signification, each field contributes to the composite sign system with its (integrative) meaning. Our embodied response to a particular operatic scene is typically shaped by the combination of material, sensory, and spatiotemporal modalities of experience. For example, in Peter Sellars's mise-en-scène for Adams's *Doctor Atomic,* the interlude that begins the third scene in Act I depicts a powerful electric storm that threatens the cancellation of the test explosion (DVD #1: 48'47"). Counterpointing the fast, syncopated music with offbeat accents, the strobe light flickers at odd intervals and obscures the view on stage; the workers frantically run from one end of the stage to the other. In lieu of spoken or sung text, the physical and psychological state of panic is registered through the visual semiotic fields in synchrony with Adams's agitated "filler" music. Listening to the same interlude in the absence of the visual dimension in the 2008 concert setting failed to induce the embodied sensation of "panic" I experienced in watching the DVD or attending Sellars's staged productions. These somatic effects we experience are by no means trivial. As Elleström explains, the *semiotic* modality is in effect all along as an integrative device; "the creation of meaning already starts in the unconscious apprehension and arrangement of sense-data perceived by the receptors and it continues in the conscious act of finding relevant connections within the spatial temporal structure of the medium. . . ." (22).

Focusing further on the semiotics of reception, Linda and Michael Hutcheon introduce the concept of *multimodal narrative* to refer to the embodied action of viewing opera: "the physical move from what theatre semiotician Keir Elam (1980: 8) calls the 'dramatic texts' – or the *design* – to live performance with actual material bodies in actual physical space is an act of narrative *production* of both the verbal libretto and the musical score" (2010: 66). They argue that, even if the story of Wagner's *Ring* cycle is familiar to us, the *way* it is told defines our multimodal experience. While acknowledging that vocal music is clearly the defining feature of opera, Hutcheon and Hutcheon also emphasize the importance of language, gesture, visual architectural form, color, and other fields as vital components of the multimodal production. Unlike those who claim that the performative mise-en-scène replaces the authors' printed texts, Hutcheon and Hutcheon argue that *production* adds to *design* to the accumulation of meaning(s) and helps "organize the interpretive strategies of the audience members" (67). That is to say, even if the story is already familiar to the audience, the way it is told *holistically* defines our multimodal narrative experience. They remind us that while no two audience members respond to an operatic performance in the same manner, it is "the task and responsibility of the mise-en-scène to constrain and direct the variety of possible interpretations and responses" (68). The director's aesthetic intention, indeed, *constrains* our narrative experience in a definitive manner. This is especially true if the production is converted into a filmic format. The DVD format or high-definition broadcast of a given production establishes a narrative angle through filmic devices (e.g., camera angle, shot sequence) that shape the viewer's multimodal experience in an entirely different way from attending a live performance of opera in a theater.

To further complicate the picture, Carolyn Abbate defines the *narrating voice* as marked by "multiple disjunctions" with the music surrounding it, and she emphasizes the fugitive nature of viewing opera as "a rare and peculiar *act,* a unique moment of performing narration within a surrounding music" (1991: 10). In "Is Music Drastic or Gnostic," she views performance in real time as a polysemic experience that is fundamentally disconnected from the kind of hypostasized readings that we construct in hindsight, predicated on the notion that sonic media embody expressive signification or contain cultural/poetic associations (2004: 521). Does this necessarily mean that our perception remains provisional and resists being anchored to a fixed interpretation? Yes, if we refer to experience in the moment when we do not perceive something exactly in the same way twice. But if we attend to a particular recording (visual/auditory) of a performance as an artifact for study, the answer is clearly "no." We form habituated responses to a given work – and more specifically, organize our experience through recognition of patterns and stylistic constraints, which Leonard B. Meyer identify as *schemata* (1989).[5] Robert Gjerdingen, in extending this concept, defines schema more generally as an abstracted prototype, a well-learned exemplar, or a theory intuited about the nature of things we rely upon to make useful comparisons (2007: 11). Building on such notions, David Huron claims that when similar stimuli are experienced many times over a long period of time, then "the memory will be transformed into a mental schema that provides the basis for schematic expectations" (2006: 266). Applied to the present study, we can assume that while our initial multimodal response draws on an ephemeral (moment-to-moment) mode of experience, schematic (habituated) expectations build and shape our cognitive understanding of narrative of a given production in its archived medial form.

The concept of multimodality gains particular prominence in the study of postwar operas, owing to the increased level of sophistication in staging production. In *New Music Theater: Seeing the Voice, Hearing the Body,* Eric Salzman and Thomas Desi claim that the text (libretto, or book and lyrics in the case of a musical) has receded in importance in comparison to the increased creative role of stage directors and choreographers in music theater. Since the 1980s, stage directors have transformed the setting of classical and grand operas by generating a postmodern collision of time, place, text, and/or musical style, as witnessed by Peter Sellars's setting of Mozart's *Marriage of Figaro* in New York City's Trump Tower, Zhang Yimou's staging of Puccini's *Turandot* in Beijing's Forbidden City, and Jonathan Miller's staging of Verdi's *Rigoletto* in a recreation of New York's Little Italy. The last quarter of the twentieth century constitutes the Age of the Director, as directors have titillated and provoked opera audiences with novelties in staging (Sutcliffe 2005: 334). Indeed, at times, the director's staging aesthetic is blatantly disconnected from that of the music, as exemplified by the Opera Bastille's 2009 staging of Karol Szymanowski's *Le Roi Roger* with the shepherd clad in a Mickey Mouse costume. At other times, the director may create a stunning spectacle through state of the art technology (using interactive 3D projection), as demonstrated by Robert Lepage's 2008 staging of Berlioz's *La Damnation de*

Faust and his 2011–12 staging of Wagner's *Ring* cycle for the Metropolitan Opera. Such new adaptations – what Sutcliffe calls "interventionist" stagings – bring new insights into the production and consumption of opera as a popular genre that is continually shaped and transformed by new medial and aesthetic trends.

The decades of the 1970s and '80s bear witness to the most radical and avant-garde transformation of opera and theater; nonlinear or anti-narrative orientations replaced linear, goal-directed forms of narrative. Salzman and Desi remind us that in such contexts, myth, metaphor, and symbolism re-emerge as important components of storytelling (2008: 63). The operas under study here were created and produced in the first decade of the twenty-first century and have embraced this new aesthetic approach to varying degrees. While the extent of their nonlinear orientation varies from work to work, each embraces myth and metaphor in a provocative manner by examining the expressive range and scope of human conflict resulting from war. Let us now turn to the relevance of myth in constructing a multimodal discourse on operatic narrative.

Unpacking Myth

Fundamental to the present inquiry are questions of what myth entails and how its narrative content has been adapted toward different aesthetic ideals involved in operatic production. Myth typically involves an ancient story that deals with supernatural beings, ancestors, or heroes and establishes a particular worldview by explaining aspects of the natural world or delineating the psychology, customs, or ideals of a society. Mythologies and legends form the basis of Western operas, going back to Peri's *Euridice* (1600), Monteverdi's *La favola d'Orfeo* (1607), Gluck's *Orfeo ed Euridice* (1762), Mozart's *Die Zauberflöte* (1791), Berlioz's *Les Troyens* (1856), and Wagner's *Der Ring des Nibelungen* (1848–74), among others. Depending on the aesthetic aims of the librettist and composer, the dramatic trajectory of a given myth can be radically altered. Take, for instance, the myth of Orpheus. Commentaries on the Greek source (Konon) suggest that the myth centers not on his love for Eurydice but rather on his death resulting from his unwillingness to hand over his secret rites to the Thracian and Macedonian women (Blakely 2013).[6] In Virgil's *Georgics,* the focus of the tale shifts to the beekeeper Aristaeus's pursuit of Eurydice, in which Orpheus plays a subsidiary role (Detienne 2009: 278). In the Middle Ages, as exemplified by the story's treatment in Boethius's *Consolation of Philosophy,* the myth turned into a Christian allegory and a stern warning against excessive passion. Then, in Monteverdi's Baroque opera and subsequent operatic retellings of the myth, Orpheus is glorified as lover, musician, and hero. In the Romantic adaptation by Gluck, the tragic ending is completely reversed through the device of *deus ex machina;* Cupid (*Amore*) intercepts Orfeo, who tries to kill himself after losing Eurydice for the second time, but Cupid ultimately breathes life back into Eurydice. The opera ends with a celebration of the power of love, as the lovers are ultimately united. Then, around two hundred years later, in *The Mask of Orpheus* (1973–84), Harrison Birtwistle, collaborating with librettist Peter Zinovieff, reinvents Orpheus as a victim of his own age by amplifying the tragic ending using postmodern fragmentation.[7] In this pessimistic version, the contrapuntal narrative focuses on the multiple deaths suffered by Orpheus and the ritual of *performing* lament (Cross 2009: 24). How is it that the same myth could be used as a vehicle to express such varying aesthetic ideals?

Let us explore this question further by comparing three different perspectives on myth and narrative:

> It can now be seen how music resembles myth, since the latter too overcomes the contradiction between historical, enacted time and a permanent constant. (Lévi-Strauss 1969: 16)
>
> Myth, at least at its best, is a recognition of natural conflicts, of human desire frustrated by nonhuman powers, hostile oppression, or contrary desires; it is a story of the birth, passion, and defeat by death which is man's common fate. Its ultimate end is not wishful distortion of the world, but serious envisagement of its fundamental truths; moral orientation, not escape. That is why it does not exhaust its whole function in the telling, and why separate myths cannot be left entirely unrelated to any others. (Langer 2009: 67)
>
> Myths are stories told over and over, in many ways, and they provide themes woven into new myths, including those of stage and screen: that is all part of the process. (Ellwood 2008: 5)

Anthropologist Claude Lévi-Strauss in *The Raw and the Cooked* remarks on the similarity between music and myth based on a temporal dichotomy. Like a musical work, myth operates on the basis of the temporal dimension (physiological time) in which it unfolds, and the listener's apprehension of its hidden structures and meanings (psychological time). From the perspective of structuralism, Lévi-Strauss understands this dichotomy as a form of communication based on grammatical rules and a logical system of organization (*langue*), as complemented by those divergences based on individual variations (*parole*).[8] Most importantly, Lévi-Strauss claims that both music and myth lead us to grapple with "unconscious truths, which follow from them" (18). Next, philosopher Suzanne Langer's definition of myth addresses ethical and philosophical questions. Building on a Freudian conception of concealed or latent meaning in myth, Langer urges the reader to expose those hidden layers. And unlike folktales, which are focused on wish fulfillment, she claims that myths and legends pose profound moral and ethical questions that demand serious engagement on the part of the listener/reader. Particularly relevant for the present discussion is Langer's point (cited earlier) that myth "does not exhaust its whole function in the telling." This relates to Robert Ellwood's remarks that reinforce the telling of myth as a discursive practice; old myths are constantly retold and woven into new myths through adaptations in new media forms. All three perspectives – underlying narrative grammar, moral and ethical implications, and the discursiveness of myth – shape my interpretive approach to reconfiguring myth in the contemporary operas under study.

It is important to keep in mind that mythic action tends to be deliberately ambiguous with respect to time and place; as in the opening line from *Star Wars,* "A long time ago in a galaxy far, far away . . . ," mythic narrative gives the impression of having taken place in a time so far back that a precise date cannot be ascertained. It evokes a different kind of temporality where "magic and miracles could still happen" (Ellwood 2008: 18). Jeppe S. Jensen further remarks that in a religious context, the mythical world typically consists of three domains: the first world and the factual one in which humans live; a second, ideal world in which the sacred is located; and a third domain in which the human and the superhuman cohabitate. And it is through the construction of the second world that religious groups conceive of and understand the first world. In a circular sense, the world is made by myth, and myth tells how the world operates around us (2009: 13–14).

Furthermore, mythic action operates on the paradox that through a fictitious or invented tale one seeks some form of truth or ethical rule of conduct. In everyday conversation when we describe something as a myth (e.g., "democracy is a myth"), we often mean to say that it is either invented or not supported by facts. Yet, as a discursive practice, we constantly engage in *mythologizing* a subject through the act of retelling. Take, for example, Elvis Presley, who has been transformed into an immortal icon in American popular culture. One of the most significant trends in postwar operas involves mythologizing by actively merging or juxtaposing aspects of a historical figure and his/her worldview with those of a familiar myth or legend. Consider, for example, the legend of Faust, which has been reinterpreted by Auden, Kallman, and Stravinsky in *Rake's Progress* (1951). Tom Rakewell, a spendthrift subject from William Hogarth's eighteenth-century paintings, is the protagonist who recalls Faust. In exchange for Tom's three wishes and their magical powers, he contracts his soul to Nick Shadow, the devil in disguise. Another example is found in Jean Cocteau's film *Orphée* (1951); Orpheus is turned into a left-bank poet in postwar France who struggles with social alienation in the aftermath of World War II. And in Philip Glass's "portrait" operas such as *Satyagraha* (1979), mythical figures from the Bhagavad Gita, a sacred Indian text, interact with Gandhi in his quest for liberation from British colonization.

Thus, an important function of myth has to do with the continual process of *reinterpretation,* a renewal of signification based on intertextual references embedded in the telling of the story. This dynamic and pragmatic function of myth is an integral part of its evolution. According to Lévi-Strauss, myths are anonymous: "from the moment they are seen as myths, and whatever their real origins, they exist only as elements embodied in a tradition" (1969: 18). Eero Tarasti explains that the Greeks distinguished *mythos* (pure fiction) from *logos* (knowledge based on reason) and gradually drained the concept of mythos of all its religious and metaphysical connotations; thus *mythos* meant for the Greeks something that cannot really exist (1979: 19). Tarasti further observes that "German [R]omanticism's interest in myths was based on an aesthetic-philosophical interpretation of the relation between myths and the unconscious" and that "the whole Wagnerian idea of *Gesamtkunstwerk* in its entirety can be regarded as a re-construction of all the relevant aspects of the primal mythical communication" (19). Mary Cicora takes an ironic stance on Wagner's treatment of myth by argu-ing that Wotan's modern psychic reflection relativizes the mythological universe portrayed onstage and dematerializes or deconstructs it; she argues that this is in keeping with Wagner's writing in *Oper und Drama,* in which the composer states that "myth is constantly relativized by history, and thus it becomes ungenuine and ironic" (1998: 143).

The idea that myth is constantly relativized calls to mind Roland Barthes's double articulation of myth, in which he emphasizes the revolving relationship between its form and concept/meaning. Using the spatial metaphor of a con-stantly moving turnstile, Barthes argues that the mythologist occupies himself with a static method of deciphering the mythic form on the one hand and a dy-namic understanding of its latent, hidden meanings on the other (1972: 124).[9] As "a second-order semiological system," myth reconstitutes its older form by dis-placing and distorting previous references and associations.

Barthes's double articulation of myth leads us to the consideration of tempo-rality in mythic narrative. According to Paul Ricoeur, narrative encompasses two temporal dimensions: *chronological* and *configurational.* The chronological char-acterizes the story insofar as it is made up of events, while the configurational "grasps together" the succession of events into a meaningful whole and gives rise to a "new quality of time" through this reflective act (1984: 67–68). In a standard operatic narrative, the chronological timeline ensures that the story has a be-ginning, middle, and ending. In contemporary operas based on myth, the con-figurational timeline demands the reader to grapple with, say, a cyclical dimen-sion of time that extends beyond the story's diegesis: often the death of a hero leads to a birth of another.[10] Victoria Adamenko claims that when myth is pre-sented as linear narrative, the synchronic dimension of myth is lost: "The reiter-ation of the initial precedent in rituals is no less real than the precedent itself, so the events of the past, the present, and the future becomes interlocked with each other. Mythic time is thus formed" (2007: 19). Frequently, contemporary operas distort the linear progression of time in the unfolding of the story to allow for slippage into a mythical time and place where the boundaries between present and past are purposefully blurred.

How, then, do new aesthetic approaches to operatic production complicate or reconfigure mythic narrative? Expanding on Salzman and Desi, I call at-tention to two strategies by which operas appropriate mythic elements by fore-grounding metaphor and symbolism within a nonlinear narrative framework. The first has to do with the strategy of turning historical subjects into *textual-ized* representations. Under the aegis of semiotic criticism, Shlomith Rimmon-Kenan identifies textuality as "segments of a closed text," where characters are re-duced to "patterns of recurrence, motifs which are continually recontextualized in other motifs" (2001: 32).[11] John Hartley further argues that, rather than pro-viding a correct interpretation, textual analysis is "interested in the cultural and political implications of representations" (2002: 227). In an operatic context, this means that the narrative presents an ideological representation rather than a biographical characterization of a subject. An example *par excellence* is Philip Glass and Robert Wilson's groundbreaking work *Einstein on the Beach* (1975) – the first in the trilogy of "portrait" operas by Glass. Lacking a definitive plot, the four acts explore Einstein's contribution as a humanist, scientist, and amateur musician through the recurring visual themes of a train, a trial, and a spaceship, along with musical themes connected with these images, in a series of tableaux vivants. Abstract interludes called "knee plays" are inserted between them. Composed primarily for the Philip Glass Ensemble (flutes, saxophone, bass clarinet, synthesizers), Glass's minimalist style makes use of a ground bass in the slower theme and employs additive and subtractive rhythmic procedures to effect changes in the melodic constitution of the faster themes. Clad in plain white shirts and trousers with suspenders, the chorus recites numbers and solfège syllables and engages in menial everyday tasks.[12] In Trial 2/Prison, a courtroom trial setting with judges, bailiff, and clerks is juxtaposed with another setting featuring two inmates sitting behind bars. In front of the stage, a young woman in a white satin dress recites Lucinda Childs's text, entitled "Prematurely air-conditioned supermarket," repeating words such as, "I have been avoiding the beach," with different inflection and speed. Even the title of the opera, *Einstein on the Beach,* emanates from two nouns ("Einstein" and "beach") strung together in the otherwise disconnected images of the opera's tableaux vivants. In short, the opera explores Einstein's symbolic role in postwar American society in lieu of anything that resembles a biographical narrative.

Related to the textualizing strategy is *transhistoricity*: interspersing anachronistic references to older myths within the main historical and cultural context of narrative. *Satyagraha* (1979), Glass's second "portrait" opera, is loosely based on Mohandas Gandhi's early years in South Africa, where he formed a nonviolent civil disobedience movement marked by the concept of Satyagraha ("truth-force"). This opera juxtaposes Gandhi on stage with mythological armies from the sacred Indian text, the Bhagavad Gita. In addition to Krishna and Arjuna, other historical figures associated with Gandhi are introduced in each of the three acts: Tolstoy (Act I), who represents Gandhi's past; Tagore (Act II), who represents Gandhi's present; and Martin Luther King, who represents Gandhi's future. In this way, Glass plays with multiple temporalities, and a non-linear narrative emerges through the images and actions presented within each act as symbols of collective struggle. Similarly, in *Akhnaten* (1984), the last of the trilogy, Glass presents an "episodic-symbolic portrait" of the Egyptian Pharaoh (Richardson 1999: 37). Divided into three acts that illustrate Akhnaten's rise to power, his purging of polytheism, and his subsequent loss of power, the narrative transhistoricizes myth by calling attention to the Pharaoh's incestuous relationship with Queen Nefertiti and a self-mutilation modeled on the Oedipus myth.[13] Rather than accounting for the eclecticism as simply postmodern, John Richardson argues that Glass's strategy is Brechtian in that it promotes a kind of alienation technique by embedding *objets trouvées* or archeological materials into the opera as his way of grounding our perceptions of historical events in the present (49).[14]

These two strategies mythologize operatic subjects by transforming them into archetypal figures at a higher level of narrative discourse. Often, the protagonist can be identified as a known character in the opera's diegesis and as its archetypal representation at the meta-diegetic level; for example, consider how Akhnaten in Glass's opera can be identified simultaneously as the Egyptian Pharaoh and a reincarnation of Oedipus. This is compounded by the fact that contemporary operas deploy various non-linear narrative strategies, often foregrounding metaphor and symbolism to create new multilayered forms of storytelling. The four operas I examine reinterpret myth and enact narrative strategies that depart from conventional forms of storytelling. In Golijov's *Ainadamar* (chapter 2), the protagonist García Lorca is represented simultaneously as a revolutionary and a Christ-like figure within Xirgu's remembrance of the past; in Saariaho's *Adriana Mater* (chapter 3), Adriana represents *Mater Dolorosa* – a suffering Madonna – in a narrative context that alternates between a surrealistic dream world and diegetic world of the narrative; in Adams's *Doctor Atomic* (chapter 4), Robert Oppenheimer simultaneously inhabits the mythic worlds of Vishnu and Faust in a context where the boundaries between the diegetic and virtual worlds collapse; and in Tan Dun's *The First Emperor,* a prehistoric emperor, Qin Shi Huang, is closely identified with Mao Zedong in modern Chinese history to emphasize his role as antihero. Without these "shadow" representations that constitute Barthes's "second-order semiological order," the mythological dimension fails to materialize.

Analytical Methodologies

The remainder of this chapter discusses analytical methods for examining narrative, myth, and multimodality in application to contemporary operas. I examine structuralist and semiotic approaches for explaining the grammar of myth and narrative; psychoanalytic approaches for exploring the role of the unconscious in relation to myth and music; and multimodal and intermedial approaches for analyzing operatic narrative. Fundamental to my inquiry is how different components of an operatic production interact to tell a story with multiple references; while the elementary narrative structure can be extracted from the initial source materials (libretto and music), production components add other layers that complicate our multimodal narrative experience.

As a starting point for discussion, I will summarize several semiotic theories that have laid the foundation for analyzing the structure and signification of narrative in literary and musical contexts: A. J. Greimas's semiotic square and extension and application of the semiotic square to operatic narratives by Raymond Monelle (Wagner) and Andrew Davis (Puccini); James Liszka's hierarchal theory of narrative, transvaluation, and archetypes and Byron Almén's application of Liszka's theory to instrumental music; and finally, discussion of music's agential

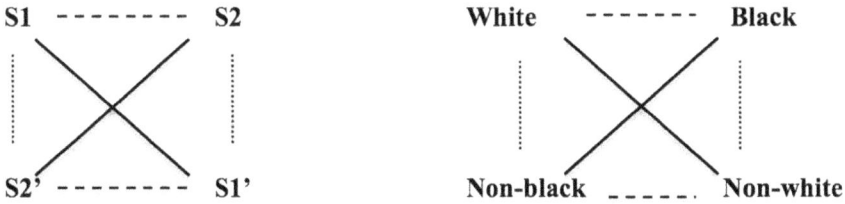

Figure 1.2. Semiotic Square

role in shaping opera's narrative dimensions, drawing on Robert Hatten's theory of *virtual* agency. Levels in narrative discourse correspond with the degrees of abstraction we traverse in our schematic understanding of operatic narrative; we proceed from identifying character roles and functions at the surface to extracting underlying patterns and dramatic oppositions that govern the narrative structure. I further extend Almén and Hatten's concept of tropological narrative to account for the juxtaposition of contradictory or incongruous intertexts in the multimodal production that sparks a new association or trajectory in the construction of meaning at a broader level of discourse. Let us first turn to the semiotic square.

A. J. Greimas and the Semiotic Square

In *Semiotics and Language: An Analytical Dictionary,* A. J. Greimas and J. Courtés introduce the semiotic square, which they define as "the visual representation of the logical articulation of any semantic category. The elementary structure of signification, when defined – in a first step – as a relation at least between two terms, rests only on a distinction of opposition which characterizes the paradigmatic axis of language" (1979: 308). Figure 1.2 summarizes the axes of the relationship as follows: S1 and S1' (or S2 and S2') form relations of *contradiction* or negation; S1 and S2 (or S1' and S2') form those of implication or *contrariety* in which the terms belong to the same semantic category; and S1 and S2' (or S2 and S1') form those of *complementation.* So, for example, if S1 = black and S2 = white, S1'= non-black, and S2'= non-white. Black and non-white are related by complementation; there is an overlap between these categories, yet they are not strictly oppositional, since non-white could include colors other than black.

Greimas then develops the semiotic square as a device that organizes narrative largely as a process of value creation. In *Structural Semantics,* he establishes two classes of narratives that accomplish the circulation of, or mediation between, certain objects of value situated according to the rules of narrative grammar, either in terms of narratives that affirm the present order or those that depart from it. Simply put, the relations between any of the four terms can be used to construct elementary narrative transformations.[15] As a system of semantic values, the semiotic square can then be used to represent systems of opposition that govern the formation of a narrative subject and actions that transform the narrative. To this end, Greimas examines Vladimir Propp's analysis of Russian folktales (2012). Propp supplies the term *roles* to distinguish the fundamental characters of the dramatis personae (e.g., villain, hero) from their thirty-one *functions* in the tale (e.g., stealing, killing, obtaining power). Greimas then substitutes the term *actants* to refer to Propp's roles, which are defined by their abstract qualities rather than the literal roles they assume in a given story. Within Propp's study of folktales, an inventory of seven actants can be established: 1) the villain, 2) the donor/provider, 3) the helper, 4) the sought-for person, 5) the dispatcher, 6) the hero, and 7) the false hero (Greimas 1983: 201). At the next level, Greimas reduces Propp's inventory of thirty-one functions to twenty, some of which are based on oppositions: 1) absence, 2) interdiction vs. violation, 3) inquiry vs. reformation, 4) fraud vs. complicity, 5) villainy vs. lack, and so forth (224–25). He then proceeds to construct logical models of transformation based on functions and actants to illustrate the different stages of the narrative in which rupture of the initial order leads to the acceptance and eventual restoration of order or in which narrative mediation involves the denial of the present order in favor of another (246).

In *Semiotics and Language: An Analytical Dictionary,* Greimas and Courtés broaden the range of what an actant encompasses with a systematic definition: "beings or things that participate in processes in any form whatsoever" and "a type of syntactic unit, properly formal in character, which precedes any semantic or ideological investment"; it also constitutes "the resultant terms of the relation known as the function" (1979: 5). Thus, unlike Propp, who restricted the term to refer to the dramatis personae, Greimas and Courtés consider sentient beings, objects, or concepts as potential actants. They further devise four categories of actants based on communication, narration, syntax, and function; any actant can then be projected onto the semiotic square, and, as the narrative discourse progresses, a given actant may assume a number of actantial roles – thus, a hero may function as a hero in only certain parts of the narrative (6).

In *Linguistics and Semiotics in Music,* Raymond Monelle applies Greimas's theories to his interpretation of the narrative structure of *Das Rheingold* from Wagner's Ring cycle. First, Monelle summarizes the basic unit of narrative utterance, NU, as defined by the function of an actant, $NU = F(A)$, e.g., "Siegfried kills a dragon." The *translative* utterance (TU) presents a more complex structure that includes three actants: sender (S1), object (O), and receiver (S2) within a function. For example, "Wotan gave the ring to the Giants" is represented by $TU = S1 \rightarrow O \rightarrow S2$ (Monelle 1992: 247). A sequence of NU or TU can be constructed to explain the course of action in a narrative. Second, Monelle constructs two semiotic squares, one showing the relations involving actants and the other showing the actantial functions that underlie the plot, as shown in figure 1.3a, which presents my summary of his analysis. Wotan, the primary sender, assumes different functions. While highly reductive, Monelle's schematic representation assigns specific actantial roles and functions to the main characters in order to reveal the underlying logic that guides the narrative unfolding of *Das Rheingold.*

a.

Actants (roles)   Functions

hero-god [Wotan] _ _ _ _ anti-hero [Alberich]   contract - - - - - - - - theft minus trickery

dream _____ dupe [Giants]   theft plus _____ spurious
women [Rhinemaidens]   trickery   contract

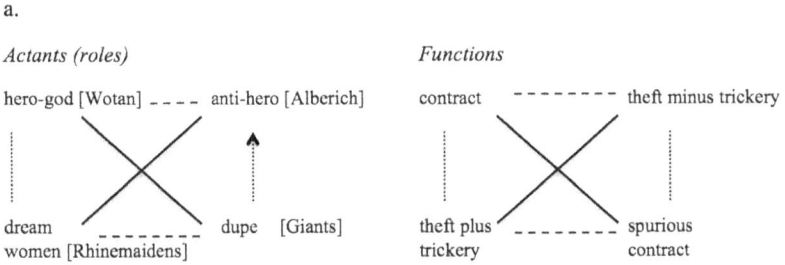

Wotan (the hero-god) obtains power from the giants (the dupes) by contract. Alberich (the anti-hero) obtains power from the Rhinemaidens (the dream-women) by theft (theft minus trickery). Wotan steals Alberich's power (theft plus trickery) and recovers his power from the giants with a spurious contract (249-50).

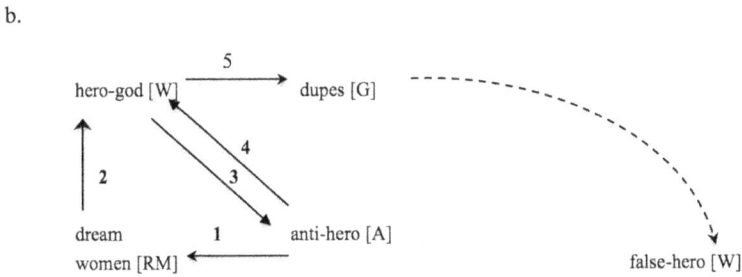

b.

5
hero-god [W] ——→ dupes [G]   - - - - - -

2   4
         3

dream   1   anti-hero [A]
women [RM] ←——   false-hero [W]

Figure 1.3a/b. Actantial Progression in Wagner's *Das Rheingold*

Building on Monelle's scheme, we can go further by using the square to show how Wotan's actantial position changes in the unfolding of the narrative. Greimas accounts for transformations in which the dramatis personae assume the roles of more than one actant through changes in function. In fact, in this narrative, the rupture in the initial order (theft of the Rhinegold) does not lead to the restoration of the initial order because Wotan's actantial role irrevocably changes from that of a hero-god to that of a false or fallen hero – all because he, too, becomes blinded by the power of the ring. In spite of the surface victory of obtaining Valhalla, Wotan's victory is ironically undermined by his fall from grace. Thus, a dynamic model illustrates how the progression reflects the change in Wotan's role (figure 1.3b). Here the actants are rearranged in such a way that hero-god and anti-hero are situated as contradictory elements that shape the dramatic opposition. The actantial progression revolves around the pursuit of power, and Wotan's contact with the anti-hero (Alberich) robs the hero (Wotan) of his virtue. Although Wotan relinquishes the ring to the Giants in order to save Fricka's sister Freie, his fate has forever been changed due to Alberich's curse. As is made evident later in *Siegfried,* when Wotan seeks Erda for council, the Goddess of Earth tells him that he has become a false ruler (hence, false-hero) of Valhalla and will soon be defeated by a race of humans (the Wälsung). In this way, *Das Rheingold*, the first of the tetralogy, ends with the seeming restoration of the existing order (Wotan as ruler of the newly acquired Valhalla) undercut by the implicit change in Wotan's role from hero-god to false-hero on a path that leads to the eventual demise of the gods.[16]

The semiotic square can thus be expanded into a dynamic tool for uncovering the theme of deception that runs throughout the Ring cycle. In *Mythology and Metaphor*, Cicora argues that the supposedly mythological world Wotan inhabits is a deceptive one; Wotan's self-fulfilling prophecy – that the curse on the ring will bring the demise of the gods – in the end reveals his own mortality (1998: 142). In the rest of the tetralogy, the actantial role of the hero is continuously undermined; Siegfried, who emerges as the hero by slaying the dragon Fafner in *Siegfried*, also turns into a false-hero when he falls prey to Hagen's trickery, loses his memory, and tricks Brünnhilde into becoming Gunther's wife in *Götterdämmerung*.

Other music theorists have expanded the Greimassian square by assigning agential roles to music within a progression of actants – dramatic oppositions that govern the transformative dimension of narrative. For example, Andrew Davis, in his dissertation on Puccini's *Turandot*, incorporates distinctive musical styles (what Harold Powers calls *tinta*) as signifiers of dramatic oppositions that govern the progression within each Act (2003: 177–85).[17] Figure 1.4 presents Davis's mapping of actants for Act I into four quadrants: "attraction" to Turandot's kingdom (S1), "attraction" to other familiar clans (S2), "repulsion" by Turandot's kingdom (S1'), and "repulsion" by other familiar clans (S2'). He then locates five different musical styles to illustrate their fixed or changing orientation within the square. The scene begins with the dissonant (Diss) music that accompanies the execution of the Persian prince. Throughout Act I the recurrence of the dissonant music signifies Turandot's cruelty and reinforces the repulsive image of the icy princess. The romantic style (Rom), in contrast, shifts in its actantial orientation, as indicated by the movements of the arrow (downward, then across to the upper left-hand corner). First, it conveys Calaf's, Timur's, and Liù's expression of love for the Tartary kingdom at reh.4 (as indicated in Davis's diagram) Then the romantic style occurs during Timur's admonitions of Calaf's reckless pursuit of Turandot (reh. 25). Finally the romantic style accompanies Calaf's admission of his love for Turandot in his aria "Non piangere, Liù" (reh. 43). The last style, the exotic-Chinese style, is associated with the "Mo-li-hua" theme, first heard when the children's choir sings the tune to glorify Turandot's kingdom (reh. 25). But then, the exotic-Chinese, romantic, and dissonant styles become associated with the trio of ministers who dissuade Calaf from his pursuit of the princess, and this scene contributes further to the negative image of Turandot.

Overall, Davis illustrates how the musical shift from "negative" to "positive" orientation toward Turandot is fully realized when Calaf rejects Liù's pleas in favor of his pursuit of the princess. He continues his analysis for the next two acts with appropriate changes in the structure of dramatic oppositions.[18] Act II hinges on the competition between Turandot and Calaf for dramatic leverage.

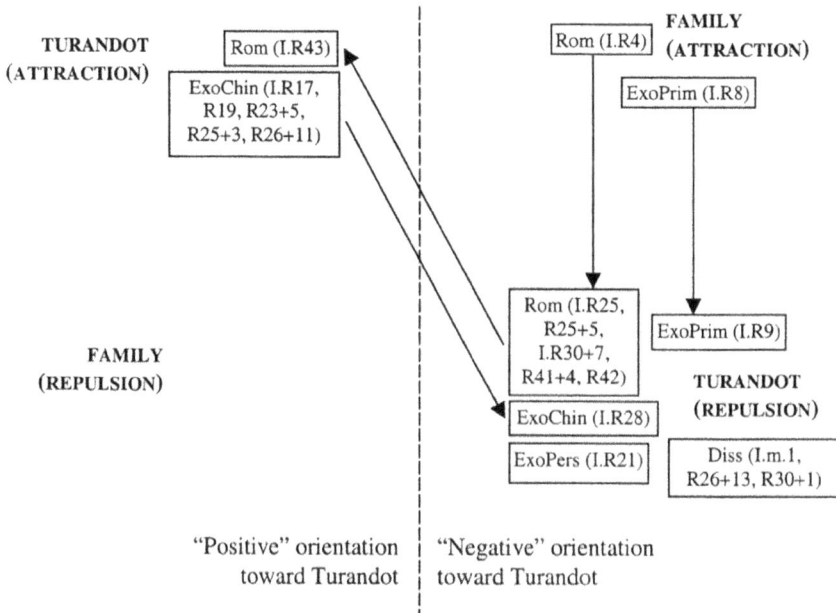

| TURANDOT (ATTRACTION) | Rom (I.R43) | Rom (I.R4) | FAMILY (ATTRACTION) |
| ExoChin (I.R17, R19, R23+5, R25+3, R26+11) | | ExoPrim (I.R8) | |

TURANDOT
(ATTRACTION)

Rom (I.R43)

ExoChin (I.R17,
R19, R23+5,
R25+3, R26+11)

FAMILY
(ATTRACTION)

Rom (I.R4)

ExoPrim (I.R8)

FAMILY
(REPULSION)

Rom (I.R25,
R25+5,
I.R30+7,
R41+4, R42)

ExoPrim (I.R9)

ExoChin (I.R28)

TURANDOT
(REPULSION)

ExoPers (I.R21)

Diss (I.m.1,
R26+13, R30+1)

"Positive" orientation
toward Turandot

"Negative" orientation
toward Turandot

Figure 1.4. Dramatic Oppositions in *Turandot* (Act I) (Davis 2003: 184)

Turandot begins as the dominant figure, and the ministers' lament encourages Calaf to abandon his quest; in the pivotal moment when Calaf solves the riddles, Turandot asks him to reconsider before he gives her a riddle to solve. Davis points out how, for the first time, exotic-Chinese music ("Mo-li-hua") is heard in association with Calaf's shift in rank to the victor. Calaf redirects the conflict so that Turandot, ironically, is placed in the position of having to solve the riddle (of Calaf's identity) if she wishes him to live. In the third act each character makes the final struggle for victory over the other. While the romantic aria "Nessun Dorma" signifies Calaf's vision of victory, the ministers' attempt to dissuade Calaf, and the re-association of "Mo-li-hua" with Turandot's glory, shift the balance. Davis expands the semiotic square to illustrate how dramatic oppositions are articulated via shifts in musical styles in the narrative unfolding of the opera. Davis's analysis shows how music and libretto co-articulate the shift from one actantial position to the next on the Greimassian square.

Extending the Greimassian square in this way transforms the static oppositions into a dynamic chain of events at the agential level of a multimodal narrative. The underlying dramatic oppositions (actants) can then be extracted and organized into an actantial progression that drives the narrative trajectory at a higher level of discourse. In so many instances, the initial condition that defines a character's role based on binary oppositions dissolves in the course of the narrative – say, a villain ends up being perceived as a non-villain. But how and where does this transformation take place in the narrative? If the libretto and music constitute the semiotic fields that define the basic narrative, how do other fields co-articulate broader metaphoric themes in the multimedial production? My analysis of Saariaho's *Adriana Mater* (chapter 3) demonstrates how the libretto and music jointly articulate four expressive registers (hope, rage, nurture, despair), which are organized into dramatic oppositions that shape the chronological dimension of the narrative. Adding the production components, these expressive states give way to temporal and psychological oppositions (reality, nonreality, conscious, unconscious) that shape one's tropological understanding of trauma at the actantial level of narrative discourse. In the following section, I will explain how one's schematic understanding of narrative can be formalized through a hierarchical framework.

Mythoi, Narrative Archetypes, and Transvaluation

In order to establish a more dynamic system of narrative analysis, literary theorists and semioticians have developed theories for their study of myths that embed valuative oppositions within a hierarchical framework of narrative archetypes. Let us now turn to the construction of myth as narrative in relation to Northrop Frye's *mythoi,* James Liszka's adaptation of Frye's categories in his broad cultural analysis of myths, and Byron Almén's formalization of Frye's and Liszka's theories into narrative archetypes for application to musical analysis.

In *The Semiotics of Myth* (1989), James Liszka examines myth from literary and semiotic perspectives in order to extract the underlying structure of myth as narrative. Taking cues from Charles Peirce's semiotics, he introduces the term *transvaluation* to refer to the condition that "any sign-referent relation is always mediated by a process which reevaluates the perceived, conceived, or imagined valuation of the referent within the pragmatic value structure of a sign user" (1989: 15).[19] Just as Freud envisioned dreams as transvaluative, Liszka sees myths as neither passive nor simply ideological representations of cultural life. Instead, myths are reflexive in the sense that the participants view and reflect on their own culture through the events they narrate. The process of transvaluation finds its locus in the act of narration, which entails the following basic scenario:

> The narration focuses on a set of rules from a certain domain or domains of cultural life, which define a certain cosmic, social, political, or economic hierarchy, and places them in a *crisis*. There is a disruption of the normative function of these rules – they are violated, there is some transgression. The narrative then unfolds a certain, somewhat ambivalent, resolution to this crisis, depending on the pragmatics of the tale: the disrupted hierarchy is restored or enhanced or, on the other hand, the hierarchy is destroyed, leading to social anomie, or terrible tragic consequences. (15)

In furthering his explication of narrative transvaluation, Liszka turns to Propp's *Morphology of the Folktale* (2012) in which the importance of the agents' narrative roles is defined by their spheres of action; e.g., the villain functions in initiating a lack, the hero in liquidating it, the helper in aiding the hero, and so forth (102). Yet Liszka criticizes Propp for failing to develop a dynamic form of narration based on these functions, and comments on the importance of the *circulation of values* that Greimas introduces into the dynamics of the narration; "the movement from lack to its liquidation is in effect a circular transference which constitutes the narration 'as a process that creates values'" (1989: 110).[20] Liszka then establishes a dynamic system of narration based on valuation by taking Propp's thirty-one functions and assigning markedness values (U = unmarked and M = marked); the dynamic system of narration emerges as the marked situations change to unmarked ones (115). Liszka takes Propp's sequence of functions and establishes three stages marked by 1) disruption of a hierarchy, 2) prolongation of the crisis, and 3) the restoration and/or enhancement of the hierarchy. He claims that a typical narrative moves from the initiation of a lack (marked) to its liquidation (unmarked), the act of villainy (marked) to its punishment (unmarked), and the actions of the hero (marked) to his reward (unmarked). Accompanying this progression is the relative ranking of the dramatis personae in terms of their functions; e.g., a hero becomes a false-hero due to deception (marked), a victim becomes a villain due to an act of villainy (marked), and so forth. In general, the marked rankings of the character persist through the prolongation of the crisis and the resolution of the conflict, and the restoration of the initial hierarchy corresponds with the point when their rankings become unmarked.

At the next level of inquiry, Liszka incorporates these valuative relations (marked versus unmarked) within the agential and actantial levels of analysis of myth. At the agential level, the various characteristics and features of the agents are identified along with their actants, the kinds of actions performed by these agents. Characters in a given myth are agents who perform specific actions that bring about changes in rank among other characters; for example, an agent, A, changes the condition of a patient, P; if the condition of P moves from high to low rank, A is identified as a villain and P a victim; in the opposite case (where P moves from low to high rank), A is identified as a hero (127). At the level of narrative, Liszka turns to Northrop Frye's four *mythoi* as a way of coordinating the agential and the actantial levels within a comprehensive framework of narrative types.

So let's take a quick look at Frye's narrative categories called mythoi. In *Anatomy of Criticism* (1957), Frye introduces comedy, romance, tragedy, and satire/irony as mythoi that generally contain six internal phases; the first or last three phases correspond with those of the neighboring category to create subtypes. For example, the last three phases of comedy (i.e., integrity quest, reflection, and *penseroso*) may overlap with those of romance for a comedic romance, while the first three phases of romance (i.e., myth of the hero, innocence, normal quest) overlap with those of tragedy to create a romantic tragedy. Similarly, the last three phases of tragedy (i.e., hero's fall, loss of direction, horror and despair) may overlap with those of satire/irony for a tragic irony, while the first three phases of satire/irony (i.e., stable universe, skepticism, and disintegration) overlap with those of comedy for an ironic comedy. Referring to numerous examples from literature (ranging from Biblical tales to Greek mythologies and from Shakespeare to Milton), Frye elucidates how these internal phases overlap from one type of mythos to another via archetypal themes: *agon,* or conflict, as the basis of romance; *pathos,* or catastrophe, as the theme of tragedy; *sparagmos,* or the absence of heroism and the reign of confusion and anarchy, as the theme of irony and satire; and *anagnorisis,* or triumph, as the theme of comedy (1957: 192).

Frye deftly shows how a comedy can range from the most savage irony (e.g., *The Mikado*) to the dreamiest wish-fulfillment type of romance, yet the basic structure remains the same. Furthermore, potential tragedy may lurk within comedy, and a tragedy may contain comic actions within an underplot (e.g., *Romeo and Juliet* and *King Lear*). As far as agential roles are concerned, comedy typically features a *senex iratus* (a "heavenly father" figure as an imposter) who impedes the love of the hero and heroine; romance features dream-characters; satire, caricatures; irony, a hero who is unaware ("dingy" to use Frye's own wording); and tragedy, the sacrifice of a splendid, magnanimous hero. For Frye, the four *mythoi* constitute generic plots with different types of agents and with internal phases that allow for a more fluid exchange of archetypal themes as shared by the four categories. Thus, Frye's literary categories differ by degree rather than by kind and offer a bottom-up structure.

In comparison to Frye, Liszka offers a top-down structure that emphasizes difference over commonality. He focuses on the "valuative tension" that underlies the ranking of order versus transgression at the narrative level such that comedy and romance share a narrative transvaluation based on the *victory* of one hierarchy over another, while tragedy and satire/irony share one based on the *defeat* of one hierarchy over another (133). It is the successful resolution to a conflict (*agon*) that defines romance, while the recognition (*anagnorisis*) of a new order of society triumphing over the old defines comedy. Similarly, the defeat of transgression by order results from *pathos* in tragedy, while the converse results from the absence of heroism (*sparagmos*) in irony. Byron Almén summarizes Liszka's strategies of "narrative transvaluation" as follows:

> Comedy: the *victory* of a transgression *over* an order-imposing hierarchy
> Romance: the *victory* of an *order*-imposing hierarchy *over* its transgression
> Tragedy: the *defeat* of a *transgression by* an order-imposing hierarchy
> Satire/Irony: the *defeat* of an *order*-imposing hierarchy *by* a transgression. (166)

Building on Lévi-Strauss's analysis of myths in *The Raw and the Cooked* (1964), Lizska analyzes tribal myths from different cultures to examine how valuative tensions on the agential level are organized similarly at the actantial level, but he claims that it is at the narrative level that radical differences emerge. For example, he compares the Netsersuitsuarssuk tale of the Netsilik Inuit (Canadian Eskimo) and the myth of the fisherwomen of the Bororo people (South America) for this very purpose. In the former, the male hunter cannot hunt seals, and his wife refuses him water; with the aid of his helper, the bear, he regains his hunting ability. In the latter, the men of the village cannot catch fish, while the women, with the help of the otters, are able to fish; the men kill the otters in revenge, and the women transform the men into pigs. At the agential level, Liszka explains how there are obvious eco-cultural differences, e.g., fish instead of seals, bears rather than otters; but, at the actantial level, the two myths are related by the shared *conflict* between men and women and the role of animals as the mediators of the conflict. At the narrative level, however, the original hierarchy is restored in the Netsilik tale (liquidation of the lack), while the Bororo tale entails the tragic consequences of the disruption of hierarchy (villainy is punished but results in the reversal of hierarchy). The transgressions in the Bororo tale (men killing the otters followed by the women's revenge) lead to a transvaluation of the ranking order of men and women. If "+" symbolizes power and "-" lack of power, the men's ranking can be represented as the initial lack followed by attainment and loss of power (- + -), while the women's can be represented as its opposite (+ - +). However, subjects construct meaning based on different cultural values: while the Bororo views this tale as a warning against the cross-division of labor, the non-Bororo may see it as an opportunity for women to start the society anew. Liszka argues repeatedly that ambivalence of this sort prevents myths as such from becoming ideological – being used merely as a tool for legitimizing values of the dominant hierarchy (216).

In *A Theory of Musical Narrative*, Byron Almén develops theoretical criteria for analyzing musical narrative that are informed by Frye's categories of *mythoi*, Tarasti's Greimassian theory of isotopy, and Liszka's concept of transvaluation. Echoing Liszka's position, he begins with the premise that narrative is essentially an act of transvaluation; a shift in meaning/values occurs through a change in the existing hierarchy based on ranking and markedness relations (2008: 51). He further notes that the change in the *perception* of dominance determines how this revaluation is to be interpreted, pointing to the role of the interpreter or observer in registering that change. By way of example, he refers to Susan McClary's analysis of the Brandenburg Concerto No. 5 in *Feminine Endings* (1991), in which the "transgressive crisis" is brought on by the harpsichord's change in status from a rhetorically subordinate to a dominant position. This change signals "an overturning of the subordinate relationship of an individual to society" (66).

Building on Liszka's tripartite model, Almén defines the *agential* level as the place where musico-semantic units are identified, characterized, and located in time. Isotopy is Tarasti's term for musical sections that are internally bound together by a singular narrative trajectory, and the *actantial* level is where the dynamic relationship between isotopies is defined. Here each musical-semantic unit is understood to have one or more expressive function(s) within the articulation of a given isotopy. These functions are coordinated through the articulation of a fundamental opposition at the *narrative* level, through which the interactions of the expressive units are understood in relation to the playing out of tensions between an order-imposing hierarchy and a transgression within that hierarchy (74). At the narrative level, Almén adopts Frye's literary categories (comedy, romance, tragedy, irony) based on Liszka's criteria of narrative transvaluation and refers to them as *narrative archetypes*.

So how does Almén apply these narrative archetypes to musical contexts? As an example of the tragic archetype, Almén refers to Schubert's Piano Sonata in B♭ major. Here he traces the process by which a tragic narrative emerges from the temporal unfolding of musical material. Adopting Tarasti's actorial reading of the principal theme as representing the narrative subject in instrumental music of this type, Almén divides the first movement into fifteen isotopies, roughly divided among the sections of its sonata-allegro form; for example, the exposition comprises "the incapable pastoral-heroic," "vacillation," "mitigated fulfillment," "illusory victory," and "resigned reflection." In the temporal unfolding of the piece, the initial, positively-ranked pastoral theme is overcome by the tragic *topos* of the trill figure, as well as other digressions. This idealized pastoral is supplanted by competing isotopies in the narrative development, and its idealized status is further weakened in the recapitulation; "the tragic effect is heightened when repetitions or near repetitions lead continually to the same results; the inability of the narrative subject to retain or achieve a higher rank value despite repeated attempts can generate a powerful impact on the listener" (157). More specifically, Almén points out the harmonically unstable treatment of the principal theme in the recapitulation. There are sudden tonal digressions (e.g., from G♭ major to F♯ minor at m. 247, which is prefigured in the exposition) when the "reminiscence" theme returns. Furthermore, the formal stability of the initial isotopy, comprising an internal ABA' form in which the pastoral theme re-emerges victoriously against the "reminiscence" theme, is entirely lacking in the recapitulation. Almén's reading of the coda (isotopy 15) as "regret" or resignation is also convincing; the principal theme is reduced to a self-enclosed turn figure with the trill figure casting its shadow to the very end.

While the theme of *pathos* that defines tragedy is undeniably present, one can also interpret the piece as displaying traits of Romantic irony. If the principal theme constitutes the objective self (idealized pastoral), the trill figure and other digressions could constitute the subjective reflection of self (shadow/reminiscence), whereby the actantial progression unfolds dialectically as a manifestation of this conflict. And the order-imposing hierarchy of the idealized self is, in the end, defeated by a transgression, as elements of doubt and despair are cast by the trill figure. Thus one could argue that the theme of *sparagmos* (absence of heroism) dominates over that of *pathos,* which characterizes the tragic theme in the Schubert sonata. To his credit, in the penultimate chapter of his book, Almén allows for greater interpretive flexibility and refinement of these archetypes by incorporating Frye's phases in his application of the ironic archetype and by introducing what Almén calls *discursive* strategies – narrative trajectories that enable processes of motion away from or toward normative points.[21]

The question then arises as to what extent Almén's narrative archetypes provide stable categories for analyzing the operas under study. With respect to mainstream operatic works, there are those that fit the archetypes apparently without equivocation: e.g., Mozart's *Marriage of Figaro* and Rossini's *Barber of Seville* (comic), Leoncavallo's *Pagliacci* and Puccini's *Madame Butterfly* (tragic), Puccini's *Turandot* (romance), Britten's *Peter Grimes* (irony), and so forth. Yet the

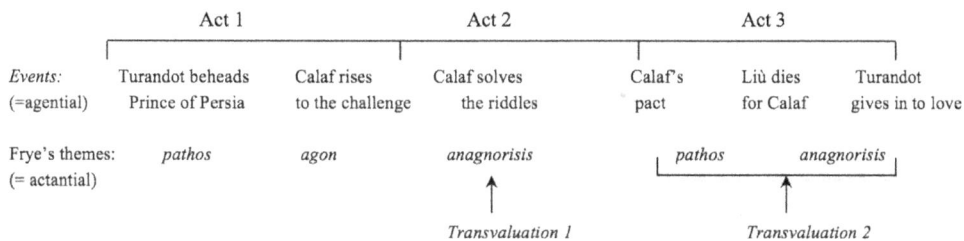

	Act 1		Act 2		Act 3		
Events: (=agential)	Turandot beheads Prince of Persia	Calaf rises to the challenge	Calaf solves the riddles	Calaf's pact	Liù dies for Calaf	Turandot gives in to love	
Frye's themes: (= actantial)	*pathos*	*agon*	*anagnorisis*		*pathos*	*anagnorisis*	
			Transvaluation 1			*Transvaluation 2*	

Figure 1.5. Actantial Progression in Puccini's *Turandot*

narrative structures of these well-known operas often resist being boiled down to one particular narrative archetype, due to the multiplicity of readings that arise from competing narrative trajectories. Take, for example, the narrative trajectory of the plot of *Turandot,* as shown in figure 1.5. The princess's agential role is divided into one of terror versus glory from the beginning; the dissonant leitmotif connotes the terror inflicted on her past suitors, while the "Mo-li-hua" theme celebrates her glory (or her glorious kingdom). Overall, the narrative encompasses themes of tragedy, romance, and comedy in the unfolding of the opera. Ping, Pang, and Pong provide comedic relief with their comic trios, Prince Calaf's proposition following his solving of the riddle presents a comedic form of transgression (transvaluation 1), while Liù's death provides a tragic turn of events (transvaluation 2). Comedy emerges as the dominant archetype when one considers how the initial hierarchy is toppled by Calaf's transgression. When Calaf solves the riddle (unmarking himself as captive), the ranking of Turandot and Calaf is reversed as he emerges as the victor and conqueror. The dramatic tension builds in yet another direction as Calaf confronts Turandot with the challenge of guessing his name (wherein Turandot becomes marked as captive). The next transvaluation occurs when Liù kills herself, honoring her love for Calaf, and this in turn compels Turandot to give in to love and embrace humanity once again (she becomes unmarked). In terms of Propp's functions, the initial lack (absence of harmony in Turandot's kingdom) is also liquidated.

Based on Almén's criteria, the narrative of *Turandot* lends itself to a comic archetype, characterized by the victory of Calaf's transgression over the order-imposing hierarchy of Turandot's kingdom and supported by the actantial state concluding with *anagnorisis* (triumph of the lovers). The challenge lies in what to make of Liù's death in light of the overall narrative since her ranking changes from an unmarked to a marked position, while Turandot's ranking changes from a marked to an unmarked one. Davis acknowledges the importance of Liù's self-sacrifice, which reinforces the element of tragedy; whether her character is central or extraneous to the dramatic narrative, it complicates the narrative trajectory of *Turandot.* Unlike other scholars who dismiss Liù as superfluous to the central drama, Davis asserts that the role of the slave girl is pivotal in compelling Turandot to acknowledge her love for Calaf in the third and final act. He argues that, musically, the opera ends with Liù's cortège (funeral progression), even if the narrative continues in order to provide actantial closure marked by the reconciliation of the lovers (2010: 221).[22] Rather than reducing a single narrative archetype, one could argue that the narrative trajectory is ambivalent precisely because the archetypal themes of *anagnorisis* and *agon* associated with comedy and romance, competes with *pathos,* central to tragedy. It isn't entirely clear whether Liù's tragic death supplements or supplants the triumphant ending. By putting the marked and unmarked rankings of the two female characters on an equal footing under the second transvaluation, my reading allows for the tragic element to occupy as important a place in the narrative as the comic or romantic. Just as Frye's original *mythoi* allow for overlapping themes between genres, most operas do not strictly conform to a generic categorization and thus require a more flexible discursive strategy to account for areas of deviation.

On Agency: Seme, Motive, and Topic

Consider now the types of agential roles one can attribute to music and other semiotic fields in analyzing opera. In *Unsung Voices,* Abbate discusses the mimetic versus diegetic role of music in nineteenth-century opera. She claims that music's function is primarily mimetic; operatic music *mimes* or dances out "the world in present time," but it cannot narrate on its own terms (1991: 53). In *Myth and Music* (1978), Eero Tarasti poses the question differently by asking whether music is "in any sense capable of representing features of external reality?" (1979: 86). For Tarasti, the answer is in the affirmative: the mimetic function of music *is* one way in which it tells a story on its own terms.[23] Edward T. Cone, in *The Composer's Voice* (1974), introduces the idea of a *master-persona* to account for various agencies that listeners identify with in their experiences of Romantic music (106). Yet neither Tarasti nor Cone addresses the intentional fallacy – the tendency for a listener/analyst to conflate the composer's intention with his/her attribution of agency to music.

In ascribing agency to music, Robert Hatten offers a taxonomy that distinguishes *actual* agents (composer and performer) from *virtual* agents (internal, external, and narrative agents) with whom listeners engage (2010: 166). He emphasizes how emergent meanings arise from the listeners' choice of identifying (co-experiencing) with or responding to a virtual agent, as follows:

> The listener may choose to map a virtual agent's presumed dramatic trajectory onto her own personal experiences, effecting a kind of para-experiencing of the emotional plot of the music's trajectory. Or the listener may choose not to invest personal emotion, but rather critically assess or appreciate the emotive expressiveness of the work, or use that evaluation as a springboard to interpret other dimensions of the work.... (168)

The present study is concerned with *how* music, as virtual or anthropomorphic agents, shapes one's reading of operatic narrative in relationship to other semiotic fields. If the libretto provides the initial narrative "map" that spells out characters and actions performed along a chronological timeline, music, along with other production components, gives voice to a range of dramatic oppositions or actantial themes in shaping the chronological and configurational dimensions of the narrative. Furthermore, in its intermedial relationship to other semiotic fields, music and libretto occupy an essential role in shaping the viewer's psychological and emotive response to opera. In short, if the music fails to complement the words and be dramatically persuasive, the entire work fails. From a semiotic perspective, music fulfills the role of virtual agent through a broad range of categories: seme, motive, topic, and isotopy, in the order of minimal to maximal unit of signification.

In *Structural Semantics,* Greimas defines a seme as the "minimal unit" of signification contained within a *lexeme,* which refers to a word or phrase. Greimas stresses that the nature of a seme is "purely relational" in that its characteristics can only be defined in relation to at least one other term within the same relational network: "it is by giving a precise logical status to constituent relations of such a structure that the concept of seme can be determined and made operational" (1983: 278). So, for example, Greimas asks readers to consider the different constellations of meaning that arise from the use of the word *la tête* (head) in French (50). While its basic reference to the "part of the body" constitutes the nuclear seme, its various connotations constitute contextual semes and effect change in meaning, as shown below:

Expressions	Semic categories
la tête d'un arbre (the top of a tree)	[verticality/superiority]
être à la tête des affaires (to be on top in business)	[verticality/superiority]
tête de ligne (head of a line)	[anteriority/horizontality]

Applied to musical contexts, Tarasti defines a musical lexeme as equivalent to a motive or a phrase. He defines a musical seme as a smaller unit defined by such categories as size, length, speed, intensity, density, continuity, tension, etc.,: "[semes] can characterize musical lexemes by organizing themselves into oppositions like long/short, slow/fast, soft/loud, thick/thin, continuous/discontinuous," and so forth (1979: 73). But this is where the connection with Greimas's operational definition for semes seems to end. In his early writing on music and myth, Tarasti treats a seme as synonymous with a musical topic or style type, which in turn corresponds with Karl Jaspers's classification of mythical types such as nature-mythical, hero-mythical, and magic-mythical (75). By taking inventory of the formulaic devices used to portray mythical elements in romantic music ranging from Liszt to Wagner, Tarasti asserts that stylistic procedures in music "imitate and reconstruct mythical messages" in the same way mythical tales have been told and retold in new contexts.[24]

In his subsequent book, *A Theory of Musical Semiotics* (1994), Tarasti introduces the concept of *actoriality,* in terms of which themes and motives operate as independent musical actants within an instrumental work. In his analysis of Liszt's *Vallée d'Obermann,* Tarasti extracts five *isotopies* based on the narrative program as follows: "ennui" (mm.1–74), "wandering" (mm.75–118), "fight or storm" (mm.109–69), "pastoral" (mm.170–203), and "pantheist apotheosis" (mm.204–16). In this context, the main theme turns into a narrative subject, and the musical narrative emerges as an anthropomorphic portrayal of Sénancour's hero, frustrated in his quest to satisfy his "unquenchable desires." The main methodological change in Tarasti's 1994 theory lies in his treatment of seme and isotopy; here, he defines seme as a minimal unit of signification equivalent to a musical motive, while isotopy is equated with a programmatic element that defines the actorial function of a given musical theme that is pervasive throughout an entire section. Márta Grabócz further develops a classification scheme in which seme occupies a minimal unit of signification in a hierarchical relationship with classeme and semantic isotopy; she applies this system to the instrumental music of Liszt circa 1840–50.[25]

In *Linguistics and Semiotics in Music* (1992), Raymond Monelle offers a working definition and musical application for seme that fall in line with Greimas's linguistic model. A lexeme constitutes the basic linguistic expression (word or phrase), which groups together atoms of meaning (semes) in a characteristic pattern (233). The invariant meaning constitutes the semic nucleus (e.g., "head" in the context of *la tête*), while variant meanings constitute contextual semes (e.g., verticality or anteriority depending on context). Applied to the Prelude to Wagner's *Tristan und Isolde,* Monelle extracts the ascending chromatic motion (seme) as a minimal unit of signification shared in common between the interlocking "desire" leitmotifs (lexemes); he then illustrates how this seme interacts with other semic attributes (e.g., dotted rhythm, falling seventh) associated with the family of related leitmotifs in giving expressive shape to the "accretion of semantic content" in the rest of the Prelude (1992: 236–41). Thus, in addition to recognizing the ascending chromatic motion as the primary seme, Monelle illustrates how a constellation of semic attributes shapes the expressive meaning of leitmotifs in *Tristan und Isolde.*

With more complex dramatic forms involving text, music, and production components, can semes and isotopies be adopted as viable tools for analyzing operatic narratives? First, building on Monelle's application, I identify a seme as a minimum unit of signification that shapes the expressive meaning of a motive, topic, phrase, or chordal unit. A *pianto* topic, for example, comprises a descending semitone as its primary seme, yet its expressive function may be altered in a given context by a constellation of other semic attributes that accompanies it. In *Adriana Mater* (chapter 3), I argue that the pervasive use of a descending semitone motive emerges as a primary seme. Yet the musical context dictates whether it functions as a topic (identifiable as *pianto* or "sigh" motive) or acquires a provisional quality that *resists* a fixed categorization because its expressive connotation continually changes in relationship to the composer's expressive indications. Moreover, in the viewer's schematic development of narrative experience, musical semes can be defined dynamically in relationship to other production components (film, objects, lighting, mime or dance) as conveyors of hidden, unconscious layers of meaning that emerge. For example, when accompanied by blue lighting and dialogue that centers on birth, the semitone descent connotes a maternal sense of yearning; when accompanied by red lighting and dialogue that centers on male aggression, it connotes despair. Similarly, in *Ainadamar* (chapter 2), color assumes a primary semic function; blue lighting is correlated with scenes depicting lament and mourning, while red lighting is associated with death and violence. To reiterate, a seme acquires expressive meaning in the context of its enunciation.

Second, leitmotifs and topics will appear as important perceptual markers of dramatic expression in two operas under study. While leitmotifs acquire expressive meaning within the context of a given work, topics are conventionalized musical signs that carry coded meanings shared by a musical community. In short, topics are signifiers with *a priori* meaning. In *The Sense of Music: Semiotic Essays,* Raymond Monelle states that "the topic is essentially a symbol, its iconic or indexical features governed by convention and thus by rule" (2000: 17). For example, the motive of a falling minor second (*pianto*) emerged as the iconic feature of weeping in Western music but came to signify grief, pain, regret, or loss through its indexical association with the physical act of weeping. In contrast, topics such as the "fanfare" motive and the Sarabande are purely indexical in the sense that they do not signify by virtue of resemblance but rather through association (Monelle 2006: 28). In an analysis of postmodern operas such as *Le Grand Macabre,* I argue that György Ligeti introduces iconic and indexical topics (e.g., *Dies Irae* as a symbol of death and destruction) to articulate the grotesque trope: his parodic procedures establish the dramatic opposition between ludicrousness and horror (Everett 2009). In Adams's *Doctor Atomic* (chapter 4) and Tan Dun's *The First Emperor* (chapter 5), the main themes of the narrative are articulated via leitmotifs and musical topics. Stylistic changes effected via topics or leitmotifs – such as the "lament" aria that conveys the moral dilemma faced by Robert Oppenheimer or the "reminiscence" aria that conveys Qin Shi Huang's nostalgia for the past – are directly linked to dramatic oppositions that govern the actantial level of discourse. In dissecting Adams's minimalistic musical language, I further distinguish emergent or proto-topics from established topics and stylized quotations; at times, Adams embeds a "clock" motive that signifies the ontological passing of time against more conventional topics such as the fanfare and military march. Over the driving, repetitive pulse that signifies the physical restlessness of the workers, Adams adds conventional topics to provide psychological commentary. Nested within the dramatic action, a network of musical motives and topics – in conjunction with dance, lighting, and sung text – effectively conveys the anxiety of the military workers who await the next command.

Third, the *episodic* temporality in these operas precludes isotopy as a functional category. This is due to the fact that episodic musical texture typically undermines the prolongation of a singular "set of semantic categories" that unify the music into clearly demarcated sections. In short, musical processes are not confined to the traditional pairing of recitative and aria, which ensures that a particular dramatic expression is prolonged across an entire section. Instead, the process tends to be erratic, marked by formal discontinuity and fragmentation where the surface musical texture continuously changes and evolves. As Davis posits in his analysis of Puccini's *Turandot,* stylistic change *becomes* the formal delineator in articulating an episodic form: "styles create their own melodramatic form, complete with their own formal functions and expressive indications" (2010: 173).[26] The episodic structure similarly governs temporality in these operas, although each differs in the deployment of semes, rhythmic motives, leitmotifs, and/or topics to articulate the agential structure. For example, in *Adriana Mater,* Saariaho alternates between episodic form and disjunct textural blocks to express the characters' suppressed desires and traumatic ruptures. And in this context, my analysis will illustrate how musical semes track the characters' psychological orientation independently of what the sung text conveys.

Lastly, the goal in the present study is not to determine a neat and tidy archetypal fit, but rather to locate moments of disruption or dissolution of oppositions that articulate shifts in narrative discourse (transvaluation), as demonstrated in my analysis of *Turandot* (figure 1.5). I begin by explaining how the music and libretto fit together to tell the basic story, then consider how the production media add new layers to our schematic understanding of the multimodal narrative. To formalize this process, I examine how semiotic fields co-articulate the structure and meaning of narrative at three levels: *agential* (sequence of events/actions in the chronological dimension), *actantial* (dramatic oppositions that structure the transformational dimension of narrative), and *tropological* (competing narrative trajectories that arise at the schematic level of multimodal discourse). Almén and Hatten, in their essay on twentieth-century music and narrative, introduce the category of "tropological" narrative to account for "a multi-level discourse, one in which the implied trajectories of the surface style are negated by the presumed ironies of the higher-level discourse" (2012: 71). Trope, for Hatten, refers to a figurative play in which the fusion of musical types or topics sparks an interpretation based on their interaction (1994: 295). Referring to Britten's *War Requiem,* Almén and Hatten argue that the troping of disparate texts and musical styles generates ironic meaning, and the connections forged serve to undermine or deconstruct traditional formal schemes. The function of this requiem is no longer a mass celebrated for the repose of the souls of the dead. The provisionality of Britten's ending – a bell tritone followed by the estranged sound of F major – calls attention instead to the *futility* of the liturgical plea for eternal peace. Moreover, Philip Rupprecht comments on the troping of tropes in the Offertorium, where the received form of the Latin *Missa pro Defunctis* is disrupted through Owen's reworking of the biblical narrative (The book of Genesis) that "harbors its own discursive shifts" (2001: 212).

In the present study, tropological narrative is *not* confined to the articulation of irony, but rather to the engendering of inconclusive and multivalent narrative trajectories that arise in the staging of opera.[27] In these operas, the juxtaposition of incongruous or contradictory intertexts in the semiotic fields often sparks a new metaphoric association in constructing narrative meaning. In many instances, the agential roles of characters (identifiable in the initial source material) may be destabilized and transformed through events and secondary intertexts that are introduced in the context of production. For example, even if a basic narrative pits the character of Ruiz Alonso as the enemy of García Lorca in Golijov's *Ainadamar* (chapter 2), his role as antihero may be undermined or put into question by the mise-en-scène. It may also be that the director adds visual themes in the staging that are not only extraneous to the basic narrative, but that change the tenor of the operatic discourse. Penny Woolcock's staging of *Doctor Atomic* (chapter 4) foregrounds the oppression of Native Americans – a theme not present in the libretto – in precisely this manner. Tropological narrative thus encourages the audience to contemplate the broader questions posed by a deliberate lack of narrative closure, much in the same way classical telling of myth impels the reader to contemplate the allegorical meanings behind the story being told.

Psychoanalytic Theories, Opera, and Myth

Returning to Barthes's dual signification of myth, psychoanalytical theories provide an important interpretive framework for the multimodal study of contemporary operas precisely because they reveal hidden layers that shape narrative at the tropological level. Additionally, the nonlinear framework of these operas reveals "apertures" into the realm of the unconscious through ruptures in the narrative progression. In *The Interpretation of Dreams* (1899), Sigmund Freud draws his psychoanalytic theories such as the categories of id, ego, and super ego from the analysis of myth. He views mythical figures as powerful symbols for how the human psyche develops at the level of the unconscious. Notably, he extracts the latent stage of development from the manifest level of a myth; the Oedipus complex is derived from the hero of Sophocles's play, who pursues a quest of self-discovery that leads him to an earlier trauma. Franz Schreker, a contemporary of Freud, incorporated Freud's psychoanalytical techniques into his music for the opera *Der ferne Klang* (1912), in which dreams represent a constant striving for an ideal.

In contrast to Freud, who conceives of these myth-derived categories as manifestations of the individual psyche, Carl Jung claims that myths are the product of the collective unconscious. In advancing the view that the collective unconscious cannot be precisely defined, Jung provides his own categories of archetypes, symbols, and allegories to refer to its surface manifestations. Myth succeeds as an intermediary when its conscious, literal meaning suggests another symbolic and psychological meaning. For Jung, the personal unconscious manifests itself through various complexes and archetypes (1980: 42). The subject acquires *individuation* (spiritual, psychological, or emotional maturation) by confronting and overcoming these complexes. Adopting Jung's "situational" archetypes, Joseph Campbell (1973) demonstrates how myths across different cultures are modeled on a hero's journey that typically involves a cycle of Quest, Initiation, Fall, and Death and Rebirth, which he further divides into seventeen stages. The term *monomyth* refers to the fundamental stages shared by numerous myths from disparate times and regions around the world. Jacqueline Furby and

Claire Hines have applied Campbell's theory of monomyth and Jungian archetypes to their analysis of the narrative structure of fantasy films such as the *Lord of the Rings* trilogy (2012: 60–64).[28]

Jungian archetypes and complexes provide us with rich character analysis in operatic narrative, especially in cases where the characters' actions are driven by desires or impulses at the levels of the unconscious (the part of the mind that is active without our being aware) or subconscious (the part of the conscious mind that is repressed). Using psychoanalysis to interpret the *Ring* cycle, for example, it is easy to understand Siegfried's quest to find his love (Brünnhilde) in terms of Jung's idea of the mother-complex: Siegfried learns fear for the first time when confronting the source of his deep-seated trauma, which was caused by his severance from his mother (Sieglinde) at birth. Siegfried achieves individuation only by confronting and overcoming his fear of the opposite sex, although in *Götterdämmerung* the same drive is used against him to entrap Brünnhilde when, under Hagen's spell, Siegfried offers her to Gunther in order to secure Gutrune as his own. Wagner's use of leitmotifs is particularly suited for expressing what lies in the character's unconscious; e.g., the "curse" motive that sounds when Siegfried encounters Hagen at the court of the Gibichungs on the Rhine signifies Hagen's deceitful influence on Siegfried as they exchange the oath of blood brotherhood.

In addition to Freud and Jung, scholars in recent years have turned to Jacques Lacan's psychoanalytical theory for understanding the role of the unconscious as it relates to language, trauma, and art. According to Lacan, a child grows up with a sense of being undifferentiated from its mother's voice, warmth, and gestures. The break from this initial state of wholeness, which Lacan calls the Real, occurs once the subject enters into the symbolic discourse of language:

> The Real is thus that which precedes discourse and that which is left unstated in the symbolic process. Although the Real cannot appear as an entity in reality, its existence affects the subject's reality, as the gap causes the creation of traumatic forms (e.g., ruptures, symptoms, stains, residues). These traumatic events create distortions in the symbolic universe, upsetting the smooth running of our discursively created universe and displaying its deficiencies, and, thus, ultimately displaying the empty kernel, the void or lack upon which reality rests. (Reichardt 2008: 78)

There has been considerable debate over what exactly the Real entails. In *The Sublime Object of Ideology,* Slavoj Žižek claims that, against the symbolic order that structures our perception of reality, the Lacanian Real is an entity that resists symbolization – "the brute, pre-symbolic reality which returns to its place" (1989: 182). And trauma is one of the symptoms of the Real that distorts our perception of reality. As Žižek elaborates:

> In the 1950s, in [Lacan's] first seminar, the traumatic event is defined as an imaginary entity which had not yet been fully symbolized, given a place in the symbolic universe of the subject; but in the 1970s, trauma is real – it is a hard core resisting symbolization, but the point is that it does not matter if it has had a place, if it has

"really occurred" in so-called reality; the point is simply that it produces a series of structural effects (displacements, repetitions, and so on). The Real is an entity which must be constructed afterwards so that we can account for the distortions of the symbolic structure. (182)

In Lacanian theory, the subject is always divided, split between ego (the conscious, but false self) and unconscious; the unconscious state of mind interrupts the flow of events in the conscious mind (Fink 1995: 45).[29] The elements of the Imaginary that resist assimilation into the Symbolic manifest as the residues of the Real. They "bubble up" to the surface via three objects that connect the Imaginary, the Symbolic, and the Real orders: *object petit a,* which links the Symbolic with the Real; S($\bar{A}$) which links the Imaginary with the Symbolic; and Φ, which links the Real with the Imaginary domain. Here I provide an abridged explanation of how these objects can be applied to the analysis of operatic narrative.

For Lacan, *object petit a* represents the desire of the Other (initially the mother) that comes to represent the subject's cause of desire. The *object a* becomes the thing that the subject seeks in all activities and relations – the "lost object" that can never be fully retrieved. For Siegfried in Wagner's *Ring* cycle, his mother's love stands as the very object that was denied to him at birth, and it emerges as the dominant force that propels him to seek out Brünnhilde and to find fulfillment in love.[30] In Tan's *First Emperor,* Qin Shi Huang's search for the perfect anthem masks his unconscious desire to recapture his youth and innocence that he shared with the slave, Gao Jianli. This loss propels his need for domination and the expansion of his kingdom.

Lacan's second object, S($\bar{A}$), constitutes a material fragment of reality that cannot be reduced to a network of formal relations proper to the symbolic structure, but which effects a positive condition as an object of exchange circulating among subjects. Consider the role of the ring in Wagner's tetralogy; as it is passed around, first as a symbol of power and then as a curse, it symbolizes something other than itself; it is an object that manifests both desire and fear. Finally, the third object, Φ, has a massive, oppressive presence, which Žižek describes as an "objectification" of the Real that is the very embodiment of *jouissance* – the psychic source that gives rise to the positive and negative poles of desire.[31] As a case in point, Žižek refers to the images of the birds in Hitchcock's *The Birds;* it is not literally the birds that we fear, but how they objectify a threat to human society through their brutal, collective force (1989: 208).

Applied to multimodal narrative involving music, the changing modes of enunciation established between the verbal (sung text) and non-verbal (music, gestures, and staging) components represent Lacan's stages of subject formation in compelling ways. The Imaginary or mirror stage is often represented by instrumental preludes and interludes in which *contrasting* expressive registers meld into one another without the symbolic intervention of words. The symbolic order, on the other hand, is represented by a clear differentiation of musical expressions at the surface – including, but not limited to sung texts and the composer's expressive indications. Sarah Reichardt, in her application of Lacan's theory to Shostakovich's String Quartets, for example, discusses how the Real is manifested as trauma via the composer's specific treatment of musical motives and gestures. Notably, she argues that Shostakovich's obsessive repetition of the D-S-C-H motive, the (0134) tetrachord, in String Quartet No. 7 functions as the *object petit a* that represents "the empty kernel upon which reality is constructed" – a signifier of that which remains ultimately unsignified (2008: 60). In her analysis of String Quartet No. 6, she interprets the role of the cadential figure exchanged between movements, which through its lack of integration into the musical texture comes to represent S(Ⱥ) as the lack in the Other (21–22).

Furthermore, Lawrence Kramer notes that what he calls the *excess remainder,* which drives the hermeneutic process, originates as ruptures of the Real and rises to the surface as immaterial, "traces of the unsaid or unseen." Kramer argues that, with utterances of a melody that occur without words, the Real is given a positive presence. Through pure vocalization, the remainder is made "material and sensuous." As a case in point, in reference to a chantey sung by the crew at the dock in Britten's *Billy Budd* (1951), Kramer points out how its metamorphosis into an orchestral chantey without words transforms the melody into a symbol of desire; in spite of Vere's silent order for Budd's execution, his unspoken dilemma is communicated by the presence of this "speaking melody" through which the men's longing becomes "manifest as the unfathomable substrate that the opera, at best, can symbolize only in part" (2006: 272). The important point is that the emotional substrate can only be symbolized in a manner that remains provisional. In my analysis of Saariaho's *Adriana Mater* (chapter 3), the semitone descent emerges as a primary semic unit that hovers in the instrumental background, detached from the protagonist's vocal form of enunciation; as an excessive element, S(Ⱥ), which is detached from the textual enunciation, it projects Adriana's inner trauma as a manifestation of "the traces of the unsaid." I interpret moments of rupture that move beyond the symbolic utterance as the site of engagement with the Real (Φ). For example, in *Adriana Mater,* the traumatic experience involving rape is conveyed through the obsessive repetition of a given chord, accompanied by the semic use of lighting. The internal trauma is expressed even more poignantly through sounds and color, disembodied from the physical act of violence.

Lacan's four discourses – schematic models that demonstrate how the subject's conscious and unconscious selves interact with other signifiers – together offer a useful framework for explaining the source of conflict at the actantial level of narrative discourse.[32] As shown in figure 1.6, these discourses depict different behavioral schemes that the "split" subject occupies in relationship to the world s/he inhabits. In the master's discourse, S1 is frequently called the master signifier because it stands for the authorial figure who addresses the Other (S2); in the process, the master bars some aspects of the truth in order to maintain a commanding presence (S̸) and the interaction results in a "dissimulated" truth (a). Any form of indoctrination into a political ideology that upholds a system of belief as truth – e.g., Hitler's fascism – is founded on this model. In the university's discourse, systematic knowledge (S2) takes place of the authorial figure (S1) by

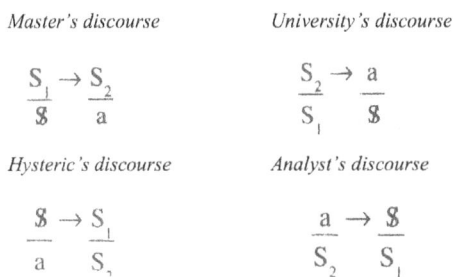

Figure 1.6. Lacan's Four Discourses
(Fink 1995: 130–36)

challenging "surplus value" (a) to reveal an alienated subject (S), as in the case of Marxist theory on capitalism. Conversely, in a hysteric's discourse, the divided subject (S) challenges the authorial figure (S1) in order to obtain knowledge (S2) that has been barred while remaining unaware of the cause of his/her desire (a). Because they proved the inadequacy of his knowledge and know-how, hysterics ultimately led Freud to develop psychoanalytic elaborations of his theories (Fink 1995: 134). What is gained through the hysteric's discourse is a new form of knowledge. Finally, in the analyst's discourse, *object a* takes the front seat as the analyst interrogates the "split" subject (S); while repressing other forms of knowledge (S2), the analyst uncovers the master signifier (S1) that had not been put into association with other signifiers. An obsessive behavioral pattern (e.g., hand washing) in an adult subject can be traced to a traumatic event from childhood that the subject has tried to repress; the analyst connects the surface behavior to other signifiers (S2) in order to identify the source of the trauma (S1).

Operatic narrative typically involves a progression of events that arises through the interaction of competing discourses. Žižek analyzes the characters from Wagner's *Parsifal* in the following manner: King Amfortas (S1) is corrupted by the magician Klingsor (S2) but is ultimately saved by Parsifal, the "pure fool" (a), who is able to resist Kundry's powers of seduction (S) (1993: 177). Unpacking this scenario a bit more, one could say that the initial stage of corruption that takes place in *Parsifal* is modeled on the hysteric's discourse: Klingsor and Kundry deceive Amfortas in order to gain knowledge about the Holy Grail. The path toward the restoration of order that follows is modeled on the analyst's discourse: by coming into contact with the hysteric sorceress, Kundry, Parsifal acknowledges Amfortas's suffering and reveals his connection to the master signifier. Through various trials and denouements, Parsifal emerges as the unknowing object of desire that unlocks the key to Amfortas's suffering and restores order to the domain of Montsalvat, where the Holy Grail is kept.[33] In a tragic narrative, however, the actantial progression typically involves the undermining of a master's discourse by others. In Saariaho's *Adriana Mater* (chapter 3), it is the shift from the master's to the hysteric's discourse that provides the long-awaited resolution to Adriana's moral dilemma of whether to perpetuate or put an end to the cycle of violence; without Yonas (as hysteric) challenging the women (as masters) about the truth of his identity, they would forever remain the victims of violence.

Thus, Jungian and Lacanian theories provide useful interpretive tools for uncovering either the archetypal complex that drives a character's actions or the music's hidden agency in commenting on the suppressed desires of the dramatis personae. In this way, psychoanalytic methods of interpreting human relations parallel narrative strategies that mythologize the subject in operatic discourse. As Jeppe S. Jensen comments, "the study of myth has mostly been an exercise in recovering something 'hidden' and then in the form of interpretive, hermeneutic attempts of understanding the deeper, or true, 'meanings' of the myths" (2009: 13).

Theorizing Multimodal Discourse and Intermediality

Returning to the idea of multimodal discourse, the methodologies discussed so far offer potential tools for explaining the mythical dimension in operatic narrative. However, we need to take into account how media elements *qua* semiotic fields relate to one another in articulating the structure and meaning of multimodal narrative. In the realm of theatrical performance and film studies, intermediality has emerged as an overarching term that defines the relative importance and interaction of media elements from various perspectives. Given the four modalities (material, sensory, spatiotemporal, and semiotic) that underlie one's experience of all conceivable media, Elleström argues that intermedial relations either combine and integrate these modalities into a unified whole – e.g., musical theatre, opera – or mediate and transform them into a new entity – e.g., a poem that describes a painting (38). For the purpose of the present study, I will qualify intermediality as the condition that defines the *relationship* between semiotic fields in co-articulating the structure of narrative at the agential level, while multimodality has to do with *representation* – what the interplay of semiotic fields signifies in the viewer's construction of narrative. In this concluding section, I will call attention to several theories that bring the intermedial and multimodal connections in line with the structure of narrative and generation of meaning.

As a means for categorizing intermedial relations, I refer to Nicholas Cook's three basic models of multimedia: conformance, complementation, and contest (1998: 98–99). The technique of "mickey-mousing" (where the soundtrack mimes every gesture) offers a simple example of conformance. According to Cook, a more sophisticated *conformant* model is based on synaesthetic and metaphysical associations between media sources. For example, the color-sound relationship in Alexander Scriabin's *Prometheus* Symphony was conceived in accordance with the composer's synaesthetic vision; Cook even provides a chart in the score that depicts the isomorphic link between each chord and a specific color. In comparison, a *contest* model articulates a "relationship of semantic difference" that cannot be resolved, as exemplified by Eisenstein's montage technique in *Alexander Nevsky*; here, the images and music elaborate the inner motion in quite distinctive ways so that "this differential elaboration establishes an asymmetry between the two media" (Cook 1998: 100). Finally, a *complementation* model allows each media source to retain its own intrinsic properties, while fitting together harmoniously with other sources. Cook refers to Schubert's settings of Heine's poems, in which the text and music retain their independence while contributing to the whole (104–105). Opposite to the dominance of the visual is what Michel Chion calls the *acousmêtre* (acousmatic effect), where the soundtrack dominates and the visible source of the sound is erased. In such instances, the sonic domain is given full agency in telling the story. Marcia Citron traces such effects of interior singing and doubling to Jean-Pierre Ponnelle's film *Le nozze di Figaro* (1976), which projects an image of Figaro as a fallen man (Citron 2002: 136–37).[34]

Cook's tripartite classification provides a starting point for analyzing how we perceive the interplay of semiotic fields within our multimodal experience. If Wagner's naturalistic conception of the staging associated with music and text exemplifies Cook's notion of conformance, then Harry Kupfer's new staging presents a contest model by overlaying a postmodern story world that purposefully deviates from the original one suggested by Wagner. In a contest model, the incongruity caused by the colliding cultural references is not intended to be resolved, but to be understood for its own sake.[35] By contrast, in the aforementioned adaptation of *Oedipus Rex* by Julie Taymor, one could argue that the story world created by Taymor *complements* that of Cocteau and Stravinsky's adaptation, since the different media retain their own intrinsic properties in spite of the disparate cultural forms that are brought together.

Furthermore, in his analysis of Disney's *Fantasia* and Stravinsky's *The Rite of Spring,* Cook introduces the idea of an audio-visual "downbeat" established through the synchronization of the two semiotic fields; he claims that coincidences established between image sequence and music articulate a "large-scale downbeat-afterbeat pattern" (1998: 184). There are many instances whereby the kinetic movement of the "machine" (comprising twenty-four wooden planks that morph into various shapes) co-articulates significant moments of arrival in the music, which are further supported by the filmic shots, camera angle, and lighting. For example, in *Die Walküre,* the dramatic moment when Siegfried (played by Jonas Kaufman) pulls the sword (Notung) out of the ash tree coincides with the sounding of the "sword" motive in C major on the downbeat (punctuated by timpani). In the live HD (high-definition) broadcast of Lepage's 2011 production, the medium-center shot of Siegfried holding the sword is followed by a long shot that captures the slow descent of the upper panel of the "machine," moving in rhythmic synchrony with the arpeggiation in the strings as the harmony changes from C to E major.[36] Following this scene, the camera shifts to a bottom-up shot angle and slowly pans from right to left to capture the joyous union of lovers; this is a common filmic technique used to prolong an expression of positive valence, and here it centers on the culmination of the anticipated union between Siegmund and Sieglinde. The visual dimension of film may dominate the viewer's attention, yet in this case it clearly works in *conformance* with the dramatic arrival in the music. In the actantial progression, this is the critical juncture in the narrative where Siegmund emerges as a hero (marked) before he meets his tragic death at the hands of Hunding, orchestrated by Wotan.

As far as the generation of meaning is concerned, intertextuality emerges as an important consideration in our multimodal discourse. Following Julia Kristeva, Michael Klein defines intertext as "the crossing of texts" where critics "often concern themselves both with the linguistic (musical) codes that bind texts together and with the tropes that transform these codes from text to text" (2005: 36). Klein lists four different types of intertextuality for music analysis:

> We may concern ourselves with just those texts that an author brought to her writing and study a *poietic* intertextuality. We may concern ourselves with the texts that a society brings to its reading and study an *esthesic* intertextuality. We may confine the text to its own time and study a *historical* intertextuality, or we may open the text to all time and study a *transhistorical* intertextuality. (Klein 2005: 12)

Applied to the present study, I argue that poietic intertexts offer primary references, while esthesic and transhistorical intertexts offer secondary references that shape the audience/analyst's multimodal reading of the narrative. As discussed at the beginning of this chapter, the subject of an opera – more often than not – evokes a mythical or historical figure from another era; Robert Oppenheimer evokes the figure of Faust, and the Qin dynasty emperor evokes the dictatorial figure of Mao Zedong for the Chinese audience. One of the reasons why multimedial productions so often resist interpretive closure is because they give rise to *secondary* intertexts that are extraneous to the basic narrative. From the viewer and listener's perspective, these intertexts are integral to the discursive strategies we bring to our multimodal narrative experience. Recognition of secondary intertexts is only one part of this strategy; following Klein, at the next stage, we look for underlying trope(s) that transform the intertextual codes from text to text; for example, the code for a diminished-seventh chord may be *Sturm und Drang* or *ombra* depending on the context (2005: 56).[37] In an operatic production, how do semiotic fields generate competing references and intertexts that give rise to a tropological narrative?

Examining narrative representation in graphic novels and comic strips, David Herman argues that multimodal narration involves multiple semiotic channels used to evoke either a single reference world or multiple reference worlds through a coordinated interplay of words and images.[38] Adapting Herman's schematic model, figure 1.7 compares Patrice Chéreau's production of Wagner's *Ring* cycle (1980) with Harry Kupfer's for the Bayreuth Festival (2010–11). Here, N stands for multimodal narration, S for semiotic fields, O for the objects referenced by the semiotic fields, and I for intertexts (code or trope in Klein's sense) referenced by various objects. While text and music reinforce the mythological dimension of Wagner's libretto drawn from various Nordic myths, Chéreau's and Kupfer's anachronistic approaches to staging complicate the viewer's understanding of the whole. Kupfer's production takes considerable liberties with the dramatic text

Kupfer's mise-en-scène:

Semiotic Fields	Objects	Intertexts
S_1 (text)	O_1 (Nordic myth)	I_1 (curse/redemption)
N S_2 (music)		
S_3 (staging)	O_2 (postnuclear holocaust)	I_2 (apocalypse)
	O_3 (television viewers)	I_3 (voyeurism)

Chereau's mise-en-scène:

Semiotic Fields	Objects	Intertexts
S_1 (text)	O_1 (Nordic myth)	I_1 (curse/redemption)
N S_2 (music)	O_2 (fairy tale)	I_2 (nature vs.
	O_3 (French aristocracy)	society)
S_3 (staging)	O_4 (industrial sewer)	I_3 (class struggle)

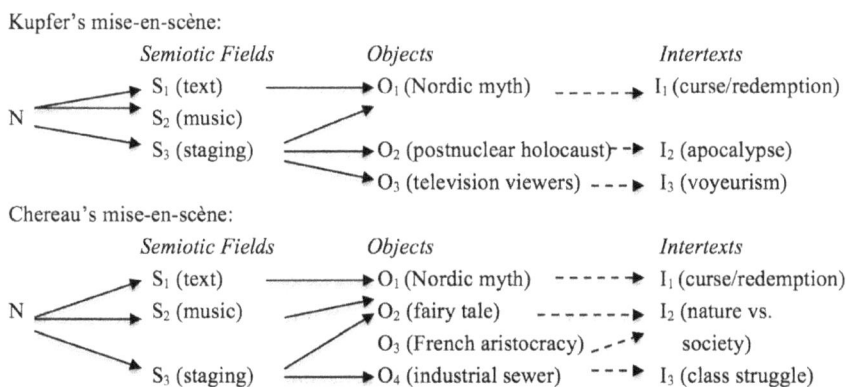

Figure 1.7. Multimodal Narration of *Götterdämmerung* (adapted from Herman 2010)

of the libretto by placing one scene after another in a ruined factory with a boiler and scattered industrial waste. Wotan makes appearances on stage even when he is not called for in the libretto, and Kupfer underscores Wotan's role as the one who controls and manipulates everything. At the conclusion, the scene swiftly changes as the stage fills with people holding cocktails and watching the gods' demise on television screens. By this time, there is nothing remaining on the stage that thematizes the elements of nature associated with Wagner's original conception.

In comparison, Chéreau's choice of costumes and staging helps reinforce the differences in the social hierarchy among the characters. While the characters associated with the category of nature/myth are clad in primitive clothing, those that represent society, e.g., the Gods in Valhalla, are given aristocratic bearings by being clad in the nineteenth-century costumes of the nobility, redolent of the court of Marie Antoinette and Louis XVI. In *Götterdämmerung,* Siegfried's transformation from fairytale hero to socially prominent member of the Gibichung's clan is underscored by the change from his tattered hunting clothes to a black tuxedo, and by his move to a fin-de-siècle European mansion.[39] The class hierarchy that distinguishes the gods from humans and the subhuman species of Nibelungen in this production is more pronounced, reflecting Adorno's view of class struggle in the Ring: "the absolute distinction drawn in the *Ring* between the different natural kinds becomes the basis of the life and death struggle . . ." (Adorno 2009: 15–16).[40]

In a multimodal context of analysis, we could stipulate that the intertexts generated by the initial source material (text and music) are primary, while those generated by the director in staging the opera are secondary. Yet secondary intertexts are hardly ancillary to our multimodal narrative experience – they can create powerful symbols and associations that enrich or complicate our interpretation. For the naïve viewer, I2 may subsume I1 in Kupfer's production: s/he may walk away with the impression that this scene of post-nuclear holocaust supplants the Nordic myth. An informed viewer, however, may recognize Kupfer's postmodern strategy – underscoring the multiplicity of subject positions – as an important message. Hutcheon and Hutcheon would argue that the tropological narrative Kupfer creates is an ironic one: he takes a satirical, "self-reflexive jab" at the audience by parodying how modern viewers consume opera (2010: 72).

In this way, multimodal narration (schematized as shown in figure 1.8) makes us grapple with contradictory references: an anachronistic inclusion of television viewers on stage, who are situated outside the opera's diegesis, and yet assess the imaginary "future" of post-nuclear holocaust in Kupfer's staging of Wagner's *Ring* cycle. In such contexts, the narrative interpretation becomes rife with tropological meaning: how does this secondary intertext relate to Wagner's mythic libretto, which draws on the medieval *Nibelungenlied,* Völsunga saga, among other sources. Herman's model of multimodal narration is especially useful in comparing two different productions of a given opera. For example, Peter Sellars's and Penny Woolcock's productions of *Doctor Atomic* yield completely different narrative trajectories by way of the cultural intertexts they generate. In Sellars's staging, different semiotic fields are brought together to articulate the horrors associated with World War II. Woolcock, in stark comparison, introduces narrative elements that are extraneous to the structure of the music and libretto; while the libretto focuses on the Faustian struggle of Robert Oppenheimer, the production components foreground the struggles of Tewa Indians against the European colonizers as an important cultural intertext.

The capturing of live broadcast in DVD format has also transformed our multimodal narrative experience in profound ways. For example, the sequence of shots, especially close-up shots of singers, gives prominence to the visual field over the aural, and constrains the material and spatiotemporal modalities of experiencing narrative in a particular way (as was illustrated in the case of Lepage's 2011 production of the scene from *Die Walküre*). Attending to opera on DVD has the capacity to undo Brecht's *Verfremdungseffekt* (alienation effect) to varying degrees – that is to say, the close-up shots eliminate the distance that would otherwise separate the viewers from the characters on stage in a live performance. Viewers tend to identify more closely with the cathartic narrative experience afforded by a range of filmic effects. Another factor to consider is that productions captured in the DVD format allow for a viewer to build *veridical* familiarity – according to David Huron, through repeated exposure, a subject can accumulate a highly refined knowledge and sensitivity to detail of a given work (2006: 241). An analyst deals with competing veridical memories of different productions of the same work – not unlike comparing exemplary recordings of any given classical music – and prioritizes one over another based on memorable attributes of each.

Toward a Multimodal Discourse

What does a multimodal discourse on opera entail? I have attempted in this opening chapter to lay down a preliminary set of criteria for analyzing operatic narrative holistically by bringing one's understanding of the structure of narrative in line with varied ways meaning is generated. My case study is limited to a narrow selection of contemporary operas composed during the first decade of the twentieth century – four operas that engage with human conflicts and trauma resulting from war. The basic tenets of my analytic orientation can be summarized as follows:

1. Contemporary operas mythologize historical subjects by transforming them into archetypal figures through textualized representation and transhistoricism. The synchronic dimension of myth in the operatic narrative is enhanced through the blurring of the temporal distinction between past, present, and future, and through references to multiple historical times and places.

2. A viewer/analyst constructs a multimodal narrative through his/her decoding of many semiotic fields – libretto, music, filmic images, choreography, action, lighting, and other production components – that can be grouped according to Elleström's four modalities (material, sensory, spatiotemporal and semiotic). These semiotic fields co-articulate the chronological and configurational (transformational) dimensions of the viewer's multimodal narrative experience.

3. Following Ricoeur, the chronological dimension of narrative refers to the sequence of events and actions that comprises the story's plot. It may be formalized through attributing roles (e.g., hero, villain) and functions (e.g., contract, theft) using the Greimassian square, as demonstrated by Monelle's analysis of *Das Rheingold* (figure 1.3a). The agential level of multimodal analysis, following Almén, comprises elements (derived from various semiotic fields), which co-articulate the main actions or events in the chronological dimension.

4. The configurational dimension is defined by any change in ranking of dramatic oppositions (actants) that creates a shift in the narrative trajectory. It involves a transvaluation in the ranking of a character and/or thematic elements, e.g., the hero is deemed an antihero, or a ring is no longer cursed. Furthermore, psychoanalytical theories by Jung and Lacan provide interpretive tools for uncovering the archetypal sources of tension/conflict that drive the mythic narrative and shed light on the transvaluative process.[41]

5. Greimas and Courtés broaden the range of what an actant encompasses from objects to functions, concepts, and states of being; an agential role of a character can be distinguished from an actantial function or theme that carries a broader significance. Music, as a virtual agent, may reinforce the character's agential role (e.g., heroic music that accompanies a hero) at a descriptive level, while articulating an actantial theme (e.g., dramatic irony) at a higher level of narrative comprehension.

6. In his/her "interventionist strategy" for staging an opera, the director often introduces cultural intertexts that are extraneous to the primary narrative, as demonstrated by Kupfer's staging of Wagner's Ring cycle. I

invoke Hatten and Almén's *tropological* narrative to account for the juxta-position of contradictory or incongruous intertexts that renders the narra-tive meaning inconclusive and multivalent.

7. For the present purpose, intermediality refers to the relationship and rela-tive importance of semiotic fields in co-articulating the structure of nar-rative, while multimodality has to do with representation – what the inter-play of semiotic fields signifies in the viewer's construction of narrative. For example, in Sellars's mise-en-scène for Saariaho's *Adriana Mater* (chapter 3), music and lighting assume a dominant intermedial function in articulating the dramatic turn of events; from a multimodal perspective, Sellars strategically combines the acousmatic function of music with red lighting to convey trauma in the non-verbal realm.

I end this chapter by acknowledging certain limitations and provisionality of the present study. As for limitations, my analysis is by no means intended to be exhaustive in covering all aspects of production and reception of those op-eras selected for study. In certain cases, interviews with the composer and libret-tist allowed for a deeper examination of the creative intention and process, while in other instances, secondary sources provided the main avenue for speculating on the creative intention and process that shaped the work. Only in the case of Tan Dun's *The First Emperor* did I have the privilege of comparing an earlier ver-sion with the revised version of the score. Additionally, the application of various theories to show how semiotic fields co-articulate narrative structure constitutes the objective portion of my study, while the hermeneutic interpretation of nar-rative meaning constitutes the subjective portion. The latter is provisional, be-cause as Lawrence Kramer states, interpretation is a *performative* act (2011: 251–52). Perhaps the object of analysis is to resist a monological interpretation and allow for the ephemeral aspects of the viewer's experience to be in dialogue with the schematic understanding of the work's structure. Multimodal discourse ac-knowledges one's embodied experience of attending to operatic production (ei-ther in theatrical or filmic settings) as a highly *mediated* and *situated* cultural practice.

Operatic analysis requires a multimodal approach precisely because of the evolving relationship between music, libretto, and more variable aspects of pro-duction. Chapters 2 and 4 provide case studies for how the structure and the meaning of operatic narrative change from one production to another. New op-eras that reconfigure older myths require the audience's active participation to complete Heidegger's *hermeneutic circle* – the interpretive act of bringing one's aesthetic experience of the work in line with its cultural and historical contexts.[42] Tom Sutcliffe remarks that opera "has in a way much greater freedom in its stag-ing precisely because it is not primarily a realistic or straightforwardly narrative form" and that "the issue of how much sense a production makes partly depends on the readiness of the audience to lend imaginative consent to what it offers" (2005: 339–40). Let us now turn to specific strategies that reconfigure myth and narrative in these operas.

2   Osvaldo Golijov's *Ainadamar*: A Myth of "Wounded" Freedom

> *Ainadamar* is about how a myth is actually being born, how Lorca that was a breathing, living, laughing, loving person became a symbol, a myth – and how we can bring him back to be that man.
>
> Osvaldo Golijov, "Interview with Adeline Sire used in the *Ainadamar* CD Listening Guide."

Ainadamar ("Fountain of Tears," 2003–05), an opera composed by Osvaldo Golijov in collaboration with librettist David Henry Hwang and director Peter Sellars, initiates the audience into an atmosphere of a bygone era in Spanish history. Over a low electronic drone, murmuring sounds of water are heard, accompanied by a solemn trumpet fanfare that reverberates in the background. Soon, electronic sounds of a galloping horse fill the hall and merge with boisterous rhythms of castanets and cajones (Peruvian drums) played live on stage. When the trumpet fanfare returns, the overture segues to a plaintive ballad sung by the female chorus lamenting the death of a revolutionary heroine, Mariana Pineda. The ballad is a reference to Lorca's 1927 play, which the Catalan actress Margarita Xirgu kept alive through her performances in Uruguay, where she lived in exile for thirty years. Golijov incorporates flamenco singing and dance rhythms, rumba, and other cultural references to create an imaginary sonic world of Lorca and Xirgu in Granada during Francisco Franco's fascist regime. Hwang and Golijov fashioned the work as a "ritualized poetic theater" that evokes the musical characteristics of three civilizations, Christian, Muslim, and Jewish.

By integrating flamenco with classical, mythical, and religious culture, *Ainadamar* explores Lorca's quest for a utopian, mythic universality. In part, this opera is conceived as a narrative of ritual passion in which Lorca is elevated to a Christ-like figure and Xirgu as a Madonna figure who mourns for her "son." In part, it is a tale about nostalgia and remembrance of a lost time and place in Spanish history. Music serves as an important marker of Andalusian culture: electronic sounds of gunshots and trickling water signify Lorca's execution at Ainadamar – a site where thousands of "liberals" were executed during the Spanish

Civil War (1936–39). Golijov's music is replete with references to *cante jondo* ("deep song") and *duende* – the existential anguish that lies at the essence of Andalusian flamenco music. The somber chant sung by the female chorus at the beginning and end of the opera comments on the revolutionary figure Mariana Pineda's self-sacrifice as a symbol of "wounded" freedom – a struggle passed on from one generation to the next in the course of Spanish history.

The making of *Ainadamar* attests to the constantly evolving nature of operatic collaboration. As Peter Lefevre puts it, the much anticipated premiere at the Tanglewood Music Festival in 2003 "was met with muted praise," and called for an extensive retooling (2012). Not only was the student production somewhat amateurish, Hwang fashioned theatrical devices, such as having the younger and older Margarita Xirgu interact with one another – a plan he abandoned soon after the premiere. For the Santa Fe Opera production in 2005, Sellars oversaw a complete rewrite of the libretto and musical score. By bringing the political dimension of the story to the foreground, the theme of the opera crystallized into one of fighting for artistic freedom against military dictatorship by the Falangists during the Spanish Civil War. Mark Sved, in his review of the Santa Fe production, wrote that *Ainadamar* became "a distilled statement of [Sellars's] spiritual and social concerns and one of his most personal productions" (2005). The new production featured Dawn Upshaw and Kelly O'Connor in the title roles of Xirgu and Lorca and received rave reviews.

In an artistic climate where new operas are typically produced once and never seen again, *Ainadamar* is highly unusual in having transformed itself under new directorship. In 2005, the Atlanta Symphony Orchestra presented a semistaged concert performance under Robert Spano; the recording of this concert version was subsequently released by Deutsche Grammophon in 2006 and received a Grammy for the best contemporary composition in the following year. *Ainadamar* quickly became an overnight sensation, with eleven performances in the course of 2007–08. In the season repertory of the Staatstheater Darmstadt, Mei Hong Lin directed a new production featuring Katrin Gerstenberger, Allison Oakes, Sonja Borowski-Tudor, Aki Hashimoto and others. Opera Boston presented Sellars's production featuring the original cast of Upshaw, O'Connor, and Jessica Rivera. In its Australian premiere, *Ainadamar* was featured as the Adelaide Festival's opening event in a new production directed by Graeme Murphy. Concert performances of the opera also include ones by the Chicago Symphony Orchestra, the City of Birmingham Symphony Orchestra, and the Phoenix Symphony.[1] More recently staged productions took place in Granada, Spain (2010) and Los Angeles (2012).

Considering its rich production history, *Ainadamar* offers an excellent case study for multimodal narrative analysis. As the genre and mode of production shift from opera to concert setting and from oratorio to theater, how has its narrative structure and meaning been affected? If we are to consider the Deutsche Grammophon recording as the exemplary musical performance of this work, how have subsequent productions of the work enriched and modified its basic narrative framework? Do we come to understand the agential roles of Lorca, Xirgu, and Alonso any differently? To shed light on such questions, this chapter uncovers *Ainadamar*'s narrative in four stages: 1) historical background of Lorca and *cante jondo;* 2) Hwang's libretto: the making of *Ainadamar;* 3) Golijov's musical setting: *Ainadamar* as myth; and 4) a multimodal comparison of productions that ranges from full-staged operas to oratorio to theater.

Historical Background: Lorca and Cante Jondo

According to various accounts, Lorca was a creative artist in many arenas – a gifted musician as well as a poet and playwright – and a charismatic character. After Lorca befriended Manuel de Falla in his early twenties, the older composer's influence on Lorca was formidable. From de Falla, Lorca learned to strive for perfection, cultivated different methods for stylizing traditional materials, and became acquainted with Gypsy music and traditional Andalusian songs (Stainton 1999: 91). Notably, he came to appreciate *cante jondo* (deep song), which contains themes of love, pain, and death – the wellsprings of his own creative writing. Unlike his contemporaries, artists like Manuel Machado and others who sought to evoke Gypsy song in a modernist context, Lorca hoped to bring about "a radical new synthesis of the traditional and the avant-garde" (97). Christopher Mauer argues that Lorca "hoped to imbue [*cante jondo*] with prestige among Spanish Intellectuals, and distinguish it from the commercially adulterated professional 'flamenco' heard in urban cafes and theaters" (Lorca 1998: vii). In 1921, when Lorca was twenty-three years old, he wrote a series of poems called *Poema del cante jondo,* based on the Gypsy song forms of *soleá, petenera, siguiriya,* and *saeta,* that were dominated by the sentiments of grief and lament. Especially in the *siguiriya,* Lorca found the perfect "poem of tears." "Their sadness is so irresistible, their pathos so strong, that they cause all true Andalusians to weep inside, with tears that cleanse the spirit and carry it away to the burning lemon grove of love" (18). The guitar appears as a common motive in Andalusian poetry and many of Lorca's poems contain the musical rhythmicity of *cante jondo* songs sung by flamenco singers. Here is one of Lorca's Gypsy Siguiriya poems, called "La Guitarra" ("The Guitar"):

Empieza el llanto	The weeping
de la guitarra.	of the guitar begins.
Se rompen las copas	Wineglasses shatter
de la madrugada.	in the dead of night.
Empieza el llanto	The weeping
de la guitarra.	of the guitar begins.
Es inútil	It's useless
callarla.	to hush it.
Es imposible	It's impossible
callarla.	to hush it.
Llora monótona	It weeps on monotonously

como llora el agua,	the way water weeps,
como llora el viento	the way wind weeps
sobre la nevada.	Over the snowdrifts.
Es imposible	It's impossible
callarla.	to hush it.
Llora por cosas	It weeps for things
lejanas.	far, far away.
Arena del Sur saliente	Sand from the hot South
que pide camellias blancas.	asking for white camellias.
Llora fleche sin blanco,	It cries, arrow with no target,
la tarde sin mañana,	evening with no morning,
y el primer pájaro muerto	and the first bird
sobre la rama.	dead on the branch.
¡Oh guitarra!	Oh guitar!
Corazón malherido	Heart mortally wounded
por cinco espadas!	by five swords!

In a manner typical to many of his poems, an everyday object becomes a vehicle for conveying human suffering. In "La Guitarra," there is a metonymic progression that links different objects and phenomena to the act of "weeping"; it is first attributed to the guitar, water and wind, sand, and then for things "far, far away." In the concluding line, the guitar's "weeping" is linked to the human heart, wounded by five swords. The poem's internal rhythm is governed by the musicality of the partially rhyming words, "guitarra," "madrugada," and "callarla," that punctuate each line. Once the word for weeping, "llora," appears, the subsequent rhyming words such as "agua" and "nevada" appear with greater intensity to build momentum to the phrase, "Es imposible callarla," that sets up the refrain. In introducing his English translation of the poems, Carlos Bauer reminds us that they do not imitate *cante jondo* lyrics in Gypsy songs, but rather they explore "the soul of this Gypsy-Andalusian-flamenco cosmos," as well as recreate "a tapestry of Andalusia's mystery and pain" (Lorca 1987: iii). The appropriation of the flamenco deep song would influence Lorca throughout his entire career as playwright and poet.

In 1923, while living in Madrid, Lorca turned to the story of Mariana Pineda, a revolutionary heroine who participated in a liberal underground network that tried to undermine the repressive monarchy of Ferdinand II during the 1830s – she was later executed by garroting.[2] Lorca struggled to find a producer for his play on Pineda; it was not until he met Margarita Xirgu in the summer of 1926 that he found an actress, a theatrical star, who would commit to staging the play. Xirgu quickly became his muse and the featured actress in his plays. On June 24, 1927, *Mariana Pineda* received its premiere at Barcelona's Goya Theater, featuring Xirgu in the title role, with sets and costumes designed by Salvador Dalí (Kellner 2005: 76). The staging of this play marked the beginning of a long friendship and artistic collaboration between Lorca and Xirgu.

Similar to his *cante jondo* poems, the play *Mariana Pineda* exhibits a metonymic association that links stone with water and the human cry. The memory of

Pineda as a revolutionary heroine was celebrated in popular ballads Lorca grew up hearing in Granada. His play begins and ends with little girls singing a ballad offstage:

¡Ay, qué día tan triste en Granada,	What a sad day it was in Granada,
que a las piedras hacía llorar	the stones began to cry;
al ver que Marianita se muere	seeing Marianita die,
en cadalso por no declarer!	because they could not make her speak!
Ay, qué día tan triste en Granada,	What a sad day it was in Granada,
¡ . . . las campañas doblar y doblar!	. . . the bells tolled and tolled!

In Lorca's retelling of the story, Mariana falls in love with Don Pedro de Soto-mayor, one of her fellow liberals, whom she believes will return to rescue her from a convent. However, Pedro, who appears to be passionate and heroic, turns out to be a coward who flees to England to avoid retribution. In spite of others who try to save her, including the officer Pedrosa and a young admirer, Fernando, Mariana chooses death rather than give away the names of the conspirators. When Fernando tries to change her mind, she answers, "I give myself so freedom's flame may never fade." Pedrosa's character unites cruelty with authoritarianism and libidinous impulses in pressuring Mariana to turn herself in. At first, she is threatened by him and contemplates giving in to him, but later grows more confident in her conviction to die for freedom. As in many of his other plays, the theme of "hopes destroyed, and at best heroically endured," emerges in Lorca's representation of the heroine; Mariana's dreams of love and happiness may have been destroyed, but not her conviction to die for her principles (Edwards 1995: xix).

Throughout this play, Lorca references objects and natural elements to comment on dramatic turns in each of the three scenes called "engravings": the flickering candlelight in the first engraving mirrors Mariana's fear and hope, the sounds of wind and rain signify impending danger, and tolling bells signify Mariana's death. Toward the end, she even compares her own heart to a wounded bird: "Now I know what the nightingale and the tree say. Man is captive and cannot set himself free" (Cuitiño 1994: 60). Yet, by infusing comedic elements – Mariana's dialogue with her female friends, Amparo and Lucia, about a bullfight in the first engraving as well as her interaction with her two children in the second – Lorca interprets Pineda's life as a mixture of comedy and tragedy.

By the fall of 1931, liberal representatives sparred with conservatives over the newly drafted constitution making Spain "a democratic republic of workers of all classes"; it nullified all titles of nobility, renounced war, legalized divorce, and granted voting eligibility to both men and women (Stainton 1999: 282). The Second Republic (1931–35), marked by political liberalism and attacks on the power of the Catholic Church, enabled Lorca to found a theater troupe called La Barraca. As artistic director, he worked tirelessly to distinguish his own brand of popular theater, influenced by Stanislavsky, from mainstream Spanish theater. To this end, he traveled all across Spain with this troupe to revive great plays from the Spanish Golden Age, as well as to introduce contemporary foreign plays (286–87).[3] Especially popular was Lorca's play Yerma and his adaptation of a Lope de Vega's play called *La dama boba;* the critics praised the latter as a "delicate and careful" adaptation of a classical Spanish author's work (403).

Although Lorca did not stage his own plays, he often appeared as an actor, provided accompaniment on traditional instruments, and sketched many of the costumes himself. During this time, he also embarked on writing a three-part tragic play called *Blood Wedding* (1932), where a bride elopes with her cousin and the two meet their death in a dank forest. Based on an event that took place in Almería in 1928, Lorca fashioned the play as a tragedy that would strike at the hearts of Spanish people and their ties to pagan superstition (Stainton 1999: 298). Expressionistic influences are found in Lorca's use of visual and musical symbols: for example, immediately before the two male protagonists kill each other, the stage turns blue, the moon emerges, and a violin duet sounds; then two screams shatter the air and the music stops; finally, a beggar woman steps onto the stage with her back turned to the audience and spreads her cloak like a prehistoric bird (301).[4] Based on the enigmatic array of symbols, Stainton claims that Lorca created the genre of *meta-theater* long before the term came into existence; in the later plays that constitute his "impossible theater," notably *The Audience, Once Five Years Pass,* and *The Dream of Life,* Lorca examines the ways in which "theater conflates and expands time and at the ways it alters our perceptions of the physical world" (2005: 83). In all three of these plays, the characters are trapped in roles from which they cannot escape.

Lorca's own fate was doomed as well. By 1934 Francisco Franco's campaign of repression took hold of Spain, and right-wing Spaniards upheld Franco as their savior. Two years later, in February 1936, Granada was taken over by the fascist Falangists (aided by Italy's fascist group) and by July, the civil war between Franco's Nationalists and the Republicans broke out. Lorca became a visible target for persecution by the Falangists due to his homosexuality and his support for pro-communist causes. Although Luis Rosales, an admirer of Lorca who was nonetheless forced to join the Falangists, provided protection, Lorca was arrested on August 15, 1936. Lorca was executed the following day, and many lamented his death. Xirgu, who was performing in Havana at the time, claimed upon hearing the news: "they have murdered my child" (Stainton 1999: 449). The uprising on July 17, 1936 marked the beginning of the Spanish Civil War, which lasted nearly three years until the end of March 1939. During the war, the Falangists' firing squads killed as many as five thousand people in Granada alone. Apparently, Franco's government never accepted responsibility for Lorca's death (457). Lorca's works were officially banned in Spain until 1953. Furthermore, Xirgu, who fled to Uruguay, was not allowed to set foot in Spain due to her liberal political leanings. She remained a faithful promoter of Lorca's legacy in the Americas until her own death in 1969, six years before the end of Franco's regime.

Given this history, it is understandable that David Hwang and Osvaldo Golijov decided to create an opera that tells the story from the point of view of the Catalan actress. But how does Hwang mythologize Lorca as a tragic hero, and to what end? Furthermore, how does Golijov's musical setting shape the mythic trajectory of *Ainadamar?*

Hwang's libretto: The Making of *Ainadamar*

Following his immense success adapting Puccini's *Madame Butterfly* to a modern play called *M. Butterfly* (1988), David Henry Hwang turned to writing libretti for opera (*The Sound of a Voice*, 2003; *The Fly*, 2008) and musicals (a revision of Joseph Field's *Flower Drum Song*, 2002). In constructing the libretto for *Ainadamar*, Hwang assembled a wide range of cultural, aesthetic, and political themes to create a mythical narrative around Lorca. Hwang chose to distance the audience from a biographical narrative of Lorca by purposefully skewing the perspective. The story is told *through* Xirgu and her recollection of Lorca during the Spanish Civil War. It is through her memory and desire that Lorca is brought back to life. Hwang enacts this narrative strategy by embedding a play within a play: each of the three scenes ("images" according to Hwang) begins with the ballad of Mariana Pineda (Mariana de Pineda Muñoz) from Lorca's play. Alex Ross's synopsis of the opera captures the dramatic essence that underlies this reconfiguration:

> *Ainadamar* means "fountain of tears" in Arabic. It is the name of an ancient well near Granada, where, in August 1936, during the early stages of the Spanish Civil War, the poet Federico García Lorca was killed by Fascist Falangist forces. Osvaldo Golijov's opera *Ainadamar* is centered around the scene of the poet's murder, but its main character is the Catalan tragedian Margarita Xirgu, who collaborated with Lorca on several of his plays. The story begins in Uruguay, in 1969, as Xirgu is about to perform the lead role in Lorca's *Mariana Pineda*, the tale of a revolutionary martyr from another century. She is haunted by memories of Lorca, by the thought that she might have saved him. By the end, she has surrendered to the strange beauty of fate, and she bequeaths her longing for freedom to her students. The opera ends as it began, with the prophetic Ballad of Mariana Pineda: "What a sad day it was in Granada. The stones began to cry." (Ross 2006a)

In constructing the libretto for the opera, Hwang strikes a careful balance between narrative and biography. Especially poignant is Hwang's replication of Lorca's execution. Lorca chooses to stay in Granada at the home of his friend Luis Rosales. Historical accounts tell us that a loud, belligerent Falangist named Ramón Ruiz Alonso, who detested the Left and hated Lorca, came to arrest him at the Rosales's residence on August 16, 1936.[5] The night before the execution, Lorca was held captive by a guard named José Tripaldi. Together with the schoolteacher Galindo Gonzaléz and two bullfighters, Lorca was executed at Ainadamar before dawn (Stainton 1999: 454). All of these characters make their way into *Ainadamar* in the critical scene of Lorca's execution. Among the evidence that provides historical authenticity for the narrative are quotes from Falangist officers in Spanish newspapers from 1936.

Furthermore, Hwang not only pays specific homage to Lorca by adapting the ballad that opens *Mariana Pineda* as a refrain, but more generally by anthropomorphizing natural elements – e.g., using water to represent human suffering through its connection with tears shed for Lorca. In his adaptation of the story, Hwang adopts the tripartite framework of *Mariana Pineda* – the three "engravings" – and turns them into three scenes (called Images) that link Pineda, Lorca, and Xirgu. In the first Image, Xirgu plays the role of Mariana Pineda in the verse-play by Lorca, a performing tradition that she kept alive in Latin America until her death in 1969. The second features Xirgu's recollection of Lorca in 1936, in which Lorca is brought back to life and his execution is reenacted during the Spanish Civil War. The final Image depicts the interior world of Xirgu as she prepares to die. All traces of reality vanish, as she is reunited with the ghost of Lorca and enters into a quasi-Eucharistic ritual of consecration with protégé Nuria: "here is my blood shed for thee, drink it and tell my story." Rather than turning bread and wine into the body and blood of Christ, however, this ritual is about Xirgu's espousal of "freedom." Mark Sved comments on Sellars's reworking of the opera in the *Los Angeles Times* as follows:

> [Sellars] also has created a theater of delirium. He has staged the opera as a representation of the spirit leaving the body. It is an opera of unfinished business, on the passing on of the knowledge and experience of one generation to the next. The young Margarita is now a student. A great poet died with a teacher as a repressive government set itself up in the business of restricting knowledge, freedom of expression and education. Margarita becomes the symbol that ideas cannot be killed. (Sved 2005)

The ritual of consecration is not just about Xirgu's spirit leaving her body but the metaphysical union between Pineda and Xirgu. Just before she is garroted, Pineda proclaims: "I give my blood, which is your blood, and the blood of every single human being. The human heart cannot be bought" (Lorca 1995: 53). Hwang made a significant revision in the version for the Santa Fe Opera in order to bring out this reference to Pineda's words in Lorca's original play. Sellars, who directed the revised version for the Santa Fe Opera, had a decisive influence on Hwang's revision in adding political and dramatic fervor to the narrative (Ross 2006a: 6). In the revised version, Xirgu's student named Nuria replaces Xirgu's younger self. Nuria is a fictitious character who is transformed from an innocent bystander to one who will carry on her mentor's fight for freedom. The dramatic thread in the opera hinges on Xirgu's conflicted desire for Lorca, which parallels Lorca's yearning for Pineda in Xirgu's recollection. Xirgu cannot be released from her own state of suffering until Lorca (in his spirit form) brings her in unity with Pineda. An important pivotal moment occurs in "De Mi Fuente Tú Emerges" where Lorca acknowledges Xirgu and Pineda as "one and the same":

Margarita, de mi fuente tú emerges,	Margarita, you emerge from my fountain
vas bañada en el agua	bathed in the water
y la luz de mi poesía . . .	and light of my poetry . . .
Tu espíritu está	Your spirit lives
en cada una de tus alumnas.	in each one of your students.
Tú y Mariana	You and Mariana
ya sois solo una	are already one
y la misma.	and the same.

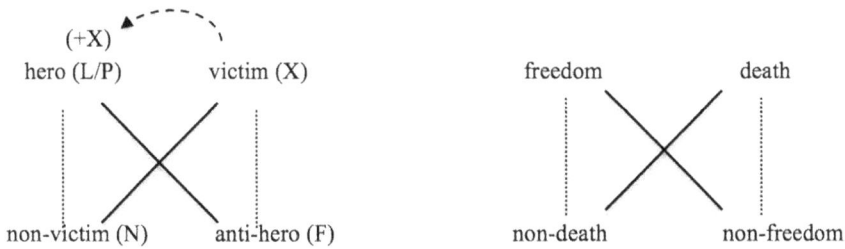

Figure 2.1. Agential Roles and Functions in *Ainadamar*

The agential roles of the main characters and the accompanying functions can be mapped onto the Greimassian square, as shown in figure 2.1. At the onset of the narrative, the four characters occupy opposite ends of the square as follows: Lorca (L) is a hero who sacrifices his life for artistic freedom, just as Pineda (P) does before him; Alonso (F) is the Falangist and anti-hero who obstructs Lorca from attaining artistic freedom; Xirgu (X) is a victim of Lorca's death, who haplessly performs the title role in *Mariana Pineda* until the end of her life; and Nuria (N) is Xirgu's protégée who remains an innocent bystander (non-victim) until the end. Xirgu, who has kept the memory of Lorca alive by playing the role of Pineda night after night in Uruguay, relives her memory of Lorca's assassination; she is, however, unable to escape her suffering until she calls forth the spirit of Lorca and enters into a ritual of consecration prior to her death. The main change in ranking occurs when Xirgu is released from her position as victim and enters into union with Lorca and Pineda: she attains her status as heroine in death (as indicated by the dotted arrow).

Golijov conceived Pineda, Lorca, and Xirgu as those who become "freedom," while Alonso and others as those who "love freedom" and will kill for their ideas: "they fear those who are [*sic*] freedom itself" (McKinnon 2005). In the same way that the statue of Mariana Pineda spoke to Lorca, the spirit of Lorca appears to Xirgu at her death and thanks her for keeping his legacy alive; it is at this moment that Nuria is able to see what Xirgu sees and to share her teacher's vision. In her final moment, Xirgu recalls Pineda's last words in Lorca's play: "yo soy la libertad" (I am freedom). While Pineda follows this up with "herida por los hombres!" (by mankind abused!), Xirgu's parting words are, "herida y sangrando esperanza" (wounded and bleeding hope).

In this context, the fountain Ainadamar emerges as an important symbol and metonym for "wounded" freedom: Hwang refers to Ainadamar as "the source [of freedom] from which you drink." The image of water thus carries a dual significance as anthropomorphic agent. Much in the same way the guitar "weeps" for human suffering in Lorca's poem, the fountain sheds tears for those who died for freedom, but it is also seen as the *source* of freedom. The moment of transvaluation occurs when Xirgu's "wounded" freedom is transformed into a positively charged symbol for carrying on the struggle. On her deathbed, she tells Nuria that while an actor's individual voice can be silenced, the hope of a people will not die. The final number ("Yo Soy la Libertad") is about Xirgu's "resurrection," whereby she declares that she *is* freedom and "the source [the fountain] from which you drink."

Where the historical Lorca departs from Hwang's idealized representation is in his political indifference. Historical accounts tell us that Lorca lived in the world of theater and artifice. While remaining sensitive to the social ramifications of political strife, he was preoccupied with aesthetic questions such as the nature of reality and artifice, the role of dreams, and the artist's responsibility in society (Stainton 2005: 425). Stainton's biography of Lorca indicates how terrified he was of his eventual capture by the Falangists; when he was first arrested in his home on August 9, he insisted that he had no political allegiances (448). When the guard Tripaldi asked him to make a confession in the holding cell for condemned prisoners, Lorca cried out that he hadn't done anything to deserve this fate (454).

In *Ainadamar,* Hwang and Sellars turn Lorca into a revolutionary figure – a martyr who is not afraid to die for his country. Lorca's martyrdom is reflected in the duet from the second Image, where Xirgu persuades him to go to Havana with her to escape from the growing political unrest in Granada. In "Quiero Cantar Entre las Explosions," which follows the duet, Lorca sings these lines, intercepted by the Falangists' radio broadcast:

Yo me quendo entre los meurtos	I will stay among the dead
yo voy cantando mi canto immenso.	singing my immense song.
Canto el canto de quienes callan,	A song for the silenced
de quienes mueren.	and the dead.
Me quedo aquí . . .	I will stay here . . .
con mi canto y con mi llanto.	with my singing and with my weeping.

Lastly, Hwang introduces an embedded narrative structure that shifts back and forth between the present (April 1969) and past (summer 1936) within the opera's diegesis. Adopting Gérard Genette's theory of narrative discourse, three diegetic levels can be distinguished based on the narrator's voice and spatiotemporal domain invoked: the *extradiegetic,* the narrator who tells the story outside its context; the *diegetic,* the voices of the characters who inhabit the narrative proper; and *metadiegetic,* the voices of those who inhabit a story within a story (1980: 228). Mapping A, B, and C to the spatiotemporal domains of *Ainadamar,* the female chorus's telling of the story in the form of a ballad constitutes the extradiegetic (A), Xirgu's last days in Uruguay the diegetic (B), and Xirgu's remembrance of Lorca in Spain the metadiegetic (C). The chorus sings the ballad in past tense ("the bells tolled and tolled"), while Xirgu and Lorca speak to each other in present tense. In the first Image, entitled "Mariana," Xirgu performs her role as Mariana Pineda (B) and recalls the time when she first met Lorca as a young man in Madrid (C). The entire second Image, entitled "Federico," is situated in summer of 1936 during the wake of the Spanish Civil War (C). The third and final Image, entitled "Margarita," takes us back to April 1969, where Lorca's spirit emerges from Ainadamar (C) and appoints Nuria to be Xirgu's successor who will carry on the tradition (B). The chorus's singing of the refrain (A) frames the progression in the narrative at the beginning of each Image and concludes with it. All in all, the libretto establishes an interpolated narrative structure as follows: A – B – C | A – C | A – C/B – A.

By assigning Lorca to speak in first person ("I give you my thanks and I love you"), Hwang brings centrality to Lorca as the mythologized subject, but also as a catalyst in the chain of martyrs who fight for artistic freedom. From a Lacanian perspective, the idea of freedom emerges as *object petit a* – the object of desire, ultimately unattainable, which is passed on from Pineda to Lorca, then from Xirgu to Nuria. Xirgu in the first Image represents a divided self – someone who cannot reconcile her state of alienation with her desire to become united with Lorca and Pineda. The re-enactment of Lorca's assassination is the focalization of traumatic rupture – yet it is the site of engagement with the Real, the confrontation with longing and sorrow that allows Xirgu to embrace death. Thus Xirgu's role as victim (marked) changes to that of martyr (unmarked) through her reenactment of Lorca's death. By the third and final Image, Xirgu passes on the torch to Nuria and embraces "freedom" in a victorious manner. She overcomes her divided self and is elevated to the status of a martyr. The female chorus is the principal narrator – comparable to the *turba's* role in the Passion – whose refrain changes its expressive nuance at the beginning of each Image to mark time and the actantial progression in the narrative.

Golijov's Musical Setting: *Ainadamar* as Myth

If Hwang's libretto sets up an embedded narrative bookended by the ballad of Mariana Pineda, Golijov's music further deepens the mythical trajectory of this story through a variety of compositional means. The metadiegetic domain refers to what the character imagines seeing in his or her head; by extension, Robynn Stilwell defines metadiegetic music as the sounds that express "feelings that we can identify as those of the character onscreen" in the context of film (2007 195). In *Ainadamar,* the electronic soundscape sets up the metadiegetic domain (C) of the story world by evoking the time and place of Lorca's execution in Granada. He intersperses sampled electronic sounds and recordings as "found objects" (*objets trouvés*) to create a portal into the past: the Falangist's radio broadcast, children's prayers that are heard at the site of Lorca's execution, and the trickling water in *Ainadamar.* It complements the mimetic function of song forms, like rumba and vocal improvisation in the flamenco style, which expresses longing, lament, *duende,* and transcendence in the diegetic domain (B).

Second, Xirgu's transformation from victim to heroine is articulated through the shift in Golijov's music that signifies lament and longing to that which signifies transcendence, coinciding with her departure from the phenomenal world. This transformation resonates with Golijov's explanation of her role in the opera as follows: "I see its action as a process, the peeling off the layers of Margarita's [Xirgu's] spiritual make up. At the beginning she might resemble Celia

Cruz, buried under three inches of mascara and a flamboyant wig. Margarita is like that, but through the course of the opera, as she approaches her own death, she cleans off all those layers to approach, and even achieve, the purity of Lorca" (Keller 2005: 78).

How does Golijov achieve this transition from the phenomenal to the mythical domain? Rather than adopting an episodic form (as discussed in chapter 1), Golijov utilizes different musical numbers to distinguish temporal domains (A, B, and C), characters, and expressive registers, by varying the instrumentation, key, motivic deployment, and expressive connotation, as shown in table 2.1 Notably, the ballad that opens each Image is elaborated differently with respect to tempo, key, and texture as it progresses from a lament (A1) to a frenetic reprise (A2) and finally to a dirge (A3); it is also preceded or followed by the metadiegetic music (Co) that evokes the fountain of Ainadamar. He utilizes popular musical forms, yet often transforms them in order to make an expressive commentary on the dramatic situation at hand. For example, when the chorus sings a number built on a rumba, Golijov refers to Ravel's *Bolero* to create "a sort of hypnotic rhythm" as the chorus echoes lines sung by Margarita as a way of taunting her (Golijov 2006).

In addition to particular rhythms and form, register and key play an important function in establishing dramatic oppositions that propel that narrative forward. For example, the low drone on C♯ always accompanies Alonso's singing in the flamenco style and it is also associated with Lorca's death at Ainadamar. Lament and longing are expressed through the darker modal flavor of the Hijāz scale associated with flamenco music, while Xirgu's transcendence is underscored through a turn toward the major mode. In my analysis, I identify two recurring motives and their variants as important expressive signifiers: a descending third motive (x) associated with lament, its inversion (x') with hope, and an ascending fourth motive (y) associated with freedom. In the Prelude, the juxtaposition of motives x and y in the trumpet fanfare connote the idea of "wounded" freedom, while in the concluding number ("Yo Soy la Libertad"), the augmentation of motive x combined with the reinstatement of the trumpet fanfare in the major mode signifies the attainment of freedom.

Rather than adopting the *cante jondo* song forms literally, Golijov creates a hybrid style that incorporates certain features of flamenco music. Peter Manuel describes the flamenco repertory as consisting of a dozen or so basic song-types called *cantes,* which are distinguished variously in terms of poetic form, characteristic vocal melodies, and rhythmic units called *compás* (2006: 95). Because of their solemn character, *soleares* and *siguiriyas* are referred to as *cante jondo* ("deep song"), as opposed to the fast and festive *tangos* and *bulerías*. The Andalusian tonality forms the foundation for flamenco music, a modal system that intersects with popular Arabic *maqām* used pervasively in Arabic and Turkish vernacular music (96). Example 2.1 shows how the foundational Andalusian scale contains both the Hijāz and Bayati modes: the former is distinguished by the Phrygian second and major third degrees, while the latter is equivalent to the Phrygian mode. The upward microtonal inflection (+) on the sixth is a feature

Table 2.1. Musical Structure of Ainadamar

Movements/Form	Characters	Instrumentation	Key/scale	Motive	Expression
Prelude (C$_0$)		Electronics/trumpet cajon	Bb (Hij)	x, y	"wounded" freedom
Balada I (A$_1$)	X/ch	Choral refrain	Bb (Hij)	x, y	lament
Mariana, Tus Ojos (B$_1$)	X	Rumba	D	x', x	hope/mockery
Bar Albor de Madrid (C$_1$)	X/L	Sung dialogue w/guitar	G#/C#		
Desde Mi Vente (C$_2$)	X/L/N	Slow waltz	Am		longing
Muerte a Caballo (C$_3$)	A	Solo/flamenco style	C# drone		*duende*
Balada II (A$_2$)	F/ch	Choral refrain/guitar	G (Hij)	x, y	frenetic reprise
Quiero Arrancarme. (C$_4$).	X	X's lament/ guitar	G/Db		lament
A la Habana (C$_5$)	X/L	Cuban rhythm	G (Hij)		longing
Quiero Cantar . . . (C$_6$)	X/L	Falangists' radio broadcast	D	x	*duende*
Arresto/La Fuente (C$_7$)	A/L	Water drops → stream	C# drone		*duende*
Confesión (C$_8$)	L/G/T/B	Electronics	C#/EM		
Interludio (C$_9$)	A/L	Gunshot loop	C#		death
Balada III (A$_3$)	ch	Choral refrain/tubular bells	D-Ab	x, y	dirge
De Mi Fuente (C$_{10}$)	L	Alto flute/strings	C (Hij)	x	
Tome Su Mano (B$_2$)	X/L/N	Trio/strings/vibraphone	Fm	x	longing
Crepúsculo Delirante (B$_3$)	X/L/N	Duo guitars	C (Hij)	x	*duende*
Doy Mi Sangre (B$_4$)	X/L/N	Vocal trio	EM	x, y'	transcendence
Yo Soy la Libertad (B$_5$)					
(A$_1$/ C$_0$)	X/ch	Instrumental tutti	CM/ C(Hij)	x (aug), y	Freedom (attained)

Note: [X = Xirgu; L = Lorca; N = Nuria; A = Alonso; G = guard; T = teacher; B = bullfighter; ch = female chorus; Hij = Hijāz scale]

Example 2.1. The Hijāz and Bayati Scales (Manuel 2006: 96)

common to the Hijāz scale in ascent. What is commonly referred to as the Andalusian cadence involves a descending progression from the subdominant, which passes through the major chord built on the Phrygian second to end on a major tonic chord; e.g., Am-GM-FM-EM – as familiarized in "Chanson Bohème" from Bizet's *Carmen*. The chord based on the Phrygian second assumes the function of the dominant harmony.

Rather than identifying the periodic rhythmic patterns in Flamenco music as meter following the convention of western art music, practitioners refer to them as *compás,* distinguishable by patterns of accentuation (strong vs. weak) that organize the beats and their internal rhythmic variations. In general, flamenco rhythm is based on a twelve-beat cycle where the *compás* varies according to particular song forms associated with the genre. Robin Totton claims that the underlying rhythmic cycle (equivalent to a measure) is deeply ingrained in the flamenco practitioners and they give it "rhythmic life by varying on it, by pulling or pushing against it" (2003: 65). The most common flamenco styles are based on *compás* of 12, 4, or 3 beats. Soleá, alegría, and bulería are popular styles based on *compás* of 12. The *fandango de huelva* has a constant rhythm based on the recurring *compás* of 3, while *guajira, soleá,* and *siguiriya* have alternating *compás* of 2 and 3. Many of the rhythms used in *Ainadamar* are based on compás associated with either the fandango de huelva or guajira.

To illustrate how these musical features shape the mythical trajectory of *Ainadamar* on their own terms, I will now turn to a more specific discussion of the synoptic function of the ballad, other popular song forms, the electronic soundscape as index of lost time and place, the flamenco and *duende,* and the ritual of consecration/transcendence.

The Synoptic Function of the Ballad

The female chorus is the extradiegetic narrator, who frames the story as myth by singing the ballad of Mariana Pineda at the commencement of each Image. Yet Golijov transforms its mimetic function (parodying Lorca's play) through its juxtaposition with metadiegetic music, notably the trumpet fanfare, which articulates the shift in the actantial theme from the desire for freedom to its attainment in the context of *Ainadamar.* Like the military fanfare, the trumpet fanfare's main function is to impart information to the participants by signaling (Monelle 2006: 136).[6] Emerging out of the B♭ minor ostinato chord in the

Example 2.2. The Trumpet "Fanfare" (mm.9–13)

"Water and Horse" prelude, the trumpet fanfare merges with the sounds of water and a galloping horse. The head motive, characterized by an ascending semitone followed by a fourth (marked y), is derived from scale degrees, 1-♭2–5, from the Hijāz scale on B♭, as shown in example 2.2. The distinctive feature of this fanfare lies in the long melodic descent, suggestive of a lament. From a Lacanian perspective, one may interpret the trumpet motive in the overture as the circulating musical element, S(A̶), that embodies desire for freedom in its material form. The idea of "wounded" freedom, one could argue, is conveyed by the long-winded descent that hobbles between the modal inflections of D5 and D♭5 and lingers on the Phrygian second, C♭5, prior to making its descent to B♭4. In Lorca's original play, it is the embroidered flag, sewn by Mariana Pineda, which symbolizes freedom; while it remains an object that is never shown on stage, it remains a powerful symbol that binds Pineda to her political cause and her loved ones. Similarly, the trumpet motive is disconnected from anything visible on stage, yet it symbolizes the idea of (fighting for) freedom in Golijov's music through his appropriation of the fanfare topic.

An abridged version of the trumpet fanfare segues into the first statement of the ballad, sung by the female chorus. Golijov explains that the text of the recurring ballad was actually a popular poem that Lorca knew and incorporated into the opening of his play *Mariana Pineda* (2006). The haunting quality of the ballad centers on the anthropomorphic image of stones crying for Mariana's death as the bells tolled and tolled. Example 2.3a shows the melodic contour of the refrain, which draws on the upper pentachord of the Hijāz scale on B♭. The lament topic is evoked by the pervasive repetition of the descending minor third motive (marked x) in the melodic line. The first section (A) comprises a sentence construction (2+2+4) and the final phrase ornaments the descending line through the addition of neighbor notes and grace notes.[7] The second section (B) features the ascending fourth (marked y) on the accompanying words "the bells tolled." In common with the y motive of the trumpet fanfare, it is associated with the tolling of the bell for Pineda's death. The two parts of the refrain serve as the cyclical module upon which Xirgu makes her solo entries as the *cantaor* of a *cante jondo*.

Upon this eight-bar cyclical module, Xirgu sings her lament, expressing her anguish over playing the role of Mariana Pineda night after night in the theater

a. Choral refrain (mm.29-33)

Translation: "What a sad day it was in Granada; even the stones began to cry, seeing Marianita die because they could not make her speak. The bells tolled...."

b. Xirgu's solo (mm.50-72)

"My whole life in such a place: alone, in the wings of a theatre, waiting to become Mariana Pineda again."

Example 2.3a/b. Ballad I

in Uruguay. As shown in example 2.3b, her initial entry floats on D5, the major third of the scale before making her chromatic descent to A♯ (= B♭).[8] Note how her melody is characterized by repeating the motive of lament (marked x) on the words "toda una vida" (my whole life). Her ending the first phrase on F5 coincides with the choral entry of the ballad melody. The consequent phrase (mm.61–72) is characterized by a circle-of-fifths sequence on the closing text, "waiting to become Mariana Pineda again." The pervasive repetition of motive x captures Xirgu's burdensome existence in Uruguay playing Pineda night after night without relief.

In the following stanza Xirgu expresses how her womb "aches" for Lorca. Here, her vocal line reaches the melodic apex on A♭5 before dropping to D♭5, the minor tenth above B♭4, on the word "vientre" (ache). Xirgu indulges in her reminiscence of Lorca as the chorus continues to sing about the bells tolling (part B of the refrain). In the final solo entry, she addresses Nuria, her protégé, about growing old, over the same melody that parallels the first entry. In this way, Xirgu's solo is intertwined with the chorus's singing of the ballad to convey lament and longing in the diegetic setting of Uruguay.

When the ballad returns at the commencement of the second Image, it turns into "a crazed, frenetic reprise" of the first. Golijov's intention in this scene was to depict Xirgu "losing her mind in a way, so everything starts to spin furiously inside her head" (2006). Anchored to G in the bass, with chords that alternate rapidly between B♭♭9/11 and G♭9/11 in the guitars and cajones, the female chorus sings in parallel fourths at a much faster, frenzied tempo (example 2.4a). The phrase structure of part A of the refrain is condensed into six bars and its second repetition is accompanied by a fast, chromatic planing of the ornamented melody with inverted triads (⁶₃ and ⁶₄). Following two cycles of verse and refrain, a distorted recording of the Falangist party's political speech interrupts the musical continuity.[9] Simultaneously, guitars and cajones maintain the frenetic pace of the ostinato, while distorted fragments of the trumpet's fanfare motive are also heard, dispersed in the flute and oboe. The radio broadcast contains the following text, condemning those who oppose the Falangist's fascist ideology, which sets the tone for the scene of execution at Ainadamar:

Nuestros jóvenes deben estar preparados	Our youth must be ready
a derramar su sangre generosa	to shed their blood generously
por la causa sagrada de España	for the sacred cause of Spain.
Quien no esté con nosotros	Whoever is not with us
está contra nosotros.	is against us.
Exterminaremos las semillas	We'll exterminate the seeds
dela revolución	of the Revolution,
aun en los uterus de las madres.	Even in the wombs of their mothers.
Viva la muerte!	Long live death!

At the beginning of third Image, the ballad is transformed into a dirge, accompanied by the tubular bells that sound the fourth, D-G, over the chordal fifth

a. 2nd Image, mm.22-29: a frenetic reprise

"[Gra]nada; the stones began to cry, seeing Marianita die because they could not make her speak."

b. 3rd Image, mm.1-7: a dirge

"What a sad day it was in Granada; even the stones began to cry...."

Examples 2.4a/b. Recurrences of the Ballad Melody

on every other downbeat. As shown in example 2.4b, Golijov entitles it balada-la-berinto ("ballad maze") with an expression indication, "fatal." The female chorus sings the ballad in a declamatory manner a minor third below the original. As Xirgu collapses and gasps for air, Nuria sings her soliloquy over the slow, recurring motive (y) that imitates the contour of the refrain with the downward appoggiatura (E♭-D), urging Xirgu to rest and not go on with the performance. See her vocal entry that mirrors the contour of the choral refrain (y) on the word "Margarita" at mm.6–7.

In the following passage, the choral entries are harmonized in parallel fourths, synchronized with the bell chords (struck every two measures) to emphasize the dire nature of this scene. Xirgu can hardly speak, while Nuria's vocal tessitura rises higher and higher as she comes to realize the importance of keeping the tradition alive.

Cuando nuestras voces callan,	When our voices are silenced
desaparecemos;	we vanish from memory.
Cuando mueren quienes nos rodean,	When those around us die,
morimos también.	we die as well.

The ballad refrain is heard for the final time at the end of the opera over a chordal drone on C major, preceded by the trumpet fanfare motive. Although the context and harmonic support change to give a positive valence to the idea of "freedom," the return of the ballad at the end reinforces the mythical and synchronic dimension of the narrative by calling attention to its circular design. Just as the story began with the chorus' ballad lamenting Pineda's death, it ends with the refrain melody from the ballad, sung in canon by two singers, which gradually fades into the distance.

Other Popular Song Forms

Golijov masterfully incorporates lighter song forms to offset the somber characteristics of the framing ballad and flamenco music. In the first scene, a rumba, a light-hearted Cuban dance form, accompanies Xirgu's nightly performance of *Mariana Pineda*. As shown in example 2.5 a/b, the female chorus sings the refrain over the dotted rumba ostinato, featuring the rising third, which is echoed by other instruments. The circularity of the ostinato rhythm associated with the rumba parallels her re-creation of Lorca's play night after night. Golijov speaks also of how the chorus "taunts" Xirgu through a refrain that compares her to "a brilliant, shining star" (2005). Musically, the three phrases make up a sentence structure, where each phrase opens with a chromatic third leap, D to F major, E♭ to G♭ major, and F to A♭ major, and capture the air of playful mockery. By inverting the signifier of lament (descending third) to an ascending one (marked x'), the chorus portrays Xirgu's role as Mariana Pineda in a positive light, yet with a touch of playful mockery.

Following this number, Nuria questions Xirgu about the first time she met Lorca, and the music turns to a light duet that recounts their first meeting in a bar in Madrid, accompanied by a solo guitar. The expressive character changes rapidly when the following number features a slow, melancholy waltz with a lament bass. In "Desde Mi Ventana" ("From my window"), Lorca recalls how he looked out onto the statue of Mariana Pineda as a young child and identified with the woman who represents "light, warmth, and most of all, love." The song conveys Lorca's yearning and love for Pineda.

a. the choral refrain (mm.29-45)

"Mariana Pineda, your eyes shine brighter than stars in the night ..."

b. Xirgu's solo entry (mm.388-400)

"The Spain of freedom we dreamt was choked, massacred, and buried by the Falange."

Example 2.5a/b. Excerpts from "Mariana, Tu Ojos"

The meandering nature of this song is supported by the lack of tonal ground-ing of the melody; while the starting bass note is anchored to G minor, the bass pattern leaps from G to E to B♭, and Lorca's initial vocal entry on C♯ avoids a se-cure footing on G. After two verses of Lorca's solo that weakly tonicize C minor and F minor, Xirgu and Nuria join in. The key then shifts to D minor when Xirgu and Nuria enter on the words "eran una solo" (be as one), as shown in example 2.6. This signifies the moment when the women recognize that Lorca knew that

Example 2.6. "Desde Mi Ventana" (mm. 168–77)

he would share the same fate as Pineda in dying, not just for the revolution, but for love.

Electronic Soundscape: Indices of a Lost Time and Place

Throughout *Ainadamar*, Golijov uses electronically generated or sampled sounds as indices of a lost time and place. In the opening Prelude, the trumpet motive (y) is heard above the reverberating drone on B♭ and electronic sounds of water, which segue to the sounds of a horse galloping and the clatter of hooves hitting cobblestones. The immediate association is with Spain at the time of the civil war and the Falangists' persecution of liberals. But there is also an allusion to the horseback flight of the bride and her lover in Lorca's aforementioned play, *Blood Wedding*. These electronically generated sounds intersect with live performers on the cajones, who maintain a steady rhythmic ostinato based on the *Fandango de Huelva* compás.

Another sampled sound that provides a powerful index to a lost time and place is the voices of children praying for the Virgin Mary prior to the assassination of Lorca and the other prisoners. Golijov used a recording of the actual sounds of Mexican children praying to the Virgin of Guadalupe in Chiapas (2006). In addition to this sonic tapestry, the electronic sound of horse galloping music signifies the moment when Lorca's body is taken away following his execution. Most poignantly, the death of Lorca is then captured through a tape loop of one gunshot. For this, Golijov looked through a library of gunshot sounds from the 1930s; symbolically, the tape loop of a single gunshot was also meant to evoke the deaths of thousands of individuals who were killed during the Franco regime (Golijov 2006).

Finally, Ainadamar, the fountain and the site of Lorca's execution, incorporates different sounds of water as indices of suffering – blood and tears shed by those who have fought for freedom. The electronic sounds of water interact with the live voices of two female singers (off stage) who sing a variant of the lament motive (D-C♯-B-G) on "Ainadamar" in imitative counterpoint. Over this repeating ostinato layer, Xirgu sings a line that paints a picture of Lorca as Christ: "So up that hillside you carried your cross; on his left, a school teacher, on his right, a bull fighter, and the fountain itself began to cry." The shift from the second (you) to third person (his) pronoun is deliberate, as the image of Christ on the cross is metonymically linked with Lorca's impending death.

Flamenco and Duende

The *cantaor,* the singer of flamenco *cante jondo* (deep song), is historically the conveyor of suffering for the marginalized race of Romani Gypsies. The composer Manuel de Falla asserts that those who settled in Andalusia distinguished themselves from the nomadic tribes and founded the *siguiriya gitana* style from a fusion of indigenous cultural elements (Stone 2004: 7). The modernist movement at the turn of the twentieth century also pursued the art of flamenco as an embodiment of utopian ideals and collective consciousness.[10] During the 1930s, Spanish fascists and anti-fascists were equally drawn to flamenco music as a way to build solidarity. Since fascists and anti-fascists alike were often great lovers of flamenco, Washabaugh comments that flamenco became "both a disease and its antidote" (2012: 67). In lieu of the exotic appeal that characterized flamenco's identity in the nineteenth century, Spaniards embraced flamenco as a reflection of their own cultural identity. In the Andalusian flamenco tradition, *duende* refers not to an institutionalized deity but rather the spirit guide, which they believe possesses the *cantaore* with a performance that resonates with the depth of feeling and emotion (Stone 2004: 22). Thus, it is hardly surprising that Golijov assigns the role of the flamenco *cantaor* to both Lorca and the Falangist executioner, Ruiz Alonso; the existential anguish that lies at the heart of *duende* binds them together in spite of their opposed political ideologies.

In what follows, I refer to three contexts in which the flamenco vocal and instrumental textures express this somber sentiment from opposing perspectives. In "Quiero Cantar entre las Explosiones," Lorca expresses his desire to stay in Granada against Xirgu's wishes, as he compares his fight for Spain to "a bull burning alive." As shown in example 2.7, Lorca's vocal line fits the contour of the Bayati scale on D in descent as it captures Lorca's fighting spirit. The rhythm of the accompaniment in the cajón part is derived from the compás of the tango (3+3+2), while the sequential oscillation between D (m.1) and E♭ (m.3) in the bass reinforces the Arabic modal inflection associated with the Hijāz scale.

Alex Ross comments that when Alonso orders Lorca's death, he sings in the florid, flamenco style, which is the style of singing most steeped in *cante jondo*

"I want to sing amidst the explosions, I want to sing an immense song."

Example 2.7. "Quiero Cantar Entre las Explosiones" (mm.9–12)

(2006a: 7). In the Deutsche Grammophon recording, Jesus Montoya sings the part of Ruiz Alonso.[11] In his vocal improvisation on the text – "Bring him to me! By God! The one with the swollen head!" – the focal pitch of his improvisation hangs on G♯, the fifth above the C♯ electronic drone, and features ornamental notes with microtonal inflection in its descent to the tonic note C♯. This spirit of *duende* comes across most powerfully through the amplified voice of Montoya, transcending his role as executioner. As one whose desperate longing is linked with death, Montoya's singing powerfully embodies the *cante* flamenco's themes of nihilistic ideology and erotic pessimism (Stone 2004: 23). Alonso's vocal improvisation appears three times and acquires greater intensity with each repetition: "Muerte a Caballo" ("Death on Horseback," Image I), "Arresto" ("Arrest," Image II), and "Interludio de Balazos y Lamento por la Muerte de Federico" ("Gunshot Interlude and Lament for the Death of Federico," Image II).

Xirgu, too, becomes immersed in the spirit of *duende* when the chorus calls out her stage name in "Crepúsculo Delirante" ("Delirious Sunset"). This number begins with an extensive interlude for two flamenco guitars. Over a pulsating drone on C, the two guitars participate in a musical "duel" – exchanging short motives back and forth as each entry ascends in register. Eventually, they come together in unison to introduce the stepwise ascending fourth motive based on the Hijāz scale. At this critical juncture, the chorus enters with the words: "Mariana, your dark eyes," as shown under example 2.8. As the chorus sustains two chords, a minor third apart, calling out for Mariana's dark eyes, the guitar motive (y') loops over the chords in a recurring rhythmic cycle of five beats. From a topical perspective, this is where the variant of motive y based on the Hijāz scale confronts the rhythmic augmentation of the lament motive x. That is to say, the aggressive (masculine) quality of the *duende* collides with the long, sustained vertical harmony that conveys the existential anguish (feminine) of Pineda's martyrdom. Contrary to the dueling function of *cante* flamenco, Xirgu's

Osvaldo Golijov's Ainadamar 63

Example 2.8. "Crepúsculo Delirante" (mm.50–55)

association with flamenco music is softened by the sustained chords that anchor her to her primary agential role in voicing lament.

Ritual Consecration/ Transcendence

Musically, the most jarring transition occurs at the juncture of "Crepúsculo De-lirante" and "Doy Mi Sangre" ("Here is [I give] my blood"). In stark contrast to the darker coloring and register of the preceding number on the C Hijāz scale, the bright key of E major establishes a mood of *pure* bliss and signals the trans-valuation that shifts the negative connotation of freedom to a positive one. I re-fer to this movement as the music of ritual consecration. The biblical reference to the Eucharistic rite is made explicit in the opening text sung by Xirgu, Nuria, and Lorca.[12] Although through composed, the structure of this song divides roughly into two sections (I and II). In Section I the key modulates from E major to C♯ minor (on "voces") and G♯ major (on "nacido"). In Section II, the key be-gins in G♯ major on an ascending third and modulates to C major and enters into a sequence build on a cycle of fifths as Xirgu bids farewell to those around her. Note the partial rhymes that connect *muriendo* (die) with *amado* (loved), *nacido* (born), and *mundo* (world) (see italicized).

I. *Doy mi sangre,*	I give my blood,
derramada por vosotros,	shed for thee,
bebedia y contad mi historia.	drink it and tell my story.
Así es cómo voy muriendo,	This is how I am going to *die*,
sumergia en las voces	submerged in the voices
de quienes siempre yo he amado	of those who have *loved* me
y los que aún no han nacido.	and those not yet *born*.

II. *Libertad! Libertad de lo alto . . .*	Freedom! Highest freedom . . .
Libertad! Libertad verdadera!	Freedom! True freedom!
Ahora veo el mundo	I see the *world* now
con ojos de multitudes	with the eyes of multitudes.
Adiós, adiós,	Farewell, farewell,
Granada amada!	beloved Granada!

Golijov's musical setting of "Doy Mi Sangre" is simply rapturous. Over the string harmonics and lilting triplets, the vocal entries by Xirgu, Nuria, and Lorca unfold in staggered counterpoint. As shown in example 2.9a, Xirgu's melodic line ascends chromatically in parallel motion to Lorca's, while Nuria's line descends on the text "shed for thee," culminating in an elided cadence that tonicizes C♯ major in m.5. This passage continues as Xirgu's line continues to soar upward, propelled by a downward circle-of-fifths progression that ends in another cadence on C♯ minor on the text "submerged in the voices" of those from the past. Xirgu's arrival on the melodic apex on "muriendo" (dying) is accompanied by an upward arpeggiation in the guitar, coupled with a downward arpeggiation in the vibraphone to create a sense of expansiveness. In the bridge that connects the two sections, a variation of the flamenco figuration (G♯-A-C♯-B) from *Crepúsculo delirante* is exchanged between the guitar and strings. Establishing G♯ major as a point of arrival and a tonicized key area, Nuria and Lorca then partake in singing vocal lines in ascending parallel thirds on "libertad" (liberty), and Xirgu provides a melodic flourish in the higher register with "libertad de lo alto" (freedom in the highest). As shown in example 2.9b, the texture then unravels into a downward circle-of-fifths sequence on "mundo" (world) from F♯ minor to C♯ minor, as Xirgu bids farewell. Another quick sequence of chords takes us to A♭ major (= G♯M) on "amada" (beloved), followed by a short bridge that segues to the final number, "Yo Soy la Libertad." Overall, the movement emphasizes modulations by chromatic third, notably E major to C♯ major/minor and A♭ major to C major.

Although cast in a popular musical style, Xirgu's role in "Doy Mi Sangre" is comparable to Isolde's in the concluding "Liebestod" from Wagner's *Tristan und Isolde;* both heroines depart from the phenomenal world through a spiritual union with their loved ones.[13] A sequence of chromatic mediant-based modulations, coupled with undulating triplets, induces a sense of ascension into an otherworldly sphere of existence. But it is unlikely that Xirgu undergoes a transfiguration on the metaphysical plane, as in the case of Isolde. Xirgu's role is more about departing from her earthly suffering and torment with grace. As she says: "I see the world now with the eyes of multitudes"; it is about letting go of her earthly existence in order to embrace freedom. Golijov provides other intertextual references to operatic works from the past: "The music starts almost in a Straussian manner to me, Rosenkavalier-like, but then it goes on to Purcell. To me it resembles the death of Dido: that majesty, that love, that grace. It's a number about finding grace right before death" (Golijov 2006).

The final number, "Yo Soy la Libertad" ("I am freedom"), begins with the eight-bar ostinato motive introduced in the flutes and strings, which I refer to

a. (mm. 5-10)

"my blood, shed for thee, drink it...."

beginning of sequence

b. (mm.46-57)

"I see the world now with the eyes of multitudes. Farewell, farewell...."

Example 2.9a/b. *"Doy Mi Sangre"*

a. (mm.1-8)

b. (mm. 103-106)

Examples 2.10a/b. "Freedom" Motive from "Yo Soy la Libertad"

as the "freedom" motive. As shown in example 2.10a, while the motive is situated in C major, the characteristic feature of the Hijāz scale is kept intact by the retention of the Phrygian second (D♭) at the end. Over this repeating ostinato, the texture builds through the addition of instrumental layers, one by one, in a style reminiscent of Ravel's *Bolero*. The texture thickens through the addition of horns, guitars, vibraphone, and other woodwinds. Guitars add a distinctive countermelody, reinforced by the strings, as the texture builds to a big, majestic climax. Alex Ross calls this "the ragged march of liberty" (2006a: 8). It is the only time Golijov introduces an extensive, acousmatic instrumental interlude to convey the struggle for freedom. Against the steady repetition of the "freedom" motive, other musical layers are added one by one, the brightness of this C major ostinato against motives derived from the Hijāz scale that connote darkness and oppression. Following the collective entry on C-D♭-C-B♭, the music comes to an abrupt halt.

Over a low drone on C, Xirgu, now in her spirit form, sings a triumphant aria in which she proclaims that she is not only "freedom," but "the source of the fountain from which you drink." The shift from the initial $\frac{4}{4}$ to $\frac{12}{8}$ meter contributes to a sense of expansion and *plenitude* – textural saturation accompanied by euphoric fulfillment in this case (Hatten 2004: 43). A highly ornamented version of the trumpet fanfare echoes her celebratory song as the female chorus hums the ostinato motive in the background (see example 2.10b). Blended harmonically with

Osvaldo Golijov's Ainadamar 67

the ostinato motive and the drone in C major, the trumpet signifies its transformation from "wounded" freedom (initially in B♭) to a symbol of transcendent freedom, in C major. It is no coincidence that the opera ends in C major, since, for Golijov, it signifies "the possibility of resurrection" (McKinnon 2005: 39). As two members of the female chorus sing the ballad melody off-stage over the eight-bar ostinato, tolling bells and flamenco guitars echo these motives. As the voices fade away, the electronic sounds of water bring the opera to a close.

Like any good operatic composer, Golijov breathes life into the narrative of *Ainadamar* in a manner where the music takes front stage in the expression of longing, lament, and existential anguish. Certain correlations can be made – for instance, flamenco music with the ethos of duende, the descending third (motive x) with the expression of lament, and the ascending fourth (motive y) with the idea of freedom. If C♯ signifies violence and E major forgiveness and transcendence, the two numbers in which the latter (brighter) key is used are in the scenes of the confession and the consecration ("Doy mi sangre"). At other times, the tritone interval replaces the third or fifth to connote longing and suffering, as in "Desde Mi Vente" (G-C♯) or the third time the ballad is stated (D-A♭) as a dirge. Along with the overall shift in tonal orientation from B♭ Hijāz scale to C major, the initial appearance of the trumpet motive and its transformation at the end articulate the transvaluative process by which "wounded" (marked) freedom shifts to the attainment of transcendent freedom (unmarked).

Golijov's music marks this journey from "wounded" freedom to freedom attained. By the time Xirgu sings "Yo Soy Libertad," the initial spatiotemporal dichotomy established between electronically generated sounds (marking metadiegetic space) and live instrumental music (marking diegetic space) dissolves. At this moment of apotheosis, Xirgu's quest for freedom turns into a universal plea for artistic freedom, in line with Lorca's utopian vision. The opera comes to an end by merging the extradiegetic voice of the chorus with the metadiegetic soundscape of murmuring water. Golijov's music plays an indispensible role in establishing mythic time; the ballad sung by the female chorus at the closing of the opera echoes in the background as it merges with the murmuring sounds of water representing the fountain of Ainadamar. When music and libretto tell the story in such a compelling manner, how might production components contribute (positively or negatively) to its multimodal structure?

Crossing Genres and Modes of Productions: Opera, Oratorio, and Meta-theater

My initial experience of *Ainadamar* was a semi-staged concert setting by the Atlanta Symphony Orchestra in 2006, conducted by Robert Spano. The visceral power of flamenco singing and Dawn Upshaw's impassioned enactment of Margarita Xirgu made a memorable impression. The female chorus adopted a nasal style of singing in the opening ballad to imitate village girls in Granada and set them apart as the narrator of the story.[14] Golijov's intention to convey the expression of *duende* through the "grain of the voice" came across convincingly. Since then, I have attended a number of different productions and adaptations that transformed my multimodal narrative experience of this opera in profound ways. In four case studies of how the directors' aesthetic strategies subtly or radically alter the narrative structure and its trajectories, I compare the Santa Fe Opera's full-staged production (2005), Indiana University's oratorio version (2007), Staatstheater Darmstadt's theatrical production (2007), and Long Beach Opera's production (2010). In each case I bring attention to how the directors' choices embellish or detract from the myth of Lorca and the actantial theme of "wounded" freedom in the basic narrative.

Opera as Gesamtkunstwerk: the Santa Fe production (2006)

The Santa Fe Opera production, directed by Peter Sellars, presents *Ainadamar* as Gesamtkustwerk – a total work of art that transposes Lorca's theatrical sensibilities onto the operatic stage. Here, the visual dimension of the staging complements and enriches Hwang's libretto and Golijov's music equally. In addition, Sellars commissioned Chicano artist Gronk (Glugio Nicandro) for an urban mural that would cover the stage's semi-circular wall and the floor, recalling the stage design of Lorca's plays from the 1930s. Contemplating the historical significance of these urban murals, Alex Ross (2006a) comments: "Lorca's play, *Mariana Pineda,* was premiered with sets designed by Salvador Dalí (with whom Lorca was infatuated at the time). Since that play figures so prominently in the opera, it struck me as a great idea to have abstract painting as the backdrop." In this sense, Sellars's production conjures up the image of a play within a play. Moreover, Gronk's penchant for geometric patterns and mutated figures is suggestive of early twentieth-century Cubist paintings, such as Pablo Picasso's *Guernica* (1937), which he painted in response to the bombing of a village in northern Spain during the Spanish Civil War. The mural presents an additional cultural intertext, drawing a parallel between Gronk's marginalized identity as a Chicano artist in East Los Angeles with Lorca's status in 1930s Spain.

The blurring of the distinction between reality and fantasy constitutes an integral part of Sellars's mise-en-scène. The coordination of choreography, lighting, and music in Sellars's production creates an otherworldly expression of existential anguish. Lighting assumes an independent semic role in articulating the mood of each scene – a signature style of Sellars's mise-en-scène, as will be illustrated in other operas discussed in this study. The mosaic effects created through alternation between full and partial lighting transform the stage without reliance on props. Extreme contrast in lighting is created through the oscillation between red and blue: red signifies defiance (literally, the blood that was shed for freedom), while blue signifies sorrow and resignation. In between, there is neutral lighting that provides a clearer view of Gronk's mural. A striking change to green lighting takes place in "Crepúsculo Delirante." This scene mimics the ending of Lorca's play *Mariana Pineda,* where he calls for an "orange light" to conjure up the image of a sunset in Granada (Golijov 2006).

Osvaldo Golijov's Ainadamar 69

Figures 2.2a/b: Gronk's Urban Murals Used in the Santa Fe Opera Production

Two images from Sellars's production for the Santa Fe Opera illustrate the effects of lighting on Gronk's mural in setting the mood for various scenes. In "Quiero Arrancarme," Xirgu kneels in prayer and then pins Lorca to the wall as she urges him to abandon his cause; as shown in figure 2.2a, neutral lighting brings out the earthy colors in the mural to inject a sense of realism. In the second ballad, where the women are alarmed by the Falangists' radio broadcast, the dark red lighting conjures up an atmosphere that threatens destruction; as shown in figure 2.2b, the patterns in the mural appear more animated due to the partial lighting that immerses half of the stage in shadows. Sellars's production is also distinguished by an elaborate choreography of physical gestures and miming that accompany the singing. Hand and facial gestures emerge as dominant signifiers of desire, entrapment, suffering, and resignation, as can be noted in both images. Lorca, played by the mezzo-soprano, is shown to be effeminate in yielding to Xirgu's plea to escape to Havana.

From an intermedial perspective, Sellars's mise-en-scène embellishes the actantial theme of "wounded" freedom in accordance with Cook's "conformance" model of multimedia discussed in chapter 1. Sellars establishes tightly knit metaphysical associations in his multimodal telling of this narrative through choreography, lighting, and music as follows.

First, the spiritual union between Lorca, Xirgu, and Nuria is established through choreographed movements that accompany their singing. The circular movement that accompanies "Desde Mi Ventana" ("From my window") is effective in conveying yearning. The slow, languid waltz with a meandering tonal orientation is set to a soft blue light that shines on the center of the stage; Lorca, as he sings, walks to the center of the spotlight, while the women walk slowly at the perimeter of the larger circle that surrounds him. As the piece progresses, the female chorus departs from the circle, and Xirgu joins Lorca in the middle of the circle; they dance back to back in a circular motion with outstretched hands. Toward the end, Nuria joins the two as Lorca reaches over to the two women, blesses them, and the three cluster together and sing about becoming "one." Later, in "Doy mi sangre," which reconfigures the Eucharistic ritual, Lorca, Xirgu, and Nuria are brought into union with each other. As the lighting illuminating the circle turns blue, Lorca and Nuria kneel down to hold Xirgu's body as they sing, "Here is [I give] my blood, shed for thee, drink and tell my story." These two numbers are related through the choreography that brings the three characters in symbolic union with each other.

Second, lighting plays an important function in articulating tension and conflict in Sellars's production. During the Falangists' radio broadcast, dramatic change is coordinated with musical structure and lighting to create strong audio-visual downbeats. For example, toward the end of "Quiero Cantar Entre las Explosiones" ("I want to sing amid the explosions"), the lighting changes every time the Falangists' radio broadcast is inserted between the instrumental interludes, while the blue spotlight remains on Lorca. The women flee from one end of the stage to the other in response to the change in lighting and blaring sounds of the radio broadcast. As mentioned above, red lighting signifies violence and is used predominantly in the second Image featuring Lorca's arrest and execution. During the Gunshot interlude, Alonso repeatedly props Lorca up and shoots him down, while the other guards shoot the remaining prisoners. In contrast, green lighting is used in "Crepúsculo Delirante"; Sellars highlights Xirgu's earthly suffering and her departure from the phenomenal world. As the flamenco guitars deliver a duet steeped in the existential anguish associated with *duende*, Xirgu collapses on the floor, gasps for air and writhes in agony in the middle of the stage, surrounded by Nuria, Lorca, and the female chorus. In "Yo Soy la Libertad," the female chorus gathers around Xirgu in solidarity as a mosaic of red, black, and white lighting illuminates the stage. Alonso appears in military fatigues and points the gun at Xirgu, who rises and directs her song about "becoming freedom" at him; the trumpet fanfare echoes her triumphant "rebirth."

Third, the consistent presence of the female chorus on stage reinforces its role akin to the turba in Passion oratorios – as the narrator of the mythic tale. The chorus's role as principal narrator of the story is emphasized through their choreographed singing of the ballad. Their vigorous bodily gestures embody the theme of "wounded" freedom. The female chorus functions as an integral part of each scene; instead of merely commenting on the drama from the outside (like a Greek chorus), they interact with Xirgu, Nuria, and Lorca. Their choreographed gestures speak of Xirgu's oppressed existence, her love for Lorca, and her need for protection. The chorus also creates a buffer between the diegetic and metadiegetic domains – the present and the past that divide Xirgu's existence until her death and "rebirth" in "Yo Soy la Libertad."

A notable exception to Sellars's production can be found in the explicit portrayal of Alonso as antihero. It works against the grain of the otherwise mythical telling of the story. I would venture to say that bringing back Alonso at the end of Sellars's production shifts the narrative trajectory from the poetic timelessness of myth to a moralistic tale. As a symbolic gesture, Xirgu (now a ghost) gets up in the final scene and stands facing Alonso as she sings about having become "freedom." This theatrical gesture at the end, extraneous to Hwang's libretto, advances Sellars's view of this opera as a play about "morality." Rather than keeping the notion of "freedom" as an entity that is ultimately unattainable, Sellars forces closure by allowing Xirgu to assert her victorious position over her enemy. On a related note, Alex Ross comments on the gender politics in this production: "There is a striking dichotomy between the artistic side of this opera, the group of feminine voices (Lorca, Margarita Xirgu, the ensemble), and the military, male side, represented especially in the character of the arresting officer, Alonso. Standing at the back of the stage through most of the action, sometimes smoking a cigarette, he is a menacing presence, costumed in army camouflage, buzz cut, boots, and machine gun" (Ross 2006a).[15] For Hwang and Sellars, it was imperative to emphasize Lorca's artistic sensibilities over his political allegiance by exaggerating his feminine characteristics against the brutality of the Falangists.

Oratorio as Passion: Indiana University (2007)

A less politically charged but equally moving performance of *Ainadamar,* directed and conducted by Carmen-Helena Telléz, took place at Indiana University's Jacobs School of Music in 2007. In this semi-staged oratorio setting, Telléz spatialized the acoustical environment by placing the main singers on stage with the ensemble while placing the female chorus and trumpets on the balcony above the main stage. The stage remained lit for the entire performance, and actions were minimized to the soloists' movements surrounding the ensemble.

In this oratorical version, the materiality of the performers clearly trumps all other dimensions of the production. The singers and instrumentalists take center stage as the narrators of the story. The electronic soundscape emits an eerie presence as a disembodied Other – the only instance of a musical force that is not attached to visible bodies on stage. The "Water and Horse" prelude is extended to allow for electronic sources to interact more fully with live elements; the music ensemble includes a number of performers who clap the flamenco rhythm. Xirgu and Nuria are seated on stage, but, as the narrative progresses, they begin to interact with one another through their physical gestures, which convey their intimacy. In this oratorio setting, the flamenco guitars convey the universal anguish associated with *duende,* in line with Lorca's poem, in which the guitar is seen as an extension of the cry of the *cantaor.* "Crepúsculo Delirante" is showcased by the two guitars in precisely this manner. The death of Lorca is conveyed exclusively through electronic means, and it is the least dramatic aspect of the production. When the Gunshot Interlude, comprising the tape loop of gunshots and Alonso's singing, segues into the third ballad, the sense of lament reaches its peak: Nuria and Xirgu, accompanied by the slow chanting of the ballad anchored to the tolling of bells, mourn Lorca's death. In "Doy mi sangre" – the scene of consecration – Xirgu, Lorca, and Nuria stand facing the audience. In recognition of their departure from the phenomenal world, Lorca leads Xirgu away from the stage as Nuria stands with her hands clasped in front of her in acknowledgement of her role as the carrier of tradition. When the trumpet "fanfare" theme is heard over the "freedom" refrain, Nuria puts on the jacket left behind by Xirgu and walks off stage.

In an interview, Telléz (2011) commented on the importance of the Passion play genre in guiding her conception of the work. As the monophonic Passion play developed during the fourteenth- and fifteenth-centuries, its structure became divided among the three primary singers – the Evangelist, Christ, and Pontius Pilate. Keeping in mind these three roles, Telléz drew a parallel between the characters in *Ainadamar* and those in the Renaissance Passion as follows: Xirgu's role corresponds to that of the Evangelist, Lorca's to that of Christ, Ruiz Alonso to that of Pontius Pilate, and the female chorus to that of the turba. It was important for Telléz that the music communicate the power of this "passion" oratorio on its own terms; it was only at the end of the performance that she projected documentary images of Lorca and Xirgu on the screen above the stage for the audience to look at. Unlike other Latin American composers who have criticized Golijov's music for equating flamenco music with the Falangists, Telléz argues that Golijov intended a much broader association of flamenco music with Spanish culture and the aesthetics of the time. Telléz's comment that "flamenco music signifies death" echoes Lorca's position on *cante jondo*.[16]

Perhaps Telléz's decision to deploy a baritone to sing the role of Lorca was dictated by *Ainadamar*'s reference to the traditional Passion story. Indeed, the male voice infuses a greater sense of realism to the role, especially in the scene where he sings the aria "Desde Mi Ventana," recalling his love for Mariana Pineda. In other respects, however, I find that the change in voice type irrevocably alters Hwang's focus on Lorca as the subject of myth. As a heteronormative corrective, the deeper, lower resonance of the male voice takes away from the symbol of Lorca as the child-like spiritual figure that Xirgu seeks to be united with in death.

More surprisingly, this performance significantly undermines Ruiz Alonso's role as antihero from a number of perspectives. Telléz utilizes a live singer for Alonso, whose voice is, for most of the performance, amplified and distorted, lending an otherworldly quality to his disembodied presence for most of the opera. However, the singer does not sing in a traditional flamenco style, but in an operatic style, which undermines the expression of duende by its failure to convey the existential anguish connected with vocal improvisation in the authentic style. Furthermore, following Xirgu's singing of "Yo Soy la Libertad," Alonso appears on the right hand corner of the stage to pay a silent tribute to Lorca. Turning him into a visible presence next to Lorca not only undermines Alonso's role as antihero, it reduces him to a caricature of Lorca's perceived enemy. Simply put, Alonso's conciliatory gesture deflates the dramatic tension that keeps the narrative riveting. In fact, the flamenco guitarists' performance of "Crepúsculo Delirante" captures the essence of duende more poignantly than Alonso's and Lorca's singing combined. Because Xirgu and Nuria emerge as central figures in this oratorio setting, the cultural trope of *Mater dolorosa* figures heavily into my narrative reading of this version of *Ainadamar*.

Meta-theater: the Staatstheater Darmstadt (2007–08)

The theatrical production of *Ainadamar* at the Staatstheater Darmstadt ran from November 2007 to May 2008 and offered a radically different approach to the mise-en-scène from all other productions that I have encountered. Under direction by Mei Hong Lin, new visual and choreographic elements were added, and these brought to the foreground cultural elements that are extraneous to Hwang and Sellars's conception of *Ainadamar*.[17] Among many intertexts that were interwoven into Lin's mise-en-scène, the parallel she draws between the victims of the Spanish Civil War and those of the holocaust is notable. Referring to the scene of execution at Ainadamar, she comments: "In this scene, I see a parallel with the fate of Jewish people under Hitler's regime. Of course, anti-Semitism in Germany basically has nothing to do with this work, but for me, it points to the same suppression and discrimination one finds in Spain under Franco's regime, only that it takes place elsewhere" (Dietrich 2007).[18] By mixing incongruous cultural elements into the choreography, Lin generates a specific atmosphere of drama and emotion to make a commentary on the Holocaust within her mise-en-scène.

Visually, the stage is divided into distinct spaces: a rectangular field in the center occupied by singers and dancers, a wall with protruding surfaces to the left of the stage, a makeshift fountain with water streaming down to the right of the stage, and a modern lounge in the front right hand corner of the stage. To Lin, the wall conjured up the "wailing wall" in Jerusalem, a holy site where Jewish people were banned from praying when the Arabs captured the Jewish Quarter between 1948 and 1967 (Klein 2007). In addition, water flows through a semi-circular ramp that lacks any specific reference to the site of Ainadamar. Costumes turn the main characters into grotesque caricatures: Xirgu is dressed in period costume, portraying Pineda with a heavy wig and make-up, Lorca in a black and white suit (or an androgynous tuxedo-like dress), Nuria in a modern green dress (made to look like a secretary from the 1960s), the female chorus in angelic white dresses, and Ruiz Alonso in a military uniform with a fox-like mask.

Overall, Lin's mise-en-scène adds prominent contrapuntal layers that shift the focus of attention away from Lorca as the subject of myth; instead she asks the viewer to contemplate other themes of oppression in relationship to this story. In effect, she transforms the opera into meta-theater, similar to how Stainton conceives Lorca's late plays (2005: 85). By giving the dancers expressive agency over the singers, Lin's mise-en-scène generates intertexts that compete with those of the basic narrative, in accordance with Cook's "contest" model.

Here are some of the ways in which Lin's theatrical presentation decenters Lorca as the focus of the tale by foregrounding extraneous visual themes. In "Mariana, Tu Ojos," twelve dancers take center stage, while Xirgu and Nuria sing from the lounge in the front corner of the stage. With their faces covered (suggesting anonymity), the dancers move horizontally across the stage and, from time to time, thrust themselves onto the "wailing wall" to the left. Metaphorically, their dance can be read as representing the marginalized existence of nomadic gypsies who migrate from one locale to another without a permanent home. This visual theme competes with Mariana's song of lament about the tragic fate of Lorca and the Spanish Republic. Moreover, in the "Confession" scene prior to Lorca's execution, the dancers, nearly naked, cluster together in the back of the stage as if they are Holocaust victims, waiting for the death chamber. These images and actions in the background compete with Lorca and other prisoners in the front of the stage, who interact with the guard by expressing forgiveness while refusing to give into their death sentence.

The deployment of dancers as doubles reinforces the mannequin-like presence of the main characters. In "Tome Su Mano," Lorca and Xirgu are each paired with a dancer: a male dancer, clad in feathery skirt and metallic wings, and a coquettish ballerina in a bikini top and dark blue tutu. Apart from the singers whom they represent, the dancers perform their spiritual union. The phoenix-like male dancer hovers over the ghost of Lorca, who consoles Xirgu, as shown in figure 2.3. The dark blue lighting brings out odd-shaped shadows on the "wailing wall" to

Figure 2.3. Male Dancer as Phoenix in *Tome su mano*

their left. In "Crepúsculo Delirante," the two dancers engage in a duet that conveys the intimate union between Xirgu and Lorca, while the singers stand apart in front of the stage. Their dance seems at odds with the scene that speaks of "delirious sunset" as a metaphor for Xirgu's departure from the world. The idea of *duende* is communicated powerfully through the flamenco singer Ardillita, who plays Ruiz Alonso's part in this production.[19] Yet his singing voice appears disembodied from the actor, due to the lack of physical engagement with other characters and the amplification used to merge Alonso's singing with the electronic tape loop of gunshots. For the "Gunshot interlude," a solo male dancer conveys the fighting spirit of *duende* through a vigorous dance modeled on the Brazilian capoeira – a type of martial arts that combines a wide variety of kicks, spins, and sweeping motions in a form of physical defense. In total darkness, Alonso sings from the tower atop the "wailing wall," while the spotlight encircles the single dancer. At the same time, the lighting on the water that flows from the fountain turns red to symbolize death.

While the dancers are given expressive agency, the female chorus has a significantly diminished presence in Lin's mise-en-scène. Even in their frenetic singing of the ballad's reprise (Image II) accompanied by the Falangists's radio broadcast, the singers stand motionless in the middle of the stage, while the dancers frantically move in between them to convey an expression of panic. In "Desde Mi Ventana," twelve dancers engage in a slow, meditative dance to express the

Sellars's mise-en-scène:

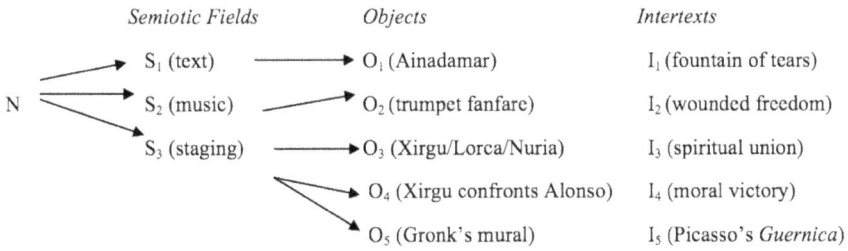

	Semiotic Fields	Objects	Intertexts
N	S_1 (text)	O_1 (Ainadamar)	I_1 (fountain of tears)
	S_2 (music)	O_2 (trumpet fanfare)	I_2 (wounded freedom)
	S_3 (staging)	O_3 (Xirgu/Lorca/Nuria)	I_3 (spiritual union)
		O_4 (Xirgu confronts Alonso)	I_4 (moral victory)
		O_5 (Gronk's mural)	I_5 (Picasso's *Guernica*)

Lin's mise-en-scène:

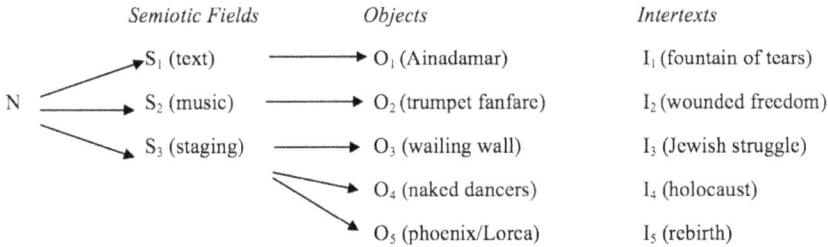

	Semiotic Fields	Objects	Intertexts
N	S_1 (text)	O_1 (Ainadamar)	I_1 (fountain of tears)
	S_2 (music)	O_2 (trumpet fanfare)	I_2 (wounded freedom)
	S_3 (staging)	O_3 (wailing wall)	I_3 (Jewish struggle)
		O_4 (naked dancers)	I_4 (holocaust)
		O_5 (phoenix/Lorca)	I_5 (rebirth)

Figure 2.4. Multimodal Narration of *Ainadamar* by Sellars and Lin

idea of Lorca's longing for the revolutionary martyr Mariana Pineda, while the female chorus assumes an ornamental role by congregating around the fountain. The singers recede to the background as the dancers move around freely. They are dressed in white, perhaps as a symbol of Pineda's innocence. Toward the end, the dancers raise their hands in gesticulations suggesting the idea of becoming one ("era una").

To summarize, Lin's theater production generates a different tropological narrative from Sellars's, as the schematic diagram of multimodal narration illustrates in figure 2.4. Sellars's mise-en-scène is tightly integrated with respect to how semiotic fields uniformly articulate the transition from the theme of "wounded" freedom to transcendent freedom. Gronk's geometric mural, which covers the entire floor and wall of the stage, represents the Spanish Civil War via its intertextual reference to Picasso's *Guernica*. The physical intimacy accorded to Xirgu, Lorca, and Nuria in his choreography foregrounds the idea of spiritual union. As mentioned earlier, the only theatrical addition that detracts from the libretto is the final scene, where the ghost of Xirgu confronts Ruiz Alonso, marking the moment in which she proclaims moral victory over the antihero. In Lin's mise-en-scène, the corporeality of the dancers overshadows the main characters who sing on stage. The site of Ainadamar loses its specificity as the place of Lorca's execution because the dancers visually represent holocaust victims during the "Confession" scene. In "Tome Su Mano," a male dancer assumes the role of a phoenix as a symbolic manifestation of Lorca's rebirth.

In fairness to Mei Hong Lin, my initial dismissal of her mise-en-scène as post-modern mishmash gave way to a schematic understanding of it as meta-theater, over the course of studying this theatrical production at Darmstadt. While her choreography generates extraneous intertexts that do not align with Hwang and Golijov's original vision of *Ainadamar*, the overall dramatic effect clearly moves beyond postmodernism, which juxtaposes incongruous actions and cultural references without reconciling them. In fact, I postulate that Lin's caricature of the singers through grotesque make-up and stilted movements builds on Lorca's aesthetics of artifice in expanding Hwang's dramatic premise of "ritualized poetic theater." As Leslie Stainton explains, "[his] characters are trapped in roles from which they cannot escape" (2005: 83). Even the idea of interjecting a phoenix-like dancer serves the purpose of using myth and metaphor to articulate the theme of rebirth. Thus, I conclude that Lin's mise-en-scène decenters the myth of Lorca in favor of advancing a trope of rebirth writ large. Rather than focusing on Lorca's struggle, she expands the scope of the narrative with a centripetal aim: her multimodal narrative expands outwardly from Lorca's story to comment on the history of oppression of Jewish people and nomadic gypsies.

Opera companies have continued to stage new productions of *Ainadamar*. In the Long Beach Opera's 2012 production, an elaborate filmic projection of light articulates changes in mood, time, and place: blue for the opening scene, blue/white rectangular lighting where Xirgu sits in a chair at the middle, blue for Aina-damar, brown/yellow for Havana, red with folds that flare out for the Falangist's radio broadcast (when actors carry Lorca away), and dark red with fragmented lines when Lorca is executed. The projection of gold lighting with cross-beaming rays creates a three-dimensional illusion for the scene where Lorca comes back from the dead. Alonso, the executioner, is shown here as a virtual character – a shadowy figure with a gun projected onto the screen. Arguably the most dramatic scene of this production occurs when the electronically looped gunshot sounds are visually synchronized with lighting and filmic projection to call attention to the violence of murder. But, because the voice of Alonso is pre-recorded, the scene involving Lorca's persecution by the Falangists appears to be more imaginary than if a live actor had sung and acted the role of Alonso. Moreover, Lorca and Xirgu never touch nor directly speak to one another in this production, which reinforces the ideas of solitude and forlornness, rather than the solidarity achieved through the artists' collective striving for freedom.

Toward the end, Lorca pulls down a large sheet that covers half the stage to reveal a room brightly lit by chandeliers. I interpret this enigmatic act as signaling the moment when the mythical world is shattered to reveal the cold, empty stage where Xirgu performs Mariana Pineda. This theatrical sleight of hand has a demystifying effect on the viewer, as if to announce that the whole story is just a play within a play. In spite of its innovative mise-en-scène, the production seemed ineffective because the singer playing the role of Xirgu could not sustain the climactic ascent to the melodic apex in "Doy mi Sangre." It goes to show that, after all, for an operatic production to be memorable, the singers have to deliver a penetrating musical performance.[20]

Conclusions

It is fascinating to observe how these productions range from subtly subverting to radically transforming the basic narrative of *Ainadamar* as originally conceived by Hwang and Golijov. Perhaps the work lends itself to a variety of mises-en-scène precisely because the music and libretto provide such a tightly knit narrative centered on the trope of "wounded" freedom. From an intermedial perspective, Sellars's production presents a complementary model, where the visual dimension enhances the theme of "wounded" freedom and politicizes Xirgu's position for an added dramatic twist at the end. In stark contrast, the Darmstadt Theater's production presents a contest model of intermediality, where the dance choreography foregrounds the theme of Jewish oppression in a manner that competes with the narrative's focus on Andalusian culture and Spanish history. The Long Beach Opera production further subverts the mythologizing effect and the trope of "wounded" freedom by the aforementioned theatrical effect that implies the play within a play was just an illusion.

Having attended these various staged productions, I was vexed by how the paradoxical notion of *duende,* the existential agony that lies at the heart of Andalusians in spite of political allegiances, got lost in translation. The more explicitly an actor depicted Ruiz Alonso as a brutish antihero, the more the character became distanced from the idea of *duende.* At the core of the narrative, *duende* is the element that drives the myth, and the visual intervention of concretizing the character of Alonso diminishes its meaning. As mentioned earlier, in the semi-staged concert performance by the Atlanta Symphony Orchestra (ASO), Alonso's presence was conveyed electronically: the character was not made visible on stage. Alonso's arrest and shooting of Lorca, when rendered through the powerful voice of flamenco singer Jesus Montoya produces a far more mysterious and engaging effect in the absence of visual signifiers. With the exception of Montoya in the ASO production, no other North American production has utilized an authentic flamenco singer to sing the part of Alonso. In my multimodal experience, Alonso's vocal improvisation in the flamenco style is crucial to the engagement of the opera's narrative as myth.

Ainadamar is highly unusual in having crossed over from opera to oratorio to meta-theater in its relatively short production history. In stark contrast, Golijov's previous work, *La Pasion segun San Marcos* (*Passion according to St. Mark"* 2000), does not allow for much flexibility in staging, owing to the participation of specific indigenous ensembles and performers. Some critics have compared Golijov's role in *La Pasion* to something akin to a traffic controller of indigenous music ensembles – implying that the strength of his work relies much more on the powerful performers he brings together to improvise in different styles than on what he contributes as a composer. Richard Taruskin, on the other hand, praises the work as a "lavish collage of musical idioms from Latin American, Afro-Cuban, and Jewish cantorial idioms" (2003: 113).

Compared with the polystylism in *La Pasion,* Golijov's musical setting for *Ainadamar* is far more stylistically integrated. But not all critics share this view. For example, Phillip Kennicott from the *Washington Post* comments on the work's stasis and lack of dramatic momentum:

> Golijov is drawn to extremes of color, ominous low gongs and bright trumpet riffs made even more nasal by the use of mutes, or the high, eerie sound of strings playing harmonics. But he is also drawn to the simple, pulse-quickening device of the crescendo, the long, slow build of sound into a juggernaut of increasing volume and intensity. And too many of the musical episodes of "Ainadamar" fall back on this device. (Kennicott 2005)

But I wonder whether this is a fair assessment. If we consider the role of opera as serving a broader narrative aim, the circularity of the music and repetitive formal devices provide an important framework for a mythic narrative that focuses on memory, trauma, and transcendence. Without the hypnotic effect induced through the repetition of elements, Golijov's music would diminish its capacity to contribute to the mythical dimensions of the narrative.

Just as Lorca's play begins and ends with children reciting the ballad of Pineda, *Ainadamar* begins and ends with a ballad as a reminder that history repeats itself – that there will be another retelling of the story of Mariana Pineda. The opera is rendered mythical precisely because the cyclical framework of the ballad prevents the story from achieving closure. It is meant to be a story that is told over and over again. Even for this listener/analyst, the ballad of *Ainadamar* has a lingering quality that reverberates in the mind's ear. In this respect, the recurring musical motives perform the same function as the phrases that constitute the refrain in Lorca's Gypsy Siguiriya poem: "Es imposible callarla" ("It's impossible to hush it").

3 Kaija Saariaho's *Adriana Mater:* A Narrative of Trauma and Ambivalence

The acousmatic voice is simply a voice whose source one cannot see, a voice whose origin cannot be identified, a voice one cannot place. It is a voice in search of an origin, in search of a body, but even when it finds its body, it turns out that this doesn't quite work, the voice doesn't stick to the body, it is an excrescence which doesn't match the body. . . .

Mladen Dolar, *A Voice and Nothing More*

Before anything takes place on stage, the overture ushers us into a sound world wrought with tension: the short, declamatory motive in the solo trumpet poses a question, which is answered by the cello's descending glissando that heaves a sigh. Following this sequence of call and response, the viola and flute exchange a mournful melody. Interjected between these sonic blocks are the *disembodied* voices of the male and female chorus. The static, cyclical motive sung by the female choir on "a" is counterpointed by the low, semitonal "sigh" motive sung by the male choir. Their voices remain wordless and invisible, disconnected from the singers who appear on stage. Who do they represent and what do they comment on? Over the course of the opera, the chorus's untexted utterances hover around the singers' voices, casting a Jungian shadow to words that are exchanged between characters. At other times, words and actions are eliminated altogether for music to comment acousmatically on the scenes of transgression.

In stark contrast to Golijov's *Ainadamar* (chapter 2), the narrative of *Adriana Mater* deliberately avoids making specific references to time and place. In a nameless country about to embark on a war, a woman is raped by a soldier from her own town and gives birth to a child. While most of the opera takes place within a constructed reality of a war zone, the plot formation is decisively nonlinear, marked by interpolated dream sequences that provide a window into the characters' unconscious desires and repressed emotions. Are we to understand the chorus's enunciation as psychic expressions of trauma endured by both the victim and the perpetrator of violence? With Saariaho's music, we enter into a mythical narrative of trauma and ambivalence where inner expression presides over spoken words.

Background

Saariaho came to writing opera rather late in her compositional career. Based in Paris since 1982, she became one of the few female composers to gain recognition at the Institut de Recherche et Coordination Acoustique/Musique (IRCAM) in Paris, her earlier compositions are characterized by spectral harmony, complex evolving forms, and real-time processing of acoustical instruments in works such as *Lichtbogen* for chamber ensemble and live-electronics (1985–86), *Du Cristal* (1989) for orchestra and live electronics, and *Amers* (1992) for solo cello, chamber ensemble, and electronics. A composer who decided in the 1980s never to write an opera, Saariaho nevertheless composed a number of important works for voice, notably *Caliban's Dream* (1993), *Château de l'âme* (1995) for soprano and orchestra, and *Lohn* (1996) for soprano and electronics, which exploit speech intonations, nature sounds, and the merging of vocal timbres with orchestral ones. However, it took years for her to identify her own relationship to the operatic tradition. Inspired by Olivier Messiaen's *Saint-François d'Assise* (1983), in 2000 she embarked on her first opera, *L'Amour de loin,* deploying electronic means, wordless choir, and thirty different kinds of instruments that expand the range of vocal and instrumental timbres. Liisamaija Hautsalo interprets this opera as an allegory of the search for the transcendent, where the theme of longing for a distant love is also understood as longing for the divine (2008).

In stark contrast to the spiritual and transcendent aura of her first opera, *Adriana Mater* is dark and contemplative in dealing with the subject of war and rape. Anthony Tommasini writes in his review of the Santa Fe Opera's production of *Adriana Mater* that Saariaho is interested in offering "opera as ritual and not an action-packed narrative" (2008); the static, non-developmental musical time in this opera is modeled on Messiaen's *Saint François d'Assise,* in which repetition of musical materials is used ritualistically to portray Francis's departure from this world. The deeply psychological aspects of this opera can also be related to earlier symbolist works such as Debussy's *Pélleas et Mélisande,* where the contrast between images of light and dark is achieved through constant shifts in orchestral timbre and mode. I argue that the metaphors of light and dark emerge as important symbols in *Adriana Mater,* manifested in the shifts in expressive registers that govern the narrative progression. The story centers on a "nameless" war where the focus is *not* on the particularities of history, but on the trauma of rape, betrayal, and war in modern times. An ambivalent narrative emerges by blurring the spatial boundaries between reality and dream.

Working with the librettist Amin Maalouf, and stage director Peter Sellars, both of whom Saariaho collaborated with on *L'Amour de loin,* Saariaho quickly developed the theme for her second opera. For Maalouf, the Latin title, *Adriana Mater,* evoked the image of a modern incarnation of a Mater Dolorosa, the mother of atoning sacrifice through whose suffering the world is saved (Maalouf

2006: 59). For Saariaho, the idea of maternity surfaced as an important theme, based on her profound experience of hearing a second heartbeat next to hers when she was pregnant with her first child years ago. She comments: "I would like to do something around maternity, because I feel sometimes that this theme is treated rather stupidly. . . . We [Maalouf] also spoke about violence and the many horrible things which have happened in past years in Europe and around Europe. But we left it in the air" (quoted in Pettitt 2006: 286). War and violence provide the context in which Adriana is put through the ultimate trial of deciding whether to raise a child born of rape. During the course of three years working on the opera, Sellars's influence on Saariaho's writing was profound, and she ultimately dedicated the opera to both him and her own mother.

Given the fact that Maalouf is Lebanese, some have identified an "oriental" conception of time in *Adriana Mater,* a view that Saariaho is quick to dismiss: "I don't think it has to do with orientalism. It has to do rather with my personality. In *Adriana Mater,* of course, his [Maalouf's] experience of war in the Middle East [Lebanon] is very important" (quoted in Pettitt 2006: 287). Drawing on his first-hand experience of war as a journalist, it was important for Maalouf to place the opera's narrative within a quasi-mythical framework. That is to say, the narrative takes place during and after a *nameless* war, without a specific time and place; in the libretto, he indicates that the diegetic time and location has to do with the "present" and the place a "country at war." Alan Riding, in his review of the opera's Paris premiere, commented that the plot inevitably evokes the Bosnian war of the 1990s, with its grim legacy of rape and ethnic cleansing (Riding 2006). Maalouf himself comments on the necessity to transfer his own experiences of war (as journalist) into an imaginary realm in order to write about it:

> The transition from the real to the imaginary realm comes about rather spontane-ously for me. That's probably due to the Lebanon war and the way I experienced it. [As a journalist] I was accustomed to going around the world covering the most tragic and bloodiest of wars, from Vietnam to Ethiopia; yet since the war broke out in my own country, in my own neighborhood, I felt unable to react as a reporter, and took refuge in writing fiction. To convey my experience, I had to pass into the imaginary realm through meditation; move toward other countries, toward other eras, absorb myself fully in those worlds, without ever making an effort to bring the matter back to Lebanon, but knowing with certainty that the essence of my intimate experience would be transmitted through what I would tell. (2006: 57)[1]

The opera, in fact, is about coping with the *memory* of war: the characters in the opera are traumatized by the memory of a recent war, which has corrupted the people and undermined their optimism for living. At the beginning of the story, all we are given is an unknown village in a war-torn country where another war is about to begin. One evening, the protagonist Adriana is raped and impregnated by Tsargo, a soldier from her own community. She gives birth to the child (Yonas) despite her sister Refka's protest, and decides to raise the illegitimate baby on her own. Much of the psychological drama is focused on the women's struggle over the fate of Adriana's son, as to whether he will grow up to be

Kaija Saariaho's Adriana Mater 83

like his mother or his father: "would he be Cain or Abel?" she asks herself. She nonetheless conceals the truth from Yonas by telling him that his father had died during the war. Seventeen years later, Yonas discovers that his father is still alive, confronts Adriana and Refka about the truth of his identity, and vows to kill his father. Yet once he encounters Tsargo, who is now blind and helpless, Yonas is unable to carry out the revenge. Adriana tells her son that his action has proven that he is truly her son and that the curse is finally broken. The nightmare is over.

At the heart of the story lies an irony: in spite of the perceived enemy, whom Tsargo fears would destroy their village and violate their women, Adriana is violated by one of her *own* people, someone who presumably would protect her. Each of the four characters, in fact, must reckon with his/her inner enemy. As Maalouf comments, bestiality and barbarism are not the Other, but they reside within ourselves (58). Aside from his award-winning novels such as *Smarcande* (1988), *Le Rocher de Tanios* (1993), and *Origines* (2004), Maalouf has written critical books where he examines the "tribal" concept of identity, which prevails in many countries around the world. In *Les identités meurtrières* ("In the Name of Identity," 1998), he comments:

> I don't think any particular affiliation, be it ethnic, religious, national or anything else, predisposes anyone to murder. We have only to review the events of the last few years to see that any human community that feels humiliated or fears for its existence will tend to produce killers. . . . There is a Mr. Hyde inside each one of us. What we have to do is prevent the conditions occurring that will bring the monster forth. (2000: 28)

Maalouf suggests that circumstances can lead people to become senseless murderers. In this respect, Tsargo is viewed not as an inherently evil man, but as a victim of war. While not condoning Tsargo's act, Adriana recognizes that the war has corrupted him and the other men who have taken false pride in fighting. He has become a monster in her eyes for blindly participating in the mission of war. Adriana is, however, not entirely innocent herself; she had flirted with Tsargo, yet treated him with contempt, and later she does not try to stop her son from taking revenge on her behalf. In the end, no one is depicted simply as villain or hero. This ambiguity adds complexity and nuance to the characterization of the dramatis personae.

The operatic narrative unfolds in seven scenes (*tableaux*), divided (by an *entr'acte*) into two acts that are chronologically separated from one another: during the war and seventeen years after the war, as shown in Saariaho's initial sketch (figure 3.1a).[2] The basic division of the opera into seven scenes had already been determined by the tentative titles: 1) before the war; 2) during the war; 3) two hearts; 4) truth; 5) rumor; 6) encounter; 7) mother. However, the sketch indicates that Saariaho and Maalouf were not quite in agreement over the placement of the dream sequences ("*rêve*" in diamond shape figures) inserted in the middle or at the end of Scenes I, III, IV, and VI. For example, what has been scratched off as the second dream sequence appears as Adriana's dream in the third scene; in the final version, however, it is transformed into Refka's dream about Adriana giving

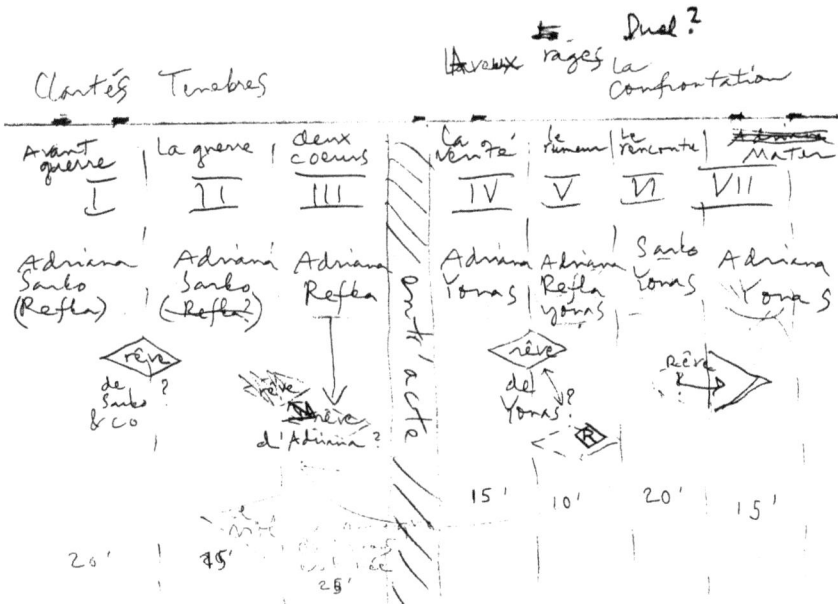

Figure 3.1a. Saariaho's Initial Sketch of the Overall Form (from October 2002)

birth, inserted in Scene III. In addition, what was initially conceived as Yonas's dream between Scenes IV and V becomes a short vision about Adriana, Refka, and Tsargo, inserted at the end of Scene V. In the final version of the score, the metaphorical titles replace the chronological; for example, "before the war" and "the war" in the first two scenes are replaced by the oppositional terms, clarity and shadow (shown in the sketch as *clartés* and *ténèbres*). The idea for clarity is manifested by Adriana's innocence and optimism before the war, while the idea for shadow symbolizes her doubt and loss of innocence, which plagues her (and Refka) for the next seventeen years. In a similar sense, Scene IV is changed from truth (*verité*) to consent (*aveux*) and Scene VI from meeting (*le rencontre*) via confrontation (*la confrontation*) to duel (*duel*) in order to amplify the dramatic confrontation between the father and son.

Furthermore, the dream sequences are interpolated into the narrative progression of the opera as an aporia from external "reality" that provides a window into each character's internalized confrontation with the trauma of war. Cathy Caruth, in *Unclaimed Experience: Trauma, Narrative, and History*, describes trauma as marked by the condition of "repetitive seeing," as follows:

> In its general definition, trauma is described as the response to an unexpected or overwhelming violent event or events that are not fully grasped as they occur, but return later in repeated flashbacks, nightmares, and other repetitive phenomena. Traumatic experience, beyond the psychological dimension of suffering it involves, suggests a certain paradox: that the most direct seeing of a violent event may oc-

cur as an absolute inability to know it; that immediacy, paradoxically, may take the form of belatedness. The repetitions of the traumatic event – which remain unavailable to consciousness but intrude repeatedly on sight – thus suggest a larger relation to the event that extends beyond what can simply be seen or what can be known, and is inextricably tied up with the belatedness and incomprehensibility that remain at the heart of this repetitive seeing. (1996: 27)

The traumatic condition does not apply solely to Adriana, who is the victim of rape. Tsargo, the perpetrator of evil deeds, is continually haunted by images from the past. Just as in post-traumatic syndromes for survivors of war, the older sister, Refka, is possessed by visions of war that surface only in her dreams. These are not ordinary dreams, but ones that are filled with ambivalent messages. When she awakes, she and Adriana ponder the meaning of her dreams as having significance beyond their comprehension. Dream sequences are thus interpolated into the narrative progression of the opera as a way for the characters to come to terms with the "belatedness" and "incomprehensibility" that accompany their experiences of traumatic repetition, as defined by Caruth. For example, in the dream sequence in Scene III, Refka relates her dream about the war, in which she imagines all the aggressors and victims to be the same:

> All had the same face, or the same mask.
> And though this face wasn't really like Tsargo's,
> In my dream I was sure that it was him –
> Sure that all of them, slaughterers
> And even the slaughtered, were him.

Often in such instances, the chorus assumes an indispensible function in providing a narrating voice that lies outside the opera's diegetic space, since the chorus's presence remains invisible to the characters and the audience. However, they possess the capacity to comment on the psychological state of the characters and to foreshadow future events. In this respect, the chorus's role in the first and final dream sequences is highly significant: in the first, because the chorus predicts the downfall of Tsargo as a "fallen angel," and in the final sequence, because the chorus participates in exonerating not only Tsargo but all other characters from the burden of the past.

Saariaho endows music with a capacity to narrate independently of the spoken words and make acousmatic commentary on violence and trauma in lieu of actions. Cyclical repetition and stasis in her music correspond with Caruth's concept of repetitive seeing. The ensuing analysis further examines how the sung text and music articulate the dramatic oppositions (e.g., maternity and violence) that govern the actantial themes in the narrative, while musical semes, in conjunction with the production components (e.g., changes in lighting), give voice to the sublimated desires and fears of the characters as a manifestation of trauma (as displaced from the sung text). To this end, I will refer to the Santa Fe Opera's 2008 production of *Adriana Mater* with set design by George Tsypin and lighting design by James Ingalls.[3]

Musical Analysis: Semic Units and Expressive Registers

Various reviews of *l'Amour de loin* and *Adriana Mater* have attributed the uniqueness of Saariaho's compositional style to her timbral soundscape, blending choral and orchestral sounds into a composite texture that builds and sustains itself over time.[4] Following the 2006 premiere of *Adriana Mater* at the Bastille Opera, Alex Ross qualified Saariaho's music as follows:

> She makes her eruptions of noise seem like natural phenomena, the aftermath of some seismic break. Shapes emerge from the chaos, and the shapes begin to sing. The latter sections of her pieces often bring apparitions of rare, pure beauty – plain intervals that sound like harmony reborn, liminal melodies that disappear the moment they are heard. They are like the wildflowers that bloom in Death Valley, their colors intensified by the nothingness around them. (Ross 2006b)

Although Saariaho is well-known for using both synthesized and processed sounds to expand the timbral scope of acoustical instruments, she claims that she no longer systematically derives her harmonies through spectral analysis, but rather arrives at the construction of chords intuitively.[5] In listening to *Adriana Mater,* I began to discern an organizing process by which significant motives, chordal structures, and timbral effects become associated with particular characters, and by which themes of maternity and violence become gendered as feminine and masculine, respectively. Saariaho comments: "The two women are linked clearly with particular modes, whereas the men are associated with themes that are more like cells. They all have characteristic rhythmic material too" (quoted in Pettitt 2006: 288).

The instrumentation for the orchestral score features four groups of percussion in addition to the standard groups of woodwind, brass, strings, harp, piano, celesta, and SATB chorus. Some unusual percussion timbres are created by five types of chimes (brass, shell, bell, bamboo, and wood), sandpaper blocks, Flexatone, Thunderstick, claves, and guiro. Extended techniques include the use of quarter tones, indeterminate high or low pitches, string tremolo behind the bridge, a trill for strings produced by alternating the finger pressure between normal and light, breath tone for flutes, and circular glissando for harp.

Saariaho's sketch (figure 3.1b) illustrates the distinctive rhythms and tempo designations she assigns to the four characters. Yonas is given the fastest tempo (♩ = 108) and a triplet subdivision to capture his youthful vigor and impatience, while Refka is depicted as a protective but weary older sister through a slightly slower tempo (♩ = 96) and a rhythmic subdivision that cuts across the three quarter notes at the polyrhythmic ratio of 4:3. Saariaho wished to emphasize the transformation Tsargo undergoes before and after the war by assigning two different tempi and rhythmic relationships, thereby capturing his vigorous disposition as a young man in contrast with his transformation into a decrepit, old man.[6] While Tsargo is assigned the same tempo and rhythmic subdivision as Yonas in his former state, his tempo slows down to ♩ = 48 and the rhythm becomes erratic in his latter state. Adriana, in comparison to others, maintains a steady tempo at

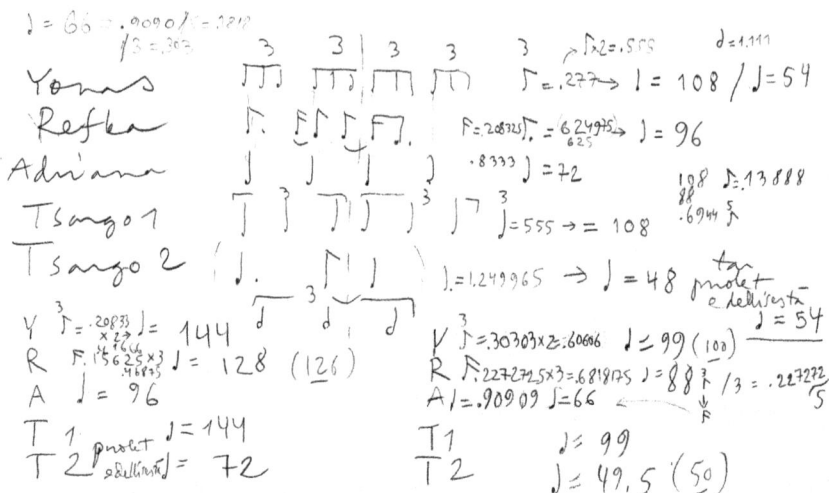

Figure 3.1b. Saariaho's Rhythmic and Tempo Designations

$\downarrow$ = 72 and an even rhythmic pacing. At the bottom half of the diagram, there are alternate sets of tempi designation for the four characters shown, but they maintain the same proportional relationship as found in the top half of the diagram. These tempo relationships actively shape the mood and structure of the individual scenes, even if the values are altered to some extent in the final version. Furthermore, unlike her earlier opera, *L'Amour de loin*, which is filled with references to the troubadour and other facets of medieval culture, Saariaho claims that the musical materials associated with the characters in *Adriana Mater* are self-referential, not borrowed from elsewhere.[7] Each of the four characters, for example, has a specific group of timbres associated with them: solo clarinet motive for Adriana, somber flute melody for Refka, trumpet, marimba, and xylophone for Yonas, and snare drum and double bass for Tsargo.

Given Saariaho's characterization of the dramatis personae, one could map their primary roles in the opera based on Vladmir Propp's inventory of agential roles and functions, as shown under figure 3.2a. Adriana is portrayed as the heroine, Tsargo the villain, Refka the helper, and Yonas the false-hero (in the sense that he tries to take revenge to honor his mother, but fails). And we can construct corresponding functions that accompany this preliminary agential mapping of characters: the heroine *hopes* for a better life after the war, the villain *despairs* over his inability to win the heroine, the helper guides and *nurtures* the heroine toward a more ethical conduct, and the false-hero *rages* over the circumstance that brought him into their war-ravaged world. However, these functions, which I designate as expressive registers, E1 = hope, E2 = rage, E3 = nurture, E4 = despair, depart from their presumed one-to-one mapping with the individual actants as the narrative unfolds.

Agential roles   *Functions (Expressive States)*

heroine [A]   - - - - - false-hero [Y]   E1 (hope)   - - - - - E2 (rage/destroy)

helper [R]   - - - - - villain [T]   E3 (nurture) - - - - - - - - E4 (despair)

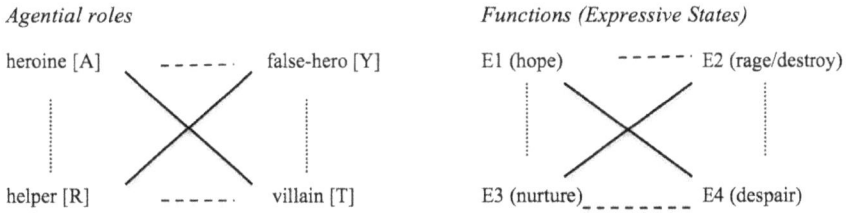

Figure 3.2. Agential Roles and Functions in *Adriana Mater*

The operatic plot is based on the following sequence: Adriana plans to build her future in a new country and is full of hope (E1), but is violated by Tsargo before the war (E2) and is led to despair (E4). Against her sister Refka's warning (E3), Adriana raises a child (E3) born of rape. Seventeen years later, Yonas grows up, learns the truth, and vows to take revenge by killing his father (E2); however, witnessing an old, decrepit man, he aborts his mission in despair (E4). Adriana reconciles her divided feelings toward Tsargo and hope is restored for all (E1). Ultimately, a tragedy is averted, yet no one emerges as a hero or villain because the characters ultimately become unmoored from their initial agential roles: Adriana turns out to be not so innocent in that she flirts with Tsargo at a ball, yet treats him with contempt; Refka, in her role as helper, is traumatized by her memory of war and cannot effectively guide her sister in her decision; although Tsargo's existence is damned from the beginning, he expresses his sincere love for Adriana by the end; and Yonas is consumed by rage over the truth, which was hidden from him, but it is unclear as to whether his motivation to kill Tsargo is motivated by actual desire for vengeance or merely the appealing idea of it.

Hautsalo, in her comprehensive analysis of topics in Saariaho's operas, identifies musical topics that range from those that signify war, rape, execution, hope, heart, and *pianto* in *Adriana Mater* (2011: 122–27). Topics are recognizable in *L'Amour de loin,* given their medieval references; I find it difficult to pin down recurring musical ideas as having consistent topical functions in *Adriana Mater,* given its episodic form and many layered textures. Instead, my analysis identifies eleven distinctive semic units, which are marked by repetition and transformation, and are set apart from music with descriptive or onomatopoeic effects, e.g., snare drum motive that establishes the presence of the military or the piano chords that simulate Tsargo's knock on the door. In short, musical semes carry psychological resonances, but resist fixed topical identification. Musical motives, chords, and timbral gestures are identified as distinctive semic units, as shown in table 3.1, based on the following criteria: 1) its inclusion or elaboration of the primary seme (i.e., the descending semitone or "sigh" motive); 2) correlation with Saariaho's expressive indications in the score; 3) presence of variants with opposing attributes (e.g., an ascending arpeggiation in the clarinet that expresses rage complements a descending one that expresses remorsefulness).

Furthermore, these semic units differ from topics in their identification with a variable range of moods or expressive registers. While many of these semic units include a semitone descent, they do not necessarily function as a *pianto* topic with the connotation of sorrow or suffering. More often than not, Saariaho's expressive indications guided my attribution of expressive registers for a given semic unit; for example, E4 (despair) for S1 corresponds with the expressive marking of *Disperato,* while E3 (nurture) for S2 with that of *Dolce* in the score. In this respect, some semes are more fluid than others in how they vary in their association with expressive registers. For example, a particular chord labeled S2 that defines Adriana's anguish (E4) is transformed into S2', which signifies rage (E2) and then S2'', which signifies maternal affection (E3) in the course of the overture. As shown in table 3.1, some semic units undergo variation with respect to contour, e.g., S8 is an upward arpeggiation played by the solo clarinet, which signifies Adriana's rage (E2), while the downward arpeggiation is associated with Tsargo's regret and yearning for Adriana (E1). Moreover, there are semic units that are defined not solely by timbre, such as the circular contour glissandi in the harp (S6) or the ascending trumpet pitch motive that recurs in a sequence of two repetitions (S1). Others are defined by a specific contour, such as S7, outlining a modally anchored trichord with a semitone descent followed by a descent by fourth or fifth. Finally, there are semic units defined by a specific mode of articulation, such as S11, which utilizes a descending glissando with a dynamic swell and the expressive indication *lugubre,* correlating with despair (E4). Although not essential, set-class identification of semic units is included to facilitate comparison of pitch collections.

Most importantly, I argue that semic units, through repetition and transformation, endow music with the capacity to comment on the characters' expressed (conscious) and unexpressed (unconscious) emotions, as in two sides of a Moebius strip. Saariaho deploys techniques of foreshadowing and flashbacks to create a web of associations among musical semes. For example, S9, associated with Tsargo's perpetration of violence, is foreshadowed in the chords that accompany his initial knock on Adriana's door and dialogues that escalate into his act of transgression. Furthermore, trauma is often communicated through the *troping* of expressive registers – a technique Robert Hatten defines as a merging of topics and textures to create an expressive language that serves a larger dramatic trajectory (2004: 89).[8] For example, the overture is characterized by opposing expressive indications (*Dolce* vs. *Disperato, Furioso* followed by *Molto espressivo*) that generate ambivalence in dramatic expression. While in the first half of the opera a given semic unit tends to maintain a fixed identification with a given expressive register, the second half of the opera bears witness to the gradual unmooring of semic units from their previous associations with expressive registers, signaling the *transvaluative* moment in which these oppositions dissolve, as will be discussed. Wherever relevant, I will refer to the complementary semic roles of lighting, gesture, and metaphoric use of text that reinforce or collide with the expressive connotation of musical semes in the 2006 Helsinki production of *Adriana Mater.*

Table 3.1. Identification of *Semic* Units in *Adriana Mater*

Semic units	Instruments/features	Contour, rhythm, pitch profile (set-class)	Expressive indication	Character/ Expressive Register
S1	Trumpet solo; sequential repetition	Ascending M7 [01] and its variants	*Disperato*	Yonas / Inquiry (E4)
S2	Sustained chord in the strings	Descending semitonal glissando [0134679]	*Dolce*	Adriana / Nurture (E3)
S2'	Rhythmic chordal motive in strings, woodwinds, chorus	Animated rhythm [0134679]	*Furioso*	Adriana / Anger (E2)
S2"	Chord sustained in the piano; "lullaby" music	Triple meter [0134679]	*Molto espressivo*	Adriana / Nurture (E3)
S3	Violin and flute; melodic exchange	Downward glissando [015]	*Dolce*	Refka / Anguish (E4)
S4	Circling figuration (woodwinds)	Upward arpeggiation [0148]	*Misterioso*	Dream (E3)
S5	Chorus	Downward glissandi	*Misterioso*	Dream (E4)
S5'	Flute/piccolo	Upward inflection; repetitive	*Molto espressivo*	Yonas (E3)
S6	Harp	Circular glissandi; downward	*Misterioso*	Refka (E3)
S7	Voice (Adriana's rondeau)	Downward [015] Upward [016]	*Sempre con molto sentimento*	Adriana / Hope (E1)
S8	Clarinet solo	Rising arpeggiation [014568]		Adriana / Rage (E2)
S8'	Clarinet solo	Falling arpeggiation [0134689]		Tsargo / Yearning (E1)
S9	Tutti	Homophonic/ *sffz* [0123456789]	*Furioso*	Tsargo / chord of violence (E2)
S10	Tutti	Ascending quarter note motive; [0134579]	*Ben sonante*	Adriana / Openness (E1)
S11	Low strings	Glissando with a dynamic swell [0134]	*Sostenuto, lugubre*	Tsargo / Death (E4)

Prologue/Overture

At the commencement, an overture initiates the listeners into the dark and mysterious world of this opera's soundscape. Anthony Tommasini describes the foreboding tone of the overture as follows: "an assaulting orchestral chord, dense, dissonant, crammed with clashing pitches, screeching slides and thwacking percussion. In the aftermath of this detonation, sonorities disperse into hazy oscillations, as melodic bits swim dazed amid the dusty music, trying to break free" (2008). The opera begins in complete darkness; the audience is initiated into Lacan's Imaginary or preverbal domain, where contrasting expressions of inquiry, despair, dream, and rage are juxtaposed without cohesion. As mentioned in the beginning of this chapter, the listener senses the tension without knowing what these oppositions entail.

My schematic understanding of the overture developed over time following my interview with Saariaho in 2009. I was especially struck by the somatic quality of the opening gestures and what the expressive oppositions entailed. As shown in example 3.1a, the solo trumpet sounds the principle dyadic motive (S1) in three parts over the sustained chords in the brass and the undulating bass drum rolls; here expressive markings alternate between *Disperato* and *Dolce,* creating an expressive opposition between S1 and S2. As the intensity of the bass drum dies down, the strings echo the chord in the brass with a softer chord, played *sul tasto;* the descending glissando (D-C♯) in the cello conveys a sense of melancholic resignation. I refer to the septachord (0134679) played by strings, labeled S2, as the *Urklang* for the opera; while here it alludes to Adriana's maternal yearning and suffering, it also forms the basis of harmonic complexes found in subsequent scenes. As the tremolo in the bass drum grows louder at m.3, this three-bar unit repeats again. Accompanied by the intensity that ebbs and flows through the bass drum rolls, the chords exchanged between the brass and strings resemble a cycle of breath – loud exhalation followed by a soft inhalation. In its somatic and organic quality, it thus captures Adriana's maternal yearning (E3) pitted against the unknown fate of the child (E4). In its third and final iteration, the trumpet motive sounds again, this time marked by an interrogatory gesture (angular leap from A to G♯), as if to pose the question: "what will become of this child?"

The next passage, labeled *Misterioso,* comprises a cyclical permutation of a four-note motive (F-A-C♯-D) in the woodwinds, accompanied by the choir, which sings the vowel "a" over sliding semitones, sustained chords in the brass, and a soft timpani roll on G. The chord in the strings derives from S2, accompanied by an upward glissando in all parts. Saariaho calls this the "dream" material, characterized by a circular and static layering of textures that provides the foundation for the dream sequences. At m.14, the melody (S3) associated with Refka is introduced, as shown in the first six measures of example 3.1b. The solo violin projects an antecedent phrase culminating in a move up to the sustained trill, which is answered by a consequent phrase in the flute, ending with a down-

a. (mm. 1-7)

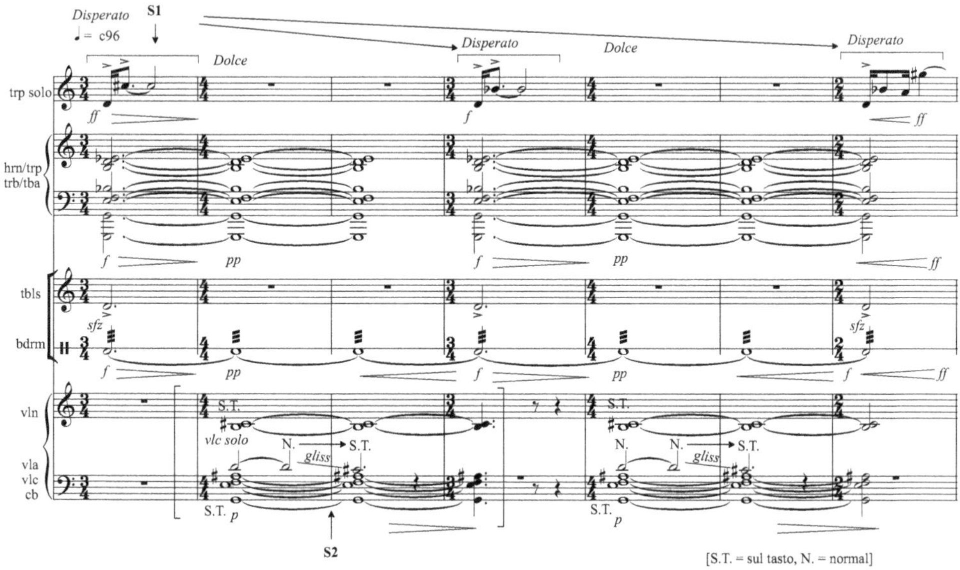

b. (mm. 14-21)

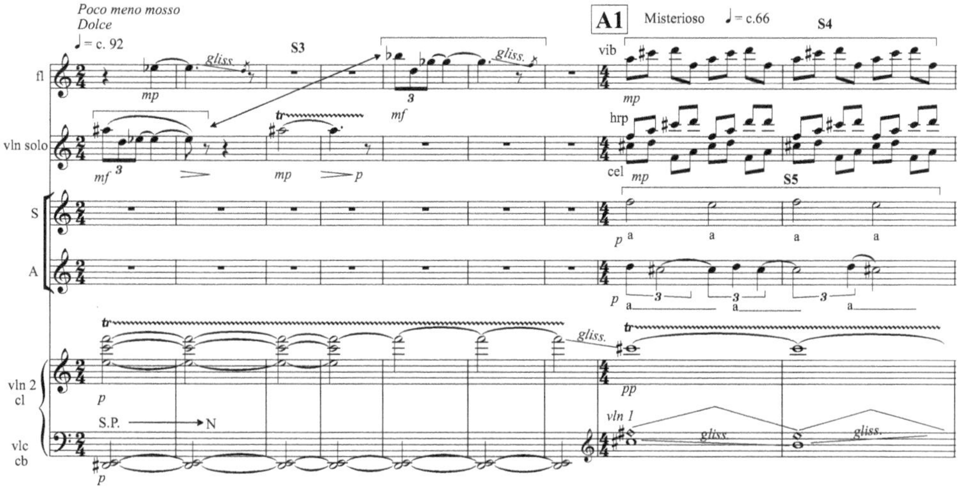

Example 3.1a/b. Instrumental Overture

ward glissando. The wistful timbres of violin and flute convey the character of the protective older sister, anxious and a bit on edge. Strings sustain a chord in the upper register, framing the motivic exchange between the violin and flute. This passage segues into that of the "dream" material (*Misterioso*), featuring the cycling four-note motive (S4), now transposed to the upper registers of vibraphone, harp, and celesta. The female chorus doubles the "sigh" motive (S5) in rhythmically staggered imitation.[9] In the third section of the overture (not shown here), a variant of the S2 chord appears in the strings, doubled by the chorus (on alternating syllables of "tsa" and "ka") and accompanied by a driving ostinato figure in the piano with metric changes that alternate between $\frac{3}{8}$ and $\frac{2}{4}$. The listener can still recognize it as a variant of S2 because it preserves its chordal make-up with the descending semitone glissando, as shown in example 3.1a. Marked *furioso*, however, this succession of short, explosive chords expresses rage as a fluid, organic counterpart to the preceding dream-like material.

An abridged return of the dream music brings closure to the overture, this time accompanied by a rising and falling circular glissando in the harp (S6), a figuration also associated with Refka. The process by which Saariaho juxtaposes contrasting moods and expressions in this short overture conforms to the traditional function of overtures; the effects are not dissimilar to the Prelude to *Tristan und Isolde,* where Wagner encapsulates the dramatic oppositions and the narrative trajectory of the opera in purely musical terms. This overture exposes the fluidity and contrasting characteristics of semic units, whose meanings have yet to be formulated. The listener is presented with Adriana's chord (S2), whose rhythmically amorphous texture in initial context (*dolce*) segues to an animated sequence of chords that conveys rage and violence in the *furioso* section. The exchange of the wistful motive between the violin and flute symbolizes Refka's role in the opera. The overture initiates the listener into an atmosphere of impending tragedy, even without specifying these associations with the characters who have yet to be introduced.

Adriana's Soliloquy: Song of Innocence

Out of the dark and mysterious overture, the light focuses on Adriana, who appears on the roof of her house and commences to sing a tender aria. While yearning for the countryside she left behind, Adriana approaches her life with assurance and a heart full of hope. This sentiment is conveyed in an eight-line rondeau form, whose parallel stanzas read as follows:

Quand les yeux de la cité se ferment,	When the eyes of the city close,
Je dévoile ma voix.	I reveal my *voice!*
Ma voix que j'ai cueillie	The voice I gathered
Dans un jardin d'automne,	In an autumn garden,
Puis couchée sous les pages d'un livre;	Then couched under the pages of a book;
Ma voix que j'ai rapportée du pays	The *voice* I brought back from my country

Entre mes draps couleur de soufre;	Between my sulfur-colored sheets;
Ma voix que j'ai glisée dans mon corsage,	The *voice* I tucked into my bodice
Sous le plis de mon coeur.	Under the folds of my *heart*.
Quand les yeux de la cité se ferment,	When the eyes of the city close,
Je dévoile mon coeur.	I reveal my *heart!*
Mon coeur que j'ai cueillie	The heart I gathered
Dans un jardin d'automne,	In an autumn garden
Puis couchée sous les pages d'un livre;	And pressed in the pages of a book;
Mon coeur que j'ai rapportée du pays	The *heart* I brought back from my country
Entre mes draps couleur de soufre;	Between my sulfur-colored sheets;
Mon coeur que j'ai glisée	The *heart* I tucked
Dans mon corsage,	Into my bodice
Sous le plis de ma peau.	Under the folds of my *skin*.
Quand les yeux de la cité se ferment,	When the eyes of the city close,
Je dévoile ma peau.	I reveal my *skin!*
Ma peau que j'ai cueillie	The skin that I gathered
Dans un jardin d'automne,	In an autumn garden
Puis couchée . . .	Then hidden . . .

This rondeau does not have any rhyme scheme – certainly not the AABBA associated with the French *rondeau*. Instead, the second stanza echoes the first as each line returns in sequence. What is unusual is the emphasis and substitution of certain words, as highlighted in italics; the repetition of a key word "voix" in the first stanza leads to "coeur" in the second, which then leads to "peau" in the third. The corporeal association established between her voice, heart, and skin is noteworthy here: first, she reveals her voice, then her heart, and her skin (or body, by implication). The metaphorical expression of the city "closing its eyes" invites Adriana in turn to expose her inner self to the world. Obviously a country girl who is displaced from her village, Adriana is filled with yearning and hope for a new beginning. Against the undulating backdrop of slow triplet rhythm in the piano and circular glissando in the harp, Adriana sings a melody set to a lyrical melody in D minor, as shown in example 3.2a. Its strophic form is underscored by the parallel phrase structure; note how the recurring semic unit (S7), B♭-A-D, in the antecedent phrase is answered by the semitone descent (S5), F-E, in the consequent phrase. Against the rising augmented fourth, B♭-E, that projects her willfulness at the close of the antecedent phrase, the semitone descent (S5) from F to E, placed at the melodic apex, imparts a sense of yearning tinged with melancholy. The concluding phrase is consistently articulated by the downward semitone glissando on the words "livre" and "coeur."

By the beginning of the third system, her vocal pitch jumps from the lowest note of the phrase (A3) to the melodic apex on "ma voix" (F5) as if to call attention to her willfulness and conviction. The orchestra provides a rhythmically amorphous and harmonically ambivalent backdrop, with solo instruments echoing the semitonal motives in rhythmic diminution. Through this opening soliloquy, Saariaho paints Adriana as an innocent but self-assured woman who has not yet been tainted by the tragic situation that will befall her. The sung text establishes an expressive register of hope (E1), tinged with melancholic yearning (E4) for her village.

By the final stanza of the rondeau, Adriana's singing is interrupted by Tsargo's knock on the door. Being interrupted from her state of reverie, the lyricism of Adriana's vocal line is replaced by short, angular musical lines, often punctuated by rhythmically accelerating arpeggios in the clarinet (S8), mirroring her anxiety and lack of trust for this drunken man. As she contemplates his worthiness, the tempo slows and her singing becomes more declamatory. When Tsargo further provokes her by asking her whether she would invite him in if he were rich, she declares that she would open the door to him if he would change his ways and tell her the words she wishes to hear. At this precise moment, the orchestra introduces an ascending chordal motive (S10) that accumulates textural density in steady quarter-note rhythm as a signifier of Adriana's firm resolution. In a musical context dominated by a fluid and non-metric rhythmic texture, the steady stream of quarter notes, ascending in register from low to high, takes on heightened signification as an aural marker of Adriana's willfulness. This chord extends from D♯1 to A7 and provides the widest registral span within this scene, which Saariaho deliberately planned as a structural point of emphasis in the first scene.[10] Later in the same scene, the chordal motive returns in a varied sequence (mm.377–91) when Adriana defends her freedom of choice against Refka's adamant warning to stay away from Tsargo. Immediately following this passage, Adriana quickly dismisses the idea of welcoming Tsargo by revealing a more cynical side of her personality, as she shouts out: "But that day will never come!" Dejected, Tsargo returns to his drinking. Adriana gives no thought to the fact that her rejection feeds his unconscious desire to possess her by brutal force. Later in this scene, when Refka encourages Adriana to stay away from Tsargo, Adriana becomes somewhat protective of him, telling her sister that he is quite innocent.

In the course of the opera, the rondeau melody emerges as an important marker of Adriana's psychology. The rondeau melody returns in a varied and fragmented form in Scene III when she sings about "two bloods flowing, blood of the victim and blood of the aggressor" as well as in the concluding scene when Adriana looks back into her past and tries to recapture her lost innocence. In Scene VII (example 3.2b), she expresses how her "pain has placed a mask" over her face and "a carapace" over her heart, and that her skin and expression have "grown tough." In this way, the corporeal references to "heart" and "skin" take on entirely different nuances from the original context seen in example 3.2a. S5, featured in the original rondeau melody, is still used prominently, but the phrase structure is far more erratic and irregular with respect to vocal contour, rhythm, and phrase structure; note, for example, the downward leap of an augmented fourth (E to B♭) at m.39 (S7') and the dissonant leap from E to B♭ that characterizes the second phrase on the words "masque" (m.45). As she describes her heart

a. Adriana's "rondeau" (Scene I, mm. 58-84)

"When the eyes of the city close, I reveal my voice! The voice I gathered in an autumn garden, then couched under the pages of a book; the voice I brought back from my country between my sulfer-colored sheets; the voice I tucked into my bodice Under the folds of my heart."

b. Rondeau fragments in Scene VII (mm.39-61)

"Pain has placed a mask over my face and a carapace over my heart. Sometimes I say cruel things and the next moment wonder if they came out of my mouth. My skin has grown tough, and so has my expression. Yet if anyone could see into my soul, one would still see..."

Example 3.2a/b. Adriana's Rondeau [voice part only]

acquiring a hard shell or carapace, her vocal line is still anchored to D minor, but the subsequent phrase tends toward B Phrygian with the emphasis on the tetrachord B-C-F#-G.

Although not shown here, the orchestral accompaniment is more animated: strings accompany her enunciation with a chordal variant of S2, along with harp's circular glissandi (S6). It is only in the last phrase, where her sung words convey the idea of looking deep inside her soul ("Pourtant, si l'on pouvait sonder mon âme. . . .") that the melody re-orients toward the initial mode of D minor with emphasis on A. Refka and the chorus join in, echoing Adriana's wish to find her old self, one who is capable of weeping and trembling with sorrow.

Dream Sequences and the Role of Chorus

When the chorus enunciates a text (as opposed to wordless utterance), it presents a prophetic voice, situated outside of the operatic diegesis, which can be heard as either mirroring the character's unconscious state or that of an unknown collective. These revelatory moments occur only in the context of the dream sequences – moments that provide access to the characters' unconscious fears and desires and where prophecies are heard. The first dream sequence that takes place at the end of Scene I is particularly foreboding in this respect: Adriana, Refka, and the chorus conjure up an image of a macabre ballroom scene in which Tsargo and Adriana dance together. This scene is preceded by the return of the musical materials (S1 and S2) from the overture. In the ensemble singing that follows, Adriana recapitulates melodic lines from the rondeau, while Refka sings about awakening dreams. As shown under example 3.3a, Refka's voice and the choir provide overlapping commentary, with one notable difference: Refka's singing of "light" (*clartés*) is overlaid with the choral enunciation of "lies" (*mensonges*). It is as if the chorus's negation presents a form of prophecy in which "lies" refer to the misfortune and suffering brought on by war, of which the characters remain unaware. One can read this to signify that the idea of light, serving as a metaphor for the people's yearning and hope, blinds them to the truth of the situation that they fail to see.

Later on, the idea of a lie is brought back when Yonas confronts the truth about the identity of his father. This dream sequence thus comments on how the women's unassuming desires collide with the chorus's prophetic voice.

As the dream segues to a sinister ballroom scene where Adriana and Tsargo dance together, the choral texture becomes increasingly more animated; they recite the words "*Adriana rirait*" ("Adriana laughs"), set to a repeating rhythmic motive. This grotesque dream is shattered when Refka sings about the dream beginning to fade, "like a drowned sailor, lost at sea." The horns play a drawn-out rendition of S5, then Adriana sings about her vision of Tsargo fleeing into the depths of darkness, like a fallen angel; her vocal contour presents S7 in rhythmic augmentation, as shown in example 3.3b. This mythic portrayal of Tsargo as a "fallen angel" is followed by the chorus's rhythmically dovetailed motive on "damned." As the texture thins out, this choral utterance on "damned" gradually fades into oblivion. Tsargo undergoes a *symbolic* form of death in Refka's dream, although the women remain unaware of the power of this prophecy.

The subsequent dream sequences interpolated between scenes are ritualistic and foreboding in a different sense from the first dream sequence. For example, the most volatile dream sequence, that of Scene III, revolves around Refka's surrealistic reenactment of war, violence, and the birth of Yonas. She sees people being slaughtered, all having the same face or mask, and witnesses Adriana giving birth in the midst of this chaos. Refka's vocal lines become angular and agitated as she sings almost exclusively in *Sprechstimme*. The chorus often dovetails the end of Refka's musical phrase with a cascading echo on "a" against the backdrop of sounds simulating gunfire. The lighting on stage turns bright yellow as two

a. (mm. 469-74 [strings and percussion omitted])

"(R) Bringing its own noises, its lights. (A) … my stone-colored sheets. (Chorus) Its own lights, its own lies."

b. (mm.551-56)

"damned, damned, damned…."

Example 3.3a/b. Dream Sequence 1

soldiers with rifles appear on stage. When a young soldier tells Refka to "wake up," the chorus provides a literal echo of this motive. Refka's entry into this traumatic remembrance of war is accompanied by a rapid change in lighting in the Santa Fe production: first the colors are split between red and blue, then shift to white, blue, gray, orange and green. In the original libretto, Maalouf envisioned a dream sequence at the end of Scene IV, where Yonas engages in a sacrificial rite: he tears off the masks of the characters and they collapse one after another in "a blaze that at once destroys and purifies." In the final version, this scene was simplified to an instrumental postlude that features music associated with Adriana, Refka, and Tsargo, one by one, in sequence.

Music of Violence: Act of Transgression

If Adriana's rondeau embodies feminine desire and yearning in this opera, Tsargo's music in Scene II embodies that of male aggression and violence. Appropriately titled "Darkness" (*Ténèbres*), the scene opens with the overture's music, here transformed into a military march accompanied by snare drum, bass drum rolls, and bass voices that sustain the syllable "o." This topical change in significance is especially important in establishing the expressive register of E2 (rage/violence). Embedded in this military march is Adriana's chord in the strings (S2') and the dyadic motives that signify fate, played by the solo trumpet (S1). This initial texture segues to the *Furioso* passage from the prologue; the chorus's utterance of "tsa" and "ka" grows in intensity and speed, anchored by the bass drum's agitated pulse, and then breaks out into an inchoate sequence of entries on "a," conveying the mood of utter desperation. The music for this entire scene is rhythmically charged and discontinuous. In the production, the semicircular domes of Adriana's house are lit bright red, as if to signal the imminent act of violence.

The duet between Tsargo and Adriana takes place in this agitated climate. Initially, Tsargo depicts himself as a victim, blaming the war for his own corruption. In his deranged mind, he tries to convince Adriana to let him in so that he can protect her from others who may "violate" her. Tsargo speaks to Adriana about their enemies who will swarm the streets and kill them all, just as they did in his father's time. Adriana tells him to take his war cries elsewhere, far from her house. The chorus accompanies her statement with a dovetailing S5 motive with glissando on "o." A dramatic combination of the choral "sigh" motive (S5), the snare drum pattern, and violins with tremolo harmonic glissandi forms the textural backdrop for Tsargo's declaration that "the war will spread everywhere like a fine dust," as shown in example 3.4a. Because the choral sounds dominate and almost drown out Tsargo's sung text, the composite effect of this passage is eerie, to say the least. Tsargo conveys his tormented desire for Adriana through his admission of being a killer and scoundrel in order to save his own people. In spite of Tsargo's earnest request to protect her from perceived enemies, Adriana sees him as being "drunk" on the idea of war instead of on liquor; her scornful attitude is conveyed through her recourse to *Sprechstimme* on the word "ivrogne" (drunk).

Example 3.4a. The Function of Wordless Choir (Scene II, mm.198–202)

"[War] will spread everywhere like fine dust."

"Don't try to make me drunk too, don't try to frighten me, Tsargo!"

Example 3.4b. Adriana's Refusal (Scene II, mm.277–81)

Example 3.5. Chords that Represent Violence (Scene II)

Adriana's refusal of Tsargo's advances is marked by a succession of rapid arpeggiations in the clarinet (S8), as shown in example 3.4b. This musical seme, signifying Adriana's willfulness, was first introduced in Scene I when Tsargo knocked on Adriana's door and she told him to "get out of her way." In this scene, it assumes a more definitive gesture, which amplifies Adriana's anger and resistance (E2): the contour of the clarinet line mirrors the angular vocal line as it anticipates the melodic peak on F# on the downbeat of the fourth measure. The male chorus adds a mournful touch with the overlapping "sigh" motive (S5) sung on the syllable "o." Her firm denial is conveyed in the music that accompanies her statement: "Don't try to make me drunk, too; don't try to frighten me, Tsargo!" As the driving sixteenth-note motive in the strings brings back a variant of S10 to sustain harmonic tension, Adriana conveys her dismissive attitude toward Tsargo with a vocal phrase that begins and ends with the tritone C-F#. Notice how the melodic apex of the clarinet motive converges with the apex of the vocal line on the pitch F#. The second violins deploy glissando harmonics in neighboring motion to add an ethereal but sinister timbral layer in the upper register (similar to the effect used in example 3.4a).

Arguably, the most significant semic unit in the entire scene is the sequence of chords, S9 (mm.372 ff.), that convey violence (E2). Example 3.5 traces the progressive contexts in which the chord of violence emerges in the course of this scene. It is initially present as a simple hexachord played by the piano; it is an iconic motive that depicts Tsargo knocking on Adriana's house, motioning her to open the door (m.67). Later, the chord develops into one played by the chorus and orchestra in *tutti*, repeated every other measure, as Tsargo tries to convince Adriana of the enemy who will invade their town and cut their throats, as they did in their fathers' time (m.112). In its fifth recurrence, this chord develops into a sustained chordal complex involving all the instruments (mm. 134–35), following Adriana's warning to Tsargo not to frighten her anymore. At the next stage, Adriana's refusal to let Tsargo enter her house leads to reiterations of "non!" preceded by rising arpeggiation in the piano, strings, and woodwinds; the chord on the downbeat forms a dissonant cluster (m.312). Finally, upon Tsargo's forceful entry into her house, Adriana shouts "non!" (NB: Saariaho marks "screaming") five times in succession, accompanied by the ten-note chord (S9) in the orchestra and chorus played *tutti* at the dynamic indication of *sffz* (mm. 372–76).

In what follows, the narrative of "rape" is conveyed exclusively through music and changes in lighting on stage; the audience sees Adriana's house and the surrounding domes turning bright red, but is not privy to the presumed action that takes place. Following Adriana's last cry of refusal, Tsargo is seen entering her house. As the house lights up, the instrumental postlude proceeds with a massive texture in which the brass and percussion pound out rhythms that convey the act of rape, alternating with an eerie, sustained passage (*Triste molto calmo*) that features the primary seme (S5) in the chorus. After another desperate cry by Adriana, reinforced by instruments and chorus, the main texture reappears (*Disperato*), augmented by strings, woodwinds, and chorus. Following another extended pause, the scene concludes with the third iteration of the main texture, now doubled in tempo and rhythmic subdivision (*Furioso*).

In the absence of visual representation (except for the bright red light on the house), the music embodies the act of rape in the most poignant and powerful manner through the structured repetition and gendering of the sound texture – as male aggression contrasting with the silenced female, or female passivity. The effect is analogous to what Michel Chion calls an *acousmatic* function of music in film: nondiegetic or diegetic sounds the viewer hears *without* seeing their originating cause (1994: 72). Here, following Chion's concept of acousmatic sound, the dramatic import of this scene is communicated through the collision of masculine and feminine sound textures, disembodied from the presumed action.[11] The bright red lighting on the house and domes also functions as a complementary seme that signifies trauma and violence.

The Beating of Two Hearts: Will the Child be Cain or Abel?

The third scene jumps to a time immediately following the war. Entitled "Two hearts" (*Deux coeurs*), the scene depicts a dialogue between Adriana and Refka as they debate whether to keep the baby, conceived as a result of the rape. Saariaho imbues this atmosphere of expectation with a new musical material that signifies the beating of the two hearts, a rhythmic formula for what she calls "heart" music (*sydän* in Finnish). The baby's heart is represented by the faster dotted rhythm against Adriana's slower triplet division, representing a kind of "lullaby" rhythm.[12] These two rhythmic motives are used pervasively throughout the third scene, where Adriana decides to keep the baby against Refka's stern warning. The

Example 3.6. "Heartbeat" Music (Scene III, mm.1–5/mm.9–10)

motives are distinguished by timbre and register to signify the relationship between mother and child: the baby's heartbeat placed in a higher register in the
piccolo (S5'), while a variant of Adriana's chord (S2") is situated in the low register
of the piano, as shown in example 3.6. The overture begins while the dome of the
house is lit bright red from the previous scene of rape. Contrary to the semitone
descent (S5) that signifies Adriana's yearning mixed with anguish in the overture
(E3/E4), the rapid rhythmic figuration presents the dyad, E-F, in ascent. S2" and
S5', combined together, articulate the nurturing spirit of a mother awaiting the
birth of her baby (E3). Skipping over to m.9, the texture thins down to a melancholy lullaby, comprised of chordal motives in piano and harp in polyrhythms;
at m.9, the descending trichord, E♭-D-A (S7' from Adriana's rondeau), reiterated
in a cycle of three beats, is superimposed over an extended triplet rhythm in the
lower register of the piano, reiterated in a cycle of four beats. In combination, the
hemiola creates a rhythmically lopsided lullaby that represents the union of Adriana and her unborn child as her "mirror" image, suitably in a register one octave
above the piano part.

The lullaby music segues to Refka's music, featured in the prologue, characterized by the exchange of melodic motive between the solo violin and flute (as was
shown in example 3.1b). Abridged fragments of music from the previous scenes
are interjected: in particular, the *furioso* passage recapitulates the act of violence

that led to Adriana's pregnancy. In this way, the overture for Scene III provides a snapshot of everything that has taken place in Adriana's life up to this point.

In the course of Scene III, when Refka blames herself for not being at home to protect Adriana, the S5' motive and circling figuration in the celesta mirror Refka's regretful state. The "lullaby" music returns whenever Adriana defends her wish to carry the child; as she claims that the child will be hers, "it will look like her," the clarinet provides a rapidly descending figuration culminating in a sustained trill (S8'). When Adriana speaks of hearing two heartbeats, a tender musical passage comprising the piccolo motive (S5) and circling figuration in the celesta (S4) is layered over the lullaby motive. The pitch content for the vocal line "I hear another heart beating next to mine" is closely integrated with those of the orchestral motives that create this acoustical envelope. The lullaby music returns as Adriana reassures Refka that she is sure that the baby will be like her; the melodic fragment from the rondeau (D-B♭-A) is heard on "je suis sûre," and the lullaby motive (S2") echoes her voice as a form of *acoustical mirroring*.[13] A short instrumental interlude amplifies the semi-tonal motive in rhythmic diminution (G♭-F-B). A moment later, however, Adriana admits to her sister that she is actually not sure about anything, except for the presence of two hearts beating inside her. Fragments of her rondeau melody from Scene I are heard in the background. After she concludes her soliloquy with the question "will my child turn out to be Cain or Abel?" another acousmatic effect takes hold: the instrumental postlude develops the three-note motive into a frenzied texture through near obsessive repetition. Other woodwind and brass instruments double the motive at the tritone and the textural density increases before it merges with the marimba's rhythmic ostinato based on the same motive. For Saariaho, the instrumental postlude represents the birth of the baby and its growth into a young man in acousmatic terms. As the music slows down and the texture begins to thin down, a trumpet motive with an ascending B♭-F♯ dyad ushers in the final chord, which signifies Yonas's coming into being as a young man.

Yonas Confronts Adriana: Who Is My Father?

The time is now seventeen years later. In the fourth scene, called "Confessions" (*Aveux*), Adriana's son, Yonas, now a young man, confronts his mother about the secret she has kept from him all these years. He finds out that his father is not a hero, as he had been told, and that his father is still alive. What follows is an animated duet between mother and son; Adriana's confession about the truth of the matter propels Yonas to declare that he will take revenge by killing Tsargo. Yonas's desire to "kill" Tsargo is not driven so much by an Oedipal complex (that is, revenge driven by a subconscious desire to possess his mother), but rather by an intense self-hatred: the discovery of being brought into this world under such a circumstance and realizing that the blood of a monster runs through his veins. Notwithstanding Adriana's pleading that blood "has no words, no voice, no memory, it can't tell you what to do," the damage has been done.

With an expressive indication of *Giocoso energico,* the instrumental prelude begins with rapid sixteenth-note figurations in the strings and woodwinds, accompanied by the rhythmic diminution of the D-E♭ motive in the xylophone (S5'), which conveys Yonas's youthful energy and impatience. As Yonas bursts through the door of their dilapidated home, he questions Adriana about his identity, his vocal phrase punctuated by the circular figurations in the xylophone, piano, and harp. When Yonas declares that his father is not dead and calls Adriana a liar ("tu mentaisi!") on a falling tritone, the orchestra responds with a succession of volatile chords (S9'), which ironically recalls the music from the rape scene. In signifying male aggression, these chords now comment on the rage that consumes Yonas (E2).

The mood suddenly shifts when Adriana begins her confession; she tells Yonas how she was afraid of the truth and what it would do to him as a child. The accompanying music returns to a somber layer of the string glissandi motive with a swell (S11) and circular glissandi in the harp (S6). A tender but sad melody in the violin accompanies her response to him – that it was wrong of her to keep the truth from him, but that she wanted to protect him from the "hateful truth" (mm. 201–208). As Yonas presses on and asks her at what age she would have told him, the increasingly agitated duet between mother and son comes to a halt on a single note, F#⁶, sustained by the first violin; over this eerily suspended note, Adriana shouts "No more questions!" to her son. Then regaining her composure, Adriana tells him the truth about the rape; a somber melody in the flute hovers over her vocal line, interspersed by the obsessive repetition of a F-G♭ dyad (S5') in the marimba against a semitone descent (S5) in the flute, celesta, and harp. As she declares her love for Yonas, the "heartbeat" music from the previous scene returns as an extended interlude with overlaid S5's. This scene presents the dramatic moment when Adriana's maternal instinct to protect her son (E3) comes in direct confrontation with Yonas's rage (E2). The child consciously breaks away from the mother figure by asserting his identity with his own highly rhythmic music, while Adriana's utterance is tied to the aimlessly repeating figurations (S7') reminiscent of the rondeau. In the instrumental interlude that follows, her lullaby music intersects with Yonas's motive (S5') – the latter fortified by the melodic elaborations in the woodwinds and trumpet.

In the semi-darkened stage, Yonas walks away from his mother; then, in a calmer voice, he asks more questions about Tsargo's identity. As Adriana tells Yonas how Tsargo has been corrupted by war, the chorus provides a rich *sonorous envelope* around her vocal entries on "o." The orchestral texture becomes more agitated as it mirrors the violence associated with the war; sudden chromatic descending figurations in the woodwinds announce Adriana's declaration that the war ended on the day Yonas was born and, therefore, he represents "the death of death." A poignant use of choral echo, interspersed by silence, occurs as Adriana tells Yonas of Tsargo's fate following the war; he was wounded and taken to a hospital, but he dared not come back to the village. Then a rapid figuration in the clarinet (S8) ushers in Yonas's declaration to kill Tsargo if he ever returns (example 3.7). Against the pulsating ostinato in the double bass, the harp sustains a

(A): "I don't think he'd dare come back! (Y): if he comes back, I'll kill him."

Example 3.7. Yonas's Declaration (Scene IV, mm.415–23)

circling quintuplet figuration, while the timpani strikes the dyad D-E♭ (S5′) over and over again, as a signifier of traumatic repetition. As Yonas declares his intention to kill his father, the F♯-B descent in Adriana's vocal line is echoed by the same dyad in ascent; pivoting on the same dyad, the mother's resignation is countered by the son's aggressive urge to take action.

In this passage, I hear a distinctive intertextual reference to the murder scene from Berg's *Wozzeck,* in which the pulsating beats in the timpani can be associated with the agitated heartbeat of the protagonist as he sets out to murder Marie. As an iconic representation of Wozzeck's heartbeat, the timpani rhythm builds dramatic momentum up to his raising the knife to kill Marie. Although the double bass pattern accompanies Yonas's declaration to kill Tsargo and not the actual murder, it builds anticipation through sequential repetition; as the ostinato in the double bass descends in register, it is preceded by the rising arpeggiation of the clarinet. Synchronized with the sounding of loud chords played *con violenza,* the lighting on stage changes to dark purple and red; Yonas declares that "the monster's blood runs in my veins." The lullaby music returns momentarily as Adriana insists that blood doesn't mean anything, though a succession of volatile chords intervenes. In the short dream sequence that concludes this

Kaija Saariaho's Adriana Mater 107

scene, the music recapitulates the semic units (S3, S4, S6, and S7) associated with the tender, maternal voices of the women, but ultimately ends with a succession of volatile chords that signify Tsargo and the act of violence.

Without pause, the music continues into the fifth scene, labeled "Rages," where Yonas confronts Refka about the secret of his identity. The lighting on stage divides into two colors, now with the dome above the house lit white and the wall of the house yellow. The confrontation between Yonas and Refka is accentuated by the alternation between two types of musical textures: an aggressive and rhythmically agitated texture with prominent use of marimba and percussion accompanies Yonas's vocal entries, whereas softer, more fluid gestures in the celesta and circular harp glissandi accompany Refka's. When Yonas interrogates Refka about her lies, abrupt chords played in *tutti* punctuate his phrase endings, marked *furioso* (m.83, mm.103–104). A tender gesture in the flute with a descending slide accompanies Refka's reply (mm.105–106), contrasted by the increasingly agitated music that accompanies Yonas, which is characterized by a fast rhythmic ostinato in the marimba. Adriana reenters the stage, but stands to one side and listens to their conversation. When she makes her appearance known, Yonas accuses both of them of betraying him. As in the previous scene, an agitated instrumental interlude follows, culminating in the fast repetition of syncopated chords played at triple forte in the strings in $\frac{6}{8}$ meter (mm. 186–89). Saariaho purposefully eliminated part of the dialogue here and replaced it with this orchestral outburst, which conveys Yonas's anger over his sense of betrayal by both his mother and his aunt.

When the music dies down, the texture resumes the lilting rhythm of the lullaby music from the previous scene, accompanied by harp's circular glissando (S6) (mm.206–12). As Refka nervously informs them about Tsargo's return to the village, the music becomes increasingly more agitated. Over a rising bass line, Yonas declares once again that he *will* kill Tsargo. After Yonas rushes off stage, an instrumental interlude that elaborates on the *Disperato* music returns, associated with the "vision" from the previous scene. The lighting on stage suddenly turns white and purplish, with the ruins around the house lit to show their ragged edges. Refka urges Adriana to do something, to chase after Yonas. Adriana shows her resignation as she utters the words, "if he must kill, he will kill" over the rising clarinet arpeggiation (S8). The orchestra interjects the dissonant chords (S9') marked *furioso* each time after Adriana repeats these words; the transformation of this passage to "if he's meant to kill him, he will kill him," is accompanied by a descending figuration in the strings followed by a slow, ascent in the clarinet motive over an ostinato motive in the double bass. A slow, downward spiraling motive played in *tutti* over Adriana's chord (S2) concludes this scene by signifying her state of resignation.

Tsargo and Yonas: The Duel

In the sixth scene, called "Duel," Yonas seeks out Tsargo with the intent to kill him. The floor of the stage and the landscape turns bright red (reminiscent of the second scene involving the rape). The opening prelude, marked *sostenuto/lugubre,* features tubular bells, which mark the passing of time through a slow, quarter-note pulse that oscillates between G and A. Tam-tam and bass drum enter with their own rhythmic cycles in counterpoint with the tubular bells. Against the upward and downward glissandi in the harp and piano, and tremolo glissandi in the strings, the flute, oboe, and the first violin present a variant of S1 in *stretto.* Combined with these layers, the bass voices sustain the vowel "o" to project an eerie, suspenseful mood. The most prominent motive featured in this scene is the "swelling" glissandi introduced in the double bass and cello (S11). As the strings shift bowing from normal to *sul ponticello,* the semitone descent at the end is accompanied by an increase in dynamic level to *sforzando.* This motive is echoed back and forth between the cello and double bass. Locally, it is associated with Tsargo's fall from grace and his lamentable existence as a blind man. According to Sellars's vision of this scene, the music emerges as a topical signifier for the voice of the haunted soldiers who, like Tsargo, are alive but forever imprisoned inside their tortured psyches.[14] The superimposition of the trumpet motive (S1) in the high register and the string glissandi (S11) in the lowest register creates suspense; one can interpret this prologue as representing Yonas's uncomfortable entry into Tsargo's world of shadows.

This slow, lugubrious music provides the backdrop for Yonas's dialogue with Tsargo. When Yonas mentions to him that his mother is Adriana, Tsargo laps into a gentle soliloquy over the woman he loved; a variation of the lullaby motive, associated with Adriana, and a fragment of the rondeau melody from Scene I, are heard in the background. As Tsargo sings the words, "we could have been lovers," the clarinet plays a melody that cascades upward and downward to convey his unfulfilled yearning for Adriana. Unperturbed, Yonas points his rifle at Tsargo and presses him to talk about the "accursed night": the chorus amplifies the heightened emotion with vocal exclamations on "ha!" alternating with slow, downward glissandi. Yonas's impatience with the old man is conveyed satirically by the dance-like rhythm in $\frac{6}{8}$ meter, as he declares: "the fact that you're ready to pay for your crimes doesn't make you innocent."

Rather than a duel between the two men, the dramatic tension of this scene culminates in a standstill; Yonas points a rifle at Tsargo, who lies on the ground, but he is unable to pull the trigger. What ensues is arguably the most static part of the opera, where long and slow instrumental interludes are inserted between the minimal exchanges of words that take place between them. After Yonas tells Tsargo that he doesn't have the right to live, the first of the instrumental passages is heard, bringing back the opening material with the tubular bells that mark the passing of time. S11 is featured in the lower strings, accompanied by an ostinato of S5's in the bass voice of the chorus (S5). Following this interlude, Yonas hesitantly asks whether Tsargo was aware of his existence all of these years. A gentle harp ostinato in triple rhythm accompanies Yonas's inquiry. A second, more prolonged instrumental interlude follows, bringing back the tubular bell motive that marks time with circular figurations dispersed among all instruments; here the glissandi motive (S11) becomes even more prominent, its static effect augmented

Example 3.8. Postlude (Scene VI, reduced score)

by tremolos in the upper strings, and the flute echoes the downward glissando with a transformed motive that signifies Refka (S3). When Yonas asks Tsargo to turn around to look at him, the third and the longest interlude follows, building suspense by further widening the register gap between the string harmonics in the upper register and the glissandi motive in the lower strings. When Tsargo turns around and lets Yonas know that he is unable to see his own son because he is blind, a rhythmically amorphous triplet pattern in the piano echoes his meandering tone of voice, punctuated by the cascading chain of S5 in the chorus. As Tsargo reaches over to touch and grope Yonas's face, the latter recoils at first, but cannot pull himself away. As they walk backward together, the stage turns pitch dark except for the red glow of the stage floor. The orchestra follows immediately with a postlude that builds up in rhythmic momentum and dynamic intensity to an explosive, cacophonic ending. As shown in example 3.8, trichords and tetrachords are formed from superimposing S5 at different transpositional levels in order to create a massive texture that builds up to an explosive ending. The descending semitone sheds itself of its topical signifier of *piano,* as it undergoes semic dissolution through cyclical repetition. Although omitted from this reduction, the chorus marks the downbeat with exclamations on "ha," derived from the S2 chord.

Thus, the title for this scene, "duel," is used ironically to depict Yonas's inability to respond to Tsargo's advances. It speaks to a psychological battle that Yonas wages against his own will as he confronts a decrepit old man who is already "dead" among the living. Other than the visual image of Yonas holding a gun steadily to Tsargo's head, the scene contains no exterior form of violence. Yet it is a duel in the sense that the purpose of their encounter is to settle a point of honor. Constituting one of the tensest moments in the opera, Saariaho suspends time by minimizing action on stage and substituting dialogue, once again with *acousmatic* use of music. Just as in the scene of rape, the character's experience of trauma is made visceral and psychological through a musical enactment of "repetition" compulsion. Saariaho has gone so far as to eliminate parts of the dialogue in Maalouf's original libretto in order to communicate the dramatic tension of the scene in purely musical terms. The slow and static music eventually builds to the volatile instrumental postlude. In spite of his revulsion, Yonas is unable to resist his father's desire to touch him. As the two depart from the stage and the music builds to an explosive end, the viewer is fully absorbed into the inner expression of trauma that accompanies this reunion.

Scene VII: the Ritual of Absolution

The final scene, called "Adriana," begins with an instrumental prelude, marked *Misterioso,* which brings back the overture music. Over the tempo slowed to ♩ = 32, the rumbling tremolos in the strings and percussion are first heard, followed by a spectral chord (a variation of S2) sustained by the woodwinds, brass, and chorus over the bass note G. As the trumpet plays another variation of the motive (S1'), now completely liquidated, the timpani provides a slow, triplet ostinato support. The harp's circular glissandi (S6) and chorus' utterances on "o" and "a" provide another layer absorbed into an ominous wash of sound. The massive textural crescendo dramatizes the moment when all four characters are brought back on stage, one by one, to confront the nightmare of the past. According to Maalouf, however, "though they are all on stage together they are not together, and each follows his or her own bent. They speak in monologues that sometimes overlap; the chorus, too, occasionally intervenes. Only the son and the mother finally come together." He further describes this scene as belonging neither to the world of dream nor to that of reality, but somewhere in between.

Following the dramatic overture, Adriana appears on stage with the floor lit blue. As she sings about "that accursed night" to refer to the night when she was raped, Refka and the chorus join in with the text, "the gates of Hell opened up." The domes of Adriana's house turn bright red in reference to the violence. As Adriana continues to sing about the pain that "has placed a mask" over her face all of those years, an ostinato motive (short-long) is sounded in the vibraphone, repeating itself seemingly endlessly like a broken record. As she speaks of her "soul" and her old self left behind, the chorus echoes Adriana's nostalgic sentiment. A glowing, orange light surrounds the women as they hold onto one another. The chorus, now in full force, echoes Adriana's tender sentiment. As the stage floor and the dome of the house glow with orange and gold light, all four characters appear together for once; with arms up in the air, they sing simultaneously, but independent of one another, in recalling what has taken place in their lives. The gold and orange lighting assumes an important semic role in this scene of absolution. The cacophonic ensemble singing returns to the trauma of the "accursed night" as a descending motive (B♭-E) in the tuba is heard (mm.96–99). The chorus emerges in full force, commenting on "how nothing ever has been able to efface" what has happened that night (example 3.9a). Notice the manner in which the word "jamais" (never) is emphasized by repetition.

Tuba and double bass anchor the modality of this passage to E minor; the frequently unresolved leading tone (D♯) and the chromatically descending bass line reinforce the idea of a traumatic event that has consumed them for over seventeen years. From this point onward, the four characters individually sing about what s/he regrets having or not having done, one by one. When Refka admits her failure to protect Adriana, she is accompanied by the timbres of flute and harp glissando (S6) that characterize her remorsefulness. Yonas then curses himself for not having the courage to kill Tsargo, and admits to the hate and fear that consume him, as variants of the chord of violence (S9) are heard in the background. Tsargo wishes that he might have died during the war, as the low strings sound the glissando motive with a swell (S11). Finally, the chorus joins in once more as Refka and Adriana, immersed in the orange and gold light, together articulate their wish for "a peaceful dawn." The chorus then brings closure to this ritualistic scene with the reassurance that the gates of Hell are "closing once again."

Refka regrets the course of events that led to the tragic rape, repeatedly claiming that she "should have taken her [Adriana] under my wings." Yonas then sings about the fear and hate that still possess him, his enunciation accompanied by a flurry of descending figurations in the woodwinds that signify his anguish. Tsargo's dark, lament-filled soliloquy follows, accompanied by a cascade of low string glissandi that swell up to *sforzando*. The tenor and bass choir provide a sonorous envelope around Tsargo's lamentation, as he declares that he should have died in the war. Against the dark blue hue of the house and the red dome, Tsargo, Adriana, and Refka take turns singing about what they "should have" done with their lives. When Yonas again regrets not killing Tsargo, the music returns to his succession of volatile chords (mm.248–61). A more tender side of Tsargo is revealed when he declares that he should have died after dancing with Adriana in the ball; as he calls out her name, "Adriana," on the falling tritone, C♯-G, a series of falling figurations in the clarinet echoes his sentiment, as shown in example 3.9b. Here, the clarinet motive (S8) that previously signified Adriana's anger projected at Tsargo, is transformed into a signifier of Tsargo's sincere regret and affection (E1) through descending arpeggiation (S8'). A descending chain of S5 in the strings accompanies Tsargo's confession, echoing his remorseful sentiment. The clarinet motive (S8), which signified Adriana's willfulness up until this point, becomes unmoored from her for the first time.

Following this scene, mother and son look at one another and realize that they are no longer filled with the idea of revenge. As the celesta enters with a lilting four-note ostinato (S4) with an upward contour, Refka and Adriana pray for "a peaceful dawn," which symbolizes relief from the nightmare. As a warm and suffused orange light surrounds the stage, the ensemble participates in sing-

a. (mm. 92-98 [percussion, woodwinds, strings omitted])

"Nothing, nothing ever has been able to efface what happened that accursed night."

b. (mm.274-77)

"...right after this dance, this unique dance with Adriana."

Example 3.9a/b. Excerpts from Scene VII

Example 3.10. Closing Melody (Scene VII, mm.632–39)

ing about "shutting the gates of Hell," complete with a choral refrain. This is the *transvaluative* moment in which the characters are freed from the burden of the past. In this way, in a final scene that hovers between dream and reality, the characters undergo a ritual of absolution from guilt, obligation, and punishment.

The stage darkens, with only the wall of the house and the red dome visible, when Yonas asks his mother for forgiveness for not being able to take revenge. For the first time, a different musical texture accompanies Yonas's singing, a gentle, rollicking ostinato in ⅝ meter accompanied by the S5 motive in the chorus. Nonetheless, the static, circling figurations that accompany Yonas's confession to his mother maintain an obsessive edge. A dramatic pause follows the two, who join together to sing about how Tsargo "deserved to die" (m.461). Then Adriana in turn confesses to Yonas that she has always wondered whether her son was capable of killing, since he is the son of a soldier who mercilessly killed others during the war; semi-tonal motive and ostinato figures repeat like a mantra to convey the nature of her obsessive inquiry. When the S5 motive sounds in the horn (mm.479–81), the music slows down to the rhythm of the melancholy lullaby heard in Scene III. As Adriana reassures herself that in the end "blood determined nothing," the orchestra interjects the *furioso* chords. The chorus literally echoes Adriana's words that it was enough that she raised him to be an honorable man (mm.516–24). The volatile chords, somewhat diffused, return as Adriana comments that if Yonas were spiritually Tsargo's son, he would have killed him without remorse. The lighting on stage turns bright yellow and gold as she tells Yonas that today she has found her life again, which she thought she had lost, and that they are saved. As the music slowly dissipates and faint echoes of the primary seme (S5) are heard in multiple layers, they embrace each other. The semitone dyad, B♭-A, becomes embedded within the trichord motive (S7') on E, suggestive of Dorian mode on G. As shown in example 3.10, the clarinet entry in the third measure further complicates the mode, outlining an Aeolian mode on G with D♭ alternating with D at the beginning. This modal fragment is passed on to the piano, then to other instruments, over the A-E drone, before it resolves to the

Example 3.11. Overview of the Harmonic Fields and Semic Units

modal tonic G with E (an added sixth) sounding above it (not shown). The ending represents not only Adriana's reconciliation with Yonas, but also with her own divided self.

By way of summary, I will examine how the primary seme (S5) can be situated within the overall harmonic orientation that governs the orchestral writing from beginning to the end. Saariaho is often asked whether she still composes with spectral harmonies (a compositional technique based on analysis of sound spectra, which she used in earlier works); her answer is an emphatic "no," insisting that she has constructed harmonies intuitively without any kind of system based on spectral analysis since her first opera, *l'Amour de loin*. Spencer N. Lambright, nonetheless, has coined the term "harmonic field" to describe Saariaho's construction of harmonies in works beginning with *Verblendungen* (1982–84), characterized by the distribution of pitches that resemble the structure of the harmonic overtone series; he traces the process by which the large-scale harmonic organization of *l'Amour de loin* is articulated by a progression to and from a given harmonic field anchored to B♭1 (2008: 65). My own analysis of *l'Amour de loin* demonstrates how the stable harmonic fields pointed out by Lambright are disrupted by the chords of rupture – dissonant chords that are interpolated into earlier scenes that foreshadow the turn to doubt and despair that consume Clémence (Everett 2012: 341–42).

Although *Adriana Mater* is a much later work, its harmonic orientation is similarly organized around the progressive transformation of S2 (the "maternal" chord), anchored to G1, as shown in example 3.11. Notice how the primary seme (S5), initially contained within S2, is embedded within all of the subsequent harmonic fields as a linear motive and/or as a primary intervallic building block. Even in the dissonant outbursts that characterize scenes of rape and confrontation (Scenes II and VI), the semitone serves as the primary building block; an extreme case can be noted in the construction of the harmonic field of the postlude in Scene VI, comprised of a superimposition of secundal clusters across a five-octave span. At the close of the opera when the son and mother

Kaija Saariaho's Adriana Mater 115

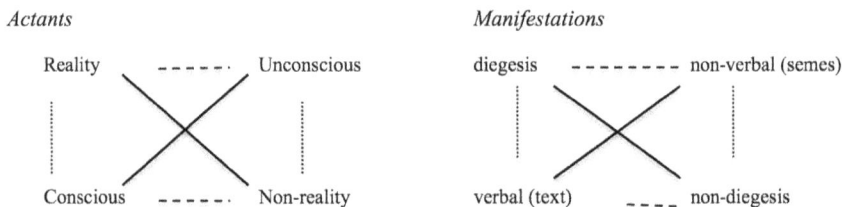

Actants		Manifestations	

Figure 3.3. Dramatic Oppositions at the Actantial Level

come to a resolution, the maternal chord returns with the fragment of the "rondeau" melody (S7), clearly anchored to the G Dorian mode.

Psychological Resonances: Traumatic Repetition and Ruptures

Focusing on the psychological resonances of trauma, I will now return to how Saariaho, Maalouf, and Sellars configure this opera into a type of redemption myth. Returning to the framework of the libretto, the chorus is used, as in Greek tragedy, to provide commentary on the drama as well as to interact with and guide the characters. The chorus provides a ritualistic framework in which to absolve the four characters from trauma, rage, and/or the collective guilt of keeping a secret for seventeen years. Adriana and Refka have repressed their guilt and shame into their unconscious, which can only be accessed at the level of a dream. Thus, one way to explain the narrative trajectory is to invoke these oppositions as higher-level actants that govern the configurational dimension of the narrative, as shown in figure 3.3.

Here, the actants correspond with their dramatic manifestations in the following manner. Reality and dream sequences set up a fundamental opposition in the temporal unfolding of the opera; the interpolation of dream sequences creates ruptures that disrupt the dramatic continuity of the otherwise linear temporal ordering of events. On the other axis, the unconscious and conscious levels of communication establish another opposition and create psychological tension in the unfolding of the narrative. However, the conscious and unconscious divide, according to Lacan, can be conceived as two sides of a Moebius strip; the impacts of the Real create turning points that allow access rather seamlessly onto the opposite side of the conscious order (Johnston 2005: 55).[15] The musical articulation of the dramatic oppositions (reality vs. non-reality, consciousness vs. the unconscious) can also be interpreted in this fashion. Generally, the enunciated text functions as the voice of consciousness and non-verbal semic units that of the unconscious, yet these domains do blur. Through juxtaposition or superimposition of layers, musical semes comment on the conscious and unconscious modes of enunciation: at times, they reinforce the denotative meaning conveyed by the sung text (e.g., S9 chords that accompany Adriana's exclamation of "non!")

and at other times, the expressive connotation of one layer collides with the sung text (e.g., the "repetition" compulsion conveyed by S5 that hovers over Adriana's declaration that "the child will be like her" in Scene III). In short, the non-verbal media provides a portal into the characters' unconscious vis-à-vis the enunciated text. The sense of trauma and ambivalence accrues from moving back and forth between these realms until the tension is resolved in the final scene.

Musically speaking, there are two primary means by which the idea of trauma is expressed throughout *Adriana Mater*. At the broader level of structure, Saariaho prolongs stasis through the interpolation of musical interludes at key moments that signal confrontation, as in Scene VI where she slows down the tempo to emphasize the encounter between the father and son. At the local level, the cyclical repetition of motive is a pervasive compositional means by which Saariaho expresses the characters' anxiety and trauma in confronting the past. In short, musical repetition presents itself as an audible manifestation of the "repetition" compulsion associated with trauma, either in passages where semic units hover above the enunciated text or when the acousmatic function of music replaces words and actions. The repeating motives that project the characters' subliminal desires and fears can be interpreted as a musical rendition of *chora,* as conceived by Julia Kristeva. In defining *chora* as an indeterminate articulation characterized by repetition, Kristeva proposes a new modality of the signifying process based on traces and marks rather than signs; as an *emergent* sign, it constitutes the kinetic functional stage of semiosis, as articulated through repetition.

> Though deprived of unity, identity, or deity, the *chora* is nevertheless subject to a regulating process, which is different from that of symbolic law but nevertheless effectuates discontinuities by temporarily articulating them and then starting over, again and again. . . . [This] kinetic functional stage of the semiotic precedes the establishment of the sign. (1984: 26–27)

While a typical musical sign is established through distinctive vocal patterns associated with each character or sharply delineated dissonances that mark scenes of violence, a musical chora is characterized by its emergent and transient quality, exemplified by circling figurations in the woodwinds and strings that repeat like a mantra, choral utterances of nonsensical syllables, and circular glissandi in the harp. The static, non-unitary enunciation of the chora may be heard as embodying the character's yearning, anger, fear, and even love. Like a broken record, these instrumental motives repeat themselves in projecting the character's unconscious desire at a preverbal, pre-symbolic level (Kristeva 1984: 26).[16] It is in this sense that Kristeva's chora can be interpreted as a specific condition within Lacan's Imaginary Order that precedes the Symbolic.

Furthermore, Kaja Silverman comments on the positive and negative inflections of the chora as follows:

> We learn that although the symbolic attempts to negate the *chora,* the maternal substratum of subjectivity surfaces to carnivalesque, surrealist, psychotic, and 'poetic' language. It is also, according to Kristeva, an inevitable feature of even the most

normative gesture. However, the *chora* is most fully showcased within infantile language, which permits the adult subject to hear what has not been fully rationalized within its own discourse, and which thereby provides it with a privileged access to the archaic mother. (1988: 106)

Indeed, the characters lapse into this "substratum of subjectivity," manifested in the dream sequences that are inserted within three of the seven scenes. Kristeva also refers to the *choric* fantasy, which forces the maternal voice to the inside of the "sonorous" envelope, figuring the oneness of mother and child – and these parts may be forms, colors, sounds, organs, or words as long as they have been invested by primordial drives (1984: 102). This is precisely the source of the tension that underlies Adriana's and Refka's relationships with Yonas. In order to find a way to reconcile with Yonas, the women must wrestle with the source of their anxiety – the traumatic experience of rape during the war, which they suppress from their consciousness for seventeen years. When Yonas's anger is externalized through a rhythmic ostinato that soon erupts into a sequence of exploding chords, the women's initial response is to retreat inside this choric space, which is represented by musical semes (S4, S5, S6) associated with the dream world. However, once the subject is severed from the oneness of the "sonorous" envelope, her mode of enunciation becomes split, as made evident by the repetition of musical semes (S4 and S5) that hovers over Adriana's or Refka's sung text as an element of excess – a semiotic object that is severed from the symbolic mode of utterance.

Based on Lacan's idea regarding the infant's experience of imaginary structures after birth and before language acquisition, David Schwarz asserts that musical analysis parallels phases in our cognitive development during which we cross from the Imaginary to the Symbolic domain of experience: "Listening as a *fantasy space* is produced when music-theoretical, musical-historical, cultural, psychoanalytic, or personal thresholds are crossed and enunciated" (1997: 4). Applied to my reading of this operatic narrative, the changing modes of enunciation established between the verbal (sung text) and non-verbal (music, gestures, and staging) components represent Lacan's stages of subject formation in compelling ways. First, I argue that the Imaginary or mirror stage is represented by the instrumental preludes and interludes in which contrasting expressive registers are presented without symbolic intervention of words. Slavoj Žižek defines the Imaginary and the Symbolic as follows:

In the *imaginary* relation, the two poles of opposition are complementary; together they build a harmonious totality; each gives the other what the other lacks – each fills out the lack in the other. ... The *symbolic* relation is, on the contrary, differential: the identity of each of the moments consists in its difference to the opposite moment. A given element does not fill in the lack in the other, it is not complementary to the other but, on the contrary, takes the place of the lack in the other, embodies what is lacking in the other: its positive presence is nothing but an objectification of a lack in its opposite element. (1989: 193–94)

Frequently, the musical passages that represent the Imaginary order juxtapose two semic units with opposite expressive registers: for example, the paired relationship between S1 and S2 (first presented in the overture) recurs throughout the opera as a reflection of the changing relationship between mother and son. The prologue of the final scene provides the most complicated transformation of S1 and S2 by placing it in the slowest tempo, accompanied by choral "sigh" (S5) and harp glissando (S6), to extend the tension between the expressive registers of hope and despair. The third dream sequence consists of a short instrumental postlude that juxtaposes music for Adriana, Refka, and Tsargo, and thus belongs to the Imaginary order.

Applying Žižek's explanation further, the Symbolic order (reality as it appears at the surface) is represented whenever music, stage actions, and text are combined as a composite form of enunciation, identifying and clearly reinforcing the differences in the characters' positions; this occurs most prominently in Scenes IV and V, where the musical texture quickly alternates between Yonas and Refka or between Yonas and Adriana via block juxtaposition. Scene VI is where stasis is maximized, as the trauma of the confrontation between father and son is conveyed through the oscillation between the Imaginary (long interludes) and Symbolic (sung dialogue) orders.

One could then argue that the residues of the Real order are manifested in Saariaho's music whenever musical semes signify something in *excess* of what the sung text conveys: that is to say, when the voiceless choir echoes the singer's text via *acoustical mirroring*, when there is choric repetition of semic units (signifying "repetition" compulsion), or in the two postludes (Scenes II and VI) where the *acousmatic* function of music conveys traumatic rupture in its own terms.[17] More specifically, the residues of the Real can be discussed in reference to Lacan's later theory concerning the three objects through which these residues "bubble up" to the surface (chapter 1, figure 1.11). One can trace Lacan's *object petit a,* the lack in the constructed reality that sets the crisis in motion, to the pairing of the trumpet motive (S1) and the Adriana chord (S2); as an ascending motive framed within a three-part phrase construction, it repeatedly poses the central enigma concerning Yonas's identity. But what of the other objects in the Lacanian order? In Lacanian theory, trauma implies fixation and blockage, which manifests itself in the forms of repetition and displacement; thus, one can interpret the musical *chora* as representing traumatic repetition and a symbolization of the Imaginary, S(Ⱥ): Sarah Reichardt describes this in musical terms as a circulating object, taking "the form of an ordinary object that comes to represent the [R]eal" through unusual repetition (2008: 11). The wordless choir functions in this capacity whenever it emerges at the musical foreground, interjecting short, wordless responses (S5) to Tsargo's and Refka's pleas. Subsidiary to S5, S4, the four-note figuration in the woodwinds functions as another circulating object, passed between the women in their dream state; this figuration reappears in Tsargo and Yonas's duel scene when they undergo a crisis of identity – the obsessive repetition signifies their quest to figure out who they are in relationship to one another.[18] Finally, I would argue that the repetition of semic units that builds up to an explosive instrumental climax at the end of Scene II represents Φ, which Žižek describes as "the mute embodiment of the impossible jouissance" (2008: 209). This is the signifier of desire, the primordial impetus that drives Tsargo to possess Adriana by physical force. Adriana, in turn, becomes a "split" subject due to the traumatic injury sustained by this heinous act.

In fact, it is important to note that the trauma inflicted upon Adriana and Yonas drives them to adopt different behavioral responses to cope with the situation, and Lacan's four discourses (discussed in chapter 1) provide a useful interpretive framework. The Master's discourse models Adriana's interaction with her son: here, the authorial mother (S1) transmits knowledge to her son (S2), while barring herself from telling the whole truth S). The dissimulated truth (a) creates a false reality under which the son and mother live in apparent harmony. The model of the hysteric's discourse represents Yonas's response to learning the truth of his identity: that Adriana lied to him about his father's existence. Here the conflicted subject S) functions as the agent who seeks out the imaginary subject (S1) – the father as villain who needs to be avenged. The imaginary father takes on a massively oppressive presence (Φ), the perceived cause of his trauma. What is barred in the process is the real source of Yonas's desire (a) – his mother's love, which he is able to embrace only after his traumatic encounter with the real father (S2) – the decrepit old man who asks for forgiveness.

So how does the psychoanalytic dimension of the narrative intersect with the function of musical semes? To recapitulate, the chronological sequence of events is interrupted by dream sequences, which catapult Adriana and Refka into a past reconstituted within a dream. While there is a consistent pattern by which semic units articulate the divided expressive registers – e.g., pounding chords (S9) with rage (E2) and semitonal descent (S5) with despair (E4) – the dramatic tension is conveyed through their juxtaposition, be it the nurturing maternal voice (E3) paired with profound feeling of despair (E4) or the rage of the impatient young man (E2) paired with the women's despair (E4). This is symptomatic of the "splitting" of the drive in the subject, which creates traumatic resonances. For example, in Scene III, Adriana professes the innocence of her unborn child in her role as a nurturing mother (E3), while the woodwinds project the despairing sigh motive (E4) in the background. The ambivalence is sustained until the transvaluative moment in the final scene where the hero/villain opposition dissolves: the unmooring of semic units from the previously established expressive registers, metaphorical reference to dawn and closing the gates of hell, and the continual change in lighting contribute to this scene of absolution. The characters are redeemed from the psychic wounds of war and freed from the burden of the past.

Musical semes articulate important shifts in narrative discourse. Notably, they disrupt the continuity of events within the chronological unfolding of the narrative as follows: semic units, such as the initial trumpet motive (S1) paired with the maternal chord (S2), *project* the central enigma over and over again as the manifestation of Lacan's *object petit a;* semic units that circulate as objects of exchange, such as the primary seme (S5) and "dream" materials (S4) *disrupt* the musical surface as unusual repetitions that voice the residues of the Real. Finally, the same semic units manifested as acousmatic music undergo textural and rhythmic forms of intensification in generating moments of traumatic rupture (Φ). The first arrow for Φ points to the scene of rape, the traumatic event accompanied by an irretrievable loss and change in ranking: loss of innocence for Adriana and the marking of Tsargo as villain. Later in Scene VI, the traumatic encounter between Yonas and Tsargo *reverses* the previous marking of Tsargo as villain, as Yonas's expectation of his father is shattered by witnessing the latter's decrepit state. Thus, the unmarking of Tsargo as villain (and his status in Yonas's mind as a "master signifier") can be represented by $-(\Phi)$. Following this symbolic moment, the characters engage in a "conscious" reckoning with the past in the final scene as a way of moving beyond the guilt and shame that have consumed them over the years. Curiously enough, the semic unit that represents "repetition compulsion," S5, disappears from the orchestral background; instead, the fragment of the "rondeau" melody (S7') returns and is anchored – for the first time – to a stable mode (G Aeolian) at the end.

One might ask why this particular production by Sellars remains the only version that exists to date. I would be inclined to say that the tightly knit collaboration between Saariaho, Maalouf, and Sellars resulted in a mise-en-scène that perfectly complements the music, libretto, and the vision behind the work. Aleksi Barrière comments that Sellars always searches for a scenic language that brings out the essence of the musical text with an absolute economy of means and stays attuned to the composer's vision without reducing the staging to a "visual repetition of the sonic content" (2013: 29–30). In *Adriana Mater*, Sellars achieves these goals by foregrounding inner expression and symbolism in a minimal and abstract setting of a war-torn village. In this context, dramatic changes in the staging are articulated by prominent shifts in color and lighting of the domes and the walls of Adriana's dilapidated house. The lighting combined with stage actions articulates the change in inner expression with self-sufficient clarity and consistency. For example, darkness correlates with despair (E4), orange and gold with warmth and hopefulness (E1), red with rage and violence (E2), blue and gold with Adriana's maternity (E3), and brown and purple with Yonas's rage and despair (E2/E4). At times, red and blue lights are juxtaposed to show visible tension in the characters' interaction with one another. The third scene is especially interesting because it begins with red lighting from the previous scene of rape, then turns blue and gold when Adriana and Refka become visible. However, as Refka enters a dream sequence in which she recalls the war, the lighting is split to blue (facade of house) and red. Each of the dream sequences is marked by a greater frequency of change in the lighting, especially in the last Scene (VII), where the characters' long repressed thoughts are brought to the foreground. The opera ends with the mother and son enveloped in gold and orange lights, as if to signal the restoration of hope and a peaceful existence. Compared to a symbolist opera that moves from darkness to light and back to darkness, e.g., Bartók's *Bluebeard's Castle* (1911), the overall shift in lighting from darkness to brightness (e.g., orange/gold hue) in *Adriana Mater* seems to signal a definitive move away from the initial order of melancholy and despair to one of hope. Yet the narrative resists being relegated to an established archetype.

Mythic Resonances

My reading of this opera resonates strongly with Suzanne Langer's remark on myth, her claim that the ultimate aim of myth is "not wishful distortion of the world, but serious envisagement of its fundamental truths, moral orientation, not escape" (2009: 67). I believe that the narrative of *Adriana Mater* is reconfigured into a modern myth precisely in order to force viewers to grapple with the human dilemma and moral orientation at stake in this narrative. Will this be a story about revenge or forgiveness? Will the child be like its mother or like its father? This ambivalence develops into a specific kind of trope that drives the hermeneutic orientation. To this end, the operatic narrative invokes mythic elements without modeling one specific type of mythic narrative. On the theme of revenge, Maalouf interweaves references to Greek tragedy: notably, it calls to mind Aeschylus's *Oresteia* (458 BCE), in which Clytemnestra kills Agamemnon for sacrificing their daughter Iphigenia; Orestes, in turn, murders Clytemnestra in order to avenge the wrongful death of his father. The chorus plays an indispensible role in commenting on the unending cycle of violence. In *Adriana Mater,* the chorus makes prophetic remarks, as when it depicts Tsargo as "a fallen angel" and proclaims that he will be "damned" in the first dream sequence (before anything happens). Other important references include Cain from the Old Testament, who commits fratricide by killing his pious brother Abel, when Adriana asks herself whether her child will be like Cain or Abel.

In spite of these mythical and literary allusions, the characters in this opera are given individual responsibility, unlike mythological subjects whose courses of action are determined to a large extent by the prophecy of an oracle or some other supernatural force. Instead, the subjects in this opera are held accountable for their actions, as made evident by Yonas's struggle to let go of his primal urge and Tsargo's plea for forgiveness. The mythical reference to "gates of hell closing" at the end of the opera signals more than Yonas's reconciliation with Adriana; it also symbolizes the act of putting an end to the cycle of violence that has plagued the people of this unknown village. Yet, in the final analysis, we do not know what this voice of alterity represents: does the chorus function as gatekeeper, allowing characters entry into and out of the mythical domain of the dream world, or does it project the voice of the dead soldiers, as imagined by Peter Sellars? The ambivalent role attributed to the chorus, I argue, is one of the strategies Maalouf uses to mythologize the drama: it is not the particularity of time and place that matters, but the ethical conduct underlying the characters' actions. As Gunther Kress and Theo van Leeuwen claim, "mythical" elements signify discourses that are never explicitly formulated and are purposefully vague, nonetheless they are "always invested with affect, with a strong sense of positive or negative evaluation" (2001: 73).

The ambivalence also extends to the narrative structure of *Adriana Mater,* which narrowly escapes the tragic archetype; the first act of transgression (rape of Adriana) is followed not by another transgression (murder of Tsargo), but by an attempt to restore the initial order. Textual references to dawn in the final scene, accompanied by orange and gold lighting, suggest the idea of a new beginning. Regardless of the historical time and circumstance, we are led to identify with Adriana's moral struggle to cope with a decision to either raise or abort a child begotten through rape. Adriana's alter ego is her sister Refka, whose conviction of Tsargo as evil and monstrous remains unchanged throughout the opera. Much of the tension within the dramatic narrative rests on the question of whether Yonas will take revenge on Tsargo for shaming his mother. When Yonas ultimately fails to do so, there is a disruption in the expectation for violence that leads to an alternative order in the social hierarchy. The transgression in this case has to do with breaking away from the vicious cycle of violence. In fact, Tsargo's role undergoes transvaluation when he is no longer seen as a villain at the end. But does anyone emerge as a real hero? Does the narrative lean toward the romantic archetype? That hardly seems to be the case. If anything, the point of the narrative lies in the dissolution of binary oppositions: none of the characters is seen as exclusively a hero or villain. However inconclusive the ending appears to be, the expected course for resolution, as modeled on older mythic narratives, gives way to a new perspective. The opera plays out an age-old myth of redemption, here presented as a promise of a new beginning for mother and son.

The notable departure from a conventional narrative lies in the emphasis given to acousmatic music and semic effects of lighting (in lieu of stage actions) in telling the story. In fact, Saariaho confided in an interview that in this production they purposefully departed from what was indicated in the libretto, leaving out the dramatic realization of certain scenes as originally intended by Maalouf. For example, Maalouf conceived the third dream sequence as "a kind of sacrificial [rite] enacted in slow motion," where Yonas tears off others' masks and throws them onto a fire. This visionary act, which was intended to link Scenes IV and V, was not realized. Instead, Sellars decided to suggest the potentiality of violence by bringing back the red lighting on stage, which conjures up the memories of war and rape from Scene II.

The ending is in no way definitive in providing narrative closure. A modern view of Adriana as *Mater Dolorosa,* a suffering Madonna, emerges in Peter Sellars's telling of the story. "In the 21st century," Sellars said in an interview, "we have a responsibility to do more than sit around and tell sad stories. Here we see there will be a future. And that future has been guaranteed all over the world by women, women who in impossible situations nourish and cultivate human dignity" (quoted in Riding 2006). In Sellars's staging for the Opera Bastille, he added a dimension of hope that was not included in Maalouf's libretto: in the final scene, Yonas and Adriana make gestures toward Tsargo as if to ask whether the circle of violence, hatred, and revenge can be stopped through forgiveness. In concluding the opera with this question, Sellars engages the audience to see the narrative as a parable for the world in which we live today.

4   John Adams's *Doctor Atomic:*
A Faustian Parable
for the Modern Age?

Doctor Atomic is more like *The Death of Klinghoffer* in that it's about a real historic event that immediately took on mythic meaning.

John Adams, quoted in Alex Ross, "The Rest is Noise: *Doctor Atomic*."

Near the end of the *Doctor Atomic,* the countdown to the test explosion of the atomic bomb in the Alamogordo, New Mexico, begins as Oppenheimer quotes from Baudelaire: "Time has disappeared; it is eternity that reigns!" John Adams's ethereal, polyrhythmic music simulates numerous clocks ticking away as the characters on stage anxiously await the test explosion. In the semi-staged 2008 production of *Doctor Atomic* by the Atlanta Symphony Orchestra, the audience watched a large image of the atomic mushroom cloud erupt on the screen as their seats began to shake from the low vibrations emanating from the surround sound system. The singers on stage stood silent as the ostinato of celesta and harp returned to mark time. The opera came to a close as the tape loop of a Japanese victim asking for water played and faded away. Many sat in disbelief, wondering what to take away from this disjunctive experience.

   Doctor Atomic is the last in the trilogy of Adams's operas based on political subjects from postwar American history. *Nixon in China* (1985–87) revolves around Nixon's historical visit to China and his meeting with Mao Zedong and then-Prime Minister Zhou Enlai; the opera cleverly satirizes the "disconnect" between the American and Chinese officials as Nixon and Kissinger engage in an one-sided conversation with the aging tyrant of communism. On a more controversial note, *Death of Klinghoffer* (1992) foregrounds the murder of an American Jewish civilian at the hands of Palestinian terrorists aboard the Italian cruise ship *Achille Lauro,* which has led critics and scholars to debate the moral authority behind the violence of one ethnic and political group against another.[1] *Doctor Atomic,* in turn, takes us back in American history to the Manhattan Project; in July 1945, a group of scientists led by Robert Oppenheimer conducted the first atomic bomb testing in New Mexico in anticipation of its use to bring an end to World War II. Here, the scientists were faced with the ethical dilemma of whether or not to carry out the test explosion of the thermonuclear bomb in the Los Alamos desert prior to dropping the bomb in Japan. The "pact with the devil" implication and Oppenheimer's subsequent fall from grace in his political career lead us to view the opera as a Faustian parable set in the modern age. Yet, considering Adams's quote in the opening line, how does mythic meaning emerge in the context of *Doctor Atomic*? How does the Faustian theme intersect or collide with allusion to other myths?

The idea for the opera began when Pamela Rosenberg, then director of the San Francisco Opera, approached John Adams about the prospect of writing a contemporary opera based on an "American" Faust.[2] Although Adams was not interested in composing another opera at the time, he was interested in exploring the subject of Robert Oppenheimer and the making of the atomic bomb. Instead of collaborating with Alice Goodman, who wrote the original libretti for *Nixon in China* and *Death of Klinghoffer*, Adams teamed with stage director Peter Sellars, who went to great lengths to compile the libretto for *Doctor Atomic* largely from fragments of written texts found in Oppenheimer's library. These included the declassified government documents on the Manhattan Project; a popular book on the atomic bomb from the 1950s; poetry by Charles Baudelaire, John Donne, and Muriel Rukeyser; and the Indian sacred text, the Bhagavad Gita, which Oppenheimer had read in its original Sanskrit. Sellars skillfully interwove dialogues and references to government documents, providing an objective account of the Manhattan project with other textual sources that give us a glimpse into Oppenheimer's subjective, interior world. Sellars describes the narrative as about time: "Every second is charged, because it is a new thing in the history of time – this massive pressure behind every minute and every second in a way that never counted before . . . You get the hands of that clock, and inside every minute is a universe" (quoted in Ross 2005). This is, indeed, the paradox that shapes the progression of events: diegetic and meta-diegetic[3] space and time merge in the countdown to the test explosion. To this end, textual sources shift from those that are anchored in historical time (e.g., declassified documents) to those that convey poetic timelessness (e.g., poetry by Baudelaire and Donne). To parallel this progression, Adams introduces a wide range of musical procedures that dichotomizes the viewer's perception of time into chronometric and psychological categories in the context of this opera. In addition to an electronic collage of machines, screaming children, and a simulation of the bomb explosion, musical motives that signify specific processes – e.g., the clock "ticking away" toward the countdown, a descending and spiraling motive in the strings portraying an electrical storm, and the slow, sustained micropolyphony indicating the "chain reaction" of chemical compounds – mark the passing of time toward the test explosion. These are juxtaposed and merged with topics and stylized quotations (referencing music by Stravinsky, Wagner, Orff, and Debussy) that signify the psychological or experiential time of those who await the countdown. The musical narrative unfolds through the oscillation between these two topical representations of temporality, but strikingly, in approach to the countdown, the boundary between these markers of time collapse. By interpolating sounds of screaming children and the disembodied voice of a Japanese woman asking for water, the concluding scene conjures up the actual horror inflicted on the victims of Hiroshima and Nagasaki in virtual space and time. In this respect, the ending catapults the audience from the once-now (Los Alamos) to the soon-to-be-now (Hiroshima) and casts the operatic narrative within a broader historical framework, enabling them to participate in the construction of its meaning. What could this spatiotemporal collapse mean for a twenty-first-century audience?

After interpreting the opera from the perspective of Peter Sellars's mise-en-scène for the Netherlands Opera (2007), I will conclude my analysis by comparing Sellars's production with Penny Woolcock's for the Metropolitan Opera (2008). *Doctor Atomic* is an unusual opera in that it pushes the spatiotemporal boundary of the viewer's experience by introducing a perspectival shift from the historical/local mode of representation to the mythological/global one during the course of the opera. The "mythic" meaning that Adams speaks of, as I will demonstrate, can be revealed through analyzing the participating semiotic fields that articulate the dramaturgical turn toward the mythological. As the story progresses, Adams's music becomes increasingly static and Sellars's libretto emphasizes poetic timelessness over realism; this orientation, combined with various aspects of staging, steers the viewer into a synchronic (as opposed to a diachronic) experience of narrative, one associated with myth. To illustrate how the process works, this chapter examines the historical background of the story, the refracted references in the libretto, Adams's post-minimalist music as markers of time, the opera's connection to archetypal myth, and the two contrasting productions of *Doctor Atomic* by Sellars and Woolcock.

Historical Background: Oppenheimer as Hero?

Robert Oppenheimer was a complicated figure in history. Renowned for his brilliance as a scientist, he was also plagued by the moral responsibility of his decision to lead the world's first test of a thermonuclear bomb. In the tense hours leading up to the testing on Monday, July 16, 1945, Oppenheimer was on the verge of collapse from exhaustion. The experiment worked, causing a huge ball of fire to rise 40,000 feet in the air outside Los Alamos. Three weeks later, similar bombs were dropped in Hiroshima and Nagasaki, which effectively put an end to World War II. Exhausted by his ordeal and falling into a deep depression, Oppenheimer resigned from his post as director of the Atomic Energy Commission (AEC) soon afterward. In his parting speech, he emphasized both the "peril" and "hope" of atomic energy by advocating for scientific openness as the key to world unity:

Today that pride must be tempered with a profound concern. If atomic bombs are to be added as new weapons to the arsenals of a warring world, or to the arsenals of nations preparing for war, then the time will come when mankind will curse the names of Los Alamos and Hiroshima. (Byrd and Sherwin 2005: 329)

In the years that followed World War II, the father of the atomic bomb ironically became the most vigilant opponent of nuclear arms development. First, Oppenheimer formed a new organization called the Association of Los Alamos Scientists (ALAS) and produced a document that frankly stated the dangers of an arms race and "the impossibility of any defense against the atomic bomb in future wars" (324). In the four years following World War II, the U.S. nuclear arsenal expanded to more than one hundred atomic bombs and became the anchor of American national security during the Cold War. Unlike the thermonuclear bomb used in Hiroshima, which packed an explosive yield of 15,000 tons of TNT, the hydrogen bomb (called the Super) was developed with the explosive force of 100 million tons of TNT (422). In 1950, Oppenheimer's petition to discourage the Truman administration from continuing to build these "genocidal" weapons was flatly denied. The situation was exacerbated by Lewis Strauss's appointment as Eisenhower's atomic energy adviser in 1953: Strauss began a vicious campaign to destroy Oppenheimer's reputation by accusing him of an alliance with the Communist Party. This led to a lengthy trial in 1954, featuring FBI files that traced Oppenheimer's connection with the Communist Party (CPUSA) back to the early 1940s and including unfavorable testimonies of fellow scientists at Los Alamos. In the end, Oppenheimer lost his case. Yet his popularity in America and abroad soared as he came to be seen as the most prominent victim and political pariah during the McCarthyite anti-communist hysteria that swept the nation. Although he was excommunicated from government circles, Oppenheimer became a symbol to liberals of everything that was wrong with the Republican Party. In the early 1960s when the Democrats assumed power in Washington, the Kennedy administration awarded Oppenheimer the Enrico Fermi Award for his service in the area of political rehabilitation (575). Until his death from throat cancer in 1967, he worked tirelessly to promote causes that brought ethical considerations to the use of nuclear weapons. Oppenheimer has subsequently been mythologized in American history by many biographers as a complex but ultimately defeated man; throughout the remaining years of his life, he struggled with his public identity as the one responsible for bringing about the nuclear age. Perhaps for this reason, biographers Kai Byrd and Martin Sherwin equate him with the mythological figure of Prometheus. Gerald Finley, who premiered the role of Oppenheimer, however, follows Adams in comparing Oppenheimer to Faust: "Faust is the obvious connection – the craving for knowledge and the cruelty of having that knowledge, if you like, and the punishment [for] having that knowledge" (quoted in Ross 2005).

In constructing the operatic narrative, however, Adams did not think that Oppenheimer's characterization as Faust "American" enough, and emphasized that his operas have always been about "the American experience":

I wanted to probe the national psyche, be it the market economy vs. social welfare, which is what *Nixon in China* is about, or the gross misunderstanding about the rest of the world, which is what *Death of Klinghoffer* is all about, and on and on. But I felt that this was a heroic story and that Aristotle says that a tragic character should be a person of noble standing and I thought that Oppenheimer, indeed, filled that role. And so, right off, I knew that I had a great story. (quoted in Sellars 2007)

Thus it was important for Adams and Sellars to portray the mercurial personality, energy, and genius of this more cultivated and idealistic Oppenheimer during the time of his greatest crisis in 1945. Reading Oppenheimer's letters revealed to them the artistic mind he possessed, unrivaled by any other scientific luminaries (even Einstein); not only did Oppenheimer read and quote from the Bhagavad Gita in its original Sanskrit, he and Kitty exchanged "coded signals" to each other based on lines from Baudelaire's poems (May 2006: 223–34). In the anxious hours leading to the countdown, it was rumored that Oppenheimer calmed his nerves by reading from his tattered copy of Baudelaire's *Les Fleurs du Mal* (Adams 2008). Adams and Sellars wanted to capture his scientific brilliance vis-à-vis his artistic sensibilities.

Dramaturgical Structure: Refracted References and Faust

Sellars wished to expand the spatiotemporal experience of time through the medium of opera in more than one sense: "What happens in opera is that it exists across time" (quoted in May 2006: 242). To this end, his production begins and ends with documentary film footage from World War II, framing the entire opera in which Oppenheimer and his team of scientists, his family, and military officials await the countdown over the course of forty-eight hours. Interspersed between dialogues are poetic texts that deflect and mirror the main characters' moral struggles in dealing with the anticipated consequences of the atomic explosion. Since its premiere by the San Francisco Opera in 2005, different versions of Sellars's production of *Doctor Atomic* have been staged in Chicago and Amsterdam in 2007 and in Atlanta and New York in 2008. Except for Penny Woolcock's staging for the Metropolitan Opera production in 2008 (to be discussed below), all these productions have used Sellars's original staging.

In the Lyric Opera of Chicago symposium (preceding the opera performances), Adams and Sellars commented on how they purposefully built in multiple historical and aesthetic points of view that would emerge and collide with one another. These included influences of the European avant-garde, surrealism, the World Pantheist Movement (WPM), cultural interaction with Native Americans, the repressed roles of women, and so forth (Sellars 2007). It is as if the minimalist rhythm provided the "glue" to maintain continuity, while the characters on stage oscillated between ontological and subjective realms of time. In turn, listening viewers are challenged to disentangle the discordant fragments – a nexus of cultural, political, and aesthetic ideals, as embedded in Sellars's libretto – and comprehend their meaningful interaction.[4] To this end, he gathered together disparate texts: fragments of poetry, a sonnet, a popular book on the atomic bomb from the '40s, declassified government documents, and dialogues taken from memoirs to form a seemingly continuous whole. The textual sources within each scene can be summarized as follows:

- The military workers sing from *The Atomic Bomb for Military Purposes* and the scientists' sung dialogues are based on declassified government documents (Act I, scene 1).
- Kitty sings from Muriel Rukeyser's "Three Sides of a Coin" and "The Motive of All of It" and Oppenheimer from Charles Baudelaire's "A Hemisphere in Tresses" (Act II, scene 2).
- Leslie Groves sings from a memoir entitled *Now It Can Be Told*; Oppenheimer's closing aria is based on John Donne, "Batter my heart, three person'd God . . ." (Act II, scene 3).
- Kitty sings from Rukeyser's "Easter Eve 1945" and Pasqualita sings "The Cloud-flower," a lullaby of Tewa Indian origin (Act II/scene 2).
- Kitty and Pasqualita sing from Rukeyser's "Seventh Elegy. Dream-Singing Elegy" (Act II, scene 2).
- Kitty and Pasqualita sing from Rukeyser's "Seventh Elegy. Dream-Singing Elegy" and "Easter Eve 1945"; the chorus sings from the Bhagavad Gita (discourse XI) (Act II, scene 3).
- The chorus continues to sing from the Bhagavad Gita, while Oppenheimer sings from Baudelaire's "benevolent demon" from the collection *Les Fleurs du Mal* (Act II, scene 4).

Paralleling strategies used by Alice Goodman in the libretto for *Nixon in China*, Sellars interjects humor between deadly serious moments, or satire in scenes where the juxtaposition of incongruous texts reveals the profound lack of communication between characters. As an example of the former, Oppenheimer and General Leslie Groves talk about how the stress of the Manhattan Project is affecting the General's waistline. Groves quips about the hardship of "the diets that were, at least in theory, intended to be followed" and goes on to tell how he meticulously calculated caloric intake of food consumed: "two brownies, two hundred calories, and on September fifteenth, three pieces of choc'late cake. . . ." This scene offers comic relief to scene 3 of Act I, which concludes with Oppenheimer's gripping "lament" aria based on John Donne's sonnet, "Batter my heart. . . ." An example of the characters ignoring the meaning of each other's words can be found in Act II, scene 2, where General Groves expresses severe doubt about the testing, while Oppenheimer waxes poetic about relative vs. absolute time, and the Tewa Indian servant, Pasqualita, recites Rukeyser's mystical poetry about "bringing back the dead."[5]

The historical dimension of the operatic narrative is emphasized most vividly in the opening scene. Oppenheimer, who has just returned from Washington, conveys his abiding conviction of leaving "political" decisions up to "the best men in Washington":

> I think it is improper for a scientist to use his prestige as a platform for political pronouncements. The nation's fate should be left in the hands of the best men in Washington. They have the information which we do not possess.

In a rather callous manner, Oppenheimer dismisses Edward Teller's reservations in conducting the testing and Robert Wilson's wish to organize a petition against using the atomic bomb without giving Japan sufficient warning. He proceeds to tell the group of scientists the civilian targets for dropping the bomb, naming the cities in Japan one by one, with an air of calculated objectivity.

The women in the domestic sphere contend with the broader sociocultural implications of the atomic bomb, speaking in poetic and metaphorical terms. In this respect, Adams intended Kitty Oppenheimer and her Tewa maid, Pasqualita, to represent the concept of the "eternal feminine" (das ewig-Weibliche) from Goethe's *Faust* (May 2006: 228). Their prophetic voices contrast and complement the male scientists' preoccupation with objective speculations about the success or failure of the testing, instead taking into account the moral compass of the experiment at hand. Adams comments on Kitty: "she carries a deep moral awareness of the consequences of what is being done . . . an awareness that apparently only came to the men much later" (228). Kitty's innocence, vulnerability, and pain are revealed in the two poems by Muriel Rukeyser that form the textual source of her dialogue with Oppenheimer in the bedroom scene (Act I, scene 2):

> Am I in your light? No, go on reading
> (the hackneyed light of evening quarrelling with the bulbs;
> the book's bent rectangle solid on your knees)
> only my fingers in your hair, only my eyes
> splitting the skull to tickle your brain with love
> in a slow caress blurring the mind, (. . . .) Love, am I in your light?
> [Rukeyser, "Three Sides of a Coin"]

The poem captures Kitty's playful spirit as she teases Oppenheimer and his obsession with his work at the end of the day. Light carries two meanings here: it is, on the one hand, the material source that is essential for growth of all living things; it refers metaphorically, on the other hand, to "being" in the presence of a loved one. Like the "hackneyed" light bulb, the poet feels neglected, taken for granted by her loved on. It is as if she asks: "is my presence (my belief system) interfering with your 'rational' light?" The wistfully playful mood in "Three Sides of a Coin" is contrasted by the second poem she sings when Oppenheimer abandons her to return to work in the middle of the night:

Kitty:	The motive of all of it was loneliness,
	All the panic encounters and despair
	Were bred in fear of the lost night, apart,
	Outlined by pain, alone. Promiscuous
	As mercy. Fear – led and led again to fear
	At evening toward the cave where part fire, part
	Pity lived in that voluptuousness
	To end one and begin another loneliness.
	This is the most intolerable motive: this
Oppenheimer/Kitty:	Must be given back to life again,

>   Made superhuman, *made human,* out of pain
>   Turned to the personal, the pure release:
>   *The rings of Plato and Homer's golden chain*
>   Or Lenin with his cry of Dare We Win (. . . .)
> [Rukeyser, "The Motive of All of It" (my emphasis italicized)]

Adams cleverly sets Rukeyser's poem to emphasize the rift between Kitty and Oppenheimer. Kitty sings the first ten lines of this poem, which identifies the cycle of loneliness that consumes her. Then Adams divides the last four lines into a musical duet between Kitty and Oppenheimer. While Kitty sings about how the attributes of panic, loneliness, and pain make her human, Oppenheimer, intoxicated with the power to change the world, interjects his "superhuman" aspirations by alluding to "the rings of Plato and Homer's golden chain" (my emphasis in italics). Plato's ring refers to the corruptibility of men in the face of power, while Homer's golden chain refers to superhuman power passed on from one generation to another.[6] This opposition between "human" and "superhuman" becomes underscored in their musical dialogue, marking the couple's opposing perspectives on the ordeal involving the atomic bomb. This is the only passage where the poetic source is divided in this way so as to amplify the "disconnect" between the scientist and his melancholic (and alcoholic) wife.

Pasqualita's role in the opera receives the most enigmatic treatment. As a character, she is profoundly connected to nature and the earthly domain. While her voice is heard only through the recitation of the Tewa Indian lullaby and a verse or two from Rukeyser, she gives voice to the cosmic force of nature through her ties to her ancestral land. Throughout Act II, Pasqualita sings verses from "The Cloud-flower" lullaby in the form of a musical refrain, alternating with Kitty's verse taken from Rukeyser's "Seventh Elegy. Dream-Singing Elegy" (1949) that convey a grim view of war[7]:

Kitty:	To the farthest west, the sea and the striped country
	And deep in the camps among the wounded cities
	Half-world over, the waking dreams of night
	Outrange the horrors. Past fierce and tossing skies
	The rare desires shine in constellation.
	I hear your cries, you little voices of children
	Swaying wild, night lost, in black fields calling
	I hear you as the seething dreams arrive
	Over the sea and past the flaming mountains.
Pasqualita:	In the west the cloud-flower blossoms,
	And now the lightning flashes,
	And now the thunder clashes,
	And now the rain comes down!
	A-a-aha,a-a-aha, my little one.
	In the south the cloud-flower blossoms,
	And now the lightning flashes,
	And now the thunder clashes,
	And now the rain comes down!

The prophetic voices of these women alternate with the men's speculations about the destructive power of the "Gadget" (Oppenheimer's nickname for the atomic bomb). It is only at the end that the individual differences become subsumed by the collective burden shared by all – across gender, generational, and racial divides – as everyone stares out into the vast space where the bomb goes off.

Arguably, the turn to the mythological occurs when the characters appeal to supernatural forces to deal with their inner turmoil. In subsequent scenes from Act I, Oppenheimer's attitude begins to shift. Toward the end of Act I, he makes a painful plea to God by reciting John Donne's "Holy Sonnet XIV." According to sources, Oppenheimer chose the name "Trinity" to refer to the testing site for the world's first atomic weapon in Alamogordo, located about thirty-five miles east of Socorro, New Mexico. Later in his life Oppenheimer claimed that it was Donne's sonnet, containing the lines "Batter my heart, three person'd God," which led him to name the testing site Trinity.[8] In Act II, the reference shifts from the Christian God to the gods and the central warrior associated with the Bhagavad Gita, where the initially despondent warrior Arjuna engages the god Krishna in a series of dialogues about achieving salvation and enlightenment. In the book of the eleventh discourse, Krishna transforms himself into the terrifying image of Vishnu and challenges Arjuna to battle. While the meteorologist Hubbard and General Groves fret about the stormy weather, Oppenheimer, disassociated, speaks as though he were Krishna from the Bhagavad Gita: "Arjuna, I am the cosmos revealed" (Act I, scene 3). Historically, following the Trinity test, Oppenheimer delivered a speech in which he claimed that he "became death, the shatterer of worlds" (Kelly 2006: 58). In the introduction to her definitive English translation, Laurie L. Patton argues that the central message of the Bhagavad Gita lies in Krishna's way of showing Arjuna how to act "without clinging to the consequences" of his action (2008: xx). Arjuna, who cannot bear the thought of killing his own kinsmen, turns to Krishna for the discovery of his own *dharma* or ethical conduct, which will bring him in greater harmony with the divine: that is, to fight wrongs that have been done, even by his own family. It is likely that Oppenheimer appeals to Krishna as a way of justifying his own conduct in bringing about mass destruction for the benefit of a (presumably) higher cause. The mythological dimension reaches its apex in the moment before the countdown, when the chorus collectively expresses its fear of the inevitable destruction by identifying with Arjuna's fear of Vishnu in the choral number, "At the Sight of This."

The continual references made to light and luminescence call attention to the figure of Prometheus in Greek mythology. In Aeschylus's version, Prometheus steals fire from Zeus and passes it on to humans, along with other arts of civilization, for which he receives eternal punishment.[9] Prometheus is seen as a benefactor for mortals by fighting against Zeus's tyranny and the god's attempt to wipe out the human race. However, Sellars invokes these "shadow" representations without privileging one over the other. Furthermore, the metaphor of light carries other references in the context of *Doctor Atomic*; Oppenheimer alludes to luminescence as if he were blinded by the splendor of the atomic bomb, while Kitty's reference to "light" (Act I, scene 2) indexes her importance in Oppenheimer's life as wife and mother. She repeatedly calls on him for affirmation as she poses the question "am I in your light?" but to no avail. Later, as the countdown scene approaches, Oppenheimer makes a passing pronouncement, "I am light" (Act II, scene 3), as he becomes increasingly delusional; by this time, he is unable to separate his personal vision from the reality of the pending destruction.

Adams attributes the doomsday scenario to American culture in the late '40s and the early '50s–popular science fiction movies with a typical plot that involves "a nuclear explosion in the desert – Nevada perhaps" (May 2006: 226). Certainly, there are numerous science fiction films that are based on a doomsday scenario from this era in American history.[10] In his study of the opera, Maarten Nellestijn argues that *Doctor Atomic* expresses a distrust of nuclear weaponry refracted through the imaginary lens of the 1960s genre of nuclear monster films; he compares the opera's narrative to the typical plot of these films: "a deserted location with a nuclear explosion, nature taking revenge in the form of an angered or mutated monster of some kind, alarmed and/or curious scientists accompanied by their beautiful female assistants, and natural hindrances seemingly preventing the monster's destruction" (2011: 10).

To sum up, the libretto for *Doctor Atomic* is structured so that the main characters speak through the voice of a historical or mythological Other. Notably, Oppenheimer maps onto Goethe's Faust and Kitty embodies Goethe's concept of "ewig-Weibliche." Adams admits a backdoor reference to Thomas Mann's *Doctor Faustus* (1947), a novel that features a German composer who gambles with his life in order to strive for artistic creativity of the highest order. Although the story conspicuously lacks the figure of Mephistopheles, Oppenheimer addresses the Gadget (metonymically) as the "devil" from time to time: he announces to the other scientists that "we are bedeviled by faulty detonators" (Act I, scene 1) and before the final countdown, he looks straight up at the Gadget and says "what a benevolent demon" (Act II, scene 3). At other times, Oppenheimer alludes to the bomb as Vishnu and identifies himself with Arjuna from the Bhagavad Gita. There are still other refracted references that complicate the agential role of Oppenheimer. Nonetheless, his role is mercurial in the sense that he becomes increasingly divided in his references to the mythic and historical Others in the narrative progression: Prometheus (as a giver of light), Vishnu (as the god of protection from the Bhagavad Gita), Baudelaire (in his unleashing of romantic yearning), and John Donne (in his expression of divine torment). Similarly, while Adams conceived the women (Kitty and Pasqualita) as possessing feminine virtues, mirroring Goethe's women at the end of *Faust,* Kitty possesses a degree of clairvoyance combined with powerlessness that conjures up the image of Cassandra, the mythological Greek seer whose prophecies no one believes because of the curse placed on her by Apollo. The women also sing lines from poetry by Rukeyser, and the voice of an agonized romantic, seeking fulfillment through identification with political and spiritual ideals, is projected through them. In the approach to the countdown, the objective and pragmatic voices of the scientists openly collide with the subjective pleas of the women and servants.

Throughout Act II, confusion and chaos reign as the different voices collide and merge. Overall, these refracted textual sources articulate the transference of dramatic opposition from the level of individual strife (e.g., Oppenheimer, Wilson, Kitty) to that of cosmic/mythological strife (e.g., Arjuna and Vishnu, Faust, Cassandra), with consequences to be examined below.

Post-minimalist Music as Marker of Time

Let us now turn to the role of music in marking time and articulating the shift from the historical to the mythological dimension of the operatic narrative. Adams's post-minimalist style has been characterized as "maximally minimal"; I understand this oxymoronic description to mean that while a ubiquitous pulse drives Adams's music and renders it minimal, the music also alludes to stylistic conventions from the past.[11] In his analysis of *Nixon in China,* William Guerin distinguishes between the "epic" and "comic" minimalist styles based on Adams's treatment of tempo, harmony, timbre, and register, in addition to stylistic conventions.[12] In the opening scene, where Chinese officials anxiously await Nixon's arrival, the chorus delivers a heroic recitation of Maoist text in the epic style, while Nixon's "News" aria uncannily mimics Figaro's aria from Mozart's *Marriage of Figaro* in the comic style. Similarly, a "lament" bass accompanies the tenor's solo "Daughter of Zion" in *Death of Klinghoffer.* Compared to these earlier operas, Adams utilizes a wider range of musical procedures to vary the temporal flow of *Doctor Atomic* by altering the tempo via systematic use of accelerando or decelerando, inserting pauses between sections, and so forth. Moreover, he utilizes a sectional form (ABAB or AAB) for the main solo arias or choral numbers, distinguishing these dramatic moments from the free, episodic textures based on repetition of a pulse. Given the range of musical styles and procedures invoked, I postulate that Adams's music for *Doctor Atomic* functions within a broad continuum that moves beyond the affective qualities associated with minimalistic repetition. With respect to their signifying potential, these procedures can be categorized into a continuum that ranges from non-referential to referential: "filler" music, proto-topics, topics, stylized quotation, and electronic collage, as shown in figure 4.1.

"Filler" music refers to a long stretch of music based on the repetition of a steady pulse (ostinato) that is minimally referential; the tempo and rhythmic texture of the ostinato may convey a particular mood, but it does not carry a fixed reference with respect to the sung text. Proto-topics, according to Raymond Monelle (2000: 16), are emergent musical topics that resemble an object (e.g., sounds that simulate a locomotive in Honegger's *Pacific 231*), and portray phenomena for which *no* expressive conventions exist. Topics, on the other hand, belong to established musical conventions (e.g., march, waltz, fanfare, lament bass) within the western canon. Stylized quotations include a form of borrowing where the composer models a particular musical style that is identifiable by a musically literate audience. Like topics, stylized quotation relies heavily on established convention to evoke a particular mood or atmosphere; for example, Adams quotes

| "Filler" music / Proto-topic / Topic / Stylized Quotation / Electronic Collage |

Non-referential   ◄- - - - - - - - - - - - - - - -►   *Referential*

Figure 4.1. Adams's Musical Procedures in *Doctor Atomic*

Wagner's *Tristan* chord in *Doctor Atomic* as a signifier of yearning and desire. Lastly, electronic sounds (sampled or not) are maximally referential in their literal allusion; for example, the sounds that simulate thunderstorm or bomb explosion at the end cannot be mistaken for anything other than that. As one develops a schematic understanding of how these musical procedures shape the opera's narrative trajectory, more subtle intertextual connections emerge (to be explored below).

The narrative of *Doctor Atomic* is about the characters' anticipation of the destruction wrought by the thermonuclear bomb. From this perspective, the different musical procedures Adams deploys to build up tension leading up to the countdown of the test explosion are interpretable in terms of Stravinsky's concepts of "ontological" and "psychological" time. In *Poetics of Music*, Stravinsky comments on these oppositional markers of musical time as follows:

> Mr. [Pierre] Souvtchinsky thus presents us with two kinds of music: one which evolves parallel to the process of ontological time, embracing and penetrating it, inducing in the mind of the listener a feeling of euphoria and, to speak, of "dynamic calm." The other kind runs ahead of, or counter, to this process. It is not self-contained in each momentary tonal unit. It dislocates the centers of attraction and gravity and sets itself up in the unstable; and this fact makes it particularly adaptable to the translation of the composer's emotive impulses. All music in which the will to expression is dominant belongs to the second type. (2000: 31)

Stravinsky proceeds to define music that represents ontological time as dominated by "the principle of similarity" while that which marks psychological time as tending to "proceed by contrast" (31). In practice, since "similarity" and "contrast" are relative rather than fixed perceptual terms, the criteria for distinguishing one from the other depends entirely on context. In *Doctor Atomic,* music that marks psychological time tends to be dominated by "emotive impulses" or "the will to expression" in Stravinsky's words. In general, Adams foregrounds the use of musical topics (e.g., the *pianto* topic) and stylized quotations for dramatic situations that amplify the psychological experiences of characters, while "filler" and proto-topical music (e.g., the "clock" motive) mark passing of time within a seemingly "unmediated" present.[13]

In this respect, Middleton's classification of "musematic" and "discursive" strategies of repetition offers a useful means for distinguishing formal processes deployed by Adams: "musematic" refers to the unvaried type of repetition (e.g., riff) which combines with other textures to form an episodic section, while "discursive" refers to the repetition of longer units – at least a phrase in length – that belongs to a section within a self-contained form (e.g., AAB or ABAB) (1990: 269).[14] In fact, repetition in *Doctor Atomic* manifests itself in terms of a rhythmic ostinato, which undergoes change in texture over time while maintaining the constancy of pulse (an instance of the "musematic"); the ostinato marks chronometric time in the same way we experience the ticking of the clock. In comparison, when solo arias and ensemble numbers constitute longer, syntactically more complex units that can be organized hierarchically in strophic or ritornello forms, they exemplify "discursive" music in Middleton's sense, and provide psychological markers of time.

In the musical unfolding of *Doctor Atomic,* however, ontological and psychological markers of time are frequently blurred through layering or juxtaposing different musical strands. For example, "filler" music consists of a reiterative pulse or non-thematic scalar pattern and is minimally referential. It can, however, assume a proto-topical function, depending on the level of iconicity or resemblance to the natural object invoked, and call attention to the characters' psychological awareness; for example, micropolyphonic texture (reminiscent of Ligeti's *Atmosphères*) accompanies the scene that describes the luminescence of the anticipated explosion, as imagined by Oppenheimer. Likewise, electronic sounds (*musique concrète*) function as non-diegetic sound sources that index an event or action (e.g., sounds of airplane taking off, children's cries, and gunshots) yet carry psychological resonances through Sellars's montage technique. In the opening documentary film from World War II, an electronic collage of mechanical sounds accompanies images of American workers manufacturing weapons. When it segues to a distorted snippet of Jo Stafford singing "The Things We Did Last Summer," the filmic images shift to those of war casualties, and the orchestral overture enters by blaring out dissonant chords over a pounding bass line (Ross 2005). This audio-visual synchronization – an abrupt shift from the electronic collage that accompanies images of manufacturing of machines to the diegetic orchestral sounds that accompany human bodies in combat during World War II – foregrounds live, animated sounds to underscore the human casualties of war.

Conversely, established musical topics such as *pianto* (lament), fanfare, march, waltz and stylized quotation foreground dramatic contrasts in emotion and mood and mark psychological time, yet are merged with signifiers that mark ontological states of being. Adams deploys style quotations, appropriating the style of orchestration, texture, scale, linear intervallic pattern, and/or signature chords from familiar compositional styles, with varying degrees of clarity: the lament topic accompanies Oppenheimer's aria based on Donne's sonnet to showcase his moral struggle at the close of Act I; a fanfare topic accompanies the chorus's announcement of the atomic bomb manual and reappears in various guises to provide commentary to the sung text. While the descending stepwise pattern in the choral number signifies the military workers' physical restlessness, the triplet subdivision of the pulse in the lament aria signifies the irregular beating of Oppenheimer's heart. In what follows, I will explain how these musical procedures shape the narrative trajectory of Sellars's "charged" time, brought on by the gradual interpenetration of the two markers of time leading up to the countdown.

The Roles of Proto-topics and Topics

The proto-topical motives are important in this opera for their iconicity and power of suggestiveness. For example, the opera proper begins with a choral number that announces the testing of the atomic bomb to be carried out. As the chorus, clad in army uniform, delivers a declamatory "chorale" in rhythmic unison, it is accompanied by an ostinato motive played by strings, comprised of a Phrygian stepwise descent from E3 to E2; this motive cyclically repeats with the addition of different chromatic inflections, creating a sense of urgency. Brass and percussion instruments enter with a "fanfare" topic that adds polyrhythmic tension ($\frac{5}{8}$) against the $\frac{2}{2}$ meter of the primary texture layer established by the stepwise ostinato.[15] The descending stepwise motive found in this opening choral passage iconically suggests the physical restlessness of those who are involved at the testing site on the one hand, and indexes the fear and anxiety shared by those who await the showdown on the other. Such sentiments are captured in the first line of the text sung by the chorus (Act I, scene 1):

> The end of June 1945 finds us expecting from day to day to hear of the explosion of the first atomic bomb devised by man. . . . A weapon has been developed that is potentially destructive beyond the wildest nightmares of the imagination.

These words, taken from a small book entitled *The Atomic Energy for Military Purposes* (1945), speculate on the destructive effects of the thermonuclear bomb.[16] Adams casts the musical setting of this text in binary form (ABAB), in which the opening section features the "step" motive and the contrasting second section introduces what I will refer to as the "clock" motive (DVD #1: 06'25"). As shown in example 4.1, the "step" motive, outlining now a descending whole-tone scale, winds down in the strings at m.53, followed by the harp, oboe, and English horn entering in C major with a staccato eighth-note motive that imitates the "ticking" of the clock, while the horn presents a muted "military" march, which is metrically aligned with the "clock" motive but not with the choral entry. The C major triad gently clashes with A♭ major, as the horns project the root and third of both chords and the chorus superimposes one triad over the other. Against this harmonic backdrop, the chorus continues to sing about the yet unknown effect of this bomb and the anticipated testing of this bomb at the Trinity site. The "clock" motive generates a heightened signification in the sense that it *brackets* the ontological passing of time in the context of musical topics that mark psychological time.

Oppenheimer famously referred to the atomic bomb as the Gadget and as if to showcase it as an object of fascination and terror, the simulated bomb (around ten feet in diameter) is hung from the center of the stage. Following Oppenheimer and Edward Teller's initial dialogue, the orchestral timbres shift to

Example 4.1. Opening Chorus (reduced score, Act 1, scene 1)

a soft and scintillating combination of percussion (glockenspiel, triangles, crotales, harp and celesta) based on an octatonic scale on C (with extraneous notes of D and F). As shown in example 4.2, the ethereal, floating texture based on this timbral combination emerges as the proto-topic that signifies the mysterious property of plutonium; the upward arpeggiation and rhythmically heterogeneous layering characterize the material basis of the chemical compound prior to undergoing nuclear fission (DVD #1: 11'20"). While the contrabass sustains C, the upper strings collectively sustain a diatonic cluster of chords with tremolo. After a couple of measures, the female chorus enters with a scientific description of the plutonium core, singing in unison at first, then in two- or four-part harmony.

Wherever this timbral combination recurs, it indexes – by virtue of its ethereal, otherworldly quality – the mysterious property of the chemical compound that makes up the bomb. In scene 3 of Act I, for example, the same octatonic-based texture reappears in the harp and celesta, accompanying the scene where Captain James Nolan sings about the metabolism of the chemical compound and how it is known to cause bone cancer. In the final countdown scene, this material is extended into an instrumental postlude that slowly accelerates over time and segues into the electronic simulation of the bomb explosion. At the end, the celesta and harp repeat chords that provide an eerie backdrop for the disembodied voice of a Japanese female who asks for water. Thus, this texture is proto-topical in the sense that it speaks to "superhuman" attributes and embodies an

Example 4.2. The "Plutonium" Motives (Act I/scene 1, mm.221–226)

aura of mystery that transcends human capacity for comprehension. While it is not related to an established topic within the art music tradition, it is very likely that Adams refers to the American science fiction television dramas that utilize similar types of sound (e.g., augmented triad or octatonic scale) to convey the mystery of the unknown.

Established topics, in comparison, are used to showcase important dramatic turning points in the opera. The *pianto* topic and "lament" bass form the basis of an aria sung by Oppenheimer at the end of Act I, which signals the transvaluative moment when the apparently callous scientist sheds his façade and confronts his inner self. The mise-en-scène for the third scene returns to the testing site at Alamogordo, where scientists quibble over the inclement weather conditions (a lightning storm), which make carrying out the experiment far more unpredictable than they had anticipated, and potentially disastrous. A distorted march topic is heard, with snare drum, timpani, and string pizzicatos, as Captain Nolan reports to Oppenheimer of scientists who have become "hysterical and had to be removed." Growing impatient with the scientists, Colonel Groves announces that he will make his own weather predictions. Against the flashes of light that appear in counterpoint with the polymetric interlude, the Gadget is mounted onto a scaffold in the center of stage. In the final scene in Act I, where Oppenheimer is left alone with the Gadget, he confronts his moral dilemma in carrying out the experiment for the first time. Following an agitated instrumental ritornello, he breaks out into a soulful aria. Its text is John Donne's "Holy Sonnet XIV":

Batter my heart, three person'd God; for you
As yet knock, breathe, and seek to mend;
That I may rise and stand, o'erthrow me, and bend
Your force, to break, blow, burn and make me new.
I, like a usurped town, to another due,
Labour to admit you, but Oh, to no end.
Reason, your viceroy in me, me should defend,
But is captived, and proves weak or untrue.
Yet dearly I love you, and would be loved fain,
But am betroth'd unto your enemy:
Divorce me, untie, or break that knot again,
Take me to you, imprison me, for I,
Except you enthrall me, never shall be free,
Nor ever chaste, except you ravish me.

To Adams, this poem speaks of an "almost unbearable self-awareness, an ago-nistic struggle between good and evil, darkness and light" (May 2006: 224). Con-trary to his exterior demeanor, this aria points to Oppenheimer's private admis-sion of doubt and guilt over what is yet to come. He directs his lament to God because he has come to view the Gadget as a symbol of eternal damnation. The sonnet is "an expression of the keenest spiritual pain, a beseeching, an appeal to God that He physically beat and batter the speaker in order that his divided self might rise up and be made whole again" (Adams 2008: 3). Adams sets it in D minor, a key that is emblematic of suffering and death in the canon of Western art music (e.g., Mozart's *Requiem*).

In the featured aria, Donne's sonnet is set to a modified binary form (ABAB'CA), which alternates between an instrumental ritornello and solo vo-cal entry (DVD #1: 1:13'04").[17] The instrumental ritornello (A) is based on a poly-rhythmic layer of motives – clarinets, flutes, trumpets, and trombones maintain a steady eighth-note subdivision in $^{12}_8$ meter against the syncopated rhythms in $^4_4$ meter in the remaining instruments, as illustrated in example 4.3a. The dia-tonic cluster that makes up each layer expands in range both melodically and harmonically, but not in rhythmic synchrony; note how the chordal cluster os-cillates back and forth between a minor third (D-F) and a major second (D-E) in the oboes/clarinets and horns against the triplet division of the beat in the flutes and trumpets. The irregularity of the internal rhythmic grouping obscures the perception of downbeat. Over the course of thirty-five measures, the texture ex-pands to approximately ten polyrhythmic layers involving fourteen instruments. The rhythmic instability of the composite effect generates a sense of urgency, as if it outwardly manifesting the irregular "beating" of Oppenheimer's own heart. In this sense the instrumental ritornello may be interpreted as proto-topical in ex-pressing Oppenheimer's psychosomatic state of turmoil.

The tension is released only at the point when Oppenheimer begins to sing the lament aria, in which the vocal melody features a *pianto* topic accompanied by bass descent (albeit scattered in register), as shown in the second system of ex-ample 4.3b. The melodic apex on F4 is reached at the beginning of the consequent

a. Ritornello

b. Aria

Example 4.3a/b. Oppenheimer's Aria (reduced score, Act 1/scene 3) phrase (m.808), which then winds downward in stepwise motion using dotted rhythms. The most dramatic and expressive leap occurs when the voice thrusts itself upward from D3 to C♯4 in m.811, on the phrase "seek to mend." Oppenheimer's emotional cries are conveyed by the lament bass, the oscillating semitonal motion, and the melodic descent of the vocal phrase on "knock, breathe, knock, breathe . . ." intensified by the rhythmic acceleration in m.808.[18] The dotted rhythm and the chain of "sigh" motives convey the idea of being physically and emotionally "battered."

This period repeats for the next stanza (using the first line as a refrain) and builds the melodic apex to G4 on "bend Your force"; the descending chain of "sigh" motives now accompany the words "break, blow, break, blow, burn and make me new." The hypermetric irregularity of the antecedent phrase (moving from $\frac{2}{4}$, $\frac{3}{4}$, to $\frac{4}{4}$ meter) is counterbalanced by the regularity of the consequent phrase with the intensification of the dotted rhythm in the penultimate measure. The accompaniment limps along without providing a secure foundation in the bass voice. Although not shown here, with each repetition, both the instrumental (A) and vocal (B) sections acquire greater complexity with respect to texture and dramatic intensity. The intensity reaches its peak in the last stanza of the vocal entry (section C), when the vocal rhythm becomes less steady and more agitated, with sixteenth-note flourishes used on the musical phrase that accompanies the text "Take me to you, imprison me, for I, except you enthrall me, never shall be free." When the instrumental ritornello is heard for the last time, Oppenheimer walks into the scaffold and weakly points his finger at the bomb in the air as if to make his pact with the "devil" for good.[19]

While Adams deploys the pianto topic to express torment in a rather straightforward manner, his deployment of the fanfare topic suggests satire or irony through the negation of its conventional signifier. Historically, the fanfare topic emerged in France, characterized by a brilliant and uplifting music assigned to trumpet and drums that signifies heroic idealism in military contexts (Monelle 2000: 34). Yet in *Doctor Atomic*, the fanfare topic is typically deployed in a manner that suggests the opposite inflection. For example, when the pacifist, Robert Wilson, makes a bold speech about the "welfare of the human race" in Act I, a rhythmically distorted horn fanfare (F-C) accompanies his singing, as if underscoring the futility of his humanitarian plea. Similarly, a trumpet fanfare is sounded after Kitty's monologue on "peace" before the final countdown in Act II in an eerily ironic manner.

Two other examples illustrate Adams's techniques for distorting the fanfare topic to make ironic commentary on the situation at hand. In Act I, scene 2, Kitty is left alone to deal with her despair and loneliness while Oppenheimer leaves for work in the middle of the night. As illustrated under example 4.4, a piccolo trumpet plays an elegiac "fanfare" melody off stage as Kitty sings from Rukeyser's poem about "the most intolerable motive" and pain that make her "human" (DVD #1: 46'14"). Oblivious to her feelings, Oppenheimer interjects by singing about the "superhuman" deeds that need to be accomplished. Against this oddly divided recitation of Rukeyser's poem, the trumpet melody delivers a fan-

Example 4.4. Kitty and Robert's Duet (Act I/sc.2, mm.283–286)

fare topic that sounds as if it has sputtered out of control: while its upward melodic contour, arriving at the apex on D♭, mimics Oppenheimer's vocal contour, it is rhythmically out of whack in the sense that it does not maintain a steady beat nor organize itself into a coherent phrase. While their singing is initially unified through the prolongation of B♭ minor pentatonic (B♭-D♭-E♭-F-A♭), Oppenheimer begins to veer off from the scale by the fourth bar, and their melodic interaction becomes increasingly more discordant. Kitty, not being able to reconcile her husband's idea of waging war "as a way to make peace," as opposed to her own horrifying vision of the aftermath of war, follows their duet with a "mad" solo aria. Her coloratura flourishes are accompanied by triplet figurations played pizzicato by the strings, as she sings:

Our conflicts carry creation and its guilt, ah –
these years' great arms are full of death and flowers.
A world is to be fought for, sung, and built.
Love must imagine the world.

In this moment she assumes the role of Cassandra in Greek mythology, the daughter of King Priam of Troy who was endowed with the power of prophecy, yet cursed so that no one would believe her. Cassandra foresaw the destruction of Troy, but was unable to act on it and reverse the fate of her fellow citizens. Kitty – like Cassandra – goes mad when she predicts the path of destruction the atomic bomb will bring about, but is helpless in putting a stop to it.

Later in Act II, scene 3, following Oppenheimer's decisive command to "fire [the Gadget] at five thirty," a stormy musical interlude follows. General Groves expresses his dissatisfaction with the scientists and their doubtful outlook, contemplating the idea of dismissing them once the test has been conducted. At the moment when an offstage voice announces "zero minus nineteen minutes," the

John Adams's Doctor Atomic 143

Example 4.5. Troping of Waltz and March Topics (Act II, scene 3)

musical projection of ontological time returns, prompted by the string pizzicato that marks the passing of time in triple meter (DVD #2: 45′12″). As Oppenheimer continues to speak in metaphor (describing himself as "demonic"), Groves contends with the dismissal of such scientists in this three-part ensemble passage where neither party listens to the other:

> Oppenheimer: O yes, time has returned, time has returned, now Time reigns absolute . . . and with this hideous old man, the whole of his demoniac retinue has returned.
> Groves: After some publicity concerning the weapon is out, steps should be taken to sever these scientists from the program and to proceed with a gen'ral weeding out of personnel no longer needed.
> Women's chorus: Eee . . . eee . . . eee. . . .

Adams's musical setting for this scene amplifies the ironic collision between General Groves and Oppenheimer through a technique Hatten refers to as *troping*: a merging of topics or textures to create a new expressive meaning. For example, in reference to the first movement from Brahms's Third Symphony, Hatten discusses the subtle ways in which the march and waltz topics are merged and how "the marchlike element adds tropological force to the minor-mode intensification of the musette theme" (2004: 76).[20] As illustrated in example 4.5, the merging of topics subverts the patriotic tone associated with a military march; while the pizzicato motive in the strings trope the march topic with a waltz rhythm in

F major, a solo trumpet delivers a "stuttering and irregular" fanfare topic that sounds like a bugle call gone haywire. While Oppenheimer sings in rhythmically irregular $\frac{3}{4}$ meter, General Groves shouts out his order in $\frac{2}{4}$ meter. The overall musical effect is one of confusion and lack of order. This passage is immediately followed by another duet in which Oppenheimer sings about his nightmares, afflictions, rages, and neuroses, while Kitty's dreamy aria gives voice to the chieftain of the Uwe Indian tribe. Gone is the calm and callous demeanor that set Oppenheimer apart from others at the beginning of Act I.

Style Quotations and Allusions: Debussy, Wagner, Ligeti, and Orff

Through stylistic quotations and allusions to other music, which carry a higher degree of referentiality than proto-topics, Adams establishes expressive change in mood and creates a portal into the psychological and mythological dimensions of the narrative. At times, these allusions or quotations are introduced fleetingly into the musical fabric; and at other times, they are developed into a full-fledged dramatic aria or an ensemble number. As an example of the former, when Oppenheimer explains the visual luminescence of the anticipated explosion, which could rise to twenty thousand feet, the orchestra "paints" the text by introducing a micropolyphonic texture in the woodwinds in a style that recalls that of Ligeti's *Atmosphères* (DVD #1: 26'45"). A series of allusions occurs when Kitty tries to pry her husband's attention away from books in the bedroom scene (Act I, scene 2). The harp and strings slowly fill out the F-minor seventh chord as she repeatedly poses a question "Am I in your light?" with an ascending sixth interval. Bored from the lack of attention, Kitty soon recites "tick, tick" along with the Glockenspiel ostinato that signifies the passing of time. When she gives up and turns her back to him, Oppenheimer finally responds to her as the musical "ticking" of the clock quickly transforms into a lush, Debussyian orchestral texture, with a muted horn melody hovering above fluttering sextuplets played by harp and celesta (DVD #1: 37'32"). Wagner's *Tristan* chord (from *Tristan und Isolde*) is ironically quoted in this transitional passage. The chord, which symbolizes the yearning between lovers who cannot be united in the phenomenal world, accompanies Oppenheimer's one-sided awakening of desire and his subsequent recitation from Baudelaire's poetry:

> Long let me inhale, deeply, the odor of your hair, into it plunge the whole of my face,
> like a thirsty man into the water, into the water of spring, and wave it in my fingers
> like a scented handkerchief, to shake memories into the air. . . .

As Oppenheimer steeps himself in the self-absorbed dream world of Baudelaire, the musical texture swiftly changes to harp glissandi and rising and falling chromatic gestures in the woodwinds. The musical moment evokes the ethereal passage from Act II of Debussy's *Pelléas et Mélisande,* when the moonlight floods the entrance to the grotto of the dark cavern in scene 3; as Pelléas cries out "Oh . . . voici la clarté!" (Here is the light), the harp breaks out into a shimmering glissandi upward and downward as the flutes and oboes introduce a Phrygian-in-flected melody on F (F-G♭-A♭-B♭-C-D♭-E♭), accompanied by the *douce et expressif* indication. The symbolism of yearning associated with light carries over to the scene in Adams's opera where Oppenheimer immerses himself in Baudelaire's Orientalist dream world, filled with tender sentiments, which reveals the poet's longing for exotic lands far away. Yet, with the parting words "I am only eating memories," he abruptly turns away from Kitty to go back to work.

Act II of the opera is about waiting: the suspenseful hours of anticipation lead-ing up to the countdown. It is the night of July 15, and the women in Oppen-heimer's household, Kitty and her Tewa Indian maid, Pasqualita, meditate on the war, death, and the resurrection of the spirit in the compound in Los Ala-mos, located two-hundred miles from the detonation area. Meanwhile, the sci-entists have mounted the plutonium bomb in the detonation tower in spite of the severe electrical storm that has set in. Colonel Groves disregards the scientists' warnings about the storm and orders all to prepare for the detonation at 5:30 AM. As Pasqualita and Kitty's domestic helpers look over the horizon and the Gadget that hangs from the center of the stage, a slow interlude called "Rain over the San-gre de Cristos," based on the rising 5–6 sequence, unfolds in the low strings, ac-companied by bass clarinet, horns, and trombones. The chordal tremolos in the strings begin in the low register on B major triad and slowly rise in register, main-taining the linear intervallic pattern across a chromatic ascent that ranges from $B1$ to $G\sharp 3$ (see example 4.6). Notice how the triadic quality shifts from major to augmented (e.g., BM → B+) for the first four chords then the chord quality be-comes more erratic (including seventh chords) as the progression moves upward toward G♯ minor.

This is another instance of "filler" music that is proto-typical: the harmonic and rhythmic instability of the rising progression portrays the unpredictable storm that grows on the horizon. The acculturated audience may hear an inter-textual reference to Wagner's incidental music from Act I of *Die Walküre*, which employs a similar ascending sequence to suggest stormy weather; the progres-sion serves as a backdrop for Siegmund's arrival at Sieglinde's doorstep after hav-ing survived a battle. In Sellars's production, Pasqualita's gaze remains fixed on the dark blue horizon as she holds a baby and contemplates the mysterious forces of nature that govern her native land, while her mistress (Kitty) sleeps (DVD #2: 13:30). The upper voice slowly moves in staggered motion against the bass voice, creating momentary dissonances that build suspense and tension. Following an octave ascent, the process accelerates as the chords shift via a SLIDE function, whereby the third of the chord is held in common while the outer voices "slide" up by a half step.[21] An electronic soundscape of thunder, rain, and airplane noises is blended into this interlude, preparing for Pasqualita's plaintive aria in G♯ Ae-olian mode.

Stylized quotation finds its most dramatic expression when the chorus sings from the Bhagavad Gita (discourse XI) to implore the Hindu God Vishnu for pro-tection.

Example 4.6. Rising 5–6 Sequence in "Rain over the Sangre de Cristos"

A: At the sight of this, your shape stupendous,	B: When I see you Vishnu,
Full of mouths and eyes, terrible with fangs,	When I see you omnipresent,
At the sight of this, your shape stupendous,	Shouldering the sky,
All the worlds are fear struck, even just as I am.	in hues of rainbow, O, O, O,
	Master.

The chorus's collective plea to the supernatural immerses the viewer in a mythological and timeless domain. The opening choral texture is conspicuously modeled after the dramatic refrain that commences "O Fortuna" from Carl Orff's *Carmina Burana*.[22] This choral number is based on a binary form, with the A section in C minor. The text that speaks of "fate" being monstrous, changeable, and villainous from the opening number of *Carmina Burana* parallels the stupendous and terrifying image of Vishnu from the Bhagavad Gita text. Over the ostinato motive in the timpani, and accompanied by the horn's syncopated beats, the chorus sings in rhythmic unison within a tight span of a minor third, as shown in example 4.7a. The A section is contrasted by the B section, in which the texture shifts to a harmonic progression built on a chromatically descending bass guided by another 5–6 intervallic pattern, as shown in example 4.7b (DVD #2: 58'42" [A]; 1:00'13" [B]).

In the B section, the sense of the macabre is conveyed not only by the angular rhythmic diminution in the piccolo, but by the meandering progression that spirals downward without a clear tonal orientation (see example 4.7b). The alternation between the $\frac{3}{4}$ and $\frac{2}{4}$ meters demarcates the phrase into a 3+3+2 grouping and accentuates the words "Vishnu" and "omni-" (from "omnipresent") as points of arrival. Notice how the 5–6 intervallic framework dissolves in the second phrase (mm.4–6), departing from the established pattern in the first phrase by interjecting unresolved dissonances. A B♭ minor chord with an added major seventh accompanies the text on "om-ni" (m.6). Although not shown here, the third phrase that follows intensifies the chromatic descent through rhythmic diminution as it drives toward a cadence, with G9 proceeding to E♭m on "O, O, O, O, Master."

Shortly after the chorus sings their number based on the excerpt from the Bhagavad Gita, Oppenheimer embarks on yet another soliloquy, staring at the Gadget that hangs from the center of stage. As he asks himself the question, "To what benevolent demon do I owe the joy of being thus surrounded?" the electronic sine waves emanate from the bomb in response to Oppenheimer's query.

a. A section

b. B section

Example 4.7a/b. The Choral Number "At the Sight of This"(Act II/scene 3)

Facing. Example 4.8a/b. Polyrhythmic Cycles (Act II/scene 4)

a. (mm.395-404)

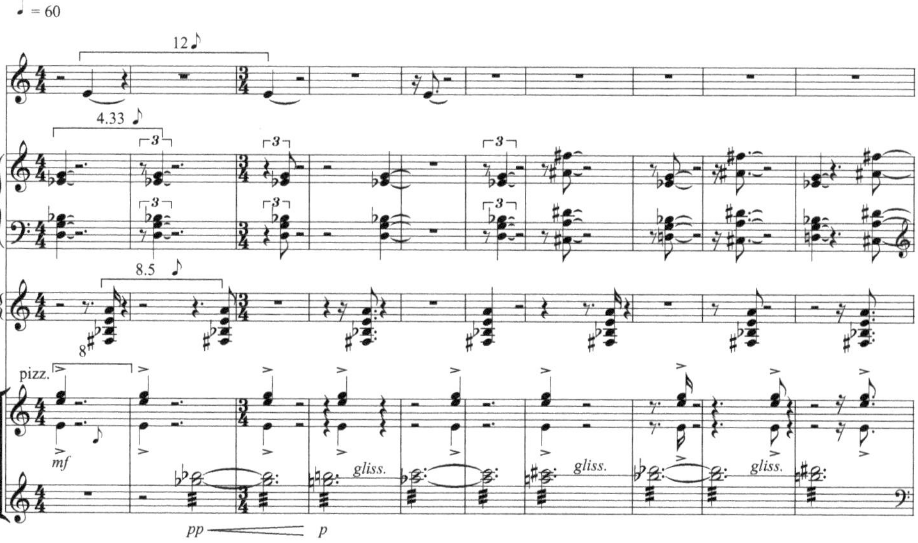

b. (mm.414-420)

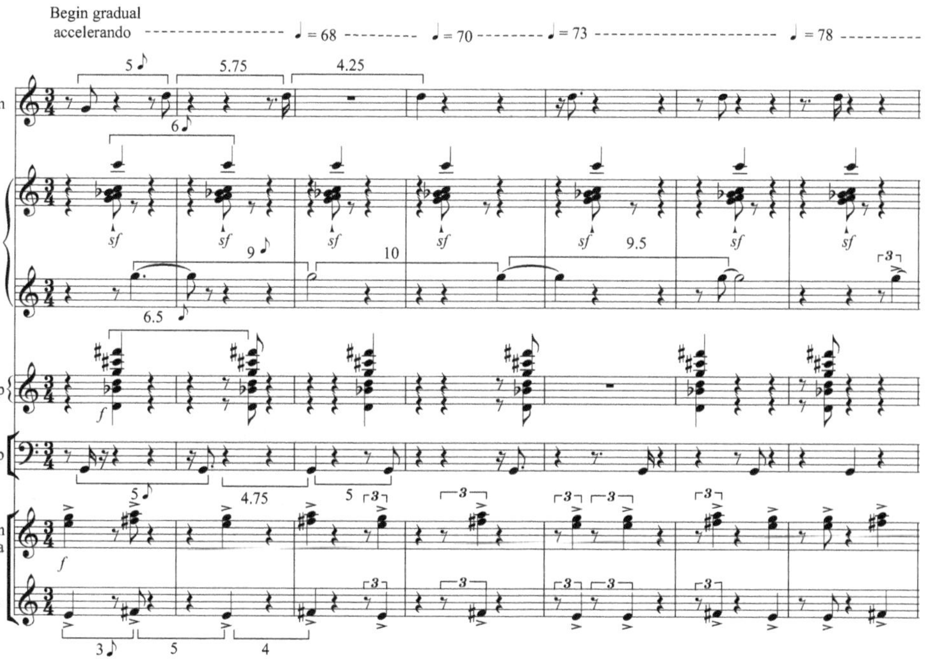

The symbolic moment of the countdown begins when Oppenheimer quotes from Baudelaire: "time has disappeared. It is eternity that reigns now." The sense of poetic timelessness collides with the realistic reminder of the impending countdown: a loud siren signals that the moment has arrived. Then Oppenheimer utters his last words: "Lord, these affairs are hard on the heart."

The instrumental music for the countdown is significant because it marks the moment in the narrative where the spatiotemporal boundary between the diegetic and meta-diegetic domains begins to blur; that is to say, we are no longer sure whether the characters are situated in Los Alamos in July 1945 or in Hiroshima and Nagasaki three weeks later, when the actual bombs are dropped. Beginning with a loud fanfare, the tempo settles down to ♩ = 60MM for a slow, polyrhythmic cycle of chords played by harp, celesta, chimes, and strings (*col legno*) that builds in textural density and speed as brass, percussion, woodwinds, and the chorus join in. The timbral combination (of chime, celesta, and harp) previously associated with the "plutonium" motive (see example 4.3), forms the basis of the initial polyrhythmic sequence, as shown in example 4.8a. Over the three steady rhythmic cycles in the strings, harp, and celesta, the chime enters with a cycle of variable duration. The second violin interjects a slowly rising tremolo glissando to add suspense. Although omitted in the reduction, the entire interlude is accompanied by an electronic soundscape comprising distant choral sounds, timpani spread, long waves, and muttering of voices (children screaming), as indicated in Adams's score.

In example 4.8b, the polyrhythmic sequence expands to six layers of shorter cycles as the tempo begins to accelerate gradually. The prominent layers are the claves, horns, and trombones that maintain a steady cycle of 6 eighth notes, the dyadic ostinato (E-F♯) in the strings that unfolds in a variable cycle of expanding and contracting durations, and the sustained but variable cycle in the trumpet. In addition, the harp maintains a cycle of 6.5 eighth notes against the variable cycles in the timpani and chimes. In the third segment, the textural density increases to ten layers as the tempo accelerates to ♩ = 162MM. In the final segment, as the anvils and castanets sound out pulses at maximum speed of ♩ = 190MM, the members of the chorus utter "ah" repeatedly on the downbeat, in anticipation of the catastrophe.

What this music embodies is the heightened experience of those who wait anxiously for the countdown to begin. The music's proto-topical function in conveying the meta-diegetic effect is, however, ambivalent. The expanding and contracting cycles and the rates of acceleration, on the one hand, resemble the human heartbeat, which accelerates at an erratic pace under pressure. The music, on the other hand, simulates a multitude of clocks of different shapes and sizes ticking away toward the countdown, spiraling out of control. Whether the viewer associates the music for the countdown with the machinery of clocks and/or heartbeats that race against time, it assumes a powerful agency in conveying the sense of "charged" time.

Sellars's staging of this scene brings out the meta-diegetic effect to its fullest. The scene focuses on Kitty, Oppenheimer, their servants, and the military workers, who anxiously await the countdown in exactly this sense (DVD #2: 1:21'30"). The camera angles provide close-up shots of each – Kitty locked in prayer, her servants holding onto Kitty's baby with a look of terror, Oppenheimer standing motionless and gazing outward – all anticipating the historical moment that will forever transform their lives. At the height of the interlude, the military workers writhe on the floor as if they have turned into the victims of the explosion themselves. In the last phase, the characters gaze outwardly onto the stage as the electronic simulation of the bomb explosion is heard two hundred miles away in Alamogordo, New Mexico. Similar to Sellars's production of *Adriana Mater* (discussed in chapter 3), the semic function of lighting plays an indispensable role in unifying this final scene. The blue lighting, initially associated with the "plutonium" motive, returns here as the polyrhythmic cycle indexes the physical process of nuclear fission. The lighting changes rapidly from red to blue during the explosion. As the low rumbling of the explosion fades away, the celesta and harp mark time over the bass drum, tam-tam, and timpani rolls. The disembodied voice of a Japanese female is overlaid; in a dispassionate and otherworldly tone, the voice asks repeatedly for water and to learn where her missing husband is. The opera comes to a halt as the woman's voice and the crowd's muttering gradually fade away.

Overall Harmonic Progression and Modal Orientation

Keith Potter defines post-minimalism as a compositional trend that emerged in the mid-1970s onward, characterized by the addition of a melodic profile, timbral variety, and harmonic progression that encompass "[a] narrative development across broader spans of time" (Potter 2000: 16). In my hearing, the harmonic formation and modal orientation in this opera contribute to its narrative development, which is marked by shifts from the individual to the collective, and from the historical to the mythological. The harmonic construction and modal orientation can be categorized roughly into three groups: 1) "Stravinskian" chordal complexes constructed via transpositional combination of triads and seventh chords; 2) diatonic and modal triads and sevenths associated with the characters' response to the impending crisis, e.g., Kitty's expression of love and loneliness and Oppenheimer's "lament" aria; and 3) symmetrical scales, such as the octatonic and whole-tone collections, and progressions based on planing parallel chords to prolong stasis. The overall harmonic and modal orientations in the opera can be summarized as shown in example 4.9a. "Stravinskian" chordal complexes are featured in the overtures at the commencement of Acts I and II and diatonic sevenths are associated with individual arias, while "planing" chords and whole-tone progression are used as connective devices. Associative, "focal" sonorities are related to specific characters and situations: Fm7 with added sixth is associated with Kitty for her expression of loneliness, D minor for Oppenheimer's "lament" aria, C minor for the chorus's apocalyptic music, and E♭ minor for Pasqualita's longing for her ancestral land.

Considering how so many of these chords are formed by transpositional combination of triads and sevenths, I mapped them onto Edward Gollin's Multiple Aggregate Double Interval cycle (MADIC) based on the chain of alternating minor third and major third (3,4).[23] As shown under example 4.9b, MADIC is a double interval cycle because it passes through the aggregate twice; when traversing the pitch classes in the clockwise direction, the pitch-class sequence alternately spells out a major-major or minor-minor seventh chord. One can also conceive the double interval cycle as linking the subdominant, tonic, and dominant chords (either major or minor in quality) in sequence. Conceiving chordal complexes as extensions of triadic relations in this manner, those that refer to ontological time ("clock" time) can be mapped onto the clockwise region of the MADIC spanning from C to G♯ (see boxed regions marked #1), while those that refer to psychological time (#2–#5) tend to be mapped onto the counterclockwise regions on the cycle. Each region contains a focal pitch, which receives contextual emphasis; as highlighted in example 4. 9b, for region #1 it is C, #2 is F, #3 is D, #4 is E♭ and #5 is C. The important choral numbers are situated in C major (opening number) or C minor (text based on the Bhagavad Gita); take, for example, the Lydian inflection (raised fourth) in the melodic contour that accompanies the second chordal formation. Oppenheimer's lament, in comparison, is clearly situated in D minor, while the women's arias are grounded in minor harmonies built on F, E♭ or C. As shown in example 4.9b, the clockwise movement on the MADIC roughly symbolizes the act of moving "with" time, while the counterclockwise is the act of moving "against" time. The upward arrow next to the stacked chords corresponds to clockwise movement, while the downward arrow next to the stacked chords corresponds to counterclockwise movement. The chords featured in the final countdown cumulatively span the largest portion of the double interval cycle, derived principally from regions #1 and #4; note, for example, the superimposition of C and D major triads at m.436 and G major triad with E major seventh at m. 472 in example 4.9a.

As in the previous passages based on the whole-tone scale and chordal planing, half-diminished sevenths, and augmented triads (B♭+), the countdown scene pits the psychological uncertainty of the individuals against the chronometric passing of time. The countdown scene is especially noteworthy in how the harmonic construction merges the harmonic regions of #1 and #4 at the same time that the spatiotemporal boundary between material and virtual domains collapses; notice how the chorus's utterance on "Ah" is accompanied by a chordal complex that occupies both harmonic regions via the inclusion of a G major triad and an E major seventh chord.

Furthermore, Adams's construction of chords alludes to those from Stravinsky's music through extra-musical associations and symbolism. As shown in example 4.9c, the chordal complex that begins the storm scene in Act I, scene 3 (marked with an asterisk * in example 4.9a), is modeled on the "Sacrificial Dance" chord from *The Rite of Spring*. Here, the chord of sacrifice is recontextualized into a proto-topical signifier of an impending storm. In addition, the bell-like chords played by harp and celesta (marked with a double asterisk **) at the end of *Doc-*

Example 4.9a. Overview of Harmonic and Modal Orientations in *Doctor Atomic*

tor Atomic are modeled on those that appear at the end of Stravinsky's *Requiem Canticles* – coincidentally, a work which Oppenheimer explicitly requested to have performed at his own funeral (Ross 2005). It is plausible that Adams planted these bell-like chords at the pivotal moment when the disembodied voice of the Japanese victim is heard as a symbol of the tolling of bells for the dead. Musical intertexts in this opera shape meaning by opening our mind's ear to associations that are thus both internal and external to the operatic narrative.[24]

John Adams's Doctor Atomic 153

b. Mapping chords onto Gollin's MADIC (3,4)

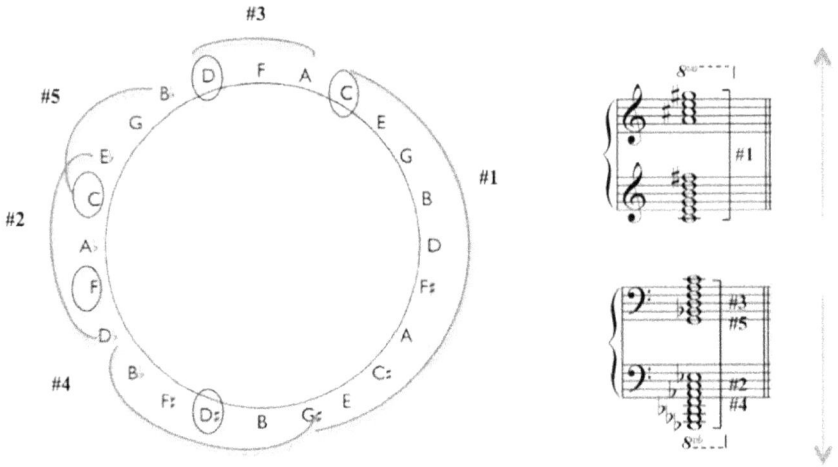

c. Stravinskian chords

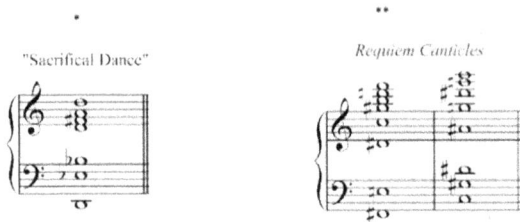

Example 4.9b/c. Mapping Chords onto Gollin's MADIC (3,4); Stravinskian Chords

Revisiting Myth: the Hero's Journey in *Doctor Atomic*

The opera critic Anthony Tommasini states that "The Oppenheimer of *Doctor Atomic* is a 20th-century Faustian figure who understands that he could be unleashing unimaginable forces within the world and even more ominous forces within mankind" (2008).[25] Having dissected the dramaturgical and musical structure of the operatic narrative, how can we view this opera as a Faustian parable in the modern age? Nicholas Boyle claims that the term "Faustian" refers to the modern human condition in which the subject strives towards some indeterminate collective goal "through the toils of necessary guilt" (1978: 129). Is Faust's vanity, his endless appetite for knowledge and worldly adventure, reflected in the portrayal of Oppenheimer alone or in the entire ensemble of military characters?

Perhaps one way in which we can draw a more concrete parallel between Goethe's *Faust* and *Doctor Atomic* is by reference to the role of a hero in myth. Joseph Campbell, in *The Hero with a Thousand Faces,* describes the archetypal hero in myth as a personage of exceptional gifts who undergoes an initiation followed by various trials in facing his oppressors; the hero achieves triumph and brings about either a restoration of social order or an entirely new order to his community. Campbell argues that the purpose of the original rituals enacted through myth was to conduct people across those difficult thresholds of transformation that "demand a change in the patterns not only of conscious but also of unconscious life" (1993: 10). Through the structure of "separation-initiation-return," the hero returns from the mysterious adventure with the power to "bestow boons on his fellow man" (30). Triumph may be achieved at the cost of bringing the hero's own demise, as in the case of Prometheus, who is punished by Zeus by being plucked to death by vultures.

To what extent do Goethe's *Faust* and the operatic adaptations of the Faustian legend by Berlioz, Gounod, and Busoni conform to the hero's journey in archetypal myth? Faust's journey in Goethe's play can be mapped onto Campbell's cycle as follows: the first stage (call for adventure) corresponds with the appearance of the devil as Mephistopheles; the second (trials) with the worldly adventures that Faust undergoes, culminating in his seduction of Gretchen; the third (apotheosis) in his choice to give his soul to Mephistopheles in exchange for saving Gretchen from eternal damnation. At the end of Part I, he falls into a healing sleep of forgetfulness. The last stage (departure) is where the story takes discursive endings: in Part II of Goethe's *Faust,* the hero is transported into a classical world where he interacts with mythological figures that range from Helen of Troy and a chorus of Trojan women, to Philemon and Baucis, within a mixed genre of lyrical, dramatic, and epic styles of narration. The portrayal of Faust as a tragic hero hinges on the choices he makes as Mephistopheles cleverly sets up traps to obtain his soul. In Goethe's telling, just when the devil tries to get his hands on Faust's departing soul, it is "filched off into heaven" at the conclusion of Part II as a chorus of mythical and penitent women (including Gretchen) blesses his soul. Other adaptations are not as kind in allowing Faust to be redeemed through a divine act of intervention. In Thomas Mann's *Doctor Faustus,* Adrian Leverkühn ultimately suffers a tragic death after he makes a pact with the devil in his dream to pursue artistic creativity at the highest level. In Hector Berlioz's operatic rendering of the legend in *La damnation du Faust* (1846), Faust undertakes a noble deed by selling his soul to Méphistophélès in exchange for redeeming Marguerite's soul; Marguerite is welcomed into heaven as the chorus sings Hosanna in praise of her deeds, while Faust, guided by the devil, is forced to descend to hell. In Charles Gounod's operatic rendering of *Faust* (1959), Faust is similarly dragged to hell while a chorus of angels saves Marguerite from damnation. Lastly, in Ferruccio Busoni's modernist opera (1924), Faust is portrayed from the beginning as a philanderer who is forced to make a pact with the devil in order to rid himself of his creditors and the women he has wronged (Gretchen and the Duchess); although he ends up a fallen man who is resigned to die, his spirit lives on within the child he begets with the Duchess. In Berlioz's and Gounod's adaptations, Faust's act of redeeming Marguerite (the apotheosis phase) defines the transvaluative moment where his ranking shifts from marked (negative) to unmarked (positive), yet his status as hero is rendered tragic when he falls prey to Mephistopheles's power at the end.

The question of whether Oppenheimer functions as a hero in the Faustian sense can be answered by mapping the chronological narrative dimension of *Doctor Atomic* onto the four phases of Campbell's mythic cycle, as follows:

- *Call for Adventure:* the opening scene that features the scientists' negotiation of then-classified documents on the Manhattan Project constitutes the initial stage of the hero's journey. Following the command from Washington, Oppenheimer is confident (to the point of being callous) about the necessity to carry on with the test explosion to bring an end to World War II. His attitude collides with Wilson's humanitarian concerns and resistance to using the bomb on human subjects. The music is comprised primarily of "filler" music and proto-topics to reinforce the sense of chronometric time.

- *Trials:* this phase begins with the personal interaction between Kitty and Oppenheimer (Act I, scene 2) and ends with the countdown scene (Act II, scene 4). In the bedroom scene, Kitty's human needs collide with Oppenheimer's preoccupation with work, driven by his "superhuman" convictions. In the concluding scene of Act I, Oppenheimer sings his "lament" aria; left alone in the company of the "gadget," the callous scientist who previously mocked other scientists' doubt as a sign of weakness begins to acknowledge his own inner turmoil; in articulating the "Crossing the Threshold" phase, the internal conflict signifies a shift in ranking from unmarked (positive) to marked (negative) in our hero. From this point onward, however, Oppenheimer becomes further and further removed from his public persona as he becomes engulfed into the mythical realm and speaks through the voices of Arjuna and Baudelaire. The women are trapped inside a mythical realm of their own: Pasqualita and other servants engage in ritualized prayers, while the scientists speculate on the destructive power of the atomic bomb. The semic role of lighting is very important in this regard: anything having to do with the objective realm of scientific research is accompanied by blue lighting, while the slippage into the mythological realm is underscored by lurid colors of red, orange, and green (see Act II, scene 3).[26]

- *Apotheosis:* what might have constituted the apotheosis in the mythic journey of a hero is cut short due to Oppenheimer's diminishing power over the initiative. Instead of glorifying Oppenheimer as the hero, the chorus's collective plea to Vishnu and their acknowledgement of divine power marks the moment of apotheosis. This turn to a supernatural force for aid is also evidenced by Sellars's inclusion of an Uwe Indian ritual dance (Act II, scene 2) prior to the countdown scene. By the time the countdown

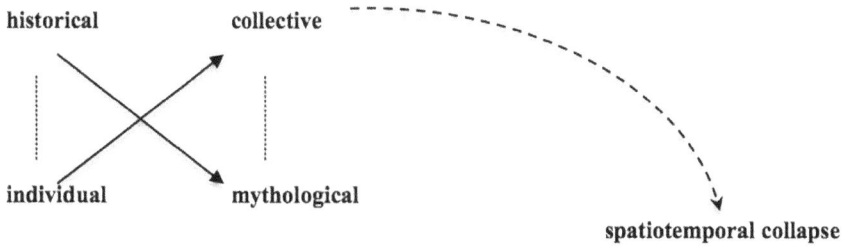

Figure 4.2. Actantial Progression in *Doctor Atomic*

begins, Oppenheimer is absorbed into the collective, unable to act on his will except to make the final pronouncement that "there is no more time!" From this point onward, the boundary between the diegetic and virtual spaces of the theater collapses as the bomb explosion in the Nevada desert is overlaid with sonic images of the bomb explosion in Hiroshima and Nagasaki. The women's prophecies have been realized.

· *Departure:* Most importantly, the journey of the hero has been supplanted by a temporal collapse. Our hero disappears into the crowd as the spatiotemporal scope of the narrative zooms outward from the local (Nevada desert) to the global (Japan). In this respect, *Doctor Atomic* articulates the shift in ranking of our hero from unmarked (indifferent) to marked (conflicted) – the reverse of what has been attributed to Goethe's Faust, but the opera omits the last stage of transvaluation (resolution of the conflict) that would offer a corrective.

From dissecting the narrative in this way, it becomes apparent that the Faustian intertexts are not literally present in *Doctor Atomic,* but figuratively present in the articulation of the individual and collective modes of striving. Just as Goethe's tale moves from the local (Faust's own study) to the global (mythical realm), the operatic narrative is marked by a shift in emphasis from the individual to collective striving toward an indeterminate future. From a broader perspective, the actantial progression of the narrative in *Doctor Atomic* may be summarized as shown in figure 4.2. Given the historical (realism) and mythological (poetic timelessness) as constituting one set of oppositions, the individual and collective modes of striving form another set of oppositions in the Greimassian square. And as the mode of representation shifts from the historical to the mythological, there is a corresponding shift from the individual to the collective mode of striving. The dynamic change in the actantial progression leads ultimately to the spatiotemporal collapse of diegetic present and future in completing the mythic journey.

The spatiotemporal collapse in the actantial progression creates a formal rupture that resists narrative closure. This rupture in the narrative invites the audience to fill in the gaps in the narrative by bringing in other historical facts and associations to bear on connections that have been eliminated. Notably, the ending of the opera fails to tell us what happens to our hero, except to suggest how Oppenheimer's crumbling psyche presages the mental breakdown the actual figure underwent many years later. The end of the opera marks the beginning of the hero's struggle to reverse the "pact" he made with the Truman administration, by advocating instead for an international sanction on the development of atomic weapons. Stretching the Faustian reference a bit more, one might claim that the government emerges as the "devil" by implication.

Tropological Narratives:
Sellars's and Woolcock's Productions

Finally, let us examine how and to what extent two exemplary productions of *Doctor Atomic* transform the narrative trajectories of the opera's initial sources (libretto and music). In Sellars's production, what stands out immediately is his effort to establish a metaphysical and synaesthetic union of semiotic fields. Recalling Cook's taxonomy (chapter 1), the intermedial relationship of semiotic fields in Sellars's production by and large follows a complementary model. Moreover, his complex stage design, lighting design, and choreography of dancers pay respect to post-Brechtian concepts of staging. Stanton B. Garner describes the contemporary manifestations of "post-Brechtian" theater in terms of the following traits: 1) the postmodern radicalizing of Brechtian aesthetics by focusing on its subversion of dogmatism; 2) the simultaneous appropriation and revision of Brechtian political theater on the part of feminists and non-Western writers; 3) experiments in decentering the function of dramatic/theatrical authorship; 4) stagings of Brecht's plays that open dialogues with Brecht's own theatrical practice; and 5) the obsessive interest in the body as a political unit, and its function within the play of political forces (1990: 146). Sellars's staging of *Doctor Atomic* embodies nearly all of these traits: the construction of the libretto in itself departs from a monolithic model of authorship; his inclusion of women's poetic voices (Rukeyser, Tewa Indian folklore) infuses the narrative with perspectives of feminist and oppressed Others, and most importantly, Sellars makes use of the human body as a political site of engagement. As figures 4.3 makes evident, the writhing bodies of the chorus members during the countdown scene visually "mirror" the images of human casualties in World War II, shown in the documentary film that precedes the opera proper (DVD #1: 1'18"). In the filmic production of Sellars's staging of this scene, close-up shots and a lurid combination of colors (orange, green, and red) call attention to individual faces and bodies as the site of political unrest. The twisted bodies and hand gestures convey physical casualties inflicted on the American military workers in a manner that suggests that they are not necessarily victors, but are portrayed as the *imagined* victims of the atomic explosion. The visual "mirroring" between this scene and the documentary footage from World War II at the beginning of the production effectively blurs the binary between victors and victims of the war.

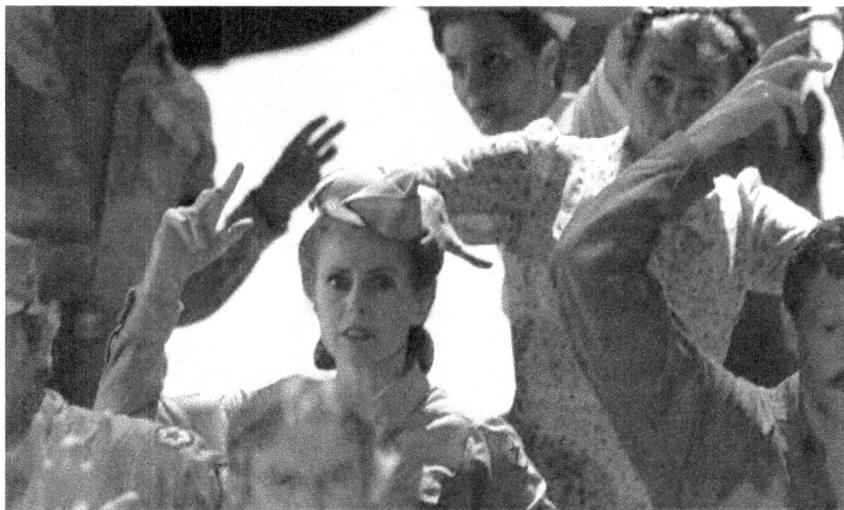

Figure 4.3. Sellars's Mise-en-Scène of "At the Sight of This" (Act II, scene 3)

Woolcock brings an entirely different political perspective to her staging of *Doctor Atomic,* stemming from her role as documentary filmmaker. Woolcock's collaboration with Adams traces back to her film production of *Death of Klinghoffer* (2003), in which she introduces a narrative strategy that departs from Sellars's theatrical production in a number of significant ways. Mainly, she has re-mediated the entire opera as a film that intersperses images from different time periods and cultural vistas to comment on the Jewish and Palestinian identities.[27] Ruth Longobardi argues that the visual domain is made primary in Woolcock's filmic opera; it provides for "a singular position from which a viewer follows events and characters, while libretto and music sustain its representations" (2009: 294–95). In Woolcock's theatrical production of *Doctor Atomic* for the Metropolitan Opera (2008), one could argue similarly for the primacy of the visual semiotic field. In her staging of the opera, she breaks up the theatrical space by placing multi-leveled panels with cubicles to segregate the scientists from the other workers and domestic servants. The scientists (all men) congregate around the table in front of the stage; the female chorus provides commentary but does not participate in dialogue; and the Native American who work as servants are "seen" but not "heard." Kitty is portrayed as a glamorous white woman, poised for the cover of fashion magazines from the time period, in contrast to Pasqualita, who is portrayed as a servant clad in her Tewa costume. In what follows, I will isolate four scenes to illustrate the differences in orientation between the two productions: the overture and the opening choral number (Act I, scene 1), discussion of the target sites in Japan (Act I, scene 1), Kitty's aria (Act II, scene 1), the staging of the "apocalyptic" music (Act II, scene 3), and the final countdown (Act II, scene 4).

At the beginning of the opera, Woolcock sets up an abstract staging of props to accompany the electronic sound collage (in lieu of Sellars' documentary film): first, a scientific table of chemical elements is projected onto a transparent screen (scrim), then a mobile of mechanical objects floats in the middle of the half-darkened stage with what appear to be machineries of war draped with a large white sheet. As the distorted sample of Jo Stafford's singing is heard, multi-layered cubicles are brought on stage. A photograph of scientists is projected onto each of the many cubicles as the music shifts from the electronic collage to the orchestral overture. Then the opening chorus sings from the book on the atomic bomb with each worker placed inside a cubicle, toiling away at his/her task. Woolcock's confinement of each worker in this manner imparts a sense of entrapment within the societal hierarchy in mid-twentieth-century America: each worker clings to the wall of his/her cubicle as a locus of identity in the societal hierarchy, whereas the top scientists are allowed full mobility in the theatrical space; women in the domestic spheres are similarly trapped inside their temporary homes, disallowed from entering into the scientists' arena of negotiation and work. Lastly, Tewa Indians are shown in various contexts as voiceless (and powerless) servants, who sweep the floor in silence. Even in the female chorus's recitation of the chemical make-up of plutonium, women sing from inside their cubicles, devoid of physical gestures and movements. The narrative trajectory (subtext) created by these visual signifiers is one of social alienation: each social group inhabits its own space without disrupting the other.

Later in Act I, scene 1, where Oppenheimer discusses the target for attack in Japan, the chorus echoes his singing in a slow, meditative manner. Timpani and harp maintain a strict eighth-note beat throughout to emphasize the calculated nature of this action. The musical setting is made ritualistic by the manner in which Oppenheimer's declaration about the targeted sites in Japan is echoed by the chorus in antiphonal dialogue (DVD #1: 25'00"). Against Wilson's passionate plea to give Japan a warning, Oppenheimer staunchly abides by his loyalty to the government. In Sellars's staging, Wilson and Oppenheimer sing to each other in close proximity, intensifying the dramatic tension generated by their conflicting views. In the same scene, Woolcock projects a geographic map of Japan and shifts the image from one map to another as Oppenheimer lists the targeted cities for bombing one by one. She skillfully places Robert Wilson, the pacifist who opposes the testing, in the highest cubicle looking down on other scientists; as he voices his humanitarian concerns from above, Oppenheimer callously boycotts Wilson's petition to put a halt to the testing.[28] In this way, Woolcock eliminates physical proximity between characters to amplify the distance between those in power and the marginalized.

Act II begins with the domestic scene featuring the women in Oppenheimer's household who can only patiently wait. As she holds a drink in her hand, Kitty rapturously sings a number called "All Things Shine" and mediates on the ritual of death; Stravinskian chords (juxtaposition of seventh chord/triads) in the celesta interact with the flowing melody in the horn to convey a sense of mystery. The second part introduces syncopated rhythms in the strings and woodwinds

to mark time again; as the trumpet ushers in a solo fanfare, a group of dancers resume their circular dance and Kitty's singing turns to the subject of death,
blood, and resurrection. Kitty extols the need for freedom and peace in her passionate yet incoherent aria. Sellars's production enhances the drama of this scene
by having her sing in the middle of a circle of dancers. The sudden interjection of
dancers' movement accentuates her state of agitation, her fear for what is yet to
come. Sellars also portrays Pasqualita as a woman who is profoundly connected
to the earth, giving comfort to Kitty and her household. As the men fret about
the safety conditions under which to conduct the test, the women make ritualistic gestures to the heavens above. In scene 3, as Oppenheimer sings that "time
has returned" and "his demoniac retinue has returned," he is accompanied by the
workers dancing in a circle, based on a ritual dance associated with Tewa Indian
culture. Pasqualita joins in and sings about "dancing to bring back the dead." Sellars's staging injects an atmosphere of primitivism, counterpointing the scientific
rationalism of Act I with the ritual and spirituality of Act II. In Woolcock's staging, the five protagonists stand in front of the darkened stage, while the remaining workers are situated inside cubicles that hold other workers and Tewa Indians. Pasqualita sings from above the cubicle, her voice associated with a mythical
Other who is fundamentally disconnected from the world inhabited by scientists.[29] Woolcock's staging continually calls attention to the marginalized existence of characters such as Pasqualita and Wilson: they are given a voice but fundamentally excluded.[30]

The most dramatic difference between the two productions is evidenced by
the visual treatment of the final scene leading up to the countdown. Immediately before the final countdown, lightning flashes in the red background and the
chorus sings about the destructive forces of the Indian god Vishnu. Figure 4.4 illustrates the completely different approach Woolcock takes in staging this scene
of the chorus's collective plea to the supernatural. Eliminating the lurid colors
and choreography featured in Sellars's production, Woolcock has the chorus
stand erect and sing the number ("At the Sight of This") devoid of any physical
gestures.[31] Behind the chorus, photographs of scientists are projected onto the
middle row of cubicles, while Tewa Indians clad in full battle gear stand in the
top row of cubicles.

Because there is no choreography that accompanies the chorus's singing,
the tempo seems to move much faster than in Sellars's production. A strong
audio-visual synchronization occurs when the projection of photographs changes
to rain-like drizzle at the beginning of the B section of this choral number. Then
the panels holding the cubicles open from the middle, revealing images of a thunderstorm on the machinery draped over in the back of the stage. The whole effect
is abstract and kinesthetically charged, but the psychological impact of terror (associated with the text from the Bhagavad Gita) is significantly undermined.

In the countdown scene where the virtual leap to the dropping of the atomic
bomb in Hiroshima and Nagasaki takes place, Woolcock's staging maintains
the separation between the diegetic/material and virtual spaces invoked; while
the stage darkens and stays nearly dark throughout the countdown and the final

Figure 4.4. Woolcock's Mise-en-Scène of "At the Sight of This" (Act II, scene 3)

scene that follows the explosion, the subtitle of the woman asking for water is projected in large prints on the transparent screen. The characters on stage dispassionately look out onto the imagined space of the explosion, as if they are oblivious to the message being communicated. Instead, the slippage between time and space is directed at the audience, as if Woolcock suggests that the dawn of nuclear age is something that each person must contend with. She makes the disembodied voice visible through the projection of subtitles onto the center of the stage, and thus presents it as historical evidence. By way of contrast, Sellars intentionally presents the disembodied voice as an acousmatic source in order to maximize the mythological effect at the end.

The two directors' approaches generate contrasting intermedial relationships in the participating semiotic fields that shape the multimodal narrative. Sellars's mise-en-scène brings together dance, miming, singing, and lighting cohesively to comment on the mythological: by incorporating Tewa Indian ritual or a choreographed singing of text from the Bhagavad Gita, the mythical Other is invoked through the physical and metaphysical union of media sources in *conformance* with the text. Woolcock's production, by contrast, purposefully avoids a facile synchronization among music, text, and visual media. The kinesthetic energy of the music does not necessarily find a visual corollary in the staging components: the chorus delivers the dramatic choral numbers devoid of physical movement, which impels the audience to focus on the visual images on stage independently of the sung text. It is as though Woolcock compels us to forget about Faust and the literary excesses built into Sellars's construction of the libretto. Even the projection of the photographs of scientists subtly undermines the agency of the "narrativized" characters on stage.

Sellars's mise-en-scène:

N $\Big\langle$ S_1 (text) $\longrightarrow$ O_1 (Vishnu) $----\blacktriangleright I_1$ (divine plea)
S_2 (music)
S_3 (lighting) $\longleftrightarrow$ O_2 (Atomic bomb) $---\blacktriangleright I_2$ (destruction)
(choreography) $\longrightarrow O_3$ (victim :: victor)

$\Big)$

Woolcock's mise-en-scène:

N $\Big\langle$ S_1 (text) $\longrightarrow$ O_1 (Vishnu) $------\blacktriangleright I_1$ (divine plea)
S_2 (music)
S_3 (staging) $\longrightarrow$ O_2 (Tewa Indians) $---\blacktriangleright I_2$ (oppression)
(film) $\longrightarrow O_3$ (Scientists) $-----\blacktriangleright$

$)\!\!\!\ast$

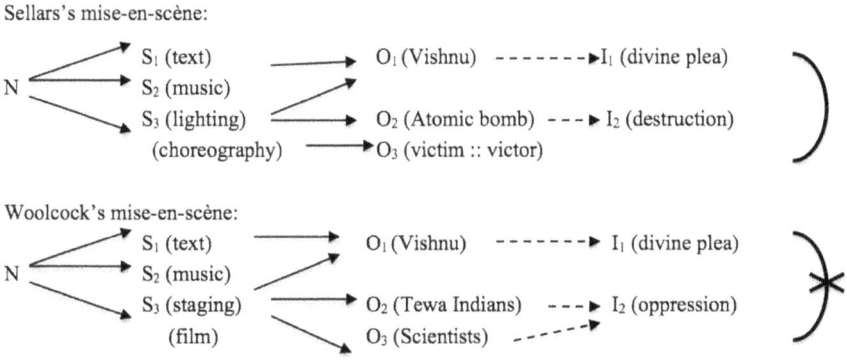

Figure 4.5. Multimodal Analysis of "At the Sight of This"

Figure 4.5 compares multimodal narration of the two stagings of "At the Sight of This"; the narration comprises a group of semiotic fields (S), which references specific objects (O) and intertextual codes (I). Sellars's production maps the text and music to the reference world of Vishnu and the staging or production components with the destruction caused by the atomic bomb. Lucinda Childs's choreography for Sellars indexes the horror associated with the atomic bomb via the aforementioned visual "mirroring," while the lurid lighting (juxtaposing purple, green, yellow, and red) indexes the phantasmagorical world of Vishnu as suggested by popular iconography of Vishnu in India. By associating the destructive power of the atomic bomb with Vishnu's godly omnipotence, the historical and mythological dimensions are metaphorically aligned. The tropological narrative that emerges is one that breaks down the binary between victors and victims of war. Perhaps the implicit message is that we are victims regardless of which side of war we belong to.

By contrast, Woolcock's staging complicates the multimodal telling of the operatic narrative by bringing historical realism into collision with the mythologizing dimension of the basic narrative. Here, realism and fantasy make uneasy bedfellows. Furthermore, she juxtaposes a visual reference to Tewa Indians in Los Alamos with that of the Anglo-Saxon scientists who engage in a parallel ethical battle. The juxtaposition of these images calls attention to the struggle of the Tewa Indians against the European colonizers who first settled in the Nevada desert. She also juxtaposes actual photos of scientists and figures of Tewa Indians to create an opposition within the material modality of experience. However, it is unclear how this historical subtext relates to the mythical world of Vishnu. Her staging represents an "interventionist" strategy that foregrounds the primacy of the visual semiotic field over the sonic and textual fields. A tropological theme that is emphasized in Woolcock's mise-en-scène is the parallel conflict between the oppressed and the oppressor in the diegetic now (WWII) and the distant past (Indians who lost their land to European settlers).

Conclusion

More than any other contemporary operas examined in this study, *Doctor Atomic* is unconventional in its treatment of spatiotemporal modality; the story takes place in a specific time and place, yet by the end, the diegetic time of the test explosion collapses and merges with the virtual space and time of the viewer, in which the distinction between past, present, and future no longer holds. In this synchronic dimension of mythic time, we are carried into a deeper experience of time that transcends the material realm. As Ricoeur explains, one's apperception of time subscribes to Heidiggerian notion of radical temporality in such instances: the experience of time is capable of unfolding itself on several levels at once, not unlike Augustine's concept of eternity in which everything can be present at the same time (86). The concept of time also resembles the second part of Goethe's *Faust,* which opens itself out to a universal, timeless domain in which Faust interacts with various mythological characters. The only difference is that in *Doctor Atomic,* the slippage and temporal collapse into the poetic timelessness is conveyed multimodally and forces the viewer to wrestle with what it means to live in a nuclear age – with the threat of nuclear disaster lurking everywhere. As a reviewer from *Newsweek* put it: "The end is suggested, not shown, as the final explosion is heard. The cast gapes at the audience as if to say: we are the bomb" (2008).

In my multimodal narrative reading of the opera, the Faustian theme resonates strongly with that of *Doctor Atomic* – not because it pertains to the Christian notion of salvation or eternal damnation, but because it emphasizes the act of striving toward the unknown at both the individual and collective levels. The jumble of different voices from different sources in the libretto parallel the structure of Part II of Goethe's *Faust;* similar to the plethora of historical and mythic figures (e.g., Helen of Troy, Philemon and Baucis) that Faust encounters in Goethe's *Faust, Doctor Atomic* tries to carve out a mythic space in mid-century America by bringing together a plethora of cultural intertexts. Perception of reality in this opera is refracted through a variety of perspectives that merge and collide.

While both productions bring out the Faustian resonances to varying degrees, it is important to note that the overall efficacy and structural balance of the opera have been called into question. Having attended live performances of both Sellars's and Woolcock's productions, I was repeatedly struck by the problem of balance in the static second act: the women's arias based on Rukeyser's poems are overly drawn out and take away from the momentum that builds up to the countdown. Additionally, some critics have expressed their concern over the incoherence of the verbal assemblage as a whole. Ron Rosenbaum was bothered by the "incoherence" and "emptiness" of the words and Clive Barnes criticized the dullness of the libretto, while calling Adams's music "terrific" (Rosenbaum 2008).[32]

Rupert Christiansen, in his review of the production at the English National Opera, praised Adams for his sophisticated writing for orchestra, while criticizing the "clunky text" and Adams's failure to animate it into "a flow of meaningful melody" (2009).

It is difficult to tell whether future productions of *Doctor Atomic* will reconcile these perceived problems. In stark contrast, the 2011 remaking of *Nixon in China* at the Metropolitan Opera was received with great accolades. Here, the libretto by Alice Goodman, music by Adams, and staging by Sellars create a synergy where the dramaturgical structure is perfectly complemented by the sparse musical language and staging. Whether *Doctor Atomic,* like *Nixon in China,* will withstand the test of time is yet to be seen.[33]

5 The Anti-hero in Tan Dun's *The First Emperor*

> The process is not based on a simple addition, but a fusion of different music, China and the world, ancient and contemporary, tradition and innovation, and so forth. The Chinese Yin-Yang master occupies the same stage as the western prophet or shaman. So do the ancient and new techniques of performing instruments, the *bel canto* and Peking opera styles of singing, the pyramid, Buddhist Nirvana, the Great Wall, and Flying Apsaras from the Dunhuang province. In short, everything that is seemingly incompatible was brought together to form an integrated whole.
>
> Jianguo Zhang, "Quanxinde Geju Chuangzuo Guannian: '1+1=1'"
> ("Completely New Opera and its Creative Concept")[1]

Drawing on the lecture Tan Dun delivered at the Beijing Central Conservatory of Music in 2006, musicologist Zhang Jianguo elaborates on Tan Dun's aesthetic ideal and the creative impetus underlying the production of *The First Emperor*. Instead of conceiving the fusion of traditions as the sum of two parts ("1+1 = 2"), Tan Dun envisioned the process as yielding an indivisible whole, coined by the paradoxical formula of "1+1 = 1." In doing so, he positions himself as an artist in pursuit of his own creative voice that transcends the conceptual binary of East and West, in spite of the label he has been given as a "neo-Orientalist" who puts a new spin on tradition of exoticism in the West.[2]

With *The First Emperor*, Tan Dun strove to compose an opera that departs from his postmodern style, exemplified by theatrical works such as *Peony Pavilion* (1998) and *Marco Polo* (1996) that freely intermix cultural elements. It all goes back to a dream he had since he first moved to New York City in the late '80s, to compose an opera for the Metropolitan Opera stage. When James Levine commissioned Tan Dun to compose a new opera for the Metropolitan Opera in 1997, he first toyed with the idea of centering the opera's subject on Jewish history in Shanghai; as he puts it, "it looked like the perfect subject matter for a Chinese opera in New York" (Lee 2006: 18). He quickly changed his mind when his wife, Jane Huang, persuaded him to consider adapting the story found in a popular Chinese film called *The Emperor's Shadow* (Qin Song, 1996). In this highly romanticized epic film, China's first emperor and his court composer engage in a psychological tug of war over the creation of an anthem to honor the Qin dynasty (221–206 BCE). Intrigued by the dramatic potential of this scenario, Tan Dun obtained the story rights from the screenwriter Wei Lu and transformed the story into an operatic libretto. Collaborating with the acclaimed novelist Ha Jin for the libretto, he strove to create a narrative that would examine the complex relationship between politics and art, incorporating materials from the *Historical Records* by Sima Qian, a Han dynasty historiographer, to provide the necessary historical framework.[3] Over the course of the next ten years, Tan Dun turned to a largely Chinese creative team, including film director Zhang Yimou, choreographer Dou Dou Huang, and costume designer Emi Wada, for staging the premiere at the Metropolitan Opera.[4] The result is the telling of a modern myth that explores the controversial and perplexing character of the First Emperor.

Anyone who attended the 2006 premiere of *The First Emperor* at the Metropolitan Opera may recall the visual splendor of Zhang Yimou's mise-en-scène: the elaborate Qin dynasty costumes, musical instruments, acrobatics, the Peking opera singer, the Shaman, spirits with waterphones, and so forth. As the staging resembled Zhang's lavish 1998 production of Puccini's *Turandot* at the Forbidden Palace in Beijing, it was understandable that the Metropolitan Opera's seasoned audience expected Tan's Dun new opera to match the *musical* splendor of Puccini's grand opera as well. It became a highly publicized event in which the audience expected Tan Dun to compose an "exotic" grand opera, while inscribing particular aspects of Chinese culture, history, and operatic traditions into the making of his own Gesamtkunstwerk.

The premiere of this opera in 2006, however, could not have elicited a more divisive reception. Chinese newspaper reviews ranged from enthusiastic to downright negative; headlines ranged from "How does *The First Emperor* move the world?" to "Tan Dun's *The First Emperor* only lacks an appealing song" and "Tan Dun's *The First Emperor* 'impeached' in the United States." While some reviewers celebrated the premiere of this opera as indicative of the growing visibility of Chinese culture in the United States, others derided the performance as "a noble opera smeared by 'clumsy' dramatic expression and vocal writing" (Zhang 2009). Expecting a grand opera that measured up to *Turandot*, Anthony Tommasini derided Tan Dun's music as "giv[ing] soaring melody a bad name" (2006).[5] Responding to such criticism, Tan Dun extensively revised the score's vocal settings and rendered them more "Pucciniesque" for the second run in 2007. Having attended the revised production a year later, I was struck by the extensive revision to the vocal and instrumental writing, which smoothed out the rough edges of the original score, but also curtailed the boisterous instrumental interludes that define his signature compositional style. It wouldn't be far-fetched to claim that the revised version compromised Tan Dun's aesthetic strategy of the "1+1=1" principle. My impression was that Tan Dun made concessions, tipping the balance more toward the "exotic" grand opera tradition in this final version in order to placate his western critics.

Further complications ensued in the cross-cultural reception of this opera. The Chinese critics objected not so much to the clumsy vocal writing, but to the moral and ethical implications of portraying the First Emperor as an arche-typal *anti-hero*. After all, the First Emperor was the first ruler to unify China, why vilify him in this way? Whereas previous literary and filmic representations as well as museum exhibitions showcased Qin Shi Huang's positive accomplish-ments, why would Ha Jin and Tan Dun turn him into an enemy of the common people by drawing a parallel with Mao Zedong? In spite of Tan's initial idea to stage the opera at the site of the Great Wall, he soon learned of the impossibility of producing the opera in China due to governmental censorship.[6] While all cul-tural heroes are mythologized in one form or another, it seemed obvious that the downright negative depiction of the Emperor in this opera did not provide the politically correct myth.

In considering the range of issues raised by this opera, this chapter discusses the historical background, musico-dramatic intertexts, multimodal narrative, and socio-political reception of *The First Emperor* in three parts. The first ad-dresses the transmedial adaptation of the film narrative into an operatic libretto. To what extent does historical scholarship on the Qin dynasty inform the narra-tive? How does Ha Jin's portrayal of the Emperor depart from the romanticized depiction of him as a tragic hero in Wei Lu's filmic counterpart? The second ex-amines the musical design of the opera in relationship to both Western and Chi-nese operatic models; Tan draws from the Chinese regional opera called *qinqiang* and its ritualistic character, as evoked by distinctive styles of vocal enunciation and the use of the guzheng (zither with twenty-one strings and bridges), stone pebbles, and waterphones. The third offers an extensive analysis of leitmotifs, themes, and cultural intertexts in association with the actantial progression that accompanies the ironic narrative. In closing, I contemplate the Emperor's role as anti-hero from different cultural perspectives. The political implications of the anthem commissioned by the Emperor and sung by the chorus openly defies the Emperor's wish: instead of glorifying the ruler with an anthem that praises him, his court composer presents him with the slaves' song demanding freedom and an end to their suffering. An anti-authoritarian reading of the opera emerges from the ironic ending that presages the downfall of the first Emperor. Is there an oblique reference to Mao Zedong, who cultivated the symbolism of the Great Wall to his political advantage during the Cultural Revolution? Or does the nar-rative allude to Shakespeare's treatment of Richard II as a fallen hero? What other resonances does this tragi-ironic narrative have for the global audience? In con-templating these questions, my analysis negotiates different cultural positions and intertexts that arise from a multimodal reading of *The First Emperor.*

Historical Background: the Making of Qin Shi Huang

Extant scholarship on the First Emperor reveals a complex and controver-sial figure, a merciless tyrant who was known for his scrupulous attention to ev-ery aspect of his kingdom. The Qin dynasty spans a relatively short period in an-cient China, but it represents a period in which Ying Zheng (the Emperor's name prior to coronation) unified his kingdom through brutal coercion. Born in 258

BCE to a descendant of the Qin king and a concubine, Zheng ascended to the throne by the time he was thirteen years of age. Leading an infamously ruthless army, Zheng conquered both the neighboring Zhao and Han kingdoms by 228 BCE. After conquering the last remaining kingdom, that of Qi, in 221 BCE, Zheng assumed the title of Qin Shi Huangdi or the First Emperor. During his reign, the Emperor set out to embark on arguably his most ambitious project, which was to link the Qin wall with those on the northern frontier of Zhao and Yan (Clements 2006: 103). On a more practical level, the Emperor introduced and standardized new scripts, currency, and forms of measurements as well as a network of roads ("Imperial Highway") that extended about 4,250 miles. Yet this was all made possible through a system of taxation and mandatory labor on public projects by all the peasants (Lewis 2007: 60). Other records indicate that "customs of Qin" placed a taboo on all criticism, thus allowing the Emperor to make errors without ever being corrected. The philosophical compendium written during the Han dynasty (206 BCE–9 AD) refers to Qin Shi Huang's barbaric customs in the follow manner:

> The customs of Qin consisted of wolf-like greed and violence. The people lacked a sense of duty and pursued profit. They could be intimidated through punishments, but could not be transformed through goodness. They could be encouraged with rewards, but could not be urged on with reputation. Enveloped in difficult terrain and belted by the Yellow River, they were cut off on all sides and thus secure. (Lewis 2007: 40)

The Emperor was notorious for shutting down dissidents. As a case in point, in 213 BCE, following the advice of his chief minister Li Si, he ordered all of the Confucian classics, histories of other kingdoms, and writings of the philosophers to be burned; in the following year he buried alive more than 460 Confucian scholars at the capital of Xianyang (Su 1991: 141). The Emperor also purportedly insisted upon including popular, regional music in his rituals in lieu of the refined court music. To this end, Li Si advocated the adoption of the music of Zheng and Wei (from neighboring provinces), claiming that: "The true sounds of Qin are to delight the ear by singing woo-woo while striking a water jar and banging a pot, strumming the zither and slapping the thigh" (43).

Wishing to be revered in posterity as an embodiment of perfection, the Emperor began making elaborate preparations for his royal tomb soon after his coronation; over 700,000 convicts and forced laborers were sent to work on his new palace and tomb (Wood 2007: 128). Due to the ruthlessness of the Emperor's command, there were at least sixteen attempts on his life. According to historiographer Sima Qian's records, Jing Ke, a master warrior sent by Crown Prince Dan of the neighboring Yan kingdom, attempted to kill the emperor by stabbing him with a dagger hidden inside a map; an attendant physician managed to ward off Jing, allowing the Emperor to get away. Jing cursed the Emperor as he was slain by the courtiers (Qian 1994: 20). Gao Jianli, a master zhu (ancient zither) player, was Jing's associate, although he managed to hide his identity and make his way into the Qin court. Even after his true identity was revealed, the Emperor blinded

Jianli and kept him close, since he was enamored of his music. However, when Jianli attempted to kill the Emperor by attacking him with his instrument, he was promptly put to death. Following this incident, the Emperor never allowed anyone else from his feudal states to come close (22). Later in life, in spite of having conquered all of the territories, the Emperor became increasingly paranoid and superstitious. He met his death in battle at the age of forty-eight. Although succeeded by two more generations (son and grandson), the Qin dynasty only lasted for fifteen years.

The privileged position occupied by the Emperor was unprecedented in Chinese history. Not only was he considered the supreme ruler and the embodiment of the political realm, he was seen as the high priest who provided "the unique link between Heaven and Earth" (Lewis 2007: 2). By instituting a cosmic cycle in accordance with "the pattern of Heaven," he declared himself to be *huangdi* ("splendid commander") and strove to transcend his human state in order to become immortal; to this end, the architecture of his palace was planned to reflect a microcosm of the universe. Moreover, the cosmological rituals established during Qin Shi Huang's reign shaped important aspects of traditional Chinese culture that are still revered today. In particular, he initiated certain sacrificial rites to claim sovereignty and immortality: the *feng* sacrifice, which involved making offerings at the foot of the mountain and then burying a written message to a high god, was initiated on special occasions, and the worship of the directional *di* (south, north, east, and west) was conducted on a regular basis as the ritual expression of his conquests. After the Han dynasty conquered Qin, these rituals were handed down to Emperor Wudi (141–86 BCE), who established the cult of Tai Yi: offerings were made to a single, high god of sacrifices, in which Tai Yi (the sky god) stood in complementary opposition to the earth god in representing the unity of Heaven and Earth (187). However, it is also Wudi who reinstated Confucianism as an ethical model for individuals and allowed poetry, literature, and philosophy to flourish. Thus, the cosmological rituals introduced by Qin Shi Huang were refined and established as the foundation of Chinese customs during Wudi's reign, while other barbaric customs associated with the Qin dynasty were eliminated for good.

Given these historical accounts of the Qin dynasty, it is no wonder that contemporary biographers and filmmakers have transformed the enigmatic First Emperor into a subject of modern myth. Zhang Yimou's film *Hero* (*Yingxiong*, 2002) models its imaginary plot on the attempted assassination of the Qin Shi Huang by a nameless killer, depicting the Emperor as a noble being who displays compassion toward the assassin (Nameless) who manages to come within ten feet of the Emperor, but gives up his plot to kill him. Building on the non-linear narrative strategy used by Akira Kurosawa in *Rashōmon* (1950), Nameless tells four different versions of the plot to kill the Emperor through the hands of other master killers, known as Sky, Broken Sword, and Flying Snow. Semic use of color (red, blue, green, and white) distinguishes the four re-tellings, as the viewer is left to wonder which version offers the truth. In the end, Nameless gives up his life-long ambition to kill the Emperor as a way to honor Broken Sword's pledge to put an end to the vicious cycle of killing. After Nameless dies at the hands of the Qin army, the Emperor gives him a proper burial as a hero. The art of calligraphy and martial arts are skillfully blended together to create a fantasy film that idealizes the Emperor as a noble figure.

In contrast, Lu Wei's screenplay for *The Emperor's Shadow* (*Qin Song*, 1996) situates the Emperor within a romanticized narrative that revolves around the themes of love, revenge, and betrayal. The film presents a historically inauthentic story in which Ying Zheng kidnaps his childhood friend, Gao Jianli, from the rival state of Yan.[7] Jianli is branded as a criminal and is ordered by Zheng to compose a national anthem suitable for the Qin state. At the height of the film, the Emperor-to-be proclaims that through music, he can "control the hearts and minds of people," echoing Mao Zedong's words from his famous speech given in 1942. Zheng promises his daughter, Yueyang, to be married to the son of his top general Wang in exchange for conquering all of the neighboring kingdoms. At the same time, he promises to hand over his daughter to Jianli, assuring the court composer that general Wang will be killed off in the next war. Although in love with Yueyang, Jianli is a stronger pacifist than lover and agrees to give up Yueyang if Zheng will stop his ruthless killing. Yet this plan backfires when Yueyang commits suicide on the night of her wedding to the general. On the day of Zheng's coronation to become Emperor, Jianli takes poison and dies. As Zheng walks down the path to undergo his coronation, the soldiers sing a march-anthem in glorifying his kingdom:

> All the dry land that is the empire
> From the western deserts to the south, ah, ah, ah
> From the eastern sea to the north
> Every human life an imperial subject
> Even animals see the emperor's virtue
> All benefit and live in peace
> Everlasting, immortal, everlasting, everlasting.

The musical setting of this anthem, sung by the chorus in the concluding scene of the film, is not in itself ironic. Set to a march topic in duple rhythm, the bombastic music makes little commentary on the sung text. However, the scene in the broader context of the film presents a *situational irony* in the sense that the words sung by the chorus, particularly the line associated with "the emperor's virtue" is flatly contradicted by the cruelty of his deeds. The indigenous sound of the *guqin* (ancient zither with seven strings), however, appears throughout the film to allude to the sacredness of music and intimate friendship. When he lights the torch at the top of the staircase, Zheng breaks down in tears; at this precise moment, the sound of Jianli's guqin is heard for the last time: the famous tune *Liu Shui* ("Flowing Water") resounds in Zheng's interior space, as if he were haunted by the memory of those whom he loved. This reference may escape the attention of a typical Western viewer, but it emerges as an important signifier to those who are familiar with the legend of Yu Boya. Boya was a renowned guqin player from the Chu province who lived during the Warring States period. When a woodcutter named Zhong Qi, who understood Boya's music better than anyone else, unexpectedly passes away, Boya breaks the strings of the instrument and vows never to play the instrument again – claiming "the world not worthy to be played to" (Van Gulik 1969: 98).[8] From this story emerged the concept of *zhiyin,* which literally translates into "knowledge through sound," but more broadly speaking, refers to the sacredness of music and the Chinese ideal of friendship. In spite of the fact that the reference is turned inside out in the film – here, it is the friend (Zheng) who mourns for the loss of his musician (Jianli), the purity and sacredness of music emerges as a central theme in the film.

Furthermore, the soundtracks in the film play an important function in demarcating the Emperor's divided psyche. The bombastic march that glorifies Zheng's kingdom is pitted against the sound of Jianli's zither as colliding signifiers of the exterior and interior spaces occupied by Zheng. In spite of his relentless drive to succeed in his role as Emperor, Zheng is depicted as a tormented being – haunted by the ghosts of those whom he has killed. With nineteen failed attempts at his assassination, Zheng is obsessed with death and seeks refuge in Jianli's music as played on the guqin. The filmic narrative also exposes the treacheries of the top ministers as people who are not trustworthy, thus underscoring the relationships Zheng has with Jianli and Yueyang as the only ones built on sincerity and unconditional love. The filmic narrative focuses on Zheng's inner defeat (loss of his loved ones) set against his ruthless desire to gain political control of his kingdom. This inner torment drives him to destroy the court musical instruments at the end of this life by throwing them down a gorge. This scene, in fact, is shown at the opening of the film and underscores the importance of the zhiyin principle – without knowledge gained through the sacredness of music, the instruments are just empty shells, not worth keeping at all. Through this poignant cultural intertext, the Emperor emerges as a tragic hero who is defeated by his own greed and ambition.

The operatic narrative follows the film's basic plot while departing from its main depiction of the Emperor as a tragic hero. Ha Jin's libretto for *The First Emperor* takes a strikingly different path by undermining the Emperor's authority in the opera's final scene. As an expatriate of mainland China, the trauma of growing up during the Cultural Revolution has been an indispensible factor in shaping Jin's view of the world. After moving to the United States in 1985, Jin studied American literature at Brandeis University, yet it was only after the Tiananmen Square massacre in 1989 that he seriously pursued a career as a novelist. His award-winning novels such as *Waiting* (1999), *The Crazed* (2002), and *War Trash* (2004) are centered on themes of conflict between the individual and society in modern China, where Jin wrestles with questions of justice and injustice in uncompromisingly realistic terms. His novels and short stories often deal with the timeless universality of the human heart pitted against a shifting sociopolitical landscape. Rather than providing neat and tidy closure, Jin also infuses a nihilistic outlook in his protagonist at the end.[9] It is thus understandable that he would similarly inject irony, designed from a Brechtian perspective, into the narrative of *The First Emperor* in order for the audience to wrestle with the allegorical questions he poses.

The operatic plot revolves around the tragic deaths of Princess Yueyang and Jianli, who sacrifice their own lives for love. The Emperor, who wishes Jianli to compose a glorious anthem in order to commemorate his new kingdom, finds out much to his dismay that the anthem is based on a slave song about endless suffering. Here, the anthem does not glorify, but openly condemns the Emperor and the sacrifices made by numerous slaves to build his fortress (which came to be part of the Great Wall of China). Thus Jin's libretto aims at the articulation of *dramatic irony* through Jianli's creation of an anthem that overtly criticizes the Emperor's command, while the latter remains blind to this outcome until the very end. Unlike the anthem sung by the soldiers in the film, the opera's anthem speaks directly to the suffering endured by the slaves:

> Oh, we are building the dream to keep out the barbarians.
> Oh, we are bearing an eternal curse that has confused gods and man.
> [Refrain] Lord of Heaven, how long is this wall? Longer than the hundred wars!
> Lord of Heaven, when will our wars end? When water's heavier than sand!
> Oh, wide and rich is this land, nourished with blood and endless hope.
> Oh, we are building a dream we will never see,
> Dying for a peace we will never know.
> [Refrain]

The words here speak against the injustice of war and oppression. It situates the audience outside the opera's diegesis to contemplate the long history of suffering and death associated with building the Great Wall of China. In short, Jianli projects his own stance on the history of injustice through presenting the slaves' song as the anthem. In this respect, one could also say that the subversive tone of the anthem sets the stage for a form of *Socratic irony* – one that questions the received truth of what an anthem ought to represent (Colebrook 2004: 28). Dramatically, Tan emphasizes the role of the anthem via foreshadowing: presenting the melody first as part of an aria sung by the Emperor, then as a working song sung by slaves at the beginning of Act II, and finally as the official anthem that accompanies the Emperor's coronation – this time, sung by everyone in his palace.

The allegorical significance of the opera hinges, indeed, on this form of *Socratic irony*. To this end, the story is cast within a mythical world through the abundant use of metaphor and symbolism. Jin foregrounds the cosmological symbolism of *yin* and *yang* by underscoring the idea of "shadow" vs. "light" and other complementary forces that govern the natural order of the universe, according to Daoism in Chinese philosophy. A mythical framework is established through the inclusion of the Shaman and Yin-Yang Master as narrators, who introduce and comment on the story, while occupying extra-diegetic roles.[10] Their presence contributes to the theatrical mode of storytelling typically found in traditional Chinese operas, yet their function is not all that different from the Greek chorus's role in providing commentary.

Finally, Tan's music dramatizes the tension by juxtaposing different types of music that speak to the inner and outer psyches of the *dramatis personae*. While the ceremonial aspects of the Emperor's kingdom are conveyed through the bombastic and ceremonial instrumental music that one hears at the beginning of the opera, the psychological longing and desire that comment on the interiority of characters are conveyed through static and resonant use of softer, resonant instruments. More specifically, the pitched ceramic chimes, stone pebbles, temple bell, and other percussive instruments represent the outer glory of the Qin dynasty, while softer, continuous timbres generated through the Tibetan singing bowl and waterphones represent the inner longing and desires of the main characters.[11] For example, when Yueyang and Jianli fall in love, their arias are embedded within this background layer of resonant, ethereal sounds.

To what extent, though, does Tan's compositional strategy based on the "1+1=1" principle add to the tradition of grand opera? How does this opera contribute to the Western tradition of "exotic" grand operas in the global age?

Inscribing Chineseness into Exotic Grand Opera

In *Musical Exoticism: Images and Reflections,* Ralph Locke defines musical exoticism as "the process of evoking in or through music a place, people, or social milieu that is *not* entirely imaginary and that differs profoundly from the home country or culture in attitudes, customs, and morals" (2009: 53). In surveying musical literature from the eighteenth century to the present, he introduces two paradigms: the Exotic-Style paradigm (ESP), where music is intended to be foreign as it incorporates specific musical signifiers of Otherness that register as "exotic" to the Western listener, for example, Rimsky-Korsakov's *Capriccio Espagnol* and *Sheherazade,* works that contain modes and scales with chromatically altered notes as signifiers of an imagined, alien land (48). The Full-Context paradigm (FCP), in contrast, engages almost any stylistic and formal resources in order to convey exotic characters and uses a wide range of musical materials to construct situations and moods (62). With regard to the latter, Locke further comments:

> The words and visual elements in an opera, oratorio, or film "place" the character or group in a given Elsewhere. The music then marks the character or group indelibly as 'barbarous,' 'seductive,' or whatever. And the audience melds the two forms of information into an indissoluble whole "This unfamiliar Elsewhere [Japan, North Africa, etc.]," they sense, "is a place of barbarity" (or seduction, etc.). Were one to hear the music on its own, it might not convey any immediate geographic or ethnic overtones. In context, the audience accepts it as consistent with the exotic setting and with the exotic character' or group's apparent proclivities. (2009: 63)

As examples of FCP, Locke refers to operas and musical theaters that provide a broad range of possibilities for representing the exotic Other within the canon of Western art music. His listing includes, but is not limited to: Handel's *Tamerlano*

(1724), Bizet's *Carmen* (1875), Saint-Saëns's *Samson et Dalila* (1875), Gilbert and Sullivan's *Mikado* (1885), Puccini's *Madam Butterfly* (1904) and *Turandot* (1925), and Sondheim's *Pacific Overtures* (1976). Depending on the opera, the music may or may not directly reference the Other; for example, the seductive aria Carmen sings ("L'Amour est un oiseau rebelle"), based on the Habañera rhythm, situates her as the exotic Other to a group of Spanish officers – as a gypsy woman who lives a carefree, amoral life.

Coining the phrase "exoticism in the global age" to account for the impact of globalization on new trends and their cross-cultural dissemination, Locke discusses how exoticist conceptions and discourse continue to play out in a variety of different settings. Notably, he calls attention to the composers' disavowal of overt forms of exoticism, while pursuing ways to extract structural aspects of foreign traditions and fit them into their own modernist or postmodernist musical language (Locke 2009: 278). Locke discusses Tan's opera *Marco Polo* (1996) as a quintessential postmodern work that offers an eclectic merging of cultural styles: elements of Beijing opera, Kabuki theater, Tibetan throat singing, Gregorian chant, and Wagner's *Parsifal*. Together with librettist Paul Griffiths, Tan structures the opera around concurrent journeys undertaken by Marco Polo and the Mongolian warrior Kublai Khan. As a non-narrative opera *par excellence,* traditional narrative is replaced by the metaphor of a journey, in which Marco Polo is transformed into the very symbol for the different "journeys" that we undertake in the postmodern world. Having two separate identities at first, Marco and Polo meet natural forces as well as Dante, Shakespeare, and Sheherazada (a variation of Scheherazade); through their encounter with the Chinese poet Li Po and Gustav Mahler in their spiritual journey, Marco and Polo meld into one.[12] Musical and cultural references are tossed back and forth as refracted fragments without congealing into a hybrid entity. When Marco and Polo arrive in Tibet they are greeted by Tibetan monks who chant using throat singing, accompanied by the deep, guttural sounds of Tibetan horns. When they finally reach the Great Wall of China, the ghost of Gustav Mahler appears and sings "Der Trunkene im Frühling" from *Das Lied on der Erde.* Then Li Po, the author of the original Chinese poem interrupts and sings it in Chinese with vocal inflections in the style of Peking Opera. Invoking Tan's own system of hybridization, the structure of *Marco Polo* is based on the formula of "1+1+1+1+1=5": here, no one of the borrowed styles dominates over the others, but they are seamlessly woven into a fluid, postmodern web of changing references. This perspective accords with Tan's own commentary on *Marco Polo:*

> Sounds and different musical cultures guide my own development, leading me through a deeper journey before the work can reach technical refinement. From Medieval to Mongolian chants; from Western Opera to Beijing Opera; from orchestra to sitar, pipa, and Tibetan ritual horns – the fusion of musical sounds came [sic] from all corners of the globe is the definition of 'Marco Polo' to me. Did Marco Polo's journey actually happen? Did someone dream it up? Or did the journey imagine us? (Tan 2007: 10–13)

In contrast to the stylistic eclecticism of *Marco Polo,* Tan presents a unified construction of themes and leitmotifs in articulating the ironic narrative of *The First Emperor.* Rather than debate the exoticness of the music as leaning exclusively toward Pucciniesque or indigenous Chinese operatic traditions, my analysis examines how different traits extracted from Puccini, *qinqiang,* and Beijing operatic traditions contribute to Tan's "1+1=1" principle. The program notes from the premiere at the Metropolitan Opera speak to his new approach to exoticism in the global age:

> Tan Dun's musical vocabulary seeks to bring together dualistic elements: East/West, classical/non-classical, avant-garde/indigenous, old/new. The score combines the expressive power of traditional ancient Chinese singing with the long musical lines of Italian opera. The operatic orchestra is augmented both by historically-inspired Chinese instruments, which the composer researched in remote areas around Qin Shi Huang's capital at Xian[,] and by newly created instruments intended to express the music of ancient times as Tan Dun has imagined it[,] based on extensive research and scant historical evidence.

The program notes emphasize the conceptual binary of East and West in valorizing the expectations of the Metropolitan opera audience. What most Western critics and scholars take for granted is that appropriation of Western music has a longstanding history in the modernization of East Asian nations. From an indigenous perspective, ethnomusicologist Joseph Lam argues that Chinese concert music *is* synonymous with the music that Chinese composers create with the language of Western or international concert music (Lam 2008: 47). This tradition of appropriating western music harkens back to the model operas and ballets that flourished during the Cultural Revolution, but can also be traced back to the Yellow River Cantata composed by Xian Xinghai in 1931 during the Sino-Japanese war. Thus, Western music has held a highly valorized niche in Chinese society throughout the course of the twentieth century. In the globalized world today, Lam argues that modern Chinese construct their identity through strategically implementing fundamental paradigms such as the inner (*zhong*) vs. the outer (*wai*) and the civilized (*ya*) vs. the vulgar/vernacular (*su*) (51). He further claims that Tan inscribes Chineseness in his Western music-based compositions by drawing from the vulgar/vernacular elements of culture, that is to say, the popular theatrical forms of Beijing and other regional Chinese operas. At the same time, *The First Emperor* demonstrates Tan's self-conscious attempt to write an opera in the grand opera tradition, complete with leitmotifs and recurring themes; the blend of cultural elements is seamless, *not* oppositional or eclectic as in the case of *Marco Polo.* However, to see this work as catering to the East/West binary is a position Tan himself is known to dismiss: "no East anymore, no West anymore. . . . My purpose . . . is to create my own unity" (Locke 2009: 334).

Thus from a modern Chinese cultural perspective, one can argue for a hybridized operatic style that cuts across multiple dimensions – cultural, historical, and aesthetic – of regional Chinese and Italian *bel canto* operatic traditions, without invoking discourses of exoticism or Orientalism. Yet this positionality does not conflict with Locke's assertion that Tan, as a modernist and cosmopolitan composer, writes for the western consumers of "exotic" grand opera: after all, the commission came from the Metropolitan Opera – renowned for its championing of traditional operas. What the Western critics fail to acknowledge and elaborate upon is the fact that Tan's extensive research took him back to the Qin region in China and the study of the rapidly vanishing *qinqiang* vocal style; as he became acquainted with the authentic style of singing from listening to practitioners of this school, he eventually decided to extract certain aspects of the singing and adapt them to Western operatic style.

As one of the oldest regional operas, *qinqiang* originated in the Shaanxi province in northern China. Drawing from regional folk songs as well as drum and woodwind music, this operatic form became an established genre by 1800 and made its way down to the Guangdong province in the south and up to Xinjiang province in the northwest. The famous female impersonator, Wei Changcheng, contributed to the spread of *qinqiang* in 1779, laying the groundwork for Peking opera; however, the stylistic development of Peking opera in the course of the twentieth century, in turn, influenced *qinqiang* so that its vocal mode of delivery became softer and the actors' gestures became more precise (Wang-Ngai and Lovrick 1997: 17). There are around 2700 pieces in the repertoire, mostly based on historical drama, classical stories, and myths. There are thirteen role types that include various male and female roles, the painted face, and the clown. The performance style is akin to German *Singspiel* or modern musicals in its alternation between spoken dialogue and sung aria. While the spoken dialogue is typically accompanied by a percussion instrument (usually a clapper), a small silk and bamboo instrumental ensemble accompanies the arias in heterophony.

The melodic framework of *qinqiang* derives from one of two scales derived from the classical operatic genre called *kunqu* as shown below:

Huayin:	**5**	6	(7)	**1**	**2**	3	(4)	5
Kuyin:	**5**	6♭	7	**1**	**2**♭	3	4	5

Although the scales depart from an equal-temperament tuning system, the first, called *huayin* ("florid tone") is based on the major pentatonic scale (in plagal disposition), with added scale degrees 4 and 7 used intermittently. The second, called *kuyin* ("bitter tone"), uses all seven tones with flatted scale degrees on 3 and 7 (equivalent to a plagal form of the Dorian mode). As highlighted in bold, scale steps 5, 1, and 2 are the same in both scales; however, *huayin* emphasizes 3 and 6, whereas *kuyin* emphasizes 4 and ♭7. As far as thematic and textural associations are concerned, joyous and celebratory themes are accompanied by melodies that derive from the *huayin* scale (corresponding with the major pentatonic scale), while themes that connote sorrow and pain derive from the *kuyin* scale.

For example, in a well-known *qinqiang* opera called *San Di Xie* ("Three Drops of Blood"), an old man named Zhou Renrui loses his fortune; because his younger brother fails to acknowledge kinship with Renrui's oldest son (due to a faulty system of determining bloodlines in his county), he becomes estranged

$\hat{5}$ $\hat{4}$ $\hat{5}$ $\hat{4}$-$\hat{3}$-$\hat{2}$-$\hat{1}$ $\hat{5}$ $\hat{1}$ $\hat{5}$ $\hat{1}$ $\hat{5}$ $\hat{4}$ $\hat{3}$ $\hat{2}$ $\hat{1}$ $\hat{♭7}$

wo haxia | gu_an_ | den | mo gul ha | an

"The Wutai county's magistrate is really ignorant…."

Example 5.1. The "Lament" Aria from *San Di Xie*

from his own son. He sings a "lament" aria based on the *kuyin* scale, complaining about the ignorance of the county's magistrate and vowing to the son's fiancée that he will continue to look for his son against all odds. As illustrated in example 5.1, the vocal line fluctuates between the two pillar scale degrees (5 and 1) and often highlights the fourth ascent within the *kuyin* scale on C. While the first vocal phrase hangs on scale degree ♭7, the instrumental interlude echoes the downward contour and resolves the tone to C at the downbeat of the fifth bar. The metric framework expands and contracts to $\frac{4}{4}$ meter by the addition of a beat at phrase endings. Such lament arias are contrasted by joyous or celebratory arias cast in the *huayin* scale, featured elsewhere in the same opera.

The vocal style of delivery in *qinqiang* is decisively rougher than that of standard Peking opera; with a predominantly nasal sound, the singer incorporates slides and noise-like elements into the vocalization. Considering how the authentic vocalization of *qinqiang* would not be compatible with Western opera, Tan made a conscious decision not to quote melodies from this operatic genre directly, but rather extract certain properties of this regional operatic practice, combined with those associated with Peking opera. Here, Locke coins the term *transcultural* composition to refer to works that incorporate certain stylistic and formal conventions of another culture's music, merging them in such a way that cultural traditions draw on and influence one another (2009: 228–29). In accordance with such a principle, Tan abstracted certain features from the *qinqiang* tradition and fused them into a hybrid style that expands the Western operatic tradition. To parallel the symbolic significance of the three colors (red, black, and white) that represented the Qin Dynasty, he discovered that the *qinqiang* vocal style has three distinctive formal characteristics: the tritone interval, the leap of a fourth, and the practice of moving from the highest note to the lowest.[13] Tan comments: "I treated these as the 'old three' in my music, to match the visual 'old three' in color on stage. So I treat my tritone [interval] as black, my continuance of the fourth as white, and the highest note to lowest as red, because it is so intense" (Kors 2008: 7).

Tan's own way of inscribing Chineseness in *The First Emperor* is documented by the video footage that accompanies the Met Player's HD broadcast of the opera.[14] In the documentary footage, Tan is seen conducting the rehearsal of *The First Emperor* at the Met with the orchestra, the singers, and his collaborators. In conducting the orchestra, he demonstrates by singing to the musicians how he wants the musical gestures shaped in conformance with the rounded, sliding vocal inflections of Peking Opera: "only Indian and Chinese music has this kind of music where every beat is a [*sic*] start – pong, pong, pong. Swing a little bit between the silence. . . ." In order for the orchestra members to make vocal effects in tandem with instrumental effects, he also demonstrates the proper Chinese intonation and slides. In another segment, Tan demonstrates to Plácido Domingo how "Zhongguo" (China) needs to be pronounced in order for the acclaimed tenor to sing the word with precise linguistic intonation. Another rehearsal scene illustrates Tan teaching the Flying Apsaras (heavenly maidens) who perform the waterphones the precise effects he wants by actively demonstrating how to play the instruments and the specific sound he is after. With respect to physical gestures, the choreographer Dou Dou Huang worked with every one of the singers and instrumentalists to acquire precise hand and foot movements associated with Peking Opera. Elizabeth Futral, who plays Yueyang, worked especially closely with a choreographer to imitate the role of an aristocratic female (*qingyi*). Furtal comments on the new genre that Tan has established in describing her role as "lyrically set in the [W]estern operatic style," although in certain passages she was asked to adopt vocal inflections drawn from the Peking opera vocal style. Such practical considerations that went into training the musicians in preparation for the Metropolitan operatic production speak most strongly to Tan's "1+1=1" ideal.

Finally, the mythological framework is shaped by the theatricality of Zhang Yimou's stage production. At first glance, there are many aspects of the production of The First Emperor that overlap with Zhang's 1998 staging of Puccini's *Turandot* at the Forbidden City in Beijing.[15] The opening scene recreates the bombastic music modeled on the barbaric custom of having soldiers beat on their chest and thighs while chanting and drumming. All of the soldiers are cast in military uniforms that match those worn by terracotta soldiers unearthed from the Qin dynasty. The colors of black, red, and white, representing the Qin dynasty, are used in abundance to illustrate Qin Shi Huang's wealth. When Jianli is first presented, he is branded as a slave by the mark on his forehead. Through the addition of an acrobatic dancer from the Peking Opera, the Yin-Yang master, the Shaman, the "erotic" spirits that accompany the lovers on resonant waterphones, and other aspects of Chinese culture – old and new – are brought into the hybridized production.

Leitmotif, Themes, and Musico-dramatic Intertexts

Let us now turn to the analysis of the music in the multimedial production of *The First Emperor*. I will be referring to the Metropolitan Opera's DVD release of the 2007 HD broadcast, featuring Plácido Domingo in the title role of Emperor Qin. Tan crafts the melodic and harmonic materials in the grand opera tradition by interweaving leitmotifs and other themes as unifying musical agents. The opera is framed by two non-diegetic actors/singers who provide narration and commentary to the story being told. In lieu of a standard overture, the Yin-Yang master appears on stage, vocalizing in the Peking Opera style as he introduces the story of the First Emperor over the pounding beats of the bass drum:

> [English translation]: More than two thousand years ago wars ravaged China, where seven states faced one another striving for dominance. Among them the king of Qin was the most powerful. He wiped out the other six states, walled the northern border and unified the land under heaven. Thus, he became China's first ruler – the First Emperor!

The Taiwanese actor, Wu Xin-guo, delivers this dramatic recitation by skillfully intermixing two Beijing opera roles and the style of vocal recitation associated with these roles: *qingyi* (noble woman) and *hualian* (painted face) (DVD #1: 6'17"). In between his recitation, the strings sound out what I call the "fate" motive, as shown in example 5.2a. This motive sounds in the background as the Yin-Yang master explains how he served in the Qin palace as the one who maintains the royal calendar and reads the country's feng shui (an age-old Chinese system of divination). As shown in example 5.2a, this leitmotif comprises a seven-note melody with interlocking tritones and major thirds; although the composite harmonic succession of the first six chords is highly dissonant and varied in constitution, each simultaneity combines the tritone B-F with a combination of major thirds, e.g., Ab-C, Db-F, and F#-A# in the first chord. The last chord (F^7) fails to provide harmonic closure to the harmonic progression, and its sustained effect presents an ominous backdrop for the Yin-Yang master's recitation about how Qin Shi Huang came into power by defeating his enemies to become the first emperor. Notice how the tritone emphasized in the first measure resolves to the perfect fifth, F-C, in the second measure.

The surface features of this leitmotif recall the five-note motive played in unison that opens Puccini's *Turandot* (example 5.2b): the dissonance set up by the falling tritone, E#-B, resolves to F# via its dominant C#. As the Mandarin announces the execution of the Prince of Persia who failed to solve the riddle posed by Turandot, this motive recurs in rhythmic diminution and provides a negative commentary on Turandot as a merciless princess. However, from a broader perspective, the rhetorical function of the two motives differs considerably. In the course of *Turandot,* this signifier of barbarism is replaced by the "Mo-li-hua" theme in Eb pentatonic, which glorifies Turandot's kingdom. In contrast, the "fate" leitmotif in *the First Emperor* does not have a positive counterpart: it recurs in various forms at key junctures in the opera, not unlike the "fate" motive in Bizet's *Carmen,* to call attention to the inescapable fate that awaits the principal characters. The voicing of the chords that cycle through tritones, fifths, and major thirds extends Puccini's textural "planing" of diatonic chords, but not in a manner that suggests direct borrowing from *Turandot.* Its effect is unsettling precisely because the progression lacks forward momentum.

a. The "fate" leitmotif

b. The opening motive from Puccini's *Turandot*

Example 5.2a/b. The "Fate" Leitmotif from *The Last Emperor* and the Opening Motive from Puccini's *Turandot*

After the Yin-Yang master orders the musicians to "strike the stones and urns" and "slap your sides as you sing" in a manner that is suggested by Sima Qian's *Historical Records,* an animated instrumental variation of the "fate" motive performed by the indigenous ensemble follows.[16] As an acrobat dances to a tune played on the guzheng that is based predominantly on the tritone (F-B), the shaman, the other non-diegetic character, appears and calls for the spirits. Unlike the Yin-Yang master, she is a mythical character who prophesizes that a sacrifice will take place, involving killing and burning, in order to "build an imperial dream," events that will ensue in the Qin palace. She summons the spirits in order to find out "who will kill, burn, and make sacrifice." After her initial dramatic appearance, the chorus joins her in singing the music of sacrifice (Theme 1), as shown in example 5.3. This melody is presented first with tritone (B-F) as the head interval, but later the phrase undergoes modal transformation; the perfect fifth (C-F) replaces the tritone to set a more optimistic tone for the fate of Qin's kingdom (DVD #1: 16':58"). Given F as the focal pitch, the whole-tone inflection of the antecedent phrase (F-G-A-B-C#) is complemented by the more stable and consonant Mixolydian modal inflection of the consequent phrase; note how

Example 5.3. Theme 1: Music of Sacrifice

the tritone accompanies the word "sacrifice" at the end of the antecedent phrase. As the chorus joins in, the music builds in density, concluding with a full brass fanfare. This theme returns at important dramatic turning points in the narrative as the signifier of sacrifice; notably, when the Emperor forces Jianli into accepting his terms for marrying Yueyang – allowing General Wang to marry Yueyang first, then waiting for the general to die in battle.

The opera proper begins when the Emperor enters the palace to complain that this music "neither moves Heaven nor Earth" because it fails to "touch the heart." While his minister and general remind him that this "loud" music has served their kingdom since ancient times, the Emperor insists that he needs a different kind of music that "dispels shadows" and that "loud music weakens our spirit." It soon becomes apparent that his friend from his youth, Jianli, is the Shadow whom the Emperor speaks of. At this point, the Emperor (played by Plácido Domingo) reminisces about the earlier years when he and Jianli played together as children (DVD #1: 23'38"). As shown in example 5.4, a descending Mixolydian melody on D with sliding tones is featured at such moments, hinting at the intimacy shared between the two men in earlier times, when Jianli's mother also took care of the Emperor. As the theme signifies reminiscence and longing for a past that cannot be reclaimed, the long, descending contour is interrupted by the sliding ascent of an octave from C2 to C4 at each phrase ending. Rather than constructing the second phrase to provide closure to the first, Tan cyclically varies the first phrase in a manner that accentuates the sense of yearning. In the next reiteration of this theme, the vocal phrase is punctuated by the gong, doubled in the oboe, and harmonized in fourths – familiar exotic musical signifiers.

When the solo violin plays a variation of this theme, the warriors in the background pair up and place their arms around each other in gesture of friendship; meanwhile the Emperor gazes outward in deep thought. During this moment of intimacy, the percussionists create a resonant soundscape by bowing the side of the Tibetan singing bowls, while the Emperor shifts to a declamatory mode of recitation, praising Jianli's transformative sound of guzheng. It becomes quickly apparent that the Emperor thinks Jianli's music is the only music that can harmonize Heaven, Earth and Man. He then promises General Wang his consent to a marriage with his daughter if Jianli is found and brought back to his kingdom. Elated by this offer, General Wang sings a tender aria in D Ionian mode, profess-

The Sha-dow that_ haunts me___ where- ever___ I___ go___

Ten years he and I___ lived to ge__ ther when I was a

hos - tage in___ the state of___ Zhao.

Example 5.4. Theme 2: Signifier of Yearning

ing his love for Yueyang: "like the river that flows, I will follow you. . . ." How-ever, the tritone in the accompaniment undermines his sincere expression of love for Yueyang. The first scene concludes with the Emperor vowing to search his kingdom for Jianli in order for him to compose an anthem. At this point, Theme 1 returns in full, as the chorus and Shaman join in and sing: "How many wars must we fight?" As the brass offers a brilliant fanfare, the postlude quickly shifts to the battle music built on the "fate" motive, during which the Yin-Yang master dances.

The second scene of Act I begins with an overture based on a succession of open fifth chords in the strings, accompanied by airy, pentatonic chords in the woodwinds. Coming down the majestic staircase in the symbolic colors of the Qin dynasty, the Emperor extols the beauty of his palace with adulatory declamation, "Zhongguo, Zhongguo!" ("China, China!") (DVD #1: 35' 40"). Speaking to his chief minister, he comments on the need to standardize weights and measurements, currency, and road conditions in order to unify his kingdom. The rhythmic division alternates between the asymmetrical metric grouping of 3+3+2 and symmetrical 4+4 to lend a light and whimsical air to the Emperor's meditations concerning his plans to systematize every aspect of his kingdom. The D Ionian mode and steady pattern of perfect fifths in the accompaniment parallel contexts in which the *huayin* scale is used in *qinqiang* operas to signify a joyous or celebratory mood. This lighter number shares the same dramatic quality as the comical ensemble number that opens Act II of *Turandot,* where the court ministers, Ping, Pong, and Pang sing about the splendor of Turandot's kingdom. The music steers away from this steady accompaniment only when the Emperor complains about undesirable music and ("worst of all," he sings repeatedly) the "heretic" writings by scholars that do not conform to Qin dynasty script. Qin Shi Huang's merciless act of burning all religious texts and scholarship that do not align with his ideals receives a rather callous treatment in Ha Jin's libretto.

Example 5.5. "Fate" Leitmotif

Jianli, who is brought to the Emperor as a slave, refuses to acknowledge his past relationship with the Emperor and rejects the Emperor's request to compose an anthem in his honor. In angry defiance, Jianli parodies a portion of Theme 2, proclaiming that he would rather cut off his tongue than to call the Emperor "Elder Brother." "I loathe to share the same sky with you, tyrant," Jianli further retorts. His state of fury subsides only when Yueyang interjects and sings: "The shadow survives the heat of the sun, a hero shows his mettle." The persistent use of Daoist symbolism is one of the key elements differentiating Ha Jin's libretto from Puccini's.[17]

In the final scene of Act I, Yueyang attends to Jianli in her chamber. As she sings a tender lullaby, the Emperor and his chief minister enter to check on Jianli, who has gone on a hunger strike. Flirtatiously, she asks the Emperor for his promise to "give" her Jianli if she manages to turn him around. After half-heartedly conceding to her wish, the Emperor leaves her to tend to Jianli, who gradually awakens to his desire for her. In a characteristic manner, they express their erotic desires in poetic terms: simply put, the image of winter gives way to spring. As she strokes the strings on the guzheng, Yueyang describes herself as a "lotus flower" longing for a spring shower or a light-hearted bird who whistles with other birds. As she describes her yearning in terms of a "lotus flower" that "opens shy, thirsty for your sweetest wine," the percussion ensemble creates and sustains a resonant timbral field with waterphones and Tibetan singing bowls (DVD #1: 1:00′32″). With her kiss, Jianli expresses his desire for love in terms of "green leaves" that are "breaking crusted ice." As the chief minister and general Wang agonizingly eavesdrop on them, the two consummate their love. As the stage turns dark, the three female spirits (representing lust) perform their waterphones by bowing on the side of the instruments to produce translucent and ethereal sounds. The "fate" motive played by the flutes is heard faintly in the background.

Soon afterward, Yueyang, who has been paralyzed from the waist down from falling off a horse, regains sensation in her legs and is able to walk again (DVD #1: 1:08′53″). As Yueyang sings her line that hangs on the ascending tritone, F-B, a variation of the fate motive returns, as shown in example 5.5. The accompaniment arpeggiates the "fate" motive in contrary motion to Yueyan's vocal line, accentuating this dramatic turning point.

As the music gains momentum through the addition of a combative rhythmic ostinato, the Emperor appears and is at first overjoyed to hear of his daughter's sudden recovery. Then he accuses Jianli of "ruining" his daughter, telling him that Yueyang has already been promised to General Wang. A red sash that the Emperor yanks away from Jianli signifies her loss of virginity. Yueyang, in turn, pleads with her father to keep Jianli alive. The Shaman warns Jianli to "beware of the sun" and her repeated declamation of "shadow" to refer to Jianli is accompanied by the central tritone (B-F). The first act builds to a climactic ending as the lovers elaborate on the power of love based on Theme 1, amid interjections by the fate motive. When the general and the top minister advise the Emperor to kill Jianli right away, the Emperor gives the order, and then quickly changes his mind to keep Jianli alive until he finishes composing the anthem for his kingdom. The Emperor's final outcry is accompanied by the animated repetition of the "fate" motive in the strings.

Throughout the course of Act I, the sun/shadow metaphor symbolizes the relationship between the dominating (the Emperor) and the dominated (Jianli). Figuratively speaking, it also alludes to the interdependence between the contrary forces of yin and yang that governs dynamic forces in nature, according to the cosmological principle of Daoism. In the course of Act II, the power relationship becomes inverted when Jianli assumes dominance over the Emperor by striking at his vulnerable point – that is to say, the Emperor's dependence on Jianli for music that unites "Heaven, Earth, and Mankind."

The Prelude to Act II features the solo guzheng player, who engages in a quasi-improvisatory musical exchange with two harps. The wild and chaotic glissandos eventually give way to the theme of the love duet sung between Yueyang and Jianli, in F Mixolydian mode (DVD #2: 1'51"). The lyrical tune in three-four meter speaks of cattle and goats grazing in the field. This pastoral theme is accompanied by a fifth-based ostinato motive (F-C-G-C). The lovers slip into melodic fragments taken from the "Reminiscence" theme as they pause to reflect on their peaceful existence. Similar to the Emperor's "Zhongguo" aria that opened scene 2 of Act I, the mood of this aria parallels that associated with the *huayin* scale in *qinqiang*.

Then the lovers pause to hear a slave song coming from afar. As the guards crack the whip on the slaves, the Shaman bemoans the cruelty imposed on the slaves in building the Great Wall: "the wolves are fat, feeding on corpses. Red, the cranes are red spattered with blood. Has the Lord of Heaven no eyes to see how humans die?" The slaves then begin to sing about "bearing an eternal curse that has confused gods and man." On the stage, Jianli observes the slaves in complete disbelief. When the Emperor approaches him and asks how his composition is coming along, Jianli bluntly responds and tells him that the slaves inspire him. Ignoring his comment, the Emperor then describes Yueyang as his "sun, who gives off light," while Jianli represents the "earth under the sun." Over a tritone harmonization, Yueyang retorts by singing that "the sun never tells the earth: 'you belong to me'" (DVD #2: 15'55"). Yueyang insists that music is her "light" and that she loves no one but Jianli. When Yueyang threatens to kill herself if her wish in not granted, the Empress intervenes by singing an aria in F Mixolydian mode (with falling fourths) to calm the Emperor. The two women sing a duet in which they remind themselves that they should let their happiness and virtues to be dictated by the Emperor. It is clear that Yueyang is conflicted, torn by her wish to follow her own path to happiness. The Emperor joins in the concluding trio by emphasizing the point that their own happiness is "nothing compared to the cause of our nation." As the Emperor schemes to marry Yueyang off to the General and convince Jianli to finish the anthem, they sing a duet based on Theme 1 (first with the tritone B-F) as the slaves' song is heard in the background. While they both sing that the music must be "the sound of Heaven," it is apparent that the two disagree on what that entails. Scene 1 comes to a brilliant close as Jianli swears that the Emperor will not be able to hear the anthem until the day of his coronation.

In stark contrast to the end of the film's narrative, the final scene of the opera is deeply subversive and ironic. As Jianli undergoes preparation to be appointed as Chief Minister to preside over the imperial inauguration, another variation of the "Fate" motive is heard in the brass section, followed by the choral entry on Theme 1, transposed now to G major. The grandeur of this scene is reminiscent of *Turandot*. Jianli plays his part faithfully in commencing the inauguration as Tan's music, recalling Stravinsky's *Sacre du printemps,* accompanies Dou Dou Huang's ritual dance.[18] The HD broadcast of the opera is especially effective in capturing the ironic juxtaposition of the distraught Emperor and the splendor of the coronation scene (DVD #2: 41'45"). Every step of the staircase is decorated with Qin dynasty calligraphy; the ministers on both sides wear red and black robes, while the courtiers on the furthest left and right wear multi-colored robes with calligraphic insignia on the back. Jianli, on the right, wears the official robe for the master of ceremony. The Emperor appears in an elaborately embroidered golden robe and salutes his courtiers with his arms outstretched.

Yet the sounding of the imperial bell comes to an abrupt halt when the Shaman announces that "the princess refused to enter the bridal chamber and the general strangled her" on the dyad, B and F. Yueyang then appears as a ghost to tell the Emperor that she killed herself because she could not sacrifice love for filial duty (DVD #2: 44'21"). Her sung text is filled with allegorical symbols of cold and dryness to depict her withering spirit devoid of love. As shown in example 5.6, her aria begins with a melody that merges properties from previous themes in disjunct phrases, punctuated by a downward slide and the blaring brass chord. When speaking in metaphor, her style of delivery shifts toward the Peking opera vocal inflections, characterized by portamento and slides: "when Jianli failed me, he took away spring. Dry husks of leaves rattled in my heart, where no dew would fall. . . . I could not sacrifice love for you." As highlighted in example 5.6, even as Yueyang's style of singing veers more toward the ornamentation of Peking opera, it contains the five-note fragment of Theme 2. Typical of Peking Opera pro-

Example 5.6. Yueyang's Ghost Song

ductions, ghosts are shown without hands or feet and dressed in white; here, dark blue lighting is used to mark Yueyang's ghostly appearance.

As Yueyang bids farewell to her father, begging him to forgive her, melodic fragments of Theme 2 saturate her vocal line, echoed by the solo cello. Next, following the Shaman's announcement about seeing "shadows rising and falling," the ghost of General Wang appears and tells the Emperor that he did not take his own life, but rather that he was poisoned by Jianli. As a ghost, the General warns the Emperor to beware of Jianli: "Be warned. Jianli's your enemy. His revenge for his mother and village lurks coiled like a serpent in a tree." Unlike the film narrative, where the ministers and generals are the ones not to be trusted, here the General is depicted as a loyal follower of the Emperor who meets a wrongful death.

As the two ghosts vanish, the distraught Emperor sings in agony about "feeling death in his bones" – how it "crushes him and sinks him into the earth." As the courtiers resume ringing the temple bell, Jianli reappears in plain clothes. The camera deploys medium and close-up shots of the two men who talk at cross purposes: while the Emperor begs for peace for his own withered heart, the despondent Jianli shouts: "blood rising. . . . The blood of the innocent!" Rejecting the Emperor's plea to call him "Elder Brother," Jianli laughs at him in disdain, shouts out "The First Emperor of China!" in mockery. Then he smashes the guzheng, cursing as he crushes it in the middle of the stage. As a final, horrific gesture of defiance, he proceeds to cut out his own tongue (DVD #2: 1:02'30"). Those familiar with Sima Qian's *Historical Records* recognize the shadow of Jing Ke, the assassin who mocked the Emperor, in Jianli's final act of defiance. As the Emperor witnesses this gruesome act, he takes a step back and sings about "the pain stabbing deeper into his heart," the "fate" motive is heard for the last time. Suddenly, as if possessed by a fit of madness, the Emperor thrusts his sword into Jianli's chest and kills him.

Example 5.7. Theme 3: Signifier of "Eternal" Suffering

Turning to the audience, the Emperor then feebly declares to the world that he *is* the First Emperor. As the chorus follows up by singing "long live the Emperor, long live China" to a variation of Theme 1, the orchestra cadences gloriously in F♯ major; yet this moment is punctuated with Theme 2 that ends ominously with the tritone. Running out of patience, the Emperor rings the Imperial bell once more and orders his men to sing the anthem Jianli has composed for him. Much to his dismay, the Emperor discovers that Jianli's anthem is based on a song sung by slaves about their suffering and being eternally cursed, as shown in example 5.7 (DVD #2: 1:11'24"). It is no coincidence that the oscillation between G and C (as shown in the first bracketed passage) and the overall contour that descends to ♭7 in the first phrase are features that parallel those in the "lament" aria of *qinqiang* opera, shown in example 5.1. The oscillating fourth motive on the words "building the dream" signifies the essence of the lament, as the slaves sing of the eternal curse place on them by the Qin Emperor. Other features of this theme, such as the four-part homophonic texture, mark it as a choral anthem.

Dejected, the Emperor slowly walks up the staircase as he questions whether there will be an end to his suffering. The final scene in which the Emperor is reduced to an utterly helpless figure, betrayed by all whom he loves, is bitterly ironic. He cannot accept Jianli's anthem since it does not paint a glorious picture of his kingdom. In stark contrast to the film *Qin Song,* the opera's concluding scene delivers an anthem that has little to do with the internal music the Emperor hears as a token of affection for Jianli. At this moment it becomes clear that the anthem is Jianli's revenge – he has the final word telling the world that the Emperor has, in effect, no clothes.

How Pucciniesque is the Opera?
Actantial Themes and Progression

It is no surprise that Western critics and opera connoisseurs, upon hearing *The First Emperor* for the first time, turned to Puccini's *Turandot* as a point of reference. There are definite parallels one can draw between the two operas with respect to their modal coloring. Puccini faced the challenge of integrating Chinese folk songs with modernist harmonic idioms (i.e., whole-tone scale) that were in vogue in the first quarter of the twentieth century; he relied heavily on penta-tonic and quartal-based harmonies to convey the exotic quality of an imagined past filled with imaginary characters. The clarity with which Puccini articulates modal colors has led scholars to adopt the idea of *tinte* (stylistic "colors") in clas-sifying themes. Following Ashbrook and Powers's (1991) analysis of *tinte* in Puc-cini's *Turandot*, Anthony Sheppard attributes three major *tinte* and sources of stylistic influence in *The First Emperor:* 1) a late Romantic and lyrical style based in part on Puccini; 2) a primitivist style resembling Tan's own earlier avant-garde works; and 3) a Chinese operatic and folk style drawing on Peking op-era and other traditional forms (2009: 290). For example, Sheppard attributes Theme 2 (the "reminiscence" aria shown in example 5.5) that the Emperor sings to remind Jianli of their shared youth as an example of the lyrical, late roman-tic "Puccini" *tinta* (295). The primitivist *tinta,* on the other hand, is associated with the orchestral interludes that involve percussion music accompanied by vo-cables, which imparts a ritual and ceremonial image of Qin's court music (300). Lastly, Sheppard refers to the omnipresent tritone interval as a marker of the "dissonant" *tinta* (category 3), exemplified by the "fate" motive that accompanies the Yin-Yang master's recitation in the Peking opera style (as shown in example 5.2a). In spite of what appears to be a highly reductive approach, Sheppard con-cedes that: "Tan's oeuvre and particularly *The First Emperor* is contradictory and ambiguous in a number of dimensions as well as compelling." Furthermore, he states that "any one passage or stylistic feature in the opera suggests multiple le-gitimate sources and it proves impossible to settle their competing claims of in-fluence" (286).

In my assessment, Sheppard appears to fudge the issue by claiming that the sources of influence cannot be settled. In fact, his taxonomy masks the differ-ences between the two operas in favor of foregrounding their musical common-alities. His primary aim is to make comparisons and find stylistic allusions to Western music in Tan's setting of *The First Emperor,* including Stravinsky's *Rite of Spring,* Puccini's *Turandot,* and Sondheim's *Pacific Overtures.* Puccini corre-lates themes and motives with expressive or emotional states of the characters in a manner that enables the listener to navigate the dramatic twists and turns.[19] Certainly, the tritone interval shares a similar expressive function in *Turandot* as in *The First Emperor.* It is featured in dramatic contexts that foreground Turan-dot's cruelty and mercilessness: in addition to the opening scene where the Man-darin declares the execution of the Prince of Persia, Puccini deploys the tritone in the harmonies that accompany what Ashbrook and Powers (1991: 23) call the "Enigma" motive, associated with Turandot's posing of the riddles to the Prince. In support of his "dissonant" *tinta,* Puccini's unequivocal use of the tritone to signify the Princess's cruelty parallels Tan's use of the tritone interval to signify the brutality of the Qin dynasty. Nonetheless, Sheppard shies away from mak-ing a cross-cultural comparison with the role of tritone in *qinqiang* opera. By referring exclusively to Western operatic influences, Sheppard unambiguously situates the music's agential role within a monolithic cultural framework. His reading of Tan's music assumes the dominance of Western operatic models over Chinese ones in the creative process. But is this really a fair assessment?

My analysis demonstrates by contrast that Tan's compositional strategy differs from Puccini's as much as it shares certain traits in common. The main differences can be summarized as follows: 1) the lack of direct quotation of Chinese folk melodies; 2) the lack of whole-tone based or other "impressionistic" harmonies; 3) melodic contour and slides based on *qinqiang;* 4) the more subtle use of leitmotifs; and 5) timbral expansion through the addition of indigenous instruments. The avoidance of a direct quotation of Chinese folk melody was important to Tan's conception of musical hybridity based on "1+1=1." Tan also avoids overt deployment of pentatonic and whole-tone scales in favor of slides and falling contours derived from his study of *qinqiang* operas. Most importantly, in Tan's setting of *The First Emperor,* themes and leitmotifs are not associated with individual characters, but are more strongly interconnected in giving voice to the central enigma posed: what will the anthem of China sound like? Rather than using particular themes to compartmentalize characters and roles (e.g., comic vs. serious) as Puccini does in *Turandot,* Tan's motives and themes assume actantial functions at the higher level of narrative: the "fate" motive returns to warn the audience of the tragedy that lies ahead; Theme 2 migrates from character to character as the signifier of yearning, at first, but later alludes to the Emperor's longing for that which cannot be reclaimed.

Moreover, the coordination between Tan's deployment of themes and leitmotifs and the actantial progression in *The First Emperor* is far *less* circumscribed than Puccini's. In *Turandot,* the "Mo-li-hua" theme signifies Turandot's glory and its recurrences in the unfolding of the narrative reinforces her victory over her perceived enemies, while the dissonant motive associated with her cruelty (see example 5.2) does not appear after the first act. Compared to the stable expressive function of Puccini's themes and letimotifs, the central themes in *The First Emperor* can be linked to a series of actants in articulating a structure of dramatic irony. Table 5.1 outlines the recurrence of themes and motives in relationship to the actantial progression. Here, localized arias that are featured once are distinguished from recurring themes (marked 1, 2, and 3).

While Theme 1 signifies the Emperor's exterior glory by linking the Shaman's prophecy with the ceremonial music for coronation, Theme 2 undergoes a more fluid progression in its chain of signification, as indicated by its dynamic movement within the Greimassian square. Initially, Theme 2 signifies the Emperor's yearning for Jianli to compose the perfect anthem, it is then linked with Jianli's resistance (1), Jianli and Yueyang's yearning and affection for each other (2), Jianli's forced compliance (3), and the General's death followed by Jianli's curse (4). Following this sequence, Theme 2 articulates how the agential roles of the Emperor and Jianli become reversed: Jianli emerges as the victor (even in death) and the Emperor the victim, although the latter remains unaware of his status until the end. Theme 3 also participates in setting up dramatic irony; Tan introduces this theme into the vocal line of the Emperor (Act I, scene 2) and in Yueyang's ghost aria (Act II, scene 1) long before it is presented as the slaves' anthem. By the

Table 5.1. Actantial Progression Associated with Theme 2

Scene	Characters	Themes and leitmotifs	Actants
Act I/sc. 1	Yin-Yang master	"fate" motif/Peking opera	Omen
	Shaman	Th1 ("who will kill, burn, sacrifice?")	Prophecy
	Emperor	**Th2** ("the Shadow that haunts me")	**Yearning**
	General Wang	"Like a stream" aria	
sc. 2	Emperor	"Zhongguo" aria	
	Emperor	Th3 ("call me Elder Brother");	Affection
	Jianli	**Th2** ("you trampled my mother to death");	**Resistance**
	Yueyang	"Wind sent me" aria	
sc. 3	Yueyang	"Sage of music" aria/Th2' ("pity me")	Affection
	Three spirits	Waterphones	
	Yueyang/Jianli	"fate" motif ("I can walk!")	Omen
	Shaman	Th1 ("shadow, beware of the sun!")	Warning
Act II/sc. 1	Yueyang/Jianli	"pastoral" theme; / love duet **Th2'**	**Yearning**
	Shaman/slaves	("herds of cattle") "humans die . . ."/Th3	Lament
	Yueyang/Empress	Duet ("follow the Emperor's wish?")	Doubt
	Jianli	**Th2'** ("complete the anthem!")	**Forced compliance**
	Emperor/Jianli	Th1 ("your love and mine")	
	Slaves	Th3 (hummed by slaves)	Lament
sc. 2	Chorus	Th1 ("the Emperor shines!")	Glory
	Shaman	**Th2'** ("I see the shadows fall . . .")	**Prophecy**
	Yueyang	"Ghost" aria/Th1/2 ("he took away	Lament
	General	spring. . . .")/ Th3' ("be kind to Jianli")	Affection
		Th2' ("your shadow who killed me")	**Death**
	Jianli/Emperor	**Th2'** ("on this accursed day. . . .")	**Curse**
	Jianli's death	"fate" motif	Omen
	Chorus	Th3 ("bearing an eternal curse. . . .")	Lament/Curse

```
                         1
  Yearning (E/J/Y) <───────────────> Resistance (J)
                         2
        │
      3 │
        ▼
  Compliance (J) ──────────────────> Curse (J)
                         4
```

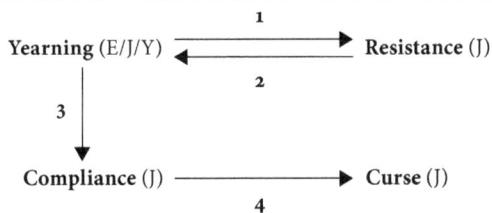

[E = Emperor, J = Jianli, Y = Yueyang]

time Theme 3 is heard as the official anthem at the end, it has accrued sufficient dramatic weight to magnify the moment in which the mystery is unveiled.

Tan also unifies the modal inflection of the central themes around the Mixolydian scale. His melodic writing is also consistently marked by the musical traits he extracts from *qinqiang* opera; in particular, the descending contour that makes use of vocal slides is not a characteristic found in Puccini's operas. As noted before, the characteristic signifier of "lament" in the *qinqiang* is the oscillating fourth interval (see example 5.1); the final anthem (Theme 3) sung by the chorus poignantly adopts this musical characteristic to connote sorrow and pain in the context of the *kuyin* scale.

From a Lacanian psychoanalytic perspective, the Emperor's quest for the perfect anthem can be interpreted as the *object a* (a) that drives the narrative engine forward. The "fate" motive is the very embodiment of the enigma that propels the narrative; from the beginning, it projects an ominous sign and serves as a signpost that steers the viewer's attention toward the ironic conclusion. The Emperor is a split subject (S) whose repressed desire (a) is fully unleashed when he comes into contact with Jianli (S2). He cannot rest until his childhood friend and captive supplies him with the anthem, not knowing that the attainment of this desire carries its own seed of destruction – the demise of those he loves and the downfall of his own kingdom. The transformation of theme 2 mirrors this process of transvaluation – the change in ranking of the Emperor from hero to anti-hero. The motive that conveys the Emperor's yearning for Jianli and the ideal anthem is linked with Jianli's resistance, his forced compliance, the Shaman's prophecy, Yueyang's death, and, later, Jianli's suicide. From a Jungian perspective, Jianli represents the "shadow" archetype that lurks within the Emperor's conscious self.[20] To the end of the narrative, the Emperor is unable to overcome and assimilate the shadow self in order to achieve individuation. Following Lacan's theory, the narrative follows a master's discourse in that S1 stands for the Emperor who tries to control the Other; yet in the process, the master bars some aspects of the truth in order to maintain his authority, and the interaction results in a "dissimulated" truth – the Emperor's false expectation that the anthem will recuperate him from the source of anxiety that eats away at his soul. It is the hysteric (Jianli) who reveals the cruelty the Emperor has exerted on his people and plants the seed that leads to the Qin dynasty's downfall. While the slave kills himself in an act of defiance, the hysteric's discourse wins over the master's by uncovering a new form of knowledge (S2) that has been suppressed. Upon Jianli's death, the "fate" motive is heard for the last time, as if to prophesize the Emperor's downfall (eleven years after the time frame of the opera).

Conflicting Reception: Socio-Political Intertexts, Allegory, and Myth

I now turn to the controversial critical reception of this opera examining it from three different perspectives: first, the Western critics' view that adheres to *The First Emperor's* association with exotic genres of Western music, drawing on specific connection with Puccini's grand opera as well as martial arts fantasy; second, the Chinese reception that focuses on the socio-political resonances of the opera's subject in relationship to other dictators (notably, Mao Zedong); third, the allegorical significance of the opera as it relates to the making of a modern myth directed at a global audience.

In response to Tommasini's incisive criticism from the premiere in 2006, Tan revised the score a year later to render it more "Pucciniesque." Principally, he abbreviated the "cross-over" music played by instrumental ensembles at the beginning of each act and adjusted the proportion of musical passages in favor of showcasing the dramatic tension between Jianli and the Emperor. Many passages with awkward text setting were amended in the process. The additions to the source material (music and libretto) further emphasize the agential role of Theme 2 in articulating the structure of dramatic irony (shown in figure 5.9), as follows:

1. Theme 2 is tossed back and forth between Jianli and the Emperor in Act I, scene 2, where Jianli openly defies the Emperor's command and calls him a tyrant "whose sacrifices had turned him into a monster."
2. Yueyang's resistance to her father's forced compliance in Act II, scene 1 is expanded to include the following dialogue: the Emperor tells Yueyang, "you are my light, Jianli is the earth under the sun," to which she responds "but the sun never tells the earth: you belong to me!" Returning once again to the metaphor of light and shadow (*yin* and *yang*), Yueyang professes Jianli's (and her own) resistance to control by the Emperor.
3. An extended aria is inserted into the scene where the Emperor orders Jianli to complete the anthem, while the Emperor forces Yueyang into a marriage with General Wang. Jianli's forced compliance to finish the anthem is set to Theme 2 in the revised version.
4. Theme 2 is more prominently featured in the Shaman's aria when she proclaims "shadows rise and fall" in anticipation of the tragedy that lies ahead; also in Yueyang's aria when she returns as a ghost and bids her father farewell. When Jianli cuts out his own tongue, his last vocal utterance incorporates Theme 2 in an ironic manner.
5. A significant change is noted in the concluding scene, where the Empress's line that criticizes the Emperor's deeds ("You have conquered the world, but you have lost your humanity, lost everything.") is omitted. It is likely that this omission was made in order to underscore the focal conflict between Jianli and the Emperor in the narrative. As a consequence, the Empress's role is further diminished as a secondary character in the opera.

However, Tommasini only slightly toned down his criticism of the second and revised version by reference to "compelling" instrumental episodes:

> Long stretches of tedious neo-Puccini, pentatonic lyricism. . . . There were some compelling instrumental episodes evocative of Mr. Tan's pulsating, Oscar-winning film score. . . . But whole spans of the opera seem to float in some nowhere land between a martial arts film fantasy and *Turandot*. (Tommasini 2007)

Allan Kozinn, on the other hand, responded more positively to "appealing moments" in the revised score:

> The arias, each an odd blend of lyricism, angular leaps, weirdly placed melismas and declamatory passages, frequently outlive their welcome. . . . But the score, which Mr. Tan conducted deftly, has appealing moments, most notably the imaginative,

otherworldly interludes and the first-act love duet between Yueyang, the emperor's daughter, and Gao Jianli. (Kozinn 2008)

Their responses emanate, nonetheless, from their unwavering stance that *The First Emperor* belongs to the genre of Western grand operas; Tan is allowed to introduce new techniques, but not exceed the comfort zone of the Met's audience, accustomed to familiar exotic signifiers in Puccini's operas. The more subtle references to Chinese regional operas like *qinqiang* were completely ignored by the Western critics.

Commenting on Tan Dun's efforts to appease western critics, Anthony Sheppard questions whether the operatic plot prompts the viewer to consider that "the stylistic and political conflict between the Emperor and his composer Jianli reflects Tan's own career" (2009: 289). In other words, do Jianli's defiance and his principled commitment to compose his own music parallel Tan's stance in opposition to the Western critics' repudiation of the original version? I doubt that this was the case, since his revisions have not fundamentally altered the "1+1= 1" principle that guided the foundational compositional strategy. Tan may occupy a "liminal" position within the community of opera consumers, as Sheppard claims, but he certainly has enjoyed the privileges that come with being a mainstream composer in the global age.

If Tan's music mattered the most to Western critics, the cultural symbolism of Qin Shi Huang seemed to matter the most to the Chinese audience and critics. For example, Ren Haijie criticizes the historically inauthentic portrayal of the emperor and Gao Jianli in the opera as follows: "the story of Qin Shi Huang [the Emperor] in the opera is highly misleading to those who know the actual history of the Qin dynasty; it is hard to accept Gao Jianli (who was an assassin and enemy) as someone whom the emperor befriended and entrusted to write an anthem" (Ren 2009: 57). Although the First Emperor remained a controversial figure throughout Chinese history, several biographers in the twentieth century have portrayed him in a more positive light. Historian Ma Feibai, for example, published a revisionist biography of Qin Shi Huang in 1941, calling him one of the greatest heroes in Chinese history; he drew many parallels with Chiang Kai-shek's role in bringing order to the Kuomintang between 1926 and 1928. Furthermore, it was during Mao's "Hundred Flowers Campaign" that Qin Shi Huang's role as a benevolent dictator was celebrated. In 1958, Mao launched a campaign which resulted in over 300,000 intellectuals being branded "rightists" and putting an end to their careers as teachers or writers (Wood 2007: 144).[21] Mao also enacted a ruse to flush out dissidents by encouraging a diversity of views and solutions to national policy issues, then proudly proclaimed in a speech directed at his party cadre in 1958 that he has "buried forty-six thousand scholars alive. . . . You [intellectuals] revile us for being Qin Shi Huangs. You are wrong. We have surpassed Qin Shi Huang a hundredfold" (Hardy and Kinney 2005: 103). Later, Hong Shidi published an enormously popular biography in 1972, which portrayed Qin Shi Huang as a farsighted ruler who centralized the state in Chinese history by rejecting the past – thus recreating the Emperor as a model for a modern dictator. Ha Jin and Tan Dun, in alluding to Mao's famous dictum ("music captures the hearts and minds of people") in the opera's libretto, were consciously drawing a parallel between Mao and the First Emperor. Ha Jin comments: "Mao worshiped the First Emperor, so our awareness of the connection must always have been there."[22]

In more recent years, however, the Chinese TV documentary called *Heshang* ("River Elegy," 1988) presented an overtly negative portrayal of the Great Wall. From an anti-authoritarian perspective, the documentary viewed important monuments within Chinese history that include the Great Wall and the Yellow River as symbols of "the sickness of China's collective soul" rather than its greatness (Su 1991: 4). I speculate that this is the critical position that has influenced Ha Jin's approach to the subject of the opera, as well as a key reason why the performance of the opera at the Great Wall and in Beijing, as envisioned by Tan Dun in 2003, has not yet come to fruition. Given the Chinese government's exercise of censorship over the arts, one cannot imagine an opera that takes an overtly critical stance with respect to such important cultural symbols as Qin Shi Huang or his anthem as being produced in China without raising controversy.[23] In the end, the opera's reception in China (so far) has had very little to do with Tan's music or the artistic merits of the opera.

By way of conclusion, I return to the allegorical significance of this opera that probes the complex relationship between art and politics. Tan claims that the Emperor's quest to find an anthem is a kind of "[a] spiritual metaphor for him to find a destiny, find a spirit of the nation" (Lunden 2006). To this end, Ha Jin uses Socratic irony to transform the subject of the First Emperor into a *modern* myth. Claire Colebrook claims "Socratic dialogue shifts the concept of irony from simple rhetorical use to complex rhetorical engagement, such that the boundary between an accepted literal meaning and an ironical meaning is shown to be political and ethical" (2004: 27). The literal meaning resides in the anti-heroic characterization of the Emperor, but the ironic meaning emerges from the heroism of those who stand up to the tyranny of dictators: should we tolerate historical figures like Qin Shi Huang, who brought enormous suffering to his people at the expense of unifying his kingdom? Is Jianli the tragic hero and the "true" protagonist of the opera, as one who stands up to tyranny? Qin Shi Huang is depicted as a split subject who cannot overcome his dependence on Jianli. Similar to Shakespeare's Richard II, the Emperor is progressively stripped of his political power. Richard's famous line about the fate of kings, "Make dust our paper and with rainy eyes. Write sorrow on the bosom of the earth . . . ," seems to apply equally well to Qin Shi Huang. Like Richard II, this Emperor is capable of action, but incapable of good judgment. The viewer is left without sympathy for the clueless dictator whose scheme to pawn his own daughter in order to keep Jianli for himself ultimately fails. From the perspective of Western dramatic sensibility, the negative portrayal of the Emperor as an enemy of the common people persuades the audience to confront the history of injustice associated with the construction of the Great Wall. Tan Dun and Ha Jin, I would like to believe, are making an anti-authoritarian statement, and this is the primary reason why the opera has yet to be staged in China. Notwithstanding the shortcomings addressed by various critics, the opera has marked its difference from the genre of merely exotic operas by pushing social and ideological boundaries.

Perhaps the complex rhetorical engagement posed by *The First Emperor*'s multimodal narrative accords with Michael Klein's view of irony as "a mode of interpretation, a master signifier that (ironically) organizes our thinking around contradictions, social failures, lapses of causality, and so on" (2009: 105). Had Tan and Ha Jin tried to recreate the Qin dynasty ritual without challenging orthodoxy, it would have ended up as another "exotic" work – a grand opera in the vein of *Turandot* or the romantic epic film *Qin Song*. From a broader sociological perspective, however, the anti-authoritarian theme in this opera remains vivid and charged in an era when China has assumed a leadership role in an increasingly interdependent world stage.

Epilogue:
Opera as Myth in the Global Age

Interpreting operatic narrative is a deeply personal activity in the sense that it is shaped by the viewer's prior knowledge of the source material, the cultural values s/he brings to the table, as well as the extent of her/his immersion into the given opera's production history. The lengthy proportion of the second act of *Doctor Atomic* seems entirely appropriate if s/he understands the operatic narrative as a Faustian parable, characterized by a slippage into a mythological realm where past, present, and future meld together. Similarly, the viewer's engagement with the irony in Ha Jin and Tan Dun's rendering of *The First Emperor* is contingent on his/her prior knowledge of Qin Shi Huang's contested role in Chinese history. In some instances, the staging can radically transform the content of the narrative, as was illustrated in the multimodal comparison of the operatic, oratorio, and theatrical productions of *Ainadamar* (chapter 2). Therefore, in claiming that these operas *reconfigure* older myths and narrative forms, I venture to say that the allegorical and tropological meanings complicate our narrative experience in ways that defy interpretive closure. The operatic narrative is rendered mythical precisely because "it does not exhaust its whole function in the telling"—to recall Suzanne Langer's dictum (2009: 67) on myth.

In closing, I would like to return to the perspectives on myth outlined in chapter 1 as I contemplate how the present case studies of contemporary opera may lead to further interdisciplinary avenues of research.

Dissecting operatic narrative in the context of the viewer's multimodal experience brings to mind Barthes's double articulation of myth, in which form and concept/meaning have a revolving relationship. In the operatic context, double articulation applies to the relationship between the basic narrative and the production components; while the initial source material (libretto and music) shapes the basic narrative, production components may alter the opera's structure and meaning from subtle to radically different ways. The postwar production history of Wagner's *Ring* cycle has demonstrated the impact of directors' interventionist strategies in reconfiguring the narrative structure and modes of presentation. Arguably, one of the most outlandish reconfigurations of this mythic narrative is Henrik Engelbrecht's mise-en-scène for the Royal Danish Opera (2006), in which Brünnhilde, who survives and conceives a child from her union with Siegfried, tells the epic story in flashbacks. Another radical reinterpretation is Frank Castorf's anarchic mise-en-scène for Bayreuth Festival (2013), which situates the epic cycle within a modern tale of a ricocheting global race for oil in which the scenery changes from a tacky motel along Route 66 in Texas (*Das Rheingold*) to the capital of Azerbaijan (*Die Walküre*). The quest narrative in the *Ring* cycle lends itself to seemingly endless staging productions with parallel plots that simultaneously enhance and compete with Wagner's initial conception. Transposed to contemporary operas, this form of double articulation is especially jarring when the director's conception significantly departs from the original, as was demonstrated in the case of Woolcock's mise-en-scène of *Doctor Atomic* or Lin's theatrical reworking of *Ainadamar*.

Mythic narrative is also about transporting the viewer from the diegetic time and place of the story to a universality of expression that transcends time. Many contemporary operas adopt nonlinear forms of narrative to enter into this synchronic dimension of myth. In the operas examined here, music emerges as an important semiotic field that articulates the sense of poetic timelessness in this respect. In *Ainadamar*, the stark shift in modality from the Andalusian scale in B minor to E major at the commencement of "Doy Mi Sangre" signifies Xirgu's liberation from her state of suffering into one of transcendence. In *Adriana Mater*, the acousmatic music (in lieu of stage action) assumes an essential function in communicating and embodying trauma. In the narrative construction of *Doctor Atomic*, Adams deploys a range of post-minimalist musical idioms to usher in a sense of timelessness as the narrative progresses toward the test explosion of the atomic bomb. Tan also strategically distinguishes between mythical and diegetic types of music by introducing resonant instruments such as the waterphone to connote the timelessness of love.

From a psychoanalytic perspective, these operas often bring shadow representations of archetypal figures into our interpretation of characters. Nonetheless, the recognition of secondary intertexts is culture-specific and explains the diverging responses we bring to our reading of narrative. For example, the shadow representation of Mao Zedong in Tan's depiction of *The First Emperor* is recognizable only to those acquainted with modern Chinese history. These narratives are also allegorical because they are charged with moral and ethical implications, to recall Suzanne Langer's point about myth. We may compare Qin Shi Huang's downfall in *The First Emperor* with the communist leader Bo Xilai's 2013 trial for abuse of power. We may relate the trauma of rape in *Adriana Mater* to other stories that involve perpetration of violence against women. The viewers are made to grapple with fundamental truths and moral imperatives by reflecting on the allegorical significance of these tales to the global age in which we live.

Moreover, in considering media as a vehicle for enhancing mythic narrative, contemporary operas' engagement with myth intersects with a wide range of artistic genres that reconfigures myth in the global age. The evolving characteristics of contemporary operas highlight the discursive aspect of myth and offer rich intertextual connections through literature, film, musical theater, and video games. Jeongwon Joe and Sander L. Gilman's *Wagner & Cinema* (2010) illustrates, for example, how Wagner's mythic ideals extend beyond the operatic arena to cinematic genres over the course of the twentieth century. Jacqueline Furby and Claire Hines' *Fantasy* (2012) discusses fantasy films in contemporary culture in relationship to myth, legends, fairy tales, Jungian archetypes, and narratological analysis. In *Body Knowledge: Performance, Intermediality, and American Entertainment at the Turn of the Twentieth Century* (2013), Mary Simonson negotiates dance, music, cultural history, gender roles, and emerging multimedia as complex sites of narrative enactment; for example, she examines how Strauss's *Salome* was reconfigured into a site of resistance and female authorship in American vaudeville in the early part of the twentieth century (29). By exploring these broader artistic intersections, concepts and approaches developed in film and media studies can be productively applied to the multimodal analysis of opera and related genres in future research.

Suffice to say, much more can be drawn from the areas of music semiotics, cognition, neuroscience, and film and multimedia studies to refine the criteria and conditions for conducting a multimodal analysis of operatic narrative. Future avenues of research may include empirical studies that examine different facets of cross-modal interaction in the viewers' response to multimodal narrative. For example, as a way to corroborate Nicholas Cook's theory of "audio-visual downbeat" (1998: 184), empirical tests may be conducted to measure what Annabel Cohen refers to as formal congruency – synchronized onsets of similarly changing audio and visual patterns – in the temporal unfolding of opera remediated as film (2014: 106).[1] The extent to which the physical environment conditions the viewer's embodied experience of narrative needs to be considered with greater care (Page 2010: 7). Another investigation may involve measuring how subjects from different backgrounds develop a schematic understanding of narrative through their identification with cultural intertexts and mythical icons. These are just a few possibilities that will continue to shed light on how we engage with opera as multimodal myth in the global age.

Glossary of Terms

Acousmatic music: According to Michel Chion, acousmatic (*acousmêtre*) refers to nondiegetic sounds, or to diegetic sounds the viewer hears *without* seeing their originating cause (1994: 72).

Actant: While Vladmir Propp restricts the term to refer to character roles in his analysis of folk tales, Greimas and Courtés broaden the range of what an actant encompasses to objects, functions, concepts, and beings that can be projected onto the semiotic square. In the present context, agential roles refer to the dramatic roles (e.g., villain, hero, victim) the characters assume in the unfolding of the narrative, while actants refer to oppositional conditions or concepts (e.g., freedom, non-freedom) that govern the transformational (*configurational* according to Ricoeur) dimension of narrative.

Agent: In ascribing agency to music, Robert Hatten distinguishes *actual* agents (composer and performer) from *virtual* agents (internal, external, and narrative) that listeners engage with (2010: 166). By contrast, the agential level of multimodal analysis, as in Byron Almén's *agential* level of narrative, refers to the main actions or events in the narrative as they are identified, characterized, and located in time.

Chora: Julia Kristeva's concept for an emergent sign whose signifying process is based on traces and marks, as articulated through repetition; distinct from the symbolic operations that depend on language, *chora* is equated with "the kinetic functional stage of the semiotic [that] precedes the establishment of the sign" (1984: 27).

Diegetic and non-diegetic music: in film, diegetic sound refers to "sound that has a source in the story world, while non-diegetic sound refers to sound "represented as coming from a source outside the story world" (Bordwell and Thompson 2004: 366). Soundtracks that are represented as coming from instruments that are visible on the screen constitute diegetic music, while those added to enhance the film's action or used for the opening and end credits constitute non-diegetic music.

Diegetic levels: In narrative fiction, Gérard Genette distinguishes between three diegetic levels: extradiegetic refers to the narrator who tells the story outside its context, diegetic to time and place associated with the primary narrative, and metadiegetic to the embedded narrative or the story told within a story (1980: 214). An enactment of the dream sequence in *Adriana Mater* and Xirgu's remembrance of Lorca's execution at the site of Ainadamar are good examples of metadiegetic narrative, where the staging transports the viewer into an imagined place and time.

Discourse: Geoffrey Leech and Michael Short define discourse as "linguistic communication seen as a transaction between speaker and hearer, as an interpersonal activity whose form is determined by its social purpose" (Mills 1997: 4). Applied to operatic analysis, discourse entails the various factors that shape the process of communication between production and reception; production further breaks down into the stages of pre-production, production, and post-production.

Intermediality: Given the modalities that underlie one's experience of all conceivable media, Elleström argues that intermedial relations either combine and integrate these modalities into a unified whole – e.g., musical theatre, opera – or mediate and transform them into a new entity – e.g., a poem that describes a painting (38). For the purpose of the present study, I will qualify intermediality as the condition that defines the *relationship* between semiotic fields in co-articulating the structure of narrative at the agential level, while multimodality has to do with *representation* – what the interplay of semiotic fields signifies in the viewer's construction of narrative meaning at the actantial and tropological levels.

Intertext: Following Julia Kristeva, Michael Klein defines intertext as "the crossing of texts" where critics "often concern themselves both with the linguistic (musical) codes that bind texts together and with the tropes that transform these codes from text to text" (2005: 13). In the present study, intertexts encompass people, object, codes and tropes that emerge in the audience's cultural-specific response to the content and meaning of operatic narrative. For example, only those acquainted with modern Chinese history will recognize the intertextual reference to Mao Zedong in the characterization of Qin Shi Huang in Tan's *The First Emperor* (the shared code is tyrant).

Mise-en-scène: As defined by Patrice Pavis, the "concretization of the dramatic text, using actors and the stage space, into a duration that is experienced by the spectators" (1998: 364).

Modality: The modal qualities of media, according to Lars Elleström (2010: 35–36), are properties that range from the material, the perceptual, to the conceptual. He categorizes four modalities that apply specifically to the analysis of multimedia as follows: 1) *material,* the corporeal interface of the medium (e.g., human bodies, digital screen); 2) *sensorial,* the physical and mental acts of perceiving the interface through sensory faculties (seeing, hearing, feeling, tasting, smelling); 3) *spatiotemporal,* the structuring of the sensorial perception of the interface with respect to space and time, and 4) *semiotic,* the creation of meaning in the medium by way of sign interpretation.

Multimedia: Different physical media (e.g., print, airwaves, radio) as they are brought together to convey information.

Multimodality: According to Ruth Page (2010: 6), how we utilize different sensory modes – indexing verbal, visual, and aural resources that are evoked by the media – and the system of choices we use to construct meaning.

Narrative: According to Paul Ricoeur (1984: 67–68), narrative encompasses two temporal dimensions: *chronological* and *configurational.* The chronological characterizes the story insofar as it is made up of events, while configurational "grasps together" the succession of events into a meaningful whole and gives rise to a "new quality of time" through this reflective act.

Schema: Robert Gjerdingen (2007: 11), in extending Leonard B. Meyer's application of this concept, defines schema generally as an abstracted prototype, a well-learned exemplar, or a theory intuited about the nature of things we rely upon to make useful comparisons (2007: 11). In the present context, schema refers to patterns and stylistic constraints that shape our habituated response to the multimodal study of opera.

Seme: Greimas (1983: 278) defines a seme as the "minimal unit" of signification contained within a *lexeme,* which refers to a word or phrase. He further emphasizes that a seme is "purely relational" in that its characteristics can only be defined in relation to at least one other term within the same relational network: "it is by giving a precise logical status to constituent relations of such a structure that the concept of seme can be determined and made operational." In the operatic context, I identify a seme as a minimal musical unit, which acquires heightened signification through recurrence and rhetorical emphasis. It may be embedded within a motive, topic, or phrase, and its expressive connotation may change according to the context. For example, the primary seme in *Adriana Mater* (chapter 3) is the descending semitone; yet the musical context dictates whether it functions as a topic (identifiable as *pianto* or "sigh" motive) or acquires a provisional quality that *resists* fixed categorization, because its expressive connotation continually changes in combination with other semic attributes in the course of this opera.

Semiotic fields: The production components, e.g., libretto, filmic images, choreography, action, lighting, and music, which become part of a composite sign system, based on the viewer's perceptual grouping according to Elleström's four modalities (material, sensory, spatiotemporal and semiotic).

Semiotic square: Greimas and J. Courtés define the semiotic square as "the visual representation of the logical articulation of any semantic category. The elementary structure of signification, when defined – in a first step – as a relation at least between two terms, rests only on a distinction of opposition which characterizes the paradigmatic axis of language" (1979: 308). Greimas then develops the semiotic square as a device that organizes narrative largely as a process of value creation. In *Structural Semantics,* he establishes two classes of narratives that accomplish the circulation of, or mediation between, certain objects of value situated according to the rules of narrative grammar, either in terms of narratives that affirm the present order or those that depart from it. Simply put, the relations between any of the four terms can be used to construct elementary narrative transformations.

Textuality: Rather than providing a correct interpretation, textual analysis is "interested in the cultural and political implications of representations" (Hartley 2002: 227). In an operatic context, this means that the narrative presents an ideological representation rather than a biographical characterization of a subject.

Topic: Topics are conventionalized musical signs that carry coded meanings shared by a musical community. In short, topics are signifiers with *a priori* meaning. Raymond Monelle (2000: 17) states that "the topic is essentially a symbol, its iconic or indexical features governed by convention and thus by rule."

Transvaluation: Following James Liszka, Byron Almén (2008: 51) defines transvaluation in the narrative context as a shift in meaning/values that occurs through a change in the existing hierarchy based on ranking and markedness relations (2008: 51). In operatic contexts, for example, Liù's role changes from a servant (unmarked) to a tragic heroine (marked) when she kills herself in honoring her love for Calaf in Puccini's *Turandot.*

Trope: A trope, for Robert Hatten (1994: 295), refers to a figurative play in which the fusion of musical types or topics sparks an interpretation based on their interaction.

Tropological narrative: Tropological narrative refers to "a multi-level discourse, one in which the implied trajectories of the surface style are negated by the presumed ironies of the higher-level discourse" (Almén and Hatten 2012: 71). Applied to the multimodal analysis of opera, "tropological" refers to the juxtaposition of contradictory or incongruous ideas that sparks a new association or dramatic trajectory that in turn renders the narrative meaning inconclusive and multivalent.

Notes

1. Toward a Multimodal Discourse on Opera

1. In the interview that accompanies the DVD, Julie Taymor explains how she intended to thoroughly transform the oratorio into a hybridized Asian theatrical form. The production defamiliarizes the Latin text by eliminating subtitles, allowing the story to be communicated only through the narrator's telling of the story in Japanese. The stage was modified from Cocteau's specification of one level to multiple levels with the addition of *hanamichi* (runways), as used in Noh drama. At the same time, Taymor pays respect to Cocteau's and Stravinsky's idea of "the geometry of theater" by utilizing puppets to symbolize elemental forces that underlie the myth.

2. Unlike the standard way in which the mise-en-scène is understood to be synonymous with the director's staging of a theatrical work, Patrice Pavis extends the notion to include the audience's reception of the work: "the structural system of a stage utterance, i.e., as the way in which the signifying systems are put together and contrasted, and placed in perspective according to their reception by an audience which is itself an active and variable factor" (1998: 94).

3. Ghazanfar and Schroeder's (2006) research point out that "the multisensory nature of most, possibly all, of the neocortex forces us to abandon the notion that the senses ever operate independently during real world cognition" (Gibbons 2006: 278).

4. The classic film example is the "shower" scene from Alfred Hitchcock's *Psycho* (1960); Bernard Hermann's soundtrack, consisting of repetition of high string glissando, captures the sensation of fright associated with Janet Leigh being stabbed by Anthony Perkins.

5. Leonard B. Meyer introduces the concept of schema (pl. schemata) in the context of musical analysis in *Explaining Music* (1973) and *Style and Idea* (1989). In the former, he comments on instances of archetypal schemata and, in the latter, he extracts specific types of schema (e.g., gap-fill) as a melodic convention associated with music from the Romantic era. Robert Gjerdingen, in *A Classical Turn of Phrase,* conducts a survey of music from the classical period that deploys the scale degrees 1,^–2,^4,^–3,^ schema and concludes that the sample population peaks during the mid-1770s (1988: 262). He also distinguishes this data-driven or bottom-up processing of schema to concept-driven or top-down processing (7).

6. Orpheus is depicted as a Muse who sang to the accompaniment of a kithara, charmed people and wild animals with his songs, and had gone down into Hades to restore Eurydice to life. However, he did not enjoy the benefits of having Eurydice come to life and thus came to hate all of the female race. He is remembered subsequently for the Orphic rites and their associations, as noted by Aristotle (Blakely 2013).

7. Centering on Orpheus's death (which occurs four times over the course of the work), other allegories are interwoven into the larger one through the intervention of electronic music. In the libretto, Birtwistle and Peter Zinovieff state: "Orpheus is an Opera or, rather, a Lyric Tragedy, in which the myth of the life and death of Orpheus is used as a carrier to otherwise express the transitions from chaos to order and back again of music, words, and thought" (Cross 2009: 39). In Act I, Orpheus the man falls in love with Eurydice, and the two are wedded; after Eurydice dies from a snakebite, Orpheus goes to the underworld in a dream and consults the Oracle of the Dead. In Act II, Orpheus believes that he has descended into the underworld, only to realize that it was a dream; following a searing climax, he commits suicide after realizing that he has lost Eurydice forever. The concluding act presents Orpheus as a mythological figure, played by a puppet. Eurydice's death and Orpheus's many deaths are viewed from different perspectives; after his final death and dismemberment at the hands of the Dionysian women, his skull becomes an oracle before being silenced by Apollo. The music becomes increasingly formalized in the third act, bringing back fragments of materials from the previous acts in disintegrated forms.

8. In his study of the Ge ("fire") myth of the Bororo tribe, Lévi-Strauss compares six different versions of the same myth by extrapolating their differences by means of valuative oppositions; for example, whether the hero's behavior is strong (+) or weak (-), whether the antagonism between jaguar and humans is positive (+) or negative (-), and so forth (1969: 77).

9. Barthes comments as follows: "Myth is a *value*, truth is no guarantee for it; nothing prevents it from being a perpetual alibi: it is enough that its signifier has two sides for it always to have an 'elsewhere' at its disposal. The meaning is always there to present the form; the form is always there to *outdistance* the meaning. And there never is any contradiction, conflict, or split between the meaning and the form: they are never at the same place" (123).

10. Cyclical time is not limited to contemporary operas based on myth. Take, for example, John Eliot Gardiner, who brings back the mythological Cassandra at the conclusion of Berlioz's *Les Troyens* in the production for Chatelet Opera (2003); following Dido's tragic suicide in Act 5, Cassandra, who is now inhabited by the spirit of Clio, proclaims "Fuit Troya, stat Roma" ("What was once Troy is now Rome") and imparts to the audience her vision of the future in which a new hero will emerge from the sacrifice made by Dido.

11. Rimmon-Kenan explains how a character in a novel is textualized into a cluster of traits (e.g., Jane Austen who writes: "Emma Woodhouse is not a woman nor need be described as if *it* were") in a manner that robs that character of his/her specificity as an individual; note how Austen textualizes Emma by the designation of her as "it" (2001: 32). In the case of Birtwistle's opera, the character of Orpheus is similarly reduced to textualized representations through inscribing multiple agential roles.

12. Other characters recite cryptic poems by Christopher Knowles, along with short texts written by choreographer Lucinda Childs and Samuel M. Johnson that refer to socio-political events ranging from the Beatles to the women's liberation movement and Patty Hearst (Page 1993).

13. The music for *Akhnaten* is by far the most operatic in the trilogy: using different types of ground bass, Glass composes lyrical solos and duets featuring Akhnaten as a countertenor. Critics such as John Rockwell and Daniel Warburton have commented on the plethora of references to operatic conventions from the past and the leitmotivic use of minimalist music in *Akhnaten* (248).

14. Richardson further explains that rather than strive for artistic unity, Brecht's theater favored elements that were at odds with one another, montage taking precedence over the linear unfolding of a plot, and counterpoints between theatrical media taking precedence over unity or harmony (1999: 43).

15. While Greimas allows paths between any of the four points of the semiotic square, recent scholars such as Jacques Fontanille distinguish between a canonical (S1 → S1', S2 → S2') and a non-canonical path (S1 → S2', S2 → S1') and forbid motion to and from contrarieties (S1 → S2, S2 → S1). See Fontanille (2006: 30–31).

16. One could argue that the relationship between a hero and an anti-hero is based on an equipollent opposition (mutually exclusive). Furthermore, one could argue that the relationship between a hero and a false-hero is based on a privative opposition: a false-hero is a type of hero who is *marked* in the sense that his status is undermined by a circumstance that results in his loss of power or heroic status. Hatten defines *markedness* as "the asymmetrical valuation of an opposition (in musical structure, language, and culture)" (1994: 291–92).

17. See also Ashbrook and Powers (1991: 94). *Turandot* is an early twentieth-century opera that straddles the fence between the melodramatic grand opera tradition of nineteenth-century France and the psychological realism and abstraction associated with modernism. Virgilio Bernardoni argues that, by embracing mythic and legendary subjects, Puccini creates a distinctly unusual protagonist, a cold and impersonal princess who exhibits a certain emotional distance; Bernardoni claims that the opera is marked by "the gradual appearance of fissures in the logic of psychological 'identification'" associated with romanticism (2005: 39).

18. See Davis 2003: 186–239. Turandot's torture of the slave girl Liù results in the latter's suicide to ensure that Calaf's name will not be revealed. Liù emerges as the dramatic catalyst whose death triggers Turandot's eventual surrender. In the end, Calaf emerges as the victor (captured by his aria "Nessun dorma"), but Turandot emerges triumphant as well by affirming the transforming power of love. See also Davis (2010: 168–221).

19. In order to illustrate transvaluation in a semiotic context, Liszka turns to Peirce's notion of *interpretant,* Edwin Battistella's explanation of markedness, and Michael Shapiro's theory of ranking to explore how the concept applies to our perception of visual and linguistic signs.

20. Quoting Ricoeur (1984: 26), Liszka criticizes Greimas for failing to make a transition from the semiotic square to the valuative function of the narration: "what occurs at best instead is the development of a logical model, on the one hand, and an axiological analysis of the narration on the other – and a forced mapping of one onto the other" (111). Consequently, there is a loss of emphasis on the dynamic aspect of narration. Liszka credits Greimas, however, for recognizing that the problem lies in transforming "an axiology, given as a system of values, into an operative syntagmatization" (112).

21. His ironic archetype ranges from the comic phase of irony in Haydn's String Quartet op. 33/2, the middle-phase of irony in Bach's Brandenburg Concerto, and the tragic phase of irony in the "Sanctus" from Britten's *War Requiem*. In the penultimate chapter, Almén discusses epiphany, emergence, and synthesis as examples of comic discursive strategies associated with works by Mahler, Debussy, and Ravel. Discursive strategies are "distinct templates for achieving a particular transvaluative result" and "they are thus concerned with the *actantial level* of analysis" (187).

22. Davis claims that the piece sounds so puzzling because Liù's cortège provides a kind of finality worthy of the work's end (in the same key as the end of Act I), but dramatically the opera must continue.

23. In this seminal work, Tarasti advances Greimas's theories toward an analysis of the function of music and myth in representative works by Sibelius, Wagner, and Stravinsky. Drawing on Karl Jasper's classification of the mythical into two principal classes – the nature-mythical and the psychic-mythical – Tarasti sets out to extract stylistic features and topics (e.g., "the tragic," "the sublime," "the pastoral") in order to construct his own categories of music that embody mythical qualities.

24. In addition, for every seme Tarasti indicates an equivalent musical "lexeme" in which the mythical seme under question is a dominant (marked) feature; however, the fact that a musical passage manifests some particular mythical seme does not preclude the inclusion of other mythical semes (or non-mythical semes) in the same musical section (86). Having established these categories *a priori,* Tarasti provides a formulaic list of timbres, harmonies, textures, and rhythms that have acquired mythical connotations in the classical and romantic eras; for example, Smetana's use of the harp evokes the mythical past at the beginning of *Ma Vlast,* while Wagner's use of the sustained woodwind pedal on E♭ at the beginning of *Das Rheingold* refers to a primeval conception of the creation of the world (77–78). Long and low sounds signify the nature-mythical in the case of Wagner. For the hero-mythical, Tarasti references the alternation between major and minor keys in Siegfried's theme that reflects the contrast between the mythical hero's life and his tragic death. Other subcategories include the magical, the fabulous, the balladic, the legendary, the sacred, the demonic, the fantastic, the mystic, the gestural, the sublime, the pastoral, and the tragic.

25. Grabócz's application of seme appears to work seamlessly because a monothematic texture governs each section of Lizst's piano music and lends itself to the prolongation of a particular narrative strategy. At the thematic level, she introduces sixteen classemes, including scherzo, pastoral, religious, *lugubre, recitativo, lamento,* and pantheistic. At the sectional level, Grabócz introduces the concept of *semantic isotopy,* finding seven types: macabre quest, heroic, pastoral-amoroso, macabre struggle, mourning, religious, and pantheistic. A given isotopy may function as the "narrative determinant" of a section of a piece or of the piece in its entirety (2009: 232). For Grabócz, these isotopies can be further generalized to explain those works of Liszt she refers to as "philosophical epics." She further stipulates three types of narrative strategies in her analysis of music by Liszt: a figurative strategy applies to pieces with one isotopy (and its variations), a simple narrative strategy applies to those with several isotopies, and a complex narrative strategy applies to those that feature a confrontation between two isotopies as the basis of the compositional evolution, as found in Liszt's Ballade in B minor (233). In her analysis of *Vallée d'Obermann,* Grabócz illustrates her reading of the simple narrative strategy via her division of the piece into four isotopies: macabre quest (mm.1–74), amorous pastorale (mm.75–118), macabre struggle (mm.119–69), and pantheism (mm.170–216) (231). Each of these isotopies comprises, in turn, a different syntagmatic sequence of semes or classemes.

26. Davis comments on how previous scholars have dealt with the taxonomy of style in Puccini's *Turandot.* Ashbrook and Power (1991) discover four *tinte* or "colors" in the work ("Chinese," "dissonant," "middle-Eastern," and "romantic diatonic"). Joanne Cassar (2000) reveals seven stylistic isotopies: "macabre," "lyrique," "la nuit," "héroïque," "grotesque," "pouvoir," and "nocturne." Davis's own stylistic taxonomy divides into Romantic, Dissonant, and Exotic, with Exotic subcategories of Chinese, Primitive, and Persian (2010: 173).

27. The tropological corresponds roughly with what David Levin calls "polylogical" staging (2007: 12).

28. Furby and Hines apply Campbell's monomyth and Jung's archetypes to track Frodo, the hero in *The Lord of the Rings,* as he begins his journey towards individuation. In the Departure stage, for instance, the protective figure, Gandalf, sends Frodo on his quest; during the Initiation stage, Frodo encounters one of his shadow selves, Gollum/Sméagol, and so forth (2012: 61–62).

29. Bruce Fink claims that the unconscious does not have full-fledged agency as Freud claims. However, Adrian Johnston argues that Lacan conceives the conscious and the unconscious as two sides of a Moebius strip; the impacts of the Real create turning points that allow access onto the opposite side of the conscious order (Johnston 2005: 55).

30. In "Altered States: Musical and Psychological Processes in Wagner," Katherine Syer discusses the psychological transitions Siegfried undergoes in the Ring cycle in terms of a type of "unconscious reckoning" associated with the Romantic idea of genius (1999: 237).

31. From a Lacanian perspective, *jouissance* refers to the repetitive condition that turns pleasure into pain or non-pleasure; it is "the energy of the superego derives from the libido of this unsatisfied drive; the more the subject fails to feel jouissance, the more libido there is to feed the superego, and the more the superego will demand new renunciations" (Laznik 2005). Thus, when a particular form of pleasure is prohibited, its prohibition leads to a compulsive drive to attain the pleasure. Salome's quest to attain the head of John the Baptist in Oscar Wilde's play presents a case in point. We do not know the cause of her desire, but it emanates from the place of jouissance.

32. Lacan offers a full-fledged explanation of the four discourses in Seminar XVII (2007).

33. Žižek reminds the reader that Parsifal's coming into being takes place in stages: in Act I, Parsifal witnesses the ritual at Montsalvat but fails to understand the significance of this act; Act II features his understanding Amfortas's suffering through his meeting with Kundry; and in the final act Parsifal delivers Amfortas from his suffering and takes his place (1993: 186).

34. In debating the role of film in opera and vice versa, Marcia Citron theorizes the relationship of dominance of one medium over another according to Wolf Werner's concepts of *overt* and *covert* intermediality. Werner claims that "if both media are directly present with their typical or conventional signifiers and if consequently each medium remains distinct and is in principle 'quotable' separately," it qualifies as *overt* intermediality; if, on the other hand, only one media dominates and the other is indirectly present within the first medium, it qualifies as *covert* intermediality (Citron 2010: 7).

35. By the same token, the 1999 production of *Turandot* at the Forbidden City in China presents a contest model; the addition of historically authentic costumes and figures work against the mythical dimension of the Persian story that inspired Carlo Gozzi's text and Puccini's romantic musical setting.

36. The timing for this passage from the 2011 production of *Die Walküre* is: DVD #1: 1'03"35–1'05"25.

37. Klein views a trope within his theory of intertextuality as "any sign or configuration of signs in one text that is a transformation of such signs in another text" (2005: 13).

38. As an example, Herman refers to the multiple diegetic levels that are evoked by the interplay between linguistic and image-based information in *The Incredible Hulk* comic books from 1962; the nuclear physicist Banner's transformations into the green behemoth, the Hulk, involve moves to and from the pre- and the post-metamorphosis realms by means of which complex layers of his personality are revealed (2010: 82).

39. By juxtaposing a world of mythology with that of modern society, Chéreau captures the idea that "the world of *Götterdämmerung* is a world in which it is difficult for anyone to believe in anything any longer." See DVD liner notes to Wagner's *Götterdämmerung* (Deutsche Grammophon DVD B0004764-09, 2005: 7).

40. Adorno, in *In Search of Wagner*, uncovers the root of Wagner's anti-Semitism in the depiction of Mime and Alberich, and claims that the entire story of the *Ring* cycle is implicated in Wagner's blind intolerance of the Jews.

41. However, not all contemporary operas are based on the standard conflict-resolution model of narrative. *Einstein on the Beach*, as discussed earlier, creates a contemporary myth around the famous physicist without any plot or character development.

42. Martin Heidegger, in *Sein und Zeit* (1927), is credited for reformulating the hermeneutic circle to "the interplay between our self-understanding and our understanding of the world" (Ramberg and Gjesdal 2013).

2. Osvaldo Golijov's *Ainadamar*

1. This information is taken from Osvaldo Golijov's main website under "latest news." See http://www.osvaldogolijov.com/news.htm (Accessed July 25, 2011).

2. Historically, Mariana Pineda is a nineteenth-century folk heroine who died for the cause of promoting liberty against the tyrannical reign of Ferdinand II. Already in the late 1820s, she had opened up her home to be used for liberals to meet. She helped people hide from the police, acquired fake passports for them, and smuggled goods for people who were jailed. Once the officials discovered that she had provided shelter for fugitives and sewed the flag of liberty, she was first put under house arrest and then transferred to a convent in Santa María Egipcíaca – a reform center and prison for Granada's prostitutes. In 1831, when she continued to refuse to tell the names of conspirators and rejected officer Pedrosa's offer of pardon, she was sentenced to death by being garroted (Edwards 1995: xvii).

3. Although political controversy dogged the company from the outset, the troupe presented famous plays by Lope de Vega, Calderón, Tirso de Molina, and Cervantes.

4. Drawing on an actual tragedy that occurred in the Almería province, Lorca darkened the story's Freudian undertones and heightened its mythic dimension by having the cousin and the bridegroom kill one another in the forest (Stainton 1999: 300).

5. Stainton also comments on Ruiz Alonso's strained relationship with the Falangists because the party had refused his request for financial compensation upon joining the party. It is presumed that Alonso was set on arresting Lorca in broad daylight as a way to exact revenge on the party (1999: 452).

6. Raymond Monelle traces the first recorded use of the trumpet fanfare for military signals to the twelfth century. As the fanfare was adopted in ceremonial occasions, it acquired more flourishes and complexity, as exemplified by the opening "Toccata" in Monteverdi's *Orfeo*, and his Vespers of 1610 (2005: 135–36).

7. The pervasive use of dotted rhythm in $^6_8$ meter suggests a connection to the Pastoral (Siciliana) topic, but I think this is coincidental. Instead, the rhythmic cycle of the refrain fits more comfortably into the flamenco music based on a *compás* of 12 beats.

8. Xirgu's solo entry is in D major in order to facilitate singing from the score, but the perceived effects match that of B♭ Phrygian.

9. Golijov claims that these were the messages printed in a number of Spanish newspapers in 1936 – quotations from Falangist officers (Golijov 2006).

10. William Washabaugh discusses the influence of Bergsonian transcendentalism, which directs attention to the perception and the aesthetic representation of the deepest conditions of life, on the spread of flamenco in Spain in the early part of the twentieth century. In modernist music by Debussy, De Falla, and Stravinsky, Andalusian flamenco represented an exemplary source of primitive cultural experience (2012: 66–67).

11. Jesus Montoya is a Gypsy flamenco singer and composer from Seville, Spain. He is the artistic director of the Montoya Flamenco Dance and Music Company. See http://jesusmontoya.net/default.htm for additional details.

12. In the King James's version, Jesus says to his disciples: "This cup is the new testament in my blood: this do ye, as oft as ye drink it, in remembrance of Me" (Corinthians 11:25).

13. Nicholas Vazsonyi emphasizes the sensory experience that consumes Isolde in her transfiguration as follows: "enveloped by sound which no one else senses, Isolde moves permanently into her alternate consciousness" (2010: 149). Patrick McCreless further comments: "It is indeed her ability to give herself over to death – to allow her love of Tristan to envelop her wholly and to transcend the limitations of earthly love – that enables her to be transfigured, and at the end to move the bystanders by her experience" (2005: 135).

14. In this respect, Brenda Pruitt from the ASO chorus recalls how Golijov, in rehearsal, encouraged them to sound like "lower class factory workers who spoke in mispronounced slang and didn't pronounce all of the letters in words." So, for example, the name of the city Granada, was sung like "Gra-now." They alternated between a technically polished "Shaw" sound (after Robert Shaw) and nasal street singing throughout the opera. (Based on correspondence with Brenda Pruitt on August 3, 2011.)

15. For the overview of the Santa Fe production and rehearsal led by Peter Sellars, go to http://www.osvaldogolijov.com/m/ainadamar.wmv).

16. Based on a phone interview with Carmen Telléz on July 29, 2011. Telléz decided to conduct *Ainadamar* at Indiana University after she attended its premiere at Tanglewood in 2003 and the Santa Fe production in 2005. She subsequently consulted Golijov about staging it as an oratorio. My commentary on the performance at the Jacobs School of Music is based on the video, which was made available by Telléz.

17. Mei Hong Lin had choreographed two other works by Lorca prior to *Ainadamar*: the play *La casa de Bernada Alba* (1936) and the poem "Es Verdad" from *Canciones* (1927). In the interview with Karin Dietrich, she explains that she stumbled upon *Ainadamar* by coincidence and was struck by the combination of Arabic, Flamenco, Cuban, and Jewish musical styles found in Golijov's music (Dietrich 2007).

18. This is my English translation of the interview Karin Dietrich conducted with Mei Hong Lin, reproduced in the program notes to Staattheater Darmstadt's premiere (2007).

19. For an excerpt of the Staatsheater Darmstadt's production of *Ainadamar,* go to "Ardillita in Ainadamar by Osvaldo Golijov." http://youtu.be/P5LeDsSX1aI.

20. Mark Sved shares this critical view of the singers in this production, in his review of the Long Beach Opera's production in the *Los Angeles Times* (2012).

3. Kaija Saariaho's *Adriana Mater*

1. Translation by Catherine Marin of the original as follows: "*Le passage du reel à l'imaginaire se fait spontanément chez moi. C'est san doute lié à la guerre du Liban, et à la manière dont je l'a vécue. J'avais l'habitude de parcourir le monde pour couvrir les événements les plus tragiques et les plus sanglants, du Vietnam à l'Éthiopie; mais lorsque la*

guerre s'est installée dans mon proper pays, dans mon proper quartier, je me suis senti incapable de réagir en reporter, et je me suis réfugié dans la fiction. Pour restituer mon experience, je devais passer par la meditation de l'imaginaire; aller vers d'autres pays, vers
d'autres époques, m'y engloutir pleinement, sans jamais faire l'effort de ramener le pro-
pos vers le Liban, mais avec la certitude que l'essentiel de mon experience intime se trans-
mettrait à travers ce que je dirais."

2. This sketch from Saariaho's private archive is used with her permission.

3. The stage and lighting designs for the Santa Fe production are closely modeled on
those for the Paris and Helsinki productions from 2006.

4. Other reviews appear in BBC Music, Ionarts, and the New York Times: Gardner
(2009), Oestreich (2002), and Ellison (2002) for *L'Amour de loin* and Tommasini (2008),
Riding (2006), and Downey (2006) for *Adriana Mater.*

5. Personal interview with Saariaho in Paris on June 15, 2009.

6. According to Saariaho, Peter Sellars initially thought of dividing Tsargo into two
roles based on the different musical characterization of this character. Personal interview with Saariaho on June 15, 2009.

7. Personal interview with Saariaho on June 15, 2009.

8. For example, in reference to Brahms's Third Symphony, Hatten discusses how the
composer transplants the march topic in the unusual $\frac{3}{4}$ meter to articulate the Romantic
topic of a pilgrims' processional (2004: 89).

9. Although Saariaho does not specify the motive characterized by a semitone descent as a "sigh" motive, it is difficult not to associate her use of this motive with its
topical meaning in Western musical canon.

10. Saariaho intended to construct a chord with the widest range within Scene I to
underscore this passage. Personal interview with Saariaho on June 15, 2009.

11. Where this concept differs from film is that the viewer is denied the opportunity
to see the action, but imagine it through sound. In filmic contexts, Chion claims: "acous-
matization is a process whereby we are made to hear without seeing after having first
been allowed to see and hear at the same time" (Chion 2014).

12. Hautsalo claims that the piccolo motive (S5') is a reference to the unborn child and
constitutes an "indexical cradle song topic" as seen earlier in *L'Amour de loin* (2011: 123).

13. The *acoustical* and *visual mirror* stages are part of what Lacan calls the Imaginary Order; in the development of a child, s/he communicates with the mother through
imitating the her voice, which produces the model for communication *with* and separation *from* the external world. In musical terms, David Schwarz suggests that an acoustical mirror is represented by many aspects of musical interaction, such as question/an-
swer structures, statement/counterstatement, melodies doubled at the octave, and so
forth (1997: 21–22). It is a mimetic process that resists being formulated into a conventional sign or symbol. Here, the lullaby motive *mirrors* Adriana's sung text as a way of re-
assuring her desire that the child will be like her, and not like the father.

14. Personal interview with Saariaho on June 15, 2009.

15. Adrian Johnston discusses how Lacan reconfigured Freud's theory of unconscious
by claiming that the unconscious and consciousness are constructed from a single surface, which is bent in a particular manner to enable one to move continually along the
"same" surface, as with a Moebius strip. The corners of the Moebius strip are the essential turning points where the traumatic Real is registered (2005: 55).

16. Kristeva defines *chora* from a number of different perspectives: "the *chora* is a modality of significance in which the linguistic sign is not yet articulated as the absence of
an object and as the distinction between real and symbolic" (1984: 26).

17. These ruptures are to be distinguished from disjunctions that occur at the surface level of the music, such as the metric changes that distinguish Yonas ($\frac{6}{8}$) from Refka ($\frac{2}{4}$) and Adriana ($\frac{3}{4}$).

18. In her analytical reading of modern subjectivity in Shostakovich's String Quartets, for example, Reichardt locates the "aural image" of the Real in the fugue subject that obsessively repeats itself without development (2008: 57–60).

4. John Adams's *Doctor Atomic*

1. Ruth Longobardi offers a penetrating analysis of the shifting representation of Palestinians and contrasting narrative orientations in pre- and post-9/11 productions of this opera. Specifically, she discusses how Sellars, Goodman, Morris, and Adams conceived the original production of *Death of Klinghoffer* at the Brooklyn Academy of Music in 1991 as a platform from which to voice disagreement and situate historical subjects within a broader narrative of tragedy; in stark contrast, Woolcock's 2003 filmic production inserts additional narrative layers that generate causal connections that are not present in the original (2009: 298).

2. Interview with Pamela Rosenberg. http://doctor-atomic.com/resources.html (accessed on April 12, 2010).

3. In this context, meta-diegetic refers to the imagined time and space that moves beyond the diegetic time and space of the main narrative in July 1945 at Los Alamos, New Mexico.

4. Moreover, Sellars's production of *Doctor Atomic* follows the multimedial structure of *Natyashastra*, a foundational Indian treatise on the performing arts, in which emphasis is given to treating literature, theater, dance, and music as a composite form.

5. In the approach to the countdown, Adams and Sellars introduce ensemble numbers like this where the characters are clearly speaking at cross purposes; here, General Groves is preoccupied with the timing of the bomb explosion, while Oppenheimer speaks in poetic terms of the end of time and Pasqualita expresses Rukeyser's anti-war sentiments.

6. Plato refers to the mythic tale of Gyges allegorically to illustrate how power can corrupt men in second book of *The Republic* (360 BCE). In the tale, the shepherd Gyges comes into possession of a ring that gives him the power of invisibility and leads him to murder the king in order to marry the queen and take over the kingdom.

7. There are ten parts to Rukeyser's poetry *Elegies* from 1949, dealing with themes that range from atrocities of war, children of refugees, and lost homelands, to the imagining of peace.

8. However, the Los Alamos historian Marjorie Bell Chambers argues that the reference to Trinity has Hindu rather than Christian roots (Kelly 2006: 56). Given Oppenheimer's intimate knowledge of Sanskrit and the Bhagavad Gita, it is plausible that Trinity also carried a reference to the three Hindu Gods as well as to the process of destruction and renewal associated with Hinduism.

9. Aeschylus's version of the myth (*Prometheus Bound*) is from the fifth century BCE and is based on Hesiod.

10. For example, *Counterblast* (1948) features a Nazi scientist's experimentation with biological warfare, *Godzilla* (1954) features a monster born of nuclear waste in Tokyo Bay in postwar Japan, *Final War* (1960) depicts the United States dropping a nuclear bomb in South Korea by accident, and *Doctor Strangelove or: How I Learned to Stop Worrying and Love the Bomb* (1964) features a megalomaniac scientist who activates the

Doomsday machine with the insanely utopian idea of rebuilding American society from scratch.

11. This attribution ("maximally minimal") appears in many reviews and websites associated with the reception of John Adams's and Steve Reich's later music; arguably, it was initiated by the release of a CD entitled *Maximum Minimalists* (Nonesuch CD B00004S1ED, 2000) that includes music by both John Adams and Steve Reich.

12. Guerin comments that while "the comic style tends to encourage the reiterative dimension of repetition," as in the "News" aria, "the epic style often tends to be larger-scale, to form textures that encourage a cyclic/static experience of time" (2010: 2–3).

13. Distinguishing between time and *markers* of time is crucial here. Musical procedures can mark time for the listener in different ways, but they cannot represent time itself. Gilles Deleuze explains the ontology of "being in time" in terms of an immersion in the undifferentiated/unmediated present as opposed to reflection, which involves temporal associations construed in terms of categories or representations (Lorraine 2003: 30). Building on Deleuze and Stravinsky, musical procedures that mark ontological time tend to anchor our perception in the present, while those that mark psychological time tend to shift our attention toward events that precede or follow that point in time.

14. Expanding on Middleton's model, Rebecca Leydon draws a typology of minimalist tropes in defining the affective qualities of ostinato techniques found in music by Arvo Pärt, Michael Nyman, and others (Leydon 2002).

15. Monelle traces the "step" motive to Albert Schweitzer's theory of topics for the music of Bach, in which a stepwise motive in the continuo part serves simultaneously as an icon for walking and an index for "confident faith" in Cantata No.159, "Sehet, wir gehen hinauf nach Jerusalem" (2000: 23).

16. The full title of the book is *The Atomic Energy for Military Purposes: The Official Report on the Development of the Atomic Bomb under the Auspices of the United States Government* (1945) by Henry De Wolf Smyth, otherwise known as the Smyth Report. In the Lyric Opera of Chicago Pre-concert Symposium, John Adams explained how the US government was dismayed by the content of this book, which explained in detail how to construct an atomic bomb (Sellars 2007).

17. This excerpt can also be found in Woolcock's production (posted on Metropolitan Opera's HD series, track #21) https://metopera.org/ondemand/index.aspx.

18. Following Christoph Bernhard's *Tractatus compositionis augmentatus* (1648–49), Monelle refers to the *passus duriusculus* as a figure that fills out the descending or ascending fourth chromatically with semitones (Monelle 2000: 73).

19. Although the harmonization is post-tonal, the passacaglia bass and the lament topic allude in part to the musical stylization of English anthems, including but not limited to John Ward's "Prayer is an endless chain," Dido's lament from Purcell's *Dido and Aeneas,* and John Bull's "Almighty God, which by the Leading of a Star."

20. More specifically, Hatten explains how the initial theme in the violins, through the hemiola in $\frac{3}{2}$ meter, presents a troping of march and triple time; it is only at the transition (m.15 onward) that the repeated quarter notes of the march are integrated with the eighth-note arabesque of the waltz topic (2004: 75–76).

21. David Lewin coined this transformation based on the voice-leading pattern of triads that "slide" in parallel fifths, while retaining the middle note in common (1987: 178). Timothy Johnson traces Adams's use of the SLIDE function (along with other Neo-Riemannian transformations) in his extensive analysis of *Nixon in China* (2011).

22. Interestingly enough, when I asked the audience at the Cincinnati Conservatory (January 28, 2011) to identify the intertextual reference for this choral number based on the Bhagavad Gita text, they unanimously heard the Orff reference.

23. I acknowledge Sean Atkinson and his work on post-minimalist operas for incorporating Gollin's multiple aggregate double interval cycle as an analytical tool. In his analysis of *Lost Objects* by Michael Gordon, Julia Wolfe, and David Lang, Atkinson illustrates how two movements from this collaborative opera use the (3, 4) cycle as a salient structural feature (2009: 99–102).

24. Adams's countdown music also references Louis Andriessen's instrumental work called *De Tijd* ("Time," 1980–81), which explores the formal opposition between temporal and non-temporal experiences of time as described by St. Augustine in his *Confessions*. Andriessen superimposes variable and fixed durational cycles in different combinations to explore different types of temporal opposition in this piece (Everett 2006: 102).

25. Anthony Tommasini, "Faust Unleashing a Destroyer of Worlds." The *New York Times*. October 14, 2008. Accessed February 15, 2011. http://www.nytimes.com/2008/10 /15/arts/music/15atom.html?_r=1&scp=4&sq=John+Adams+Doctor+Atomic&st=nyt.

26. With the lighting designer, James F. Ingalls, Sellars devised an overarching color scheme: for example, graphite represents the will to kill, blue represents whatever remains of the human impulse, gray tones represent the muddled middle, and so forth (Ross 2005).

27. The 2003 DVD of *The Death of Klinghoffer* includes an interview with Woolcock and Adams under special features; in "Filming *The Death of Klinghoffer*," Woolcock talks about coming up with the idea of making a film after hearing the concert version of *The Death of Klinghoffer* at the Barbican in 2000 and being particularly moved by the chorus's opening aria. She confesses to having no background in music nor directing opera up until that point.

28. This scene can be viewed under Track #8 in Woolcock's production of *Doctor Atomic* from the *Metropolitan Opera Live on Demand* series. http://www.metopera.org /ondemand/index.aspx?src=wlbuc.

29. This scene can be viewed under Track #36 in Woolcock's production of *Doctor Atomic* from the *Metropolitan Opera Live on Demand* series. http://www.metopera.org /ondemand/index.aspx?src=wlbuc.

30. Anthony Tommasini, in his review, expressed his criticism of Woolcock's staging in constricting some of the pivotal characters. As noted above, the pacifist, Wilson, is stuck in his cubicle as he makes his plea; by distancing him from Oppenheimer, his role is consequentially diminished (2008).

31. I speculate that due to the absence of choreography, Alan Gilbert was able to conduct this choral number at a much faster tempo.

32. Rosenbaum was under the impression that New York City's best critics were critical of the libretto, but were enthused by Adams's music; for example, the *New York Magazine* commented on the libretto being comprised of "leaden lingo" and "opaque poetry," but somehow it took a backseat to the greatness of the music and sets (2008).

33. Following *Doctor Atomic*, Adams and Sellars continued their collaboration in a smaller-scale opera, *A Flowering Tree* (2006), an adaptation of a southern Indian folktale into an opera about the rituals and trials of love. Here, the structure of multimodal narrative is more conventional. While Adams's music remains exuberant in his orchestration and choral writing that incorporates the hocket-like vocal technique of *Kechak* (Ba-

linese monkey chant), the collaborators abandon the non-linear narrative structure in favor of a linear mode of storytelling accompanied by minimal staging.

5. The Anti-hero in Tan Dun's *The First Emperor*

Chapter 5 adopts the pinyin system for Romanizing Chinese names instead of the Wade Giles's; for example, Mao Zedong (pinyin) = Mao Tse Tong (Wade Giles). In addition, some Chinese names follow the traditional order of surname/first name (as in Tan Dun, Guo Wenjing, and Zhang Yimou), while others follow the order of first name/surname (as in Dou Dou Huang and Ha Jin). All operatic and filmic characters are identified by their first names in keeping with the libretto and screenplay.

    1. Claire Wu provided the English translation of this passage. Flying Apsara refers to a female spirit of the clouds and waters in Hindu and Buddhist mythology.

    2. John Corbett situates prominent postwar Asian composers such as Tan Dun in a paradoxical role of simultaneously embracing and subverting the Orientalist ideology (2000: 180).

    3. What came to be known as the *Historical Records* (or *The Grand Scribe's Records*) by Sima Qian has remained the main source of information on the life and reign of the First Emperor for nearly two thousand years. However, other legal texts pertaining to the Qin dynasty were discovered in 1975 and shed new light on this historical period (Wood 2007: 35–36).

    4. Zhang Yimou is a film director who has won numerous awards and recognition for films such as *Ju Dou* (1990), *Raise the Red Lantern* (1991), and *Hero* (2002). Dou Dou Huang is the Artistic Director and Principal Dancer of the Shanghai Song and Dance Ensemble. His most notable works include "Dancing Dancing I," which combines multimedia, modern acoustics, and optic technology with modern dance choreography. Lastly, Emi Wada created costumes for the Academy Award winning film, *Ran* (1985) by Akira Kurosawa, and collaborated with Peter Greenaway in the film *Prospero's Books* (1991) and Zhang Yimou in *Hero* and *House of Flying Daggers* (2004).

    5. "In the Italian operas Mr. Tan has in mind – say, Puccini's *Turandot* – the pacing of vocal lines accords with the impetuosity of the moment and the flow of the words. Mr. Tan's goal in this work, it would seem, was to create a ritualistic and hypnotic lyricism" (Tommasini 2006).

    6. The newspaper, *Beijing Chenbao*, announced the possibility of staging Tan's *The First Emperor* at the site of the Great Wall as early as in 2003, but it did not come to fruition (Li 2003).

    7. Characters in the filmic and operatic narratives are identified by their first names (e.g., Zheng, Jianli, Yueyang, and so forth).

    8. Van Gulik remarks that there is hardly any Chinese book or treatise on music that does not quote this story in some form or other. The story has been elaborated further and even made into a novel (1969: 98).

    9. In his major novels like *Waiting* and *War Trash*, the male protagonists often find themselves in precarious situations and are forced to act within a moral vacuum (Fay 2009).

    10. It was Tan Dun's idea to come up with these extra-diegetic characters; the Yin-Yang master was based on the geomancer figure from the notes based on Tan's research on the Qin dynasty. Based on a phone interview with Ha Jin on June 20, 2012.

    11. A waterphone is a percussion instrument constructed largely of a stainless steel resonator "bowl" with a cylindrical neck, which may or may not contain water. A player

bows the brass rods around the rim of the bowl to create a vibrant, ethereal type of sound. Tan Dun also used this instrument in his soundtrack for *Crouching Tiger, Hidden Dragon.*

12. The opera juxtaposes the themes of spiritual, physical, and musical journeys from the past, present, and future. It hardly matters to Tan that Marco Polo in actuality never set foot in China; "we therefore have Marco (Being, Doing, It) and Polo (Spirit, Memory, I), who in reality set out on a journey together, one that is both a journey through time that takes them through the seasons and a journey in dream that carries them into themselves" (Moritz 2009: 11).

13. In his original explanation, Tan notes one of the characteristics as "the *continuance* of a fourth." I changed this to "the leap of a fourth" since, in actuality, what we find is a repetitive use of the fourth in the melodic line.

14. The video footage of the rehearsal at the Met reveals Tan Dun singing in the style of *qinqiang* to demonstrate the exact effect he is looking for. See track #35 of the video available on http://www.metoperafamily.org/met_player/players with subscription.

15. Between September 5 and 13, 1998, there were eight open-air performances of *Turandot* held at the courtyard of the palace in the Forbidden City of Beijing. Zubin Mehta and Zhang Yimou collaborated with Florence's Teatro Comunale in this elaborate production with nearly 1500 costumes modeled on Ming Dynasty apparel (Kaye 1998).

16. The opening instrumental music is based on Tan's research into the ritualistic use of music in the Qin court.

17. The libretto for Puccini's *Turandot* includes references to nature cosmology involving the moon and sun, but not to the extent that the characters address each other using such metaphors in the sung dialogues.

18. Certainly, the instrumental interlude that accompanies the ritual inauguration is filled with exotic markers. One hears an overt stylistic borrowing from Stravinsky's *Rite of Spring,* especially from part II, which is called *The Exalted Sacrifice.*

19. Andrew Davis, in his detailed analysis of *Turandot,* locates five different musical styles to illustrate the dramatic oppositions that characterize each act; to recapitulate, the exotic-Chinese music ("Mo-li-hua"), which was initially associated with the negative image of the Chinese Princess in Act I, assumes a positive role as it becomes associated with the shift in Prince Calaf's role as victor in Act II.

20. Sima Qian, in the *Historical Records,* indicate how the Emperor struggled to overcome his humble origin; as a son of a concubine who was raised in the Zhao province, he suffered from harsh conditions before being adopted by the Crown Prince of Qin (1994: 8).

21. Apparently, Mao boasted how he had outdone the First Emperor by "burying" the careers of 460,000 scholars, while Qin Shi Huang purportedly buried 460 scholars alive (Wood 2007: 144).

22. Based on email correspondence with Ha Jin on June 19, 2012.

23. On the subject of the national anthem, it is interesting to note that Nancy Guy documents the controversy regarding pop musician A-mei's singing of the Chinese national anthem in Taiwan in an article (2002: 96–119). When an opportunity arose to have this article translated in a volume in Chinese, it was denied by the Chinese government due to her critical assessment of the government's role in banning A-mei's singing of the anthem (based on an interview with Nancy Guy on November 18, 2011).

Epilogue

1. Cohen's Congruence-Associationist model (C-A M) categorizes auditory, visual, and kinesthetic information across six sensory domains to examine patterns of formal congruency; congruent information patterns from cross-modal domains are extracted into what she calls the "working narrative," which shapes long-term memory of multi-modal narrative (2014: 119–121).

Bibliography

Abbate, Carolyn. 1991. *Unsung Voices: Opera and Musical Narrative in the Nineteenth Century*. Princeton: Princeton University Press.

———. 2004. "Music – Drastic or Gnostic?" *Critical Inquiry* 30/3 (Spring): 505–36.

Adamenko, Victoria. 2007. *Neo-Mythologism in Music: From Scriabin and Schoenberg to Schnittke and Crumb*. Hillsdale, NY: Pendragon Press.

Adorno, Theodor. 2009. *In Search of Wagner*. Trans. Rodney Livingstone. London: Verso.

Almén, Byron. 2008. *A Theory of Musical Narrative*. Bloomington: Indiana University Press.

Almén, Byron and Robert S. Hatten. 2012. "Narrative Engagement with Twentieth-Century Music: Possibilities and Limits." In *Music and Narrative Since 1900*, eds. Michael L. Klein and Nicholas Reyland, 59–85. Bloomington: Indiana University Press.

"Ardillita in *Ainadamar* from Osvaldo Golijov." http://youtu.be/P5LeDsSX1aI (Accessed on August 1, 2011).

Ashbrook, William and Harold Powers. 1991. *Puccini's Turandot: The End of the Great Tradition*. Princeton, NJ: Princeton University Press.

Atkinson, Sean. 2009. "An Analytical Model for the Study of Multimedia Compositions: A Case Study in Minimalist Music." PhD dissertation: Florida State University.

Barrière, Aleksi. 2013. "Théâtre musical, théâtre de la musique. La rencontre de Kaija Saariaho et Peter Sellars." *O Tempus Perfectum. Kaija Saariaho: l'ombre du songe.* 11 (April): 25–30.

Barthes, Roland. 1972. *Mythologies*. Trans. Annette Lavers. New York: Hill and Wang.

Bernardoni, Virgilio. 2005. "Puccini and the dissolution of the Italian tradition." In *The Cambridge Companion to Twentieth-Century Opera*, ed. Mervyn Cooke, 26–44. Cambridge: Cambridge University Press.

Blakely, Sandra. 2013. "Conon (26)." *Brill's New Jacoby*. Brill Online. *Reference*. http://referenceworks.brillonline.com/entries/brill-s-new-jacoby/conon-26-a26 (Accessed on June 17, 2013).

Bolter, Jay D. and Richard Grusin. 2001. *Remediation: Understanding New Media*. Cambridge, MA: The MIT Press.

Bordwell, David and Kristin Thompson. 2004. *Film Art: An Introduction*. 7th ed. Boston: McGraw Hill.

Boyle, Nicholas. 1978. *Goethe's Faust: Part One*. Cambridge: Cambridge University Press.

Byrd, Kai and Martin J. Sherwin. 2005. *American Prometheus: The Triumph and Tragedy of J. Robert Oppenheimer*. New York: Alfred F. Knopf.

Campbell, Joseph. 1973. *The Hero with a Thousand Faces*. Princeton, NJ: Bollingen Series/Princeton University Press.

Caruth, Cathy. 1996. *Unclaimed Experience: Trauma, Narrative, and History*. Baltimore: John Hopkins University Press.

Cassar, Johanne. 2000. "*Turandot* de Puccini: Essai d'analyse sémiotique." PhD dissertation: Université de Provence.

Cheng, Li. 2003. "Tan Dun: *The First Emperor* may play on the Great Wall: Domingo cast as leader." *Beijing Chenbao/Xinhua Wang,* August 14. http://news.xinhuanet .com/ent/2003-08/14/content_1025540.htm (Accessed on January 9, 2012).

Chion, Michel. 1994. *Audio-Vision: Sound on Screen.* New York: Columbia University Press.

———. 2014. "100 Concepts pour penser et décrirer le cinema sonore." http://www .michelchion.com/v1/index.php?option=com_content&task=view&id=45&Ite mid=60 (Accessed on June 10, 2014).

Christiansen, Rupert. 2009. "*Dr. Atomic* performed by the ENO at the London Coliseum." *The Telegraph.* February 26. http://www.telegraph.co.uk/culture/music /opera/4840135/Dr-Atmoic-performed-by-the-ENO-at-the-London-Coliseum -review.html (Accessed on June 12, 2012).

Cicora, Mary A. 1998. *Mythology as Metaphor: Romantic Irony, Critical Theory, and Wagner's Ring.* Westport, CN: Greenwood Press.

Citron, Marcia J. 2002. "The Elusive Voice: Absence and Presence in Jean-Pierre Ponnelle's Film *Le nozze di Figaro.*" In *Between Opera and Cinema,* eds. Jeongwon Joe and Rose Theresa, 133–53. New York: Routledge.

———. 2010. *When Opera Meets Film.* Cambridge: Cambridge University Press.

Clements, Jonathan. 2006. *The First Emperor of China.* Gloucestershire: Sutton Publishing Ltd.

Clendinning, Jane Piper. 2002. "Postmodern Architecture/Postmodern Music." In *Postmodern Music/Postmodern Thought,* eds. Judy Lochhead and Joseph Auner, 119–39. New York: Routledge.

Cohen, Annabel J. 2014. "Film Music from the Perspective of Cognitive Science." In *The Oxford Handbook of Film Music Studies,* ed. David Neumeyer, 96–130. New York: Oxford University Press.

Colebrook, Claire. 2004. *Irony.* London and New York: Routledge.

Cook, Nicholas. 1998. *Analysing Multimedia.* Oxford: Clarendon Press.

Corbett, John. 2000. "Experimental Oriental: New Music and Other Others." In *Western Music and Its Others: Difference, Representation, and Appropriation in Music,* eds. Georgina Born and David Hesmondhalgh, 163–86. Berkeley: University of California Press.

Cross, Jonathan. 2009. *Harrison Birtwistle: The Mask of Orpheus.* Farnham, UK: Ashgate Publishing Limited.

Csapo, Eric. 2005. *Theories of Mythology.* Oxford: Blackwell Publishing.

Cuitiño, Luis Martínez, ed. 1994. *Mariana Pineda.* Madrid: Cátedra.

Davis, Andrew C. 2003. "Structural Implications of Stylistic Plurality in Puccini's *Turandot.*" PhD dissertation: Indiana University.

———. 2010. *Il Trittico, Turandot, and Puccini's Late Style.* Bloomington: Indiana University Press.

Delgado, Maria M. 2005. "Muse or Mentor: Margarita Xirgu and Federico García Lorca." *The Santa Fe Opera Program Book: 2005 Festival Season,* 84–86.

Detienne, Marcel. 2009. "The Myth of 'Honeyed Orpheus'." In *Myths and Mythologies: A Reader,* ed. Jeppe S. Jensen, 276–89. London: Equinox Publishing Ltd.

Dietrich, Karin, ed. 2007. "Musik, die nach Bewegung schreit." In the *Program Notes* to *Ainadamar.* Darmstadt, Germany: Staatstheater Darmstadt.

Dolar, Mladen. 2006. *A Voice and Nothing More.* Cambridge, MA: MIT Press.

Eco, Umberto. 1976. *A Theory of Semiotics*. Bloomington: Indiana University Press.

Elleström, Lars, ed. 2010. *Media Borders, Multimodality, and Intermediality*. New York: Palgrave MacMillan.

Ellwood, Robert. 2008. *Myth: Key Concepts in Religion*. New York: Continuum International Publishing Group.

Everett, Yayoi U. 2006. *The Music of Louis Andriessen*. Cambridge: Cambridge University Press.

———. 2009. "Signification of Parody and the Grotesque in György Ligeti's *Le Grand Macabre*." *Music Theory Spectrum* 31/1: 26–56.

———. 2012. "Counting Down Time: Musical Topics in *Dr. Atomic* (2005) by John Adams." in *Musical Semiotics: A Network of Signification,* ed. Esti Sheinberg, 263–74. Farnham, UK: Ashgate Publishing Limited.

———. 2012. "The Tropes of Desire and *Jouissance* in Kaija Saariaho's *L'Amour de loin* (2000)." In *Musical Narrative After 1900,* eds. Michael Klein and Nicholas Reyland, 329–45. Bloomington: Indiana University Press.

Fay, Sarah. 2009. "Ha Jin, The Art of Fiction No.202." *The Paris Review* 191 (Winter). http://www.theparisreview.org/interviews/5991/the-art-of-fiction-no-202-ha-jin (Accessed on December 21, 2011).

Fink, Bruce. 1995. *The Lacanian Subject: Between Language and Jouissance*. Princeton, NJ: Princeton University Press.

Fontanille, Jacques. 2006. *The Semiotics of Discourse*. New York: Peter Lang.

Frye, Northrop. 1957. *Anatomy of Criticism: Four Essays*. Princeton, NJ: Princeton University Press.

Furby, Jacqueline and Claire Hines. 2012. *Fantasy*. New York: Routledge.

Garner, Stanton B., Jr. 1990. "Post-Brechtian Anatomies: Weiss, Bond, and the Politics of Embodiment." *Theatre Journal,* 42/2 (May): 145–164.

Ghazanfar, A.A., and C. E. Schroeder. 2006. "Is Neocortex Essentially Multisensory?" *Trends in Cognitive Science* 10 (6): 278–85.

Gibbons, Alison. 2010. "I Contain Multitudes: Narrative Multimodality and the Book that Bleeds." In *New Perspectives on Narrative and Multimodality,* ed. Ruth Page, 99–114. New York and London: Routledge.

Gjerdingen, Robert, O. 1988. *A Classical Turn of Phrase: Music and the Psychology of Convention*. Philadelphia: University of Pennsylvania Press.

———. 2007. *Music in the Galant Style*. New York: Oxford University Press.

Golijov, Osvaldo. 2006. "Interview with Adeline Sire used in the Ainadamar CD Listening Guide." http://www.osvaldogolijov.com/ainadamar_listening_guide.pdf (Accessed on March 30, 2011).

Grabócz, Márta. 2009. *Musique, narrativité, signification*. Paris: L'Harmattan.

Greimas, A. J. 1983. *Structural Semantics: An Attempt at a Method*. Trans. Daniele McDowell, et al. Lincoln: University of Nebraska Press.

Greimas, A. J. and J. Courtés. 1979. *Semiotics and Language: An Analytical Dictionary*. Trans. Larry Crist, et al. Bloomington: Indiana University Press.

Grey, Thomas S. 2005. "Leitmotif, Temporality, and Musical Design in the Ring." In *The Cambridge Companion to Wagner,* ed. Thomas S. Grey, 85–114. Cambridge: Cambridge University Press.

Guerin, William. 2010. "Style, Topic, and Political Register in Act III of John Adams's *Nixon in China*." Presented at the Music Theory Midwest Conference. Miami University, Ohio. May 14.

Guy, Nancy. 2002. "'Republic of China National Anthem' on Taiwan: One Anthem, One Performance, Multiple Realities." *Ethnomusicology* 46/1 (Winter): 96–119.

———. 2011. Personal Interview. November 18.

Hardy, Grant and Anne Kinney. 2005. *The Establishment of the Han Empire and Imperial China.* Westport, CN: Greenwood Press.

Hartley, John. 2002. *Communication, Cultural and Media Studies: The Key Concepts.* London and New York: Routledge.

Hatten, Robert S. 1994. *Musical Meaning in Beethoven: Markedness, Correlation, and Interpretation.* Bloomington: Indiana University Press.

———. 2004. *Interpreting Musical Gestures, Topics, and Tropes: Mozart, Beethoven, Schubert.* Bloomington: Indiana University Press.

———. 2010. "Musical Agency as Implied by Gesture and Emotion: Its Consequences for Listeners' Experiencing of Musical Emotion." In *Semiotics 2009: Proceedings of the Annual Meeting of the Semiotic Society of America,* ed. Karen Haworth and Leonard Sbrocchi, 162–69. New York: Legas Publishing.

Hautsalo, Liisamaija. 2011. "Whispers from the Past: Musical Topics in Saariaho's Operas." In *Kaija Saariaho: Visions, Narratives, Dialogues,* eds. Tim Howell, John Hargreaves, and Michael Rofe, 107–29. Farnham, UK: Ashgate Publishing Limited.

Heldt, Guido. 2005. "Austria and Germany, 1918–1960." In *The Cambridge Companion to Twentieth-Century Opera,* ed. Mervyn Cooke, 146–64. Cambridge: Cambridge University Press.

Herman, David. 2010. "Word-Image/Utterance-Gesture: Case Studies in Multimodal Storytelling." In *New Perspectives on Narrative and Multimodality,* ed. Ruth Page, 78–98. New York and London: Routledge.

Huron, David. 2006. *Sweet Anticipation: Music and the Psychology of Expectation.* Cambridge, MA: The MIT Press.

Hutcheon, Michael and Linda Hutcheon. 2010. "Opera: Forever and Always Multimodal." In *New Perspectives on Narrative and Multimodality,* ed. Ruth Page, 65–77. New York and London: Routledge.

Jensen, Jeppe, S. 2009. "General Introduction." In *Myths and Mythologies: A Reader,* ed. Jeppe S. Jensen, 1–31. London: Equinox Publishing Ltd.

Jiang, Jing. 1995. *Zhongguo Xiqu Yinyue* [Chinese Theatrical Music]. Beijing: Renming Yinyue Chubanshe.

Jin, Ha. 2012. Phone Interview. June 20.

Joe, Jeongwon and Sander L. Gilman, eds. 2010. *Wagner & Cinema.* Bloomington: Indiana University Press.

Johnson, Timothy A. 2011. *John Adams's Nixon in China: Musical Analysis, Historical and Political Perspectives.* Farnham, UK: Ashgate Publishing Limited.

Johnston, Adrian. 2005. *Time Driven: Metapsychology and the Splitting of the Drive.* Chicago: Northwestern University Press.

Jones, Robert T. 1987. *Opera on the Beach: Philip Glass on His New World of Music Theatre.* London: Faber and Faber.

Jung, C. G. 1980. *The Archetypes and the Collective Unconscious.* Trans. R. F. C. Hull. Princeton, NJ: Princeton University Press.

Kaye, Michael. 1998. "Perspectives on Puccini." DVD Liner Notes to *Giacomo Puccini Turandot at the Forbidden City of Beijing.* New York: RCA Victor 74321-60917-2, 1999.

Keller, James M. 2005. "The Fountain of Tears." In *The Santa Fe Opera Program Book*, 75–79. Santa Fe, NM: The Santa Fe Opera.

Kelly, Cynthia C. 2006. *Oppenheimer and the Manhattan Project: Insights into J. Robert Oppenheimer, "Father of the atomic bomb."* Hackensack, NJ: World Scientific.

Kennicott, Philip. 2005. "'Ainadamar': Agony and Ecstasy in Santa Fe." *The Washington Post.* August 15. http://www.washingtonpost.com/wp-dyn/content/article/2005 /08/14/AR2005081401271.html (Accessed on November 15, 2013).

Klein, Dagmar. 2007. "Die Nacht, als die Steine Tränen weinten." *Tanznetze.de.* http:// www.tanznetz.de/blog/11250/die-nacht-als-die-steine-tranen-weinten (Accessed on November 27, 2013).

Klein, Michael, L. 2005. *Intertextuality in Western Art Music.* Bloomington: Indiana University Press.

———. 2009. "Ironic Narrative, Ironic Reading." *Journal of Music Theory* 53/1 (spring): 95–136.

Klein, Michael L. and Nicholas Reyland, eds. 2012. *Music and Narrative Since 1900.* Bloomington: Indiana University Press.

Kors, Stacey. 2008. "Tan Dun's *The First Emperor.*" DVD liner notes to *Tan Dun: The First Emperor.* The Metropolitan Opera HD Live. EMI Classics: 50999-2-1512995.

Kozinn, Allan. 2008. "Downsizing a Larger-than-life Warlord." *The New York Times.* May 12.

Kramer, Lawrence. 2006. "Speaking Melody, Melodic Speech." In *Critical Musicology and the Responsibility of Response: Selected Essays,* 263–79. Farnham, UK: Ashgate Publishing Limited.

———. 2011. *Interpreting Music.* Berkeley: University of California Press.

Kress, Gunther and Theo Van Leeuwen. 2001. *Multimodal Discourse: The Modes and Media of Contemporary Communication.* London: Hodder Education.

Kristeva, Julia. 1984. *Revolution in Poetic Language.* New York: Columbia University Press.

Lam, Joseph. 2008. "Chinese Music and its Globalized Past and Present." Ahmed Samatar, ed. *The Musical Imagination in the Epoch of Globalization.*St. Paul, MN: Macalester International 21: 29–77.

Lambright, Spencer N. 2008. "*L'amour de loin* and the Vocal Works of Kaija Saariaho." PhD dissertation: Cornell University.

Langer, Suzanne. 2009. "Life-Symbols: The Roots of Myths." In *Myths and Mythologies: A Reader,* ed. Jeppe S. Jensen, 64–85. London: Equinox Publishing Ltd. (Reprinted from "Life-Symbols: The Roots of Myths" in *Philosophy in a New Key: A Study in the Symbolism of Reason, Rite and Art,* 148–74. 1951. Cambridge, MA: Harvard University Press.)

Laznik, Marie-Christine. 2005. "Jouissance (Lacan)." *International Dictionary of Psychoanalysis.* Ed. Alain de Mijolla. Vol. 2. Gale Cengage. *eNotes.com.* http://www .enotes.com/jouissance-lacan-reference/ (Accessed on August 10, 2012).

Lee, Joanna. 2006. "Romantic Gesture: Tan Dun's *The First Emperor.*" *Opera News* 71/6 (Dec.): 16–20.

Lefevre, Peter. 2012. "Ainadamar." *Opera News* 77/2 (August) http://www.operanews .com/Opera_News_Magazine/2012/8/Reviews/LONG_BEACH,_CA __Ainadamar.html (Accessed on December 20, 2013).

Levin, David. 2007. *Unsettling Opera: Staging Mozart, Verdi, Wagner, and Zemlinsky.* Chicago: The University of Chicago Press.

Lewin, David. 1987. *Generalized Musical Intervals and Transformations.* New Haven, CT: Yale University Press.

Lewis, Mark, E. 2007. *The Early Chinese Empires: Qin and Han.* Cambridge: The Belknap Press of Harvard University Press.

Lévi-Strauss, Claude. 1969. *The Raw and the Cooked.* Trans. John and Doreen Weightman. Chicago: The University of Chicago Press.

Leydon, Rebecca. 2002. "Towards a Typology of Minimalist Tropes." *Music Theory Online* 8/4 (December). http://www.mtosmt.org/issues/mto.02.8.4/mto.02.8.4 .leydon.html (Accessed on April 10, 2011).

Liszka, James. 1989. *The Semiotics of Myth.* Bloomington: Indiana University Press.

Locke, Ralph. 2009. *Musical Exoticism: Images and Reflections.* Cambridge: Cambridge University Press.

Longobardi, Ruth. 2009. "Re-producing *Klinghoffer*: Opera and Arab Identity before and after 9/11." *Journal of the Society for American Music* 3/3: 273–310.

Lorca, Federico García. 1998. *In Search of Duende.* Trans. Christopher Mauer. New York: New Direction Publishing Corporation.

——. 1995. *Plays: Three.* Trans. Gwynne Edwards. Portsmouth, NH: Methuen Drama.

——. *Poem of the Deep Song.* Trans. Carlos Bauer. San Francisco: City Lights Books, 1987.

Lorraine, Tasmin. 2003. "Living a Time Out of Joint." *Between Deleuze and Derrida,* eds. Paul Patton and John Protevi, 30–43. New York: Continuum.

Lunden, Jeff. 2006. "Tan Dun's 'First Emperor' to Premiere at Met." NPR Music. http://www.npr.org/templates/story/story.php?storyId=6660144 (Accessed on May 10, 2012).

Maalouf, Amin. 2006. "Les portes de l'enfer doivent se refermer. . . ." In the Program Notes to *Adriana Mater,* 57–61. Paris: Opera National de Paris.

May, Thomas, ed. 2006. *The John Adams Reader: Essential Writings on an American Composer.* New Jersey: Amadeus Press.

McClary, Susan. 1991. *Feminine Endings: Music, Gender, and Sexuality.* Minneapolis: University of Minnesota Press.

McCreless, Patrick. 2005. "Isolde's Transformation in Words and Music." In *Engaging Music: Essays in Music Analysis,* ed. Deborah Stein, 125–35. New York: Oxford University Press.

McKinnon, Arlo. 2005. "Ainadamar's Architect." *Opera News* 70/2 (August): 36–39.

Meyer, Leonard B. 1989. *Style and Music: Theory, History, and Ideology.* Philadelphia: University of Pennsylvania Press.

Middleton, Richard. 1990. *Studying Popular Music.* Buckingham: Open University Press.

Miller, Jacques-Alain, ed. 1975. *Le Séminaire de Jacques Lacan,* vol. 20 ("Encore"). Paris: Seuil.

Mills, Sara. 1997. *Discourse.* London and New York: Routledge.

Monelle, Raymond. 1992. *Linguistics and Semiotics in Music.* Chur, Switzerland: Harwood Academic Publishers.

——. 2000. *The Sense of Music: Semiotic Essays.* Princeton, NJ: Princeton University Press.

——. 2006. *The Musical Topic: Hunt, Military, and Pastoral.* Bloomington: Indiana University Press.

Mortiz, Reiner E. 2009. Liner notes to *Tan Dun: Marco Polo.* DVD Opus Arte OA1010D.

Nellestijn, Maarten. 2011. *Doctor Atomic: Monster Opera?* Bachelor's thesis: University of Utrecht.

Nichols, Bill. 1987 "History, Myth, and Narrative in Documentary." *Film Quarterly* 41/1 (Autumn): 9–20.

"One Very Explosive Opera: John Adams's 'Dr. Atomic' makes its atom-smashing New York debut." 2008. *The Daily Beast.* http://www.thedailybeast.com/newsweek /2008/10/14/one-very-explosive-opera.print.html. (Accessed on June 12, 2012.)

Page, Ruth, ed. 2010. *New Perspectives on Narrative and Multimodality.* New York: Routledge.

Page, Tim. 1993. CD liner notes to *Philip Glass/Robert Wilson, Einstein on the Beach.* New York: Elektra Nonesuch 9-79323-2.

Patton, Laurie L. 2008. *The Bhagavad Gita.* London: Penguin Books.

Pavis, Patrice. 1998. *Dictionary of the Theatre: Terms, Concepts, and Analysis.* Toronto: University of Toronto Press.

Pettitt, Stephen. 2006. "A Real Opera Composer: Kaija Saariaho talks to Stephen Pettitt about 'Adriana Mater.'" *Opera* (March): 285–88.

Potter, Keith. 2000. *Four Musical Minimalists: La Monte Young, Terry Riley, Steve Reich, Philip Glass.* Cambridge: Cambridge University Press.

Propp, Vladimir. 2012. *The Russian Folktale by Vladimir Yakovlevich Propp.* Trans. Sibelan Forrester. Detroit: Wayne State University Press.

Qian, Sima. 1994. *Historical Records.* Trans. Raymond Dawson. New York. Oxford University Press.

Ramberg, Bjørn and Gjesdal, Kristin. 2013. "Hermeneutics." In *The Stanford Encyclopedia of Philosophy,* ed. Edward N. Zalta, http://plato.stanford.edu/archives /sum2013/entries/hermeneutics/ (Accessed on September 25, 2013).

Reichardt, Sarah. 2008. *Composing the Modern Subject: Four String Quartets by Dmitri Shostakovich.* Farnham, UK: Ashgate Publishing Limited.

Ren, Haijie. 2009. "Metropolitan Opera's *The First Emperor.*" *Opera* 5 (2009): 56–57.

Richardson, John. 1999. *Singing Archeology: Philip Glass's Akhnaten.* Hanover, NH: Wesleyan University Press.

Ricoeur, Paul. 1984. *Time and Narrative.* Vol. 1. Trans. Kathleen McLaughlin and David Pellauer. Chicago and London: University of Chicago Press.

Riding, Alan. 2006. "The Opera 'Adriana Mater' Addresses Motherhood in a War Zone." The *New York Times,* April 5. http://www.nytimes.com/2006/04/05/arts/music /05adri.html?_r=1 (Accessed on November 13, 2010).

Rimmon-Kenan, Shlomith. 2001. *Narrative Fiction: Contemporary Poetics.* 2nd edition. London and New York: Routledge.

Rosenbaum, Ron. 2008. "The Opera's New Clothes: Why I walked out of *Doctor Atomic.*" *Slate Magazine.* October 24th. http://www.slate.com/articles/life/the _spectator/2008/10/the_operas_new_clothes.html (Accessed on April 10, 2011.)

Ross, Alex. 2005. "The Rest is Noise: *Doctor Atomic.*" http://www.therestisnoise. com/2005/09/doctor_atomic.html (Accessed on January 14, 2011).

——. 2006a. CD liner notes to *Osvaldo Golijov: Ainadamar.* Hamburg: Deutsche Grammaphon B0006429-02.

——. 2006b. "Saariaho's Adriana." *The New Yorker.* April 24. http://www.therestisnoise .com/2006/04/saariahos_adria.html (Accessed on September 23, 2013).

Rothstein, Edward. 1993. "Two Oedipuses, One Clad in Guilt, The Other in Clay." The *New York Times.* March 31. http://www.nytimes.com/1993/03/31/movies/review -film-two-oedipuses-one-clad-in-guilt-the-other-in-clay.html (Accessed on January 14, 2011.)

Rupprecht, Philip. 2001. *Britten's Musical Language*. Cambridge: Cambridge University Press.

Saariaho, Kaija. 2009. Personal interview. June 15.

Salzman, Eric and Thomas Desi. 2008. *The New Music Theater: Seeing the Voice, Hearing the Body*. Oxford: Oxford University Press.

Schwarz, David. 1997. *Listening Subjects: Music, Psychoanalysis, Culture*. Durham: Duke University Press.

Sellars, Peter. 2005. Libretto to John Adams's *Doctor Atomic*. New York: Hendon Music Inc.

——. 2007. *Backstage at Lyric #5: Doctor Atomic: Director-librettist Peter Sellars*. October 12. http://www.lyricopera.org/watchandlisten/2007.aspx (Accessed on September 17, 2013).

Silverman, Kaja. 1988. *The Acoustic Mirror: The Female Voice in Psychoanalysis and Cinema*. Bloomington: Indiana University Press.

Simonson, Mary. 2013. *Body Knowledge: Performance, Intermediality, and American Entertainment at the Turn of the Twentieth Century*. New York: Oxford University Press.

Sheppard, W. Anthony. 2009. "Blurring the Boundaries: Tan Dun's *Tinte* and *The First Emperor*." *The Journal of Musicology* 26/3 (Summer): 285–326.

Smyth, Henry De Wolf. 1945. *Atomic Energy for Military Purposes: The Official Report on the Development of the Atomic Bomb under the Auspices of the United States Government*. http://www.atomicarchive.com/Docs/SmythReport/ (Accessed on September 19, 2013).

Stainton, Leslie. 1999. *Lorca: a Dream of Life*. New York: Farrar, Straus, and Giroux.

——. 2005. "Dreaming the Impossible: Lorca and the Stage." In *The Santa Fe Opera Program Book,* 80–83. Santa Fe, NM: The Santa Fe Opera.

Stilwell, Robynn J. 2007. "The Fantastical Gap between Diegetic and nondiegetic." In *Beyond the Soundtrack: Representing Music in Cinema,* eds. Daniel Goldmark et al., 185–201. Berkeley: Univ. of California Press.

Stone, Rob. 2004. *The Flamenco Tradition in the Works of Federico García Lorca and Carlos Saura*. Lewiston, NY: The Edwin Mellen Press.

Stravinsky, Igor. 1992. *Oedipus Rex*. DVD Philips B0003883-09.

——. 2000. *Poetics of Music in the Form of Six Lessons*. Cambridge, MA: Harvard University Press. 14th printing.

Su, Xiaokang and Luxiang Wang. 1991. *Deathsong of the River: A Reader's Guide to the Chinese TV Series Heshang*. Ithaca: East Asia Program, Cornell University.

Sutcliffe, Tom. 2005. "Technology and Interpretation: Aspects of 'Modernism.'" In *The Cambridge Companion to Twentieth-Century Opera,* ed. Mervyn Cooke, 321–40. Cambridge: Cambridge University Press.

Sved, Mark. 2005. "Out of failure, a new victory. Poorly premiered at Tanglewood two years ago, Osvaldo Golijov's *Ainadamar* is reborn in triumph at Santa Fe." *Los Angeles Times*. August 2.

——. 2012. "Review: Patchy Poetry in Long Beach Opera's *Ainadamar*." *Los Angeles Times*. May 22.

Syer, Katherine R. 1999. "Altered States: Musical and Psychological Processes in Wagner." PhD dissertation: University of Victoria.

Tarasti, Eero. 1979. *Myth and Music: A Semiotic Approach to the Aesthetics of Myth in Music, especially that of Wagner, Sibelius and Stravinsky*. The Hague: Mouton Publishers.

——. 1994. *A Theory of Musical Semiotics*. Bloomington: Indiana University Press.

Taruskin, Richard. 2003. "Sacred Entertainments." *Cambridge Opera Journal* 15/2 (July): 109–26.

Telléz, Carmen. 2011. Phone Interview, July 29.

Tommasini, Anthony. 2006. "A Majestic Imperial Chinese Saga Has Its Premiere at the Met" The *New York Times*. December 23.

Tommasini, Anthony. 2007. "New Operas at the Met: What Works?" The *New York Times*. January 11.

——. 2008. "Faust Unleashing a Destroyer of Worlds." The *New York Times*. October 14. http://www.nytimes.com/2008/10/15/arts/music/15atom.html?_r=1&scp=4&sq=John+Adams+Doctor+Atomic&st=nyt (Accessed on February 15, 2011).

——. 2008. "Compassion, Not Revenge, After a Rape in a War Zone." http://www.nytimes.com/2008/08/01/arts/music/01adri.html (Accessed on October 15, 2010).

Totton, Robin. 2003. *Song of the Outcasts: An Introduction to Flamenco*. Portland, OR: Amadeus Press.

Wang-Ngai, Siu and Peter Lovrick. 1997. *Chinese Opera: Images and Stories*. Vancouver and Seattle: UBC Press and University of Washington Press.

Washabaugh, William. 2012. *Flamenco Music and National Identity in Spain*. Farnham, UK: Ashgate Publishing Limited.

Wood, Frances. 2007. *The First Emperor of China*. London: Profile Books.

Zhang, Jianguo. 2010. "Quanxinde Geju Chuangzuo Guannian: '1+1=1'" ("Completely New Opera and its Creative Concept"). *Renminyinyue*. http://www.cnki.net (Accessed on July 21, 2011).

Zhang, Lushi. 2009. "Tan Dun 'Qin Shi Huang' Zuoqiu zai Meizao Tanhe" ("Tan Dun's *The First Emperor* 'impeached' in the United States"). December 26. *Xinjing Bao/CRI Online*.

Žižek, Slavoj. 1989. *The Sublime Object of Ideology*. London and New York: Verso.

——. 1993. *Tarrying with the Negative: Kant, Hegel, and the Critique of Ideology*. Durham: Duke University Press.

Žižek, Slavoj and Mladen Dolar. 2002. *Opera's Second Death*. New York and London: Routledge.

Discography/Videography

Adams, John. 2008. *Doctor Atomic*. The Metropolitan Opera Live on Demand. New York: The Metropolitan Opera. https://www.metoperafamily.org/ondemand/.

——. 2003. *The Death of Klinghoffer*. London: Decca. London Symphony Orchestra and Chorus. 074 189-9. DVD.

——. 2007. *Doctor Atomic*. Netherlands Philharmonic Orchestra and Chorus. Opus Arte. OA-0998-D. DVD.

Golijov, Osvaldo. 2006. *Ainadamar*. Atlanta Symphony Orchestra and Chorus.Deutsche Grammophon. B0004782-02. Compact Disc.

Qin Song ("The Emperor's Shadow"). 1999. A Co-production of Ocean Film Co. and Xi'an Film Studio. Fox Lorber Home Video: WinStar TV & Video. DVD.

Tan, Dun. 2008. *The First Emperor*. The Metropolitan Opera HD Live. New York: The Metropolitan Opera. 50999-2-15129-9-5. DVD.

Wagner, Richard. 2011. *Die Walküre*. Production by Robert Lepage. The Metropolitan Opera HD Series. Deutsche Grammaphon. 00440 073 4848. *A Theory of Musical Narrative*

Index

ture of, 51–68, *53;* mythic narrative, x–xiii, 197–98; narrative formulae, xii; oratorio as passion, 73–74; overture, 41, 55; production history, 41–43; reconfiguration of myth, 197; semic role of lighting, 27; synoptic function of ballad, 54–59, *55, 56, 57;* Telléz's staging, 211n16; tropological narrative, 29; unpacking myth, 12; "Water and Horse," 55, 73; "Yo Soy la Libertad," 49–50, 52, *53,* 65–66, *67,* 72, 74
Akhnaten (Glass), 11–12, 206n13
Alexander Nevsky (Eisenstein), 35
allegory, 197; *Adriana Mater,* 82; death of Orpheus, 206n7; *The First Emperor,* 173, 186, 192, 195; multimodal discourse, 7; mythic narrative, 197, 198; tropological narrative, 29
Almén, Byron, xii, 12, 13, 21–22, 28, 39, 207n21
anagnorisis, 20, 23–24
Anatomy of Criticism (Frye), 19–20
Andriessen, Louis, xi
anticommunism, 127
antiheroes, 72, 74, 168, 192
anti-operas, xi
anti-Semitism, 74–75, 210n40
Apollo, 133
archetypes: *Adriana Mater,* 122–23; *Doctor Atomic,* 126, 155; *The First Emperor,* 168, 192; hero's journey, 155; ironic archetype, 207n21; *The Lord of the Rings,* 209n28; Meyer on, 205n5; multimodal discourse, xiii, 39; mythic narrative, 198–99; psychoanalytic theory, 29–30, 34; situational, 29; transhistorical perspective, x; transvaluation, 18–24; unpacking myth, 12
Ardillita, 76
Argento, Dominick, xi
Aristaeus, 7
Arjuna, 11, 132–34, 156
Ashbrook, William, 189
Association of Los Alamos Scientists (ALAS), 127
Atkinson, Sean, 215n23
Atlanta Symphony Orchestra (ASO), 42, 68, 79, 124
Atomic Energy Commission (AEC), 126
Atomic Energy for Military Purposes, The, 137
Audience, The (Lorca), 46
audio-visual downbeat, 199
audio-visual synchronization, 161
Austen, Jane, 206n11

ballad, synoptic function, 54–59, *55, 56, 57*
Barber of Seville (Rossini), 22
Barnes, Clive, 163–64

Barthes, Roland, 10, 12, 29, 197, 206n9
Bartók, Bela, 121–22
Bastille Opera, 87
Battistella, Edwin, 217n19
Baucis, 155
Baudelaire, Charles, xii, 124–25, 128–29, 133, 145–46, 150, 156
Bauer, Carlos, 44
Bayati mode, 52, *54,* 62
Bayreuth Festival, 36, 197–98
Beaumarchais, Pierre, xi
Bechtolf, Sven-Eric, xi
Beijing Central Conservatory of Music, 166
Benjamin, Walter, ix
Berlioz, Hector, 6–7, 155–56, 206n10
Bernardoni, Virgilio, 207n17
Bhagavad Gita: dramaturgical structure of *Doctor Atomic,* 128–29, 132–33; harmonic region, 152; intertextual references in *Doctor Atomic,* 215n22; origin of *Doctor Atomic,* 125; source materials for *Doctor Atomic,* xii; stylistic quotations, 146–47; "Trinity" reference, 132, 213n8; tropological narratives in *Doctor Atomic,* 161–62; unpacking myth, 9, 11
Billy Budd (Britten), 32
Birds, The (1963), 31
Birtwistle, Harrison, xi, 206n7
Blood Wedding (Lorca), 46, 61
Bluebeard's Castle (Szinetár), xii, 121–22
Body Knowledge (Simonson), 199
Boethius, 7
Bolero (Ravel), 52
Bolter, Jay, xii
Bororo people, 20–21, 206n8
Borowski-Tudor, Sonja, 42
Bosnian War, 83
Boyle, Nicholas, 154
Brandenberg Concerto No. 5, 21
Brecht, Bertolt, 38, 158, 207n14
Britten, Benjamin, 22, 28, 32, 207n21
Brünnhilde, 16, 30–31, 197–98
Busoni, Ferruccio, 155
Byrd, Kay, 127

Cain (biblical), 84, 103, 105, 122
Calaf, 16–17, 23, 207n18, 217n19
Caliban's Dream (Saariaho), 82
Campbell, Joseph, 29, 155
cantaor, 55, 62, 73
cante jondo ("deep song"), 42–44, 52, 55, 62, 74
capoeira, 76
Capriccio Espagnol (Rimsky-Korsakov), 174
Carmen (Bizet), 180

Carmen (Rosi), xii
Carmina Burana (Orff), 147
Caruth, Cathy, 85–86
Cassandra, 133, 143, 206n10
Castorf, Frank, 197–98
Catholic Church, 45
Chambers, Marjorie Bell, 213n8
Château de l'âme (Saariaho), 82
Chéreau, Patrice, 36–37, 210n39
Chiang Kai-shek, 194
Chicago Symphony Orchestra, 42
Childs, Lucinda, 11, 163, 206n12
Chion, Michel, 35, 103
chora, 117–19, 132, 201, 212n16
chorus: Adriana Mater, xii, 81–82, 86, 87, 91, 92,
    94, 97–100, 106, 109–14, 113, 116, 119, 122;
    and agential roles of music, 16; Ainadamar,
    41–42, 50–51, 52, 53, 54–59, 63, 67–68, 71–
    72, 73, 75–77; Doctor Atomic, 160; The First
    Emperor, 168, 171, 173, 181–83, 186, 188, 191,
    192; proto-topics, 137
Christ figures, x, 41, 48
Christian themes, 163
Christiansen, Rupert, 164
chronological temporal dimension (Paul
    Ricoeur), 10, 39
Cicora, Mary, 10, 16
Citron, Marcia, x, 209n34
City of Birmingham Symphony Orchestra, 42
Clio, 206n10
Clytemnestra, 122
Cocteau, Jean, 1, 2, 9, 35, 205n1
Cold War, 127
Colebrook, Claire, 195
collective unconscious, 29
color (semic use), 170–71. See also lighting
comedy, 20, 45
comic archetypes, 23
Communist Party (CPUSA), 127
compás, 54
Composer's Voice, The (Cone), 24
Cone, Edward T., 24
configurational temporal dimension (Paul
    Ricoeur), 10
Confucianism, 169, 170
Congruence-Associationist model (C-A M),
    218n1
Consolation of Philosophy (Boethius), 7
contradiction, 13
contrariety, 13
conventional narrative, xi
Cook, Nicholas, 34, 158, 199
Corigliano, John, xi

counterpoint: Adriana Mater, 81; Brechtian
    montage, 207n14; Doctor Atomic, ix, 139;
    "Doy Mi Sangre," 65; lament motive, 62; mul-
    timodal discourse, 5; musical analysis of
    Adriana Mater, 109; polymetric interlude in
    Doctor Atomic, 139; primitivism in Doctor
    Atomic, 161
Courtés, J., 13, 14, 39, 201, 203
Crazed, The (Jin), 172
crescendo, 80
Cubism, 77
Cultural Revolution, 168, 172, 176
Cupid, 7
cyclical time: Adriana Mater, 81, 86, 92, 110,
    117; Ainadamar, 55, 80; Doctor Atomic, 137;
    epic style, 214n12; The First Emperor, 182; Les
    Troyens, 206n10; Mask of Orpheus, xi; tem-
    poral dimensions of narrative, 10

Dalí, Salvador, 69
damnation themes, 163
Daoism, 173
Das Rheingold (Wagner), 14–16, 15, 39, 198,
    208n24
"Daughter of Zion," 134
Davies, Maxwell, xi
Davis, Andrew, xii, 12, 16–18, 27–28
Death of Klinghoffer, The (Woolcock), xii, 124–
    25, 127, 134, 159, 213n1, 215n27
Debussy, Claude, 82, 125, 145
Deleuze, Gilles, 214n13
Der Ring des Nibelungen (Wagner): anti-Sem-
    itism, 210n40; archetypes, 209n28; multi-
    modal discourse, 5, 7, 36–39; psychoanalytic
    theory, 30–31; reconfiguration of myth, 197–
    98; semiotic square, 14, 16
Desi, Thomas, 6, 10
deus ex machina, 7
dharma, 132
Dido, 65, 206n10
Die Walküre (Wagner), 35, 146; reconfiguration
    of myth, 198
Die Zauberflöte (Mozart), 7
diegetic and non-diegetic music, 201; Adriana
    Mater, 103; agency, 24; Ainadamar, 50–52,
    54, 57, 68, 72; background of Adriana Mater,
    83, 86; diegetic levels, 21, 50–52, 54, 68, 72,
    201; Doctor Atomic, 125, 136, 150, 157, 161,
    164; The First Emperor, 173, 180–81; multi-
    modal discourse, 4; reconfiguration of myth,
    198; unpacking myth, 12
discourse: Adriana Mater, 118, 120, 122; ana-
    lytical methodologies, 12–13; described, 201;

The First Emperor, 175, 176–77, 192; intermediality, 34–38; multimodal discourse, 1–7,
3, 38–40; musical semes, 27–29; psychoanalytic theory, 30, 32–34, 33; semiotic square,
14, 17–18
discursive strategies, 22, 135–36
disembodiment, 81
distortion, xi
Doctor Atomic (Adams): Adams' musical procedures, 135; Adams/Sellars collaboration, 215n33; "All Things Shine," 160; assessment of productions, 164–65; "At the
Sight of This," 132, 147, 148–49, 159, 161, 162,
163; dramaturgical structure, 128–34; filler
music, 5, 134; harmonic progression, 151–53,
153; hero's journey, 154–58; historical background, 126–28; modal orientation, 151–53;
multimedial structure, 213n4; multimodal
discourse, 5, 38; musical semes, 27; origin,
124–26; overture, 136, 151, 159–60; "plutonium" motive, 138–39, 139, 150–51; postlude,
138; premier, ix–x; proto-topical motives,
137, 139–42, 144; reconfiguration of myth,
xii–xiii, 197–98; representation of Oppenheimer, 12; role of music in marking time,
134–37; roles of proto-topics and topics, 137–
45; SLIDE function, 214n21; stylistic quotations and allusions, 145–51; tropological narrative, 29, 158–64
Doctor Faustus (Mann), 133, 155
Dolar, Mladen, x, 81
Domingo, Plácido, 179, 182
Don Giovanni (Mozart), xii
Donne, John, 125, 129, 132–33, 136, 139–40
Dou Dou Huang, 167, 179, 186
doubling, xi
dramatic irony, 173, 190, 193
Dream of Life, The (Lorca), 46
Dream of Valentino, The (Argento), xi
Du Cristal (Saariaho), 82
duende: Ainadamar as Gesamtkunstwerk, 73–
74; "grain of the voice," 69; light design of Ainadamar, 72; music of ritual consecration,
68; musical structure of Ainadamar, 51, 53,
54; mythic function of, 79; origin of Ainadamar, 42; song forms represented in Ainadamar, 62–63; Staatstheater Darmstadt production, 76

eclecticism, xi
ego, 29
Einstein on the Beach (Glass), xi, 210n41
Eisenstein, Sergei, 34

electronic soundscapes, xii, 146
Elleström, Lars, 4, 39
Ellwood, Robert, 8
Emperor's Shadow, The (Qin Song, 1996), 166–
67, 171, 188
English National Opera, 164
"Enigma" motive, 189
Enrico Fermi Award, 127
episodic temporality, 27
Eucharist, 64
Euridice (Peri), 7
Eurydice, 7, 205n6
"ewig-Weibliche" concept, 133
exoticism, xiii, 176–77
Explaining Music (Meyer), 205n5
expressive registers, 88–92, 91, 96, 100, 118–20
extradiegetic music, 50, 54, 68, 173, 201, 216n10

Falangists: electronic soundscapes, 61; film
footage in Ainadamar, xi; flamenco and duende, 62; libretto of Ainadamar, 46–47, 49–
50; lighting design, 71–72, 76, 78; musical
structure of Ainadamar, 51, 53; origin of Ainadamar, 42; Passion play genre, 74; Ruiz
Alonso's relationship with, 210n5; synoptic
function of the ballad, 57
Falla, Manuel de, 43, 62
false heroes, 19
fandango de huelva, 54, 61
fanfare topic: Ainadamar, 41, 52, 54–55, 55, 57,
59, 67, 72–73, 210n6; Doctor Atomic, 134, 136,
137, 138, 142, 145, 150, 161; The First Emperor,
182–83; musical semes, 27
Fantasia (1940), 35
Fantasy (Furby and Hines), 199
fantasy space, 118
fascist ideology, 57
Faust (Goethe): background of Doctor Atomic,
127; concept of time in Doctor Atomic, 164;
dramaturgical structure of Doctor Atomic,
130, 133–34; hero's journey in Doctor Atomic,
154–58; multimodal analysis, 7, 36, 38; origin of Doctor Atomic, 125; reconfiguration
of myth, 197; theme of Doctor Atomic, x, xiii;
tropological narratives in Doctor Atomic,
162; unpacking myth, 9, 12
Feminine Endings (McClary), ix, 21
feminist themes, 158
Ferneyhough, Brian, ix
Finley, Gerald, 127
First Emperor, The (Tan): actantial themes and
progression, 188–92; agency in, 27; antihero
character, x, xiii; critical reception of, 192–

96; "eternal suffering" theme, 188; historical
background, 168–74; lament arias, 178, *178*,
188; leitmotifs of, 27, 179–88; multimodal
discourse, 3, 12, 40; musical exoticism, 174–
79; musical themes of, 182; origin, 166–68;
overture, 175, 180, 183; postlude, 183; psychoanalytic theory, 31; reconfiguration of
myth, 197, 198; "Zhongguo" aria, 185
flamenco: Bergsonian transcendentalism,
211n10; Golijov's musical eclecticism, 211n17;
Montoya, 211n11; music of ritual consecration, 65, 68; musical structure of *Ainadamar*,
51–54, *53*; mythic function of, 79; origin of
Ainadamar, 41–43; Pastoral topic, 210n7;
song forms represented in *Ainadamar*, 59,
62–64; Staatstheater Darmstadt production,
76; Telléz's production of *Ainadamar*, 72–74
Floyd, Carlisle, xi
Flying Apsaras, 179
folk melodies, 190
Fontanille, Jacques, 207n15
Forbidden City, 6, 179, 209n35, 217n15
Franco, Francisco, 41, 46, 74–75
Freud, Sigmund, x, 29
Frye, Northrop, 18–22, 24
Full-Context paradigm (FCP), 174–75
Furby, Jacqueline, 198–99

Gao Jianli (character): actantial progression in
The First Emperor, 189–92, *191*; background
of *The First Emperor*, 169–74; critical reception of *The First Emperor*, 193–95; musical
exoticism, 179; musical themes of *The First
Emperor*, 182–88
García Lorca, Federico (character): agency, 29;
assessment of *Ainadamar* productions, 79–
80; *cante jondo*, 43–46; electronic soundscapes, 61–62; Falangist politics, 210n5;
Freudian undertones in *Ainadamar*, 210n4;
libretto of *Ainadamar*, 47–51; light design
of *Ainadamar*, 71–72; metadiegetic narrative, 201; music of ritual consecration, 64–
65, 68; musical structure of *Ainadamar*, 51–
52, *53*; origin of *Ainadamar*, 41–43; Passion
play genre, 73–74; "Quiero Cantar Entre las
Explosiones," 63; Sellars' production of *Ainadamar*, 69; song forms represented in *Ainadamar*, 59–60; Staatstheater Darmstadt
production, 75–78; as subject of *Ainadamar*,
x–xiii; synoptic function of the ballad, 54–55,
57; unpacking myth, 12
Gardiner, John Eliot, 206n10
gender-based discourse, ix–x, 72, 199

Genette, Gérard, 50
genre crossing, 68–78
geometry of theater, 205n1
Georgics (Virgil), 7
German Romanticism, 9–10
Gerstenberger, Katrin, 42
Gesamtkunstwerk, 10, 69–72
Ghosts of Versailles (Corigliano), xi
Gibbons, Alison, 4
Gilman, Sander L., 198
Gjerdingen, Robert, 6, 205n5
Glass, Philip, xi, 9, 11–12
glissando harmonics, 102
Godfather trilogy, x
Goethe, Johann Wolgang von, 130, 133, 163
Golijov, Osvaldo: agency, 29; *Ainadamar* as
Gesamtkunstwerk, 69; assessment of *Ainad-
amar* productions, 79–80; on birth of myth,
41; electronic soundscapes, 61–62; libretto of
Ainadamar, 46–47, 49; origin of *Ainadamar*,
41–43; Passion play genre, 74; representation
of Lorca, 12; song forms represented in *Aina-
damar*, 59; Staatstheater Darmstadt produc-
tion, 78; synoptic function of the ballad, 54–
55, 57–58; use of slang, 211n14
Gollin, Edward, 152, *154*
Goodman, Alice, 125, 129, 164
Götterdämmerung (Wagner), 30, 37, 210n39
Gounod, Charles, 155–56
Goya Theater, 44
Grabócz, Márta, 26, 208n25
Great Wall of China, 166, 168, 173, 175, 185, 195,
216n6
Greek culture, 122, 133, 143, 155
Greenaway, Peter, xi
Greimas, A. J., 12, 15, 39, 157, 207n15, 217n20
Gronk (Glugio Nicandro), 69–71, *70*, 77
grotesque trope, 27
Groves, Leslie, 129, 132, 143–45, 146, 213n5
Grusin, Richard, xii
Guerin, William, 134
Guernica (Picasso), 69, 77
Guy, Nancy, 217n23
Gyges, 213n6
Gypsies, 43–44, 62, 75, 78, 175, 211n11

Ha Jin, 167–68, 172, 183–84, 195–97
Haijie, Ren, 194
Han dynasty, 167, 169–70
Handel, George Frideric, 174–75
harmonic fields, 115, *115*
Hartley, John, 10–11
Hashimoto, Aki, 42

34, 120, 192; Imaginary Order, 212n13; *object petit a*, 31, 32, 119, 192; operatic representations of death, x; preverbal domain, 92; psychoanalytic theory, 30–34; psychological resonances of trauma, 116–20; structure of multimodal analysis, 39

Lam, Joseph, 176

Lambright, Spencer N., 115

L'Amour de loin (Saariaho), ix–x, 82, 87–89, 115, 212n12

Langer, Suzanne, 8, 122

language acquisition, 30, 118

Lapage, Robert, 6–7

Le Bourgeois Gentilhomme (Lully), xi

Le Grand Macabre (Ligeti), 27

Le nozze di Figaro (Ponnelle), 35

Le Rocher de Tanios (Maalouf), 84

Le Roi Roger (Szymanowski), 6

Leech, Geoffrey, 2

Lefevre, Peter, 42

legends, 7

Leigh, Janet, 205n4

leitmotifs: *Akhnaten*, 206n13; fate leitmotif, 180–81, *181*, 183–87, *184*, 189–92, 195; *The First Emperor*, 168, 176, 179–81, *181*, *184*, 190, *191*; musical semes, 27–28; psychoanalytic theory, 30

Leoncavallo, Ruggero, 22

Lepage, Robert, 35

Les Fleurs du Mal (Baudelaire), 128

Les identités meurtrières (Maalouf), 84

Les Troyens (Berlioz), 7, 206n10

Levin, David, 1–2, 208n27

Levine, James, 166

Lévi-Strauss, Claude, 8, 9, 20, 206n8

Lewin, David, 214n21

Li Si, 169

Lichtbogen (Saariaho), 82

Ligeti, György, xi, 27, 145

lighting, 121, 151, 170–71, 189

Linguistics and Semiotics in Music (Monelle), 14, 26

Liszka, James, 12, 18–21, 203, 217n20

Liszt, Franz, 25–26

Liu Shui ("Flowing Water"), 171

Locke, Ralph, 174, 177, 178

Lohn (Saariaho), 82

Long Beach Opera, xi, 69, 78, 79

Longobardi, Ruth, 158, 213n1

Lord of the Rings trilogy, 30

Los Alamos, New Mexico, 150

Losey, Joseph, xii

Louis XVI, 37

Love for Three Oranges (Prokofiev), xi

Lu Wei, 171

lullabies, *91*, 103–109, 114, 129, 131, 184, 212n13

Lully, Jean-Baptiste, xi

Lyric Opera of Chicago, 128

Lyric Tragedy, 206n7

M. Butterfly (Hwang), 46

Ma Feibai, 194

Maalouf, Amin, 82–84, 100, 111, 116, 121–23

Machado, Manuel, 43

Madame Butterfly, x, xii, 22, 46

Madonna figures, x, 41, 123

Manhattan Project, 125, 129

Mann, Thomas, 133, 155

Manuel, Peter, 52

Mao Zedong: background of *The First Emperor*, x, 171; critical reception of *The First Emperor*, 192, 194–95; execution of scholars, 217n21; intertextual reference to, 202; multimodal discourse, 36; *Nixon in China*, 124; origin of *The First Emperor*, 168; reconfiguration of myth, 198; unpacking myth, 12

maqāms, 52

march topic, *144*, 144–45

Marco Polo (Tan), 166, 176, 217n12

Marguerite, 155–56

"Mariana, Tu Ojos," 53, *60*, 75

Marie Antoinette, Queen consort, xi, 37

Marina Pineda (Lorca), 44–45, 47–48, 69

Marriage of Figaro (Mozart), xi, 6, 22, 134

Marxist theory, 33

Mask of Orpheus, The (Birtwistle), xi, 7–8

Mater Dolorosa, x, 82–83. See also *Adriana Mater* (Saariaho)

material mode, 4, 34

Mauer, Christopher, 43

Mayer, Michael, xi

McCarthyism, 127

McClary, Susan, ix, 21

Mei Hong Lin, 74, 78

Méphistophélès, 155–56

Messiaen, Olivier, 82

metadiegetic music: *Ainadamar*, 50–52, 54, 68, 72; described, 201, 213n3; *Doctor Atomic*, 125, 150

metaphor, 10

meta-theater, 46

Metropolitan Opera: *Doctor Atomic*, 126, 128, 158, 164; *The First Emperor*, 166, 167, 177, 179; Wagner's *Ring* cycle, 3, 7

Meyer, Leonard B., 6, 205n5

Miller, Jonathan, 6

mimetic role of music, 24

Tanglewood Music Festival, 42
Tarasti, Eero, 9, 22, 25, 208n24
Taruskin, Richard, 79
Taymor, Julie, 1–2, 35, 205n1
teleology, ix
Teller, Edward, 130, 137–38
Telléz, Carmen-Helena, 73
Tewa Indians, 38, 129–31, 146, 158–63
textuality, 2, 10–11
Theory of Musical Narrative, A (Almén), xii, 21
throat singing, 175
Tiananmen Square massacre, 172
Tibetan singing bowl, 182
Tolstoy, Leo, 11
Tomasula, Steve, 4
"Tome Su Mano," *53, 75, 76, 77*
Tommasini, Anthony, 82, 92, 154, 167, 192–93, 215n30
topics, 25, 136, 137–45; iconic, 27, 102, 107, 136, 137, 203; indexical, 27, 203, 212n12; march, *144,* 144–45; Pastoral, 210n7; *pianto,* 26–27, 89–90, 110, 135–36, 139–42, *141,* 203; proto-topics, 134, 137–45; waltz, 59, *144,* 144–45. *See also* fanfare topic
Totton, Robin, 54
tragedy, 22
transcultural music, xiii
transhistoricity, 11, 39
transvaluation: *Adriana Mater,* 90, 114, 120, 123; *Ainadamar,* 64, 68; analytical methodologies, 12; described, 18, 20–21, 23–24, 203; *Doctor Atomic,* 139, 156–57; *The First Emperor,* 192; *interpretant* concept, 207n19; ironic archetype, 207n21; multimodal discourse, 39; musical semes, 28
trauma: *Adriana Mater,* 81–83, 85–86, 89–90, 100, 103, 107, 111–12, 116–21; *Ainadamar,* 51, 80; *The First Emperor,* 172; Freud's theory of unconscious, 212n15; multimodal discourse, 39–40; musical semes, 28; mythic narrative, 198; psychoanalytic theory, xiii, 29–30, 32–33; the semiotic square, 18
"tribal" concept of identity, 84
Trinity test site, 132, 213n8
Tristan und Isolde (Wagner), 26, 65, 94, 135, 145, 211n13
tropes, 90, *144,* 144–45, 209n37
tropological narrative: *Ainadamar,* 77; analytical methodologies, 13; described, 204; *Doctor Atomic,* 158–64; multimodal discourse, 36, 38, 40; reconfiguration of myth, 197; scope of study, 28–29
Truman, Harry, 127, 158
Trump Tower, 6

Tsargo (character): Adriana's soliloquy, 96; background of *Adriana Mater,* 84–86; confrontation with Yonas, 105–108, 108–11; dream sequences, 98; music of violence, 100–103; musical characterization of, 212n6; mythic resonances, 122–23; psychological resonances, 119–21; ritual of absolution, 112, 114; semic units and expressive registers, 87–90, *91*
Tsypin, George, 86
Turandot (Puccini): *The First Emperor,* 167, 175, 179–80, *181,* 183, 186, 188–90, 193, 196; Forbidden City performances, 217n15; influence on Tan, 216n5; multimodal discourse, 6; musical semes, 28; narrative archetypes, 22–23; narrative formulae, xi; nature cosmology, 217n17; role of Liù, 207n18; semiotic square, 16–18; taxonomy of style, 208n26; transvaluation, 203; use of mythic and legendary subjects, 207n17; varied musical styles, 217n19

Unclaimed Experience: Trauma, Narrative, and History (Caruth), 85–86
Unsung Voices (Abbate), ix, 24
Upshaw, Dawn, 42, 68

Vallée d'Obermann (Liszt), 25–26
valuative tension, 20
Van Leeuwen, Theo, 3, 122
VAS: An Opera in Flatland (Tomasula), 4
vaudeville, 199
Vazsonyi, Nicholas, 211n13
Vega, Lope de, 46
Verblendungen (Saariaho), 115
Verdi, Giuseppe, xi, 6
Verfremdungseffekt (Brecht), 38
villainy, 19. *See also* antiheroes
virtual agency, 13, 24–25
Vishnu, 12, 132–34, 146–48, *148–49,* 156, 161, 163
Voice and Nothing More, A (Dolar), 81
Völsunga saga, 38

Wada, Emi, 167
Wagner, Richard: analytical methodologies, 12; anti-Semitism, 210n40; *Doctor Atomic,* 125, 135; *The First Emperor,* 175; Greimas's theories, 208n23; "Liebestod," 65; multimodal discourse, 5, 7, 35–38, 39; musical lexemes, 208n24; musical semes, 25–26; mythic narrative, 10, 197–98; overtures, 94; psychoanalytic theory, 30–31, 33; reconfiguration of myth, 197–99; semiotic square, 14–15, *15;* style quotations in *Doctor Atomic,* 145–46

Musical Meaning and Interpretation

Robert S. Hatten, *editor*

YAYOI UNO EVERETT is Professor of Music at University of Illinois at Chicago and has previously taught at Emory University, University of Illinois at Urbana-Champaign, and University of Colorado at Boulder. Her research focuses on the analysis of postwar art music, film, and opera from the perspectives of semiotics, multimedia theories, cultural studies, and East Asian aesthetics. Her previous publications include *Music of Louis Andriessen* (2006) and various peer-reviewed articles on music by Kaija Saariaho, John Adams, Louis Andriessen, György Ligeti, Elliott Carter, Toru Takemitsu, Toshi Ichiyanagi, Chou-Wen Chung, and Lei Liang.

www.ingramcontent.com/pod-product-compliance
Lightning Source LLC
Chambersburg PA
CBHW070447100426
42812CB00004B/1229